Essays in
Greek History
and
Literature

A. W. GOMME
LECTURER IN GREEK AND GREEK HISTORY IN THE UNIVERSITY
OF GLASGOW

Essay Index Reprint Series

BOOKS FOR LIBRARIES PRESS, INC.
FREEPORT, NEW YORK

Originally published by:
BASIL BLACKWELL

First published 1937
Reprinted 1967

PRINTED IN THE UNITED STATES OF AMERICA

NOTE

Some half-dozen of the following papers have already appeared in print; and I wish to express my gratitude to the Editors of *The Annual of the British School at Athens, The Journal of Hellenic Studies, The Classical Quarterly,* and *Classical Philology* for permission to republish these. Except for the correction of mistakes I have left what I once wrote substantially unaltered; but I have in two cases added notes in answer to objections which had since been raised to my arguments; and in one ('A Forgotten Factor in Greek Naval Strategy') I have added a few more examples to illustrate my meaning. The two maps I owe to my wife; and a great deal of help and useful suggestions, and a reading of the proofs, to my colleague, Mr. Kitto.

A.W.G.

Glasgow, September, 1936.

CONTENTS

I

INTRODUCTORY

MANY of us in this country have listened, with pain, to the intelligent foreigner who points out that we have no word in English for *Wissenschaft, science, scienza*. With pain, partly because we know it for ourselves, partly because it isn't true. For the English word *science* is a proper translation of *Wissenschaft*, though it does not exactly correspond with it. It has a double duty to perform, with both a wider and a narrower meaning, *Wissenschaft* and *Naturwissenschaft*. In this it is only like many other words, in all languages, the most prominent in our own being the very words England and English: which may mean, according to the context, England proper (as in *England v. Wales, Scotland, Ireland, France*, or any other country, at football), England and Wales (as in *England v. Australia*, at cricket), England, Wales and Scotland, but no part of Ireland (popular usage, as in lawn tennis, where the official title is 'Great Britain'[1]), or England, Wales, Scotland and Ireland (only Northern Ireland since 1922), the popular usage again, as in 'England's foreign policy,' where also 'Great Britain' is officially correct. It will be observed that even the official title 'Great Britain' does not always mean the same thing, any more than do 'British' and 'Briton,' which so many are anxious for us to use whenever anything but English in the narrowest sense is meant: for 'the British Government' means the Government of Great Britain, 'the British Empire' sometimes very different; and 'British subjects' includes all citizens of the Empire, whereas 'Britons' would exclude the large majority. In Scotland 'English Literature' includes Scott and Burns, for it includes all that is written in the English language, which is one; but does it in America include all American writers? In spite of this nobody has yet informed us that we

[1]But there is no consistency even here: in *The Times* report of the draw for the Wimbledon Lawn Tennis Championships in 1936, one player was listed as representing Scotland, another as representing Wales, but all the other players from this country as Great Britain. In the official programme the two former were given to Great Britain.

have no English word for *England*, *Angleterre*, *Inghilterra*.
But though there is a certain pedantry and misunderstanding in this belief that we have no word for *Wissenschaft*,
yet there is cause for it in our own frequent misuse of the
words 'science,' 'scientist,' and 'scientific.' There would be
no great harm in asking the words to do double duty, no
more than the occasional inconvenience caused by every
such lack of precision, if it were not that they are very often
used in the narrow sense as though this actually excluded the
wider; and since the eminent are sometimes guilty of this, it
is not surprising that there is much popular confusion. We
have inherited or adopted the word 'science' for the official
term 'Faculty of Science' in our universities, and the word
'Arts' for the Faculty which comprises languages and history. It would be pedantic to object to this, if it had not
resulted in the popular belief (shared, it seems, by many
'scientists') that philology and history are not sciences, that
their professors are not scientists and do not work in a
scientific spirit. As an example of it, I may be allowed to
refer to a now forgotten controversy. In a criticism of H. G.
Wells' *Outline of History*, I had remarked in passing: 'this
ugly word ["Nordic"] does not seem to mean anything
other than "Northern," unless perhaps it should be applied
to people who live in the south but have those virtues of
fairness, tallness, love of truth, courage, a frank and brave
religion, which must be confined to northerners or certain
well-known theories would fall.' To which Mr. Wells replied: 'but, of course, if it did not [mean anything else],
as any undergraduate in science at Glasgow would explain
to him, then scientific people would use the word "Northern" and not a special term.' I am not here thinking of the
logic of this, which implies that ethnologists and archæolo-
gists cannot make mistakes; it is the phrase 'any undergraduate in science' that delights me, this innocent belief in
the virtue of 'science,' in the powers which it alone can give
to its students and which are denied to those who study language and history.   Yet teachers of languages have often
been reproached with paying too much attention to nice
distinctions, all designated by special terms, to moods and
tenses and cases and their various uses.

But popular thought is not entirely to be blamed for this confusion. The Royal Society since its foundation in 1660, has practically confined its activities to 'the promoting of Physico-Mathematical Experimental Learning' (to quote from the memorandum of the meeting on November 28, 1660), the 'New Philosophy,' to the neglect of 'other parts of human learning,' into which, together with natural philosophy, 'divers worthy persons' had been inquisitive in 1645; though it is clear that from the first the main interest was in physical science and mathematics, as appears from the list of subjects discussed at the informal meetings from 1645 on and in the Oxford Society from 1649. The philosophical, historical and philological sciences have been ignored.[1] On the continent and in America, on the other hand, Academies, with a better sense of the solidarity of human learning, comprise all branches of science, divided normally into two main classes, physico-mathematical and philosophical-historical.[2] So that when, in 1899, at the conference of European and American academies at Wiesbaden, a scheme was drawn up for an international association of academies, it was found that though the Royal Society represented England in the former class, there was no institution to represent her in the second. One chair at the first meeting of the federated academies was vacant. A proposal by Henry Sidgwick to add a new section to the Royal Society was rejected. Its officers 'were requested to communicate with a few distinguished men of letters with a view to a representation of the United Kingdom on the proposed Association in the Literary and Philosophical Section,' but the Society would not 'itself initiate the establishment of a British Academy.'[3] ('Men of letters,' not 'men of science' in other branches of learning, was already ominous.) In a letter from the Council of the Society to the Privy Council,

[1] Weld's *History of the Royal Society*, pp. 31–2, 65. The discussion of theology and politics was expressly barred, wisely enough at the time; but this perhaps helped the exclusion of philosophy and history later. It is possible that had Gresham's College, in whose building the Royal Society first met, continued in being, it might have developed into an Academy of Sciences on the continental model; or, perhaps, into an earlier University of London.

[2] The Royal Society of Edinburgh, also had at its foundation a philosophical and historical class, with some well-known members; but the subsequent work of this side has not been distinguished.

[3] Minute of the Council, July 4, 1901.

it was stated : 'The Records of the Society clearly show that, as a matter of fact, those activities have been, with some few exceptions in quite early days, confined for two and a half centuries to the studies with which it is now occupied. . . . The several branches of knowledge with which the Society now occupies itself form a whole sufficiently homogeneous to enable one body to deal with them effectively, and yet sufficiently large to prevent narrowness of spirit. To attempt to enlarge the sphere of the Society's activity would, in the opinion of the President and Council, expose the Society to the great danger of losing the firm hold which it now possesses on the branches of learning to which it confines itself.'[1] The result was the formation of an independent British Academy 'for the promotion of historical, philoso-phical, and philological studies.' An admirable institution; but this country still suffers from the dichotomy of science.

No one, of course, will deny that, just as there is a pro-found distinction between the exact sciences, mathematics and physics, and all others—which, as they deal with living things, might have been comprised under a general title of biology—so there is one equally important between the biological group (as it is in fact called) and the human group, philosophy, history and philology (which might have been comprised under a general title of anthropology; but these two words, biology and anthropology, have sadly restricted meanings); for the former are experimental sciences, the latter, except to a small extent, are not. But that these distinctions should not lead to complete divorce is shown by the existence of sciences that belong or should belong to both groups (medicine and geography being obvious instances), and by the curious history, in this respect, of the British Association for the Advancement of Science. It was founded on the model of the German *Naturforscherversammlung*, the object of which was to 'exalt science in general estimation.' Vernon Harcourt, at the first meeting of the Association, spoke of the value of 'a meeting at which all the sciences of these kingdoms should be convened.' It was desired to prevent the separation of the several sciences; and 'we pro-pose that all members of Philosophical Societies in the

[1]February 19, 1902, recorded in the Society's Minutes.

British Empire shall be entitled to become members.'[1]
Nevertheless philology, philosophy and history were excluded from the objects which the Association wished to
advance. One might therefore assume that the word 'science'
was used in its narrower sense to comprise only the experimental and exact sciences. But such an assumption would be
wrong; for economics, which is neither experimental nor,
despite its mathematical basis, exact, was considered from
the beginning to be worthy of advancement, in spite of the
strong objections of Whewell in the early years and of Galton
later to a study that they regarded as popular and unscientific
because it was involved in contemporary politics (compare
the avoidance of politics by the Royal Society in the seventeenth century); psychology, experimental in part, but
not exact, was admitted because it was new (it became a
section in 1921); so was anthropology (a section in 1884).
Under the aegis of anthropology, archæology crept in; and
the Association has aided financially excavations in Greece
and England, and has made recommendations to the Government for the protection of ancient monuments. These last
two sciences find themselves in consequence in strange company: admitted to the society of pure mathematics and
astronomical physics and thereby cut off from their nearest
kinsman, history. The cause of this is clear: geology and
palæontology are obviously 'science'; but they are indissolu-
bly linked with the earliest history of man, and that is even
more the business of archæology than of geology. Moreover,
early man is also one form of primitive man; so anthropology
as well, which studies the other form, helps to bring archæology within the fold. But though the cause is clear, the
result is none the less curious; for the link between prehistoric and historic man is broken. It is a science to study
present-day primitive man and prehistoric man, but not
civilized man; where the evidence is scanty and (in the
absence of the written record) difficult to interpret, it is
scientific to study and draw conclusions (generally very
positive ones) from it; the fuller the record, the less scientific,
apparently, becomes the examination of it. Yet even the thin
line which divides history from prehistory (defining here

[1]Howarth, *The British Association: A Retrospect*, 1831–1921, pp. 7, 18, 23.

prehistory as that part of the story of man preceding intelligible. written record) is not observed in the British
Association: because our knowledge of ancient Egypt and
Mesopotamia is largely the product of the spade, the *history*
of these countries is admitted under the general heading of
archæology, though the written record is abundant; so is
the story of the Bronze Age in Greece, and would still be if
many more written documents were found and they were all
interpreted; but, except for an occasional glimpse afforded
by archæology, classical, mediæval and modern history is
excluded. But no; not even this is true: economic history is a
branch of economics, and economics is a 'science'; so a partial,
a sectional history of any period or country is allowable.
Minds that are primitive, the origin or the broken elements of
a language, evidence that is weak or dug up by the spade, one
or two special aspects of history, are objects of scientific study;
the full record of civilized man, the story of human society
and human achievements, of the development of language, is
not. Psychology is a science, dealing with the human mind;
history, dealing with the past activities of the human mind,
expressed in language or music, in stone or paint or clay, in
politics or trade or engineering, is apparently not. That is
how we foster 'the essential homogeneity of science.'[1]
    It is true that we can just contemplate some of these
achievements and enjoy them for themselves alone, without
any scientific thinking; but so we can a flower or an animal
or the starry firmament. Admiring contemplation of the past
is not history, any more than a sense of the beauty of plants is
botany, of stars astronomy. The material of history, it is
also true, has often been the material for scribblers, romancers, rhetoricians and preachers; but so has the material of
the botanist and the astronomer been used in aid of supersti-
tion, both by quacks and by honest men. This, we recognize
at once, only increases the need for a scientific botany and
astronomy; and the work of scribblers, romancers, rhetoricians and preachers (all of whom may have their place in
society) increases the need and the value of scientific history.

[1] The 'creation of new sections,' and the admission of 'the widest possible range
of scientific interest' show 'the unique elasticity of the British Association among
United Kingdom scientific bodies'—Howarth, *op. cit.*, p. 78.

It is true again that some historians have at the same time been great literary artists; but this should not be allowed to confuse the issue. Gibbon was a better writer than Stubbs, but this does not make him a worse historian; Plato occupies a much larger space in the history of Greek literature than does Aristotle, but he is not less great a philosopher for that.

This has some bearing on the controversy, which has always seemed to me a barren one, whether history is a science or an art: a controversy which is surely only possible among a people which misuses the word science as we do. To collect and sift and study and properly value evidence, in doing this to reject as far as possible all pre-judgements, everything that is personal or accidental, and mere submission to authority, is to do scientific work in history as in any other branch of learning; to present the result of this work in writing in such a way as to make the meaning clear is a work of art, in all sciences, including history. It must be so. A lecture on the most highly specialized branch of the most abstruse of sciences needs a skill, τέχνη, in delivery, if it is to be made clear to the audience, even though that audience consist only of other specialists. Art and skill are shown in the doing, just as they have also been shown in the original experiment or discovery. Practical archæology, excavation, is an art guided by scientific method: that is to say, the actual application of spade to earth is art. So is the exposition of the results of study. It is true that some sciences, of which history, in some of its aspects, is one, are more amenable to attractive exposition than others, just as some have (quite apart from 'the wonders of science') a more popular appeal than others, as zoology or botany with its fascinating pictures of animal or plant life, or the fantastic figures of astronomy. There have therefore been more historians than physicists or biologists who have been great men of letters—though there have not been many of them, all told. But to suppose that history is any the less a science is to confuse either the essential with the accidental, or one part of a man's work with another.

There is, however, one danger to which history is exposed to a greater degree than any other science—the danger of patriotism: that tendency not so much to think one's own

country always right (or, what is even odder, always victorious)—that is childishness, however often it may be repeated
—as to treat it as the principal centre of interest. History is
the record of man in society, and is therefore largely concerned with frontiers (it is almost always international, and
the new term 'International History' adopted by some
universities means, or should mean, nothing new); only a
very few men are indifferent to frontiers, and not many of
these are historians; and it is a difficult thing to realize that
the society to which one belongs is not, if not the finest, at
least the most interesting and probably the most important
of all societies. Moreover a good deal of the work of the
scientist in practice consists in teaching; and it is necessary
to teach part of a subject in detail, as well as the whole of it in
general; it is inevitable, indeed desirable, that this part
should be one in which the pupil will take an immediate
interest. Regional history, like regional geography or geology or botany, is obviously a proper subject both of study
and of teaching, and the region chosen will normally be one
known to and of special interest to the pupil; but it must be
recognized as regional, not masquerade under the guise of
history as a whole. Herein lies part of the peculiar value to us
of the study of Greek history, and a justification of the
special claims that are made for it.

   The study of Greek history as such needs no justification:
it is a 'part of human learning.' So are Assyriology and
Egyptology; yet for Greek, as for Roman history, we make
an extra claim—namely that it should be among the regular
studies at schools and universities; that it should not be confined to specialists. Does this claim need justification? It has
often enough been defended, but perhaps not too often; and
the present time is one at which a defence is especially suitable. For Greek history is not simply the record of a society
in which were produced masterpieces of art, letters and
philosophy that still hold the attention of men; nor is it of
importance to us only because the Greeks faced certain
political problems and made certain political experiments
that are of permanent interest. It is that in an age of extreme
nationalism such as the present it is of the utmost importance
to keep alive and vigorous the story of the two civilizations

which form the background of that of all the warring countries of Europe and their colonies of to-day, to which all of
them can look back as a common possession as the equally
quarrelsome states of Greece could look back to Homer.[1]
Along with philosophy and the physical and mathematical
sciences it forms a common link and bond. The history of
modern European countries cannot be understood apart
from that of Rome, nor that of Rome without Greece.
They are sufficiently different from us to stimulate the
imagination, and require the learning of two languages that
are foreign but kin (and herein lies an advantage to us over
the Greeks—their classics, Homer, were in their own
language, and their outlook was to that extent narrowed);
they are sufficiently like to prevent any feeling of remoteness,
to secure our immediate interest. 'History . . . has, as a
form of knowledge and inquiry, a twofold aspect. As an
investigation of what really happened, it is as thoroughly a
science as geology or botany, or any other non-experimental
branch of learning. But as a science which selects from
among the things which have happened the things which are
of human interest, and regards only those things as being of
interest which are seen to have been instrumental in bringing
about 'the present,' History stands alone; or rather, takes
rank among those other branches of knowledge, like the
study of Art and Morals, which are concerned not only with
the discovery and record of facts, and the ascertainment of
relations between them; but also with the application of a
standard of value. History is a science of observation, it is
true; but it is also a critical science. Its standard is one of
value as well as of relevance; it relates its facts not only to
other facts, but to the judgment and service of Man.'[2]

The value of Greek history in this sense is twofold. It
depends partly on the results of Greek political thought and
experiment, on the effects which these have had on subsequent history, largely because the effects are common to all
modern European civilization: 'the wider the circle is, over
which the effects of a historical event extend, the more

[1] As I have said elsewhere, it is wrong, it seems to me, to speak of Homer as the
Bible of the Greeks. He was their 'Classics.'
[2] See J. L. Myres' admirable paper, *The Value of Ancient History* (Liverpool,
University Press, 1910), p. 7.

important is it, and the greater therefore the interest which we attribute to it';[1] partly also on the interest which we at the present time must take in events and conditions in some ways like our own. For Greek political history too presents a picture of a number of states, with hard and fast boundaries between them and yet with a common civilization, trying to find the means of a tolerable life—at first, from the sixth to the middle of the fourth century, when there were no states overwhelmingly powerful and only a few attempted, with moderate success, to dominate some of their neighbours; later, to the end of the third century, when the story is one of a struggle for existence of small powers against a few very strong, greedy and mutually quarrelsome ones and of the contest between the old idea of states with exclusive boundaries and the new idea of the world-state.[2] I do not mean by this simply that here is a grand opportunity for the present to learn a valuable lesson from the past, though that aspect of the study of history, as Thucydides foresaw, is not to be despised. I mean that the present is bound to take a special and living interest in those sections of the past where this similarity of conditions exists; where, even if analogies are dangerous, light is thrown by the past on the present and the present enables us to study the past with more understanding.

There are indeed many who believe that it is just the events of Greek political history that have lost all their interest and therefore their value for the present day (for all but the specialist); there are historians who boast that the names of Perikles and Kleon and Demosthenes hardly appear in their pages: it is only, they say, the things of the spirit that have a permanent value, the tragedies of Aeschylus, the sculpture of Pheidias, the philosophy of Plato. As though politics, the organization of society, of the means by which man can live with his fellow man, were not a thing of the spirit for the 'political animal'; as though we were not only too well aware that politics may either foster or destroy art and letters; as though, because politics has so often been ugly and destructive, we can afford (quite apart from any

[1]Ed. Meyer, quoted by Myres, *op. cit.*, pp. 6–7.
[2]See below, the essay on *The End of the City-State*.

question of scientific honesty) to put our heads in the sand
and ignore, in the study of man, all the mistakes, the crimes
and the disasters, and concentrate on the outstanding suc-
cesses. In any case Greek art and letters, perhaps more than
others, are not to be fully understood (though they may be
enjoyed) without an understanding of Greek politics.

Greek political conditions were, as I have said, in some
ways similar to our own; and though, because analogies are
dangerous, because there are many unknown and uncertain
factors in past history, if not also in the present, it is not often
possible or wise to point the moral, there is one comparison
(in which the Greeks come off the best) which is particularly
interesting and valuable. I have mentioned already the
special danger to which history is exposed more than any
other science—the danger of patriotic bias, of which the
lesser evil is the misunderstanding of the foreigner, the
greater is the magnifying of the importance and the interest
of one's own society. It is a remarkable thing, but this is a
vice of which nearly all Greek historians were free. I am not
here of course referring to the Greek attitude to the 'barbarian,'
to the non-Greek; that, always with the inspiring exception of
Herodotus, was generally as narrow and ignorant as the
most nationalist modern could desire. I mean the attitude of
the historian to his own state and to the other states of the
Greek world; for here lies the true analogy with the present
—France, Germany, Brazil, South Africa being in the
modern world of European civilization what Athens, Sparta,
Miletos or Kyme were in the Greek world. Most modern
historiography is national—histories of England, of Germany, of America; so strong is the influence of national
feeling that even mediæval history, the story of Europe before the rise of modern nations, is often written, or at least
taught, from a national point of view. I am not saying that it
is necessarily biased in the sense of being falsified to suit
national pride, though that happens often enough; but we
learn history not as the story of Europe as a whole, still less
of the world as a whole, but each one of us as the story of his
own country in relation to foreigners. His own country is
for each man the centre. Greek historians did not write like
that. Whether good historians or bad, whether professedly

writers of a universal history or of a limited period, whether
of the fifth or of the second century, Herodotus, Thucydides, Xenophon, Theopompos, Ephoros, Polybios, they
all wrote Ἑλληνικά, not Ἀτθίδες or Μιλησιακά.   An
Atthis, a *Milesiaka* was local history corresponding to our
histories of towns and counties. Here again it is not simply a
question of absence of bias; not many Greek historians
showed the even-tempered impartiality of Herodotus nor
the austere impartiality of Thucydides; Xenophon and Theopompos are notorious cases, and Polybios, for all his fine
feeling for the Roman enemy, was biased enough against the
neighbour-enemies of the Achæans in Greece. It is a question once more of balance and proportion. Thucydides did
not write a history of Athens with a fair treatment of her
enemies, nor Xenophon one of Sparta with an unfair treatment of hers; but both wrote histories of Greece. The title of
Theopompos' *Philippika* might suggest that he at least
wrote a history in the terms of one state, like our national
histories; but the inference would be wrong. His title means
A History of Greece during the Reign of Philip, of a period
when the influence of one man was so great, so dominating,
that it may rightly be called after his name, as that of the fifth
century could not be called after Athens nor that of the sixth
or the first half of the fourth after Sparta; it was not a *History
of Macedon* in the reign of Philip. Greek political boundaries
were in some ways more sharply defined, more effectively
exclusive than those of modern Europe (or rather, of Europe
before 1914—there has hardly been a parallel in the past to
the extreme nationalism of the present day); but the Greeks
had a far more lively sense of their common civilization than
we have, and in none of their work is this perhaps so clearly
seen as in their historiography, their record of their own
political history, where at first sight it is least to be expected,
but where it is implicit, taken for granted, the question not
even raised. Herodotus got much of his material for the
Persian wars from Athenian sources; but when he says that
his praise of Athens will be ἐπίφθονον τῶν πλεόνων ἀνθρώπων, he makes it plain for whom he is writing. Dionysios of Halikarnassos criticized Thucydides for his choice of
subject, for reasons so perverse that it has been left to a

writer of our own age to repeat them.[1] He said that Thucydides was wrong to choose so unpleasant a subject, a war
that was so destructive and which ended in the defeat of his
own country, Athens. The first part of this criticism Thucydides would at least have understood, and have scorned; but
he would have wondered what the second part meant, for he
was a historian, not a local antiquary, a historian of Greece,
not of Athens.[2] One of the most wrong-headed of criticisms
of ancient Greece, but often heard, is that for every man the
state, his own state, was supreme, that his actions and his
thoughts were bounded by it; that everything, art and letters
as well as political thought and action, were in the service of
the state, that small and narrow society. Apart from the
travellers, and they were many—not only the distinguished
individuals, as Simonides and Pindar, the great sophists, the
sculptors and painters, the star-actors, but also the innumerable merchants and the thousands who gave up their own
poleis and therewith their political activities to settle as
metoikoi in another state—apart from these, when we think
of names such as Homer, Aeschylus, Sophocles, Euripides,
Aristophanes, Plato, Aristotle, what meaning can we attach
to that criticism? Professor Murray has recently emphasized
what seems to us the remarkable phenomenon of Aristophanes' free attacks on his country's policy, his defence of

[1]Shotwell, *History of History*, quoted by Vlachos, *Hellas and Hellenism*, p. 293.
[2]Dr. Macan (*Camb. Anc. Hist.* v. pp. 399–400) says that before Herodotus no
history of Greece as a whole was attempted or thought of; the multiplicity of
states, of centres of Greek life, made it impossible: 'there was still no seeing the wood
by reason of the trees, and no man conceived the possibility of a common Hellenic
history, or sat down to write it. It was, then, no accident that the Prince of Ionian
History came to write his unrivalled account of the achievements of the Greek
world as he knew it, or knew of it, in the third quarter of the fifth century before
our era: that is to say, just after the Greeks had been schooled into something more
nearly approaching single, even if brief-lived incorporation, by the attacks of the
massed forces of the "Barbarian" upon their liberties and institutions.' I believe
this is only half the truth. The feeling for Greek unity had been there at least since
Olympia and Delphi had been important centres, and Homer had been sung (as
Macan, of course, recognizes); and if we were to recover the *History* of Hekataios,
I expect we should find a common Greek outlook in him as clearly as in his great
successor. We should not find the art of Herodotus, the genius, whereby he 'con-
trived to mould so far-flung an argument, with such apparent ease of heart and
lightness of touch, into so large and perfect a work of literary art'; but that is a
different matter. What the Persian wars did for Herodotus, in fact, was to bring
out not so much his pan-hellenism as his humanity, his interest in all men, barbarian
as well as Greek. The political unity of the Greek states in face of the Persian attack
was after all short-lived; but the feeling of unity throughout Greece, especially in
the historians, survived to the end.

the enemy, in war time. It was worth emphasizing; but at the same time it must be remembered that Aristophanes, though a bolder man than the rest, in this as in other ways, was not unique. It is our modern nationalism which, especially since the war, is extreme, which has reached a degree of intensity unknown hitherto. The Greeks knew how to be patriotic and yet to be 'good Greeks' as well, as few moderns have been good Europeans. Let Aeschylus be our witness, and Thucydides. It is an apparent paradox, yet clear to men of understanding, that it was often the 'good Greeks,' the men with the widest vision as far as Greece was concerned, who were most in favour of the 'narrow' local autonomy, most opposed to any unity which implied control by one state over the rest. We may guess that Aristophanes was one of these, Kleon being his opposite; and it is interesting to observe that among the most 'nationalist' of Athenian writers, most narrowly Athenian, is Isokrates; next to him perhaps Lysias, not a citizen and characteristically more intensely patriotic than the citizens; and that Demosthenes, the enemy of Macedon and so, according to the moderns, of the union of Greece, has a much wider range, is much less narrowly Athenian than his opponent Aischines.

Ἑλλὰς μέν ἐστι μία, πόλεις δὲ πλείονες,

wrote Poseidippos, and it was a commonplace. We could not substitute 'Europe' and translate it to fit the present day. Plutarch, living under the Roman Empire, was not more pan-hellenic than Herodotus and Thucydides; he also loved his own village—but his interest was in all Greece. 'Aλλ' οὐ δεῖ ψεύδεσθαι· φιλῶ μὲν γὰρ καὶ ἀσπάζομαι τὴν ἐμαυτοῦ πατρίδα, ἐπαινῶ δὲ καὶ θαυμάζω τὴν ἐκείνων.[1]

Pindar, I think, shows most clearly what is meant by this feeling for Greece (it is not quite the same thing as Pan-hellenism, and is quite different from cosmopolitanism), as opposed to state-patriotism; and an examination of a passage in Ehrenberg's excellent book, Ost und West, will make my meaning plain. He there (p. 110) would date fragments 109 and 110—

[1] Brut. anim. rat. uti. 3 (Mor. vi, 987 A.).

γλυκὺ δ' ἀπείρῳ πόλεμος·
πεπειραμένων δέ τις
ταρβεῖ προσιόντα νιν
καρδίᾳ περισσῶς
and
τὸ κοινόν τις ἀστῶν ἐν εὐδίᾳ τιθείς
ἐρευνασά-
τω μεγαλάνορος 'Ησυχίας
τὸ φαιδρὸν φάος,
στάσιν ἀπὸ
πραπίδος ἐπίκοτον ἀνελών;
πενίας δότειραν, ἐχθρὰν ⟨δὲ⟩ κουρότροφον

(as well as Theognis, vv. 761–8 and 775–82) in 480 B.C., and compares them with Herodotus vi 48 (Greek states offering earth and water to Darius): the states, he says, were simply wanting to be at peace, even if this involved submission to Persia, and Pindar in these lines is advising his own fellow-citizens to remain neutral in the war with Xerxes. Ehrenberg finds here 'Mangel am gemeingriechischem Verantwortungs-gefühl'; and writes: 'Aber gerade dass die Dichter zwischen dem Kampfe von Griechen und Bürgern gegeneinander und dem Kriege gegen Persien kaum unterschieden, zeigt wie weit sie von allem gemeingriechischen Denken entfernt waren'; and this only ten years after Marathon. This, I think, gives a wrong impression of Pindar's thought (not of Theognis'—*his* was confined to his own city and his own class). For one thing the Persian invasion might so easily lead to fighting between Greek and Greek; as indeed it did, though not to as much as might well have been expected. Secondly, Pindar is here, even supposing that these fragments are rightly interpreted (which is by no means certain), expressing the normal Greek dislike of war.[1] For he, as much as anyone, was 'Greek-minded,' he was for his generation pre-eminently the poet of all Greece. His interests were not confined to Thebes; but when war threatened his first thoughts may well have been for his own kin: φιλῶ μὲν γὰρ καὶ ἀσπάζομαι τὴν ἐμαυτοῦ πατρίδα. The conjunction of the two men, Pindar and Theognis, is enlightening: both urging neutrality in the war, the one in the interests of a

[1]See below, *The Greatest War in History.*

narrow and greedy class in a small city, the other in the hope of peace for all, because 'only to the inexperienced is war a delight.' But it is the attitude of the historians which is most memorable, because most different from that of the present day.

II

THE TOPOGRAPHY OF BOEOTIA AND THE THEORIES OF M. BÉRARD[1]

Ephoros remarked in his history that Boeotia was unique among Greek lands in having a coast well provided with harbours and fronting three seas, open to the West, the North, and the East, to Italy, Sicily, and Carthage, to Macedonia and the Euxine, and to Egypt, Cyprus, and the islands; and that it thus had ample opportunities for education, and was marked out by nature for rule over others. Strabo quotes this with approval, adding a remark of his own about the permanence of the success of the Romans due to the education they had received from contact with civilized countries: if only Boeotia had known how to educate her sons![2] The author of the *Periplus* which passes under the name of Skymnos of Chios (about 110 B.C.) says the same in almost the same words;[3] and Stephanos of Byzantium repeats it.[4]

Some modern scholars have been much struck with the wisdom of Ephoros,[5] and M. Bérard has used his statement with great effect to bring Thebes within the sphere of his law of isthmuses, and the Kadmeans into his system of a Phoenician thalassocracy.[6] The law of isthmuses is, shortly, that ancient traders travelled as much as possible by land, and as little as possible by sea, so that rather than have one sea journey, they would disembark at a port on one coast, travel across country in 'caravans,' and embark again on the

[1] First published in the *Annual of the British School at Athens*, xviii, 1911–1912.
[2] Strabo, ix 2. 1–2, pp. 400–1.
[3] vv. 485–500.
[4] *s.v.* Βοιωτία.
[5] *e.g.* Tozer, *Selections from Strabo*, p. 232 ('an excellent specimen of criticism applied to historical geography'); Tucker, ed. *Seven ag. Thebes*, p. xi; Murray, *Rise of the Greek Epic*,[2] pp. 35–6 ('I suggest that these great fortress cities [Troy and Thebes] depended for their greatness entirely upon commerce'); cf. Cornford, *Thucydides Mythistoricus*, pp. 32 ff. Forchhammer, who knew the country, did not hold this view: 'Boeotia, tribus maribus interposita, tamen portubus, qui quidem ex interioribus terrae partibus facilem praebeant accessum, minime excellit.'—*Topographia Thebarum*, p. 6.
[6] With regard to the theory of a Phoenician origin of the Kadmeans, cf. my article in *J.H.S.* xxxiii (1913), 53–72, 223–45.

opposite coast; and that consequently we find traces of these ancient trade-routes which were later deserted.[1] Several of them, says M. Bérard, passed through Boeotia, and these would all meet at Thebes. Hence the story of the foundation of Thebes by the Phoenician Kadmos, 'en pleine Béotie, au centre du pays le plus continental, semble-t-il, de toute la Grèce. Consultant nos cartes et nos habitudes actuelles, les archéologues s'écrient que voilà une jolie fable: une ville de l'intérieur, fondée par des marins, à une grande journée de toutes les côtes!' But Thebes was a meeting place of trade-routes; and it was for this reason that 'Thèbes fut un fondation du commerce étranger.'[2]

Further on, he says: 'La seule topologie nous fournirait une preuve d'origine pour cette fondation phénicienne. L'étranger Kadmos, venu de l'Orient, fonde Thèbes, et le site de Thèbes prouverait à lui seul que ce bazar et cette capitale de la Béotie supposent en effet un commerce étranger venu des mers orientales. Thèbes n'est pas au milieu de la cuvette béotienne, mais à l'une de ses extrémités. La capitale indigène et le marché agricole de la Béotie devrait être au milieu des champs et des récoltes, dans le centre de la cuvette, en quelque site comparable à l'Orchomène des Minyens. . . . Éloignée du centre, Thèbes a d'autres avantages: elle est au croisement des routes terrestres qui coupent la Béotie et qui, pour des marins orientaux surtout, serviraient à relier les mers du Sud et la mer du Nord. Une thalassocratie phénicienne implique un comptoir et une forteresse en cet endroit. . . .

Pour les peuples de la mer, la Béotie n'est pas seulement la riche et grasse plaine que nous vantent les géographes et les poètes anciens, la contrée agricole d'où les navigateurs tirent les approvisionnements, leurs chargements de blés, de fruits, de légumes, de laines et d'animaux, par l'intermédiaire des caravanes indigènes.[3] Il est d'autres raisons qui forcent les navigateurs à monter eux-mêmes, à pénétrer et à séjourner dans l'intérieur du pays, à y posséder quelques points de défense et d'entrepôt: la Béotie est un carrefour de

[1] *Les Phéniciens et l'Odyssée*, i, p. 69.
[2] *Op. cit.* pp. 78–9.
[3] Leave out 'ne . . . pas,' and this sentence expresses clearly and exactly what I wish to suggest was the case with Boeotia.

THE TOPOGRAPHY OF BOEOTIA

routes isthmiques. "La Béotie, dit Ephore, . . . touche à trois mers . . ." Cette heureuse situation de la Béotie entre les trois mers était proverbiale parmi les Anciens. Les manuels de géographie la décrivaient à qui mieux mieux et le prétendu Scymnus de Chios la célèbre dans ses vers de mirliton . . . Ceci nous ramène à notre loi des isthmes et à la traversée des continents par les caravanes des thalasso-crates.'[1]

By way of preface I would point out an inaccuracy in this statement of the ancient evidence. First, there is only one manual of geography that celebrates this happy situation of Boeotia; the *Periplus* of Pseudo-Skylax, for example, says nothing about it. Secondly, it is evident that both Pseudo-Skymnos[2] and Stephanos are only quoting Ephoros, as Strabo did; and Stephanos probably at second-hand: that therefore we have only one ancient authority to support the view, not three or four, still less an ancient proverb.[3]

Let us see moreover exactly what this one writer does say; we note at once that Ephoros says one thing, and the moderns, with him as their authority, say another. First, he does not say that Thebes was a place with large external commerce, but implies that it is strange that it was not: the two things are not quite the same. However, Kadmean Thebes may have been, though classical Thebes remained inaccessible.[4] In the second place, Ephoros does not 'explain that Thebes commanded the roads between three seas': he says nothing about roads or trade-routes, but, as Boeotia was τριθάλαττος, τὴν χώραν ἐπαινεῖ διὰ ταῦτα, καί φησι πρὸς ἡγεμονίαν εὐφυῶς ἔχειν:[5] he might have said that France,

---

[1] pp. 224–6.

[2] He names Ephoros among his authorities at the beginning of the work (vv. 109 ff.), and explicitly follows him in describing Greece proper (vv. 470–2). See Bunbury *Hist. Anc. Geogr.* ii, p. 71 (cf. i, p. 183, n. 6).

[3] 'The untrained historian,' says Professor Bury (ed. Gibbon, *Decline and Fall*, Introd. p. xlvi), 'fails to recognize that nothing is added to the value of a statement by Widukind by its repetition by Thietmar or Ekkehard, and that a record in the continuation of Theophanes gains no further credibility from the fact that it likewise occurs in Cedrenus, Zonaras, or Glycas.'

[4] This is one of the chief difficulties in the way of Bérard's explanation of a Phoenician Thebes (as in the case of Troy, Leaf, *Troy: a Study in Homeric Geography*, p. 258): Why, when the conditions were similar, as Bérard recognizes, should the effects in prehistoric and classical times have been so different?

[5] He therefore says nothing about the Phocian ports, Krissa and Antikyra, as Bérard does; these would be important for trade, but would have nothing to do with Boeotian hegemony.

having the sea on three sides, has geographically a natural tendency to hold the hegemony of the Mediterranean, the Atlantic, and the English Channel, while, England, naturally, would only rule in seas surrounding her. But this does not necessarily mean that France is more on the line of trade-routes than England.

Yet as Ephoros mentions not only the seas immediately bordering on Boeotia, the Corinthian Gulf and the straits of Euboea, but also the distant lands, Sicily and Libya, Egypt, Macedonia and the Propontis, with which Boeotia was connected by those seas, it is probable that he had foreign trade in his mind as well as hegemony; and it is perhaps in this connexion that the words ἀγωγῇ καὶ παιδείᾳ μὴ χρησαμένους are to be taken; being open to foreign lands, the Boeotians had unique opportunities for 'education,' of which they did not take advantage.[1] But again, it is necessary to point out that this passage does not imply that Thebes or Boeotia commanded a line of trade-routes, but only that it was easy of approach to foreign vessels. When you say that a town is situated on a trade-route, you do not only mean that foreign trade can easily reach it, but that foreign trade, in order to reach another place, must go through it.[2] This is perfectly understood by modern writers, who all point out

[1] The idea that their ill-success was due to want of education may seem at first sight parallel to Isokrates' idea that the success of the Megarians was due to virtuous moderation, in which case it would equally well 'illustrate the blindness of the Greeks to economic causes' (Cornford, op. cit. p. 32), and this early Greek support for the modern idea of Boeotia as a centre of trade-routes, falls at once to the ground. But it is probable that Ephoros intended to give a much wider meaning to ἀγωγῇ καὶ παιδεία—as it were, a progressive as opposed to a provincial outlook generally.

[2] At the head of his list of typical isthmic routes, M. Bérard (pp. 69–74, 233) places that from Eretria through Oropos and Dekeleia to Athens, of which we hear from Thucydides (vii 27–8) and Herakleides (Descr. Gr., F.H.G. ii, p. 256): 'Athènes, ville continentale, assise entre deux mers, avait en réalité deux ports, deux échelles, le Pirée sur la mer du Sud, Oropos sur la mer du Nord' (so too Cornford, op. cit. p. 33). But this does not mean that trade passed on through Oropos, Athens, and the Peiraeus to other places; which would necessarily have been the case, had Attica been a real isthmus. This distinction is important. Goods for Athens from the north were landed at Oropos instead of being taken round Sunion by sea; goods from the south were landed at the Peiraeus. But we do not hear that trade from Chalkis, intended for the South or West, passed overland through Attica by the Oropos-Peiraeus route. So that when M. Bérard writes, 'à travers l'isthme attique, les caravanes débarquées à Oropos viennent reprendre la mer au Pirée,' these last words are an addition of his own, which begs the question and is not warranted by the ancient evidence. England also has ports on its three seas. So has France; in fact, a perfect example of an isthmic route is to be found under modern conditions—the normal passenger-route from London to Egypt and the East via the Channel ports and then overland to Marseilles.

that Boeotia is by nature an isthmus between two seas; but Ephoros does not say so. He only says (or implies, rather) that trade could easily reach Boeotia, not that it travelled through it. It is perfectly possible to conceive that the Kadmean farmers (though not their descendants of the classical period) exported their surplus wheat in return for all the delicacies of the East, and in consequence were educated and held a hegemony; but that would not deny the truth of the statement that they were an agricultural community, nor affirm the suggestion that the great fortress city of Thebes 'depended for its greatness entirely upon commerce.' M. Bérard, and Professor Murray and Mr. Tucker after him, in referring to Ephoros as a support for their theory, are quoting him loosely, and attributing to his words an exaggerated meaning which they do not possess.[1] However, Ephoros may be understating the facts, and the moderns may be right; we must discuss first the statements of M. Bérard about the geographical position of Boeotia, and compare them with the actual nature of the routes within Boeotia from sea to sea, and afterwards examine its position as a whole in relation to the lines of trade in the Levant in prehistoric times.

In this case it is M. Bérard himself, who, 'consultant ses cartes[2] et ses habitudes actuelles, s'écria que voilà un joli isthme!' Let us examine the roads of Boeotia in turn, remembering that once within either of the two Boeotian plains, either that of Thebes or that of the Kopais, travel and transport of merchandise is easy enough; e.g.: once at Plataia or Lake Hylike, it is easy to reach Thebes; once at Haliartos or Kopai, to reach Orchomenos. It is the roads to the towns situated at the extremities of the plains that must be considered. We can take those from the south first. Five routes pass over the mountains that separate Boeotia from Attica and the Megarid; they are, from west to east—(1) that from Megara by Pagai and Aigosthena, round Kith-

[1] Leake, *Northern Greece* ii, p. 220, accepted the more limited ideas of Ephoros.
[2] I imagine he has not visited Boeotia, judging from the fact that he never gives the results of personal observation, but refers, before describing the country, 'pour tout ceci' to Herakleides, Pausanias, or Mr. Frazer (*e.g.* notes to pp. 69, 226, etc.). Cf. 'M. Bérard, as I gather from his book, is not personally acquainted with the site of Troy, and his theory is evidently the product of the study' (Leaf, *op. cit.* p. 258.) (See below, p. 40.)

airon and up the valley of the Oëroë to Plataia. This was the road twice taken by the Lacedaemonians retiring from Thespiai; its dangers were well known, and it was one of the most difficult passes in Greece; 'elle n'est qu'un sentier. . . . Dangereux, étroit, exposé aux terribles rafales du golfe, ce chemin n'était suivi qu'en cas de nécessité.'[1] (2) A route from Megara to Plataia, somewhat to the east of the Eleutherai pass: it is mentioned by Pausanias[2] and Xenophon,[3] but was very little known or used. (3) The ordinary route from Attica to Boeotia by the pass of Eleutherai. This is so important that there must have been a road here from very early times, but the pass reaches a considerable height, and is frequently snowed up in winter. The road from Eleusis ascends fairly gradually as far as the upper valley of the Eleusinian Kephissos, a stony plain between Oinoë and Eleutherai. Past the latter the road winds in between the steep mountain slopes on either side to the highest point, then opens out somewhat and descends very rapidly and with many curves past the village of Kriekoúki (just east of Plataia) down to the valley of the Asopos. With an important town on either side of the pass there will always be a great deal of traffic through it, for, though not the shortest, it is the most convenient road from Thebes to Athens; but is not so easy as to invite men to cross it for its own sake. (4) The route through Phyle, Panakton[4] and Skolos: this, too, 'n'est qu'un sentier.' It was important, because it was possible for an army invading Attica from the north to come this way and so turn the pass of Eleutherai; and it is a good deal shorter than the Eleutherai road. But it was never a trade-route; it was far too difficult. The fortress of Phyle itself is over 2,000 feet above sea-level, and it is a stiff climb from

[1] Xen. *Hell.* v 4. 16–8; vi 4. 25–6; Bérard i, p. 232.
[2] ix 2. 3; Frazer *ad loc.*
[3] *Hell.* v 4. 14. There is a mule-track in use now from Aigosthena to Plataia: it climbs Kithairon, very steeply, in a north-easterly direction till it meets another track, and the road from Vília. It crosses the mountain high up (for some three hours above snow-level in winter-time) and descends not far from Kriekoúki, whence it turns westwards to Kokla (by Plataia). It is seven to eight hours' journey. My guide told me there was a straighter path, which descended just above Kokla, but it was impassable on the day I was there (March, 1913) on account of the snow. Cf. Leake, *Northern Greece*, ii, p. 334.
[4] It is now generally believed that the ruined fort called Gyphtókastro, formerly thought to be Eleutherai, is Panakton. I am not yet convinced; and the old identification appears on my map.

Athens. The path at first ascends gradually as far as the village of Chasiá; after that the ascent is very steep, over a torrent and up a mountain sparsely wooded with pines, to the foot of the rock on which Phyle stands. Beyond Phyle the path goes through hilly, rocky, deserted, and very bare and wild-looking country, where for miles hardly anyone is now to be met with: it continues high up, with the peaks of mountains all round, until it finally opens on to the stony plain of Panakton. Past this it descends the northern slopes of Kithairon, and thence north-eastwards across the plain to Thebes. It is altogether a hard two-days' journey from Athens ἀνδρὶ εὐζώνῳ. (5) The last pass is the easiest; that due northwards by Tatói, near Dekeleia, over the shoulder of Mt. Parnes. The ascent is easy and gradual, through thick pine-forests; the summit is not sufficiently high for it ever to be blocked with snow; the descent is much more rapid and the modern road winds about with great serpentine curves down to the valley, along which the railway now runs. There it branches into two, one continuing northwards over fairly low and wooded hills to Oropos, the other turning north-westwards to Staniátes (just east of Tanagra), along level or slightly undulating ground the whole way. This pass would only have been difficult if there were no road through, for the whole district is covered with forests. This may have been the case in Kadmean times, before Oropos became important as the northern port of Athens.

Before giving the routes from the north-eastern coast-line to the interior, it will be as well to summarize what the *Mediterranean Pilot*[1] tells us about the harbours and landing places of the Euboean Channel. Ships from Egypt and Cyprus would sail between Andros and Keos, and then off the coast of Attica into the channel. On the coast of Attica are Port Ráphtis and Marathon Bay, where 'the shore is low and sandy, . . . open to the south and south-east. Temporary anchorage in summer may be taken where convenient.' The dangers of passing Cape Marathon and the south-west point of the bay are considerable. The principles of ancient sailing as laid down by M. Bérard must be remembered—the necessity for frequent places of refuge *en route* in case of some

[1] 3rd ed. (1900), iv, pp. 80 ff. (6th ed. [1929], iv, pp. 154–180.)

sudden storm such as is wont to come on unexpectedly in the Aegean; at these refuges boats were liable to be detained for several days, and so food-supplies and water must be abundant—especially the latter, for very little water could be taken on board an ancient ship.[1]

On the opposite coast is Karystos Bay, 'deep and clear of danger except on the western shore where it is rocky and foul; it is exposed to all southerly winds. . . . In entering under sail be prepared for the heavy variable squalls which blow from the high land: . . . the holding ground . . . is indifferent. . . . A sailing vessel should not, however, go too far in, as the winds may be light and baffling when leaving, and there is frequently an indraught into the bay.'

West of the Bay of Karystos and further along the same coast are the group of islands now called the Petáli Islands.[2] M. Bérard has shown the importance of small islands as affording safety in a time of rough weather. The Petáli Group afford a good refuge, but there is no fresh water, and 'the currents run strongly between the islands and are much influenced by prevailing winds. . . .' But 'midway between Trágo islet and Megálo there is a snug anchorage for small vessels in seven fathoms, sandy bottom . . . good holding ground, with a smooth sea in all winds.'[3]

The channel then narrows between the Attic and the Euboean coasts at Xero Pass which only 'offers a few difficulties,' though a little further on between the Berdúgi islets and the shore, 'the currents at times are strong.' Port Armyro Pótamo is 'seldom visited even by boats'; but Limiona Bay must presumably afford anchorage, for it is 'now used for vessels shipping iron-ore from Marathon'; but the *Directions* do not say whether it is safe for smaller boats. On the opposite shore is Alivéri Bay, where 'there is good anchorage in fifteen or sixteen fathoms, rather close in [and so constantly exposed to winds from the mountains close by the shore], but the holding ground is good. . . . No fresh

---

[1] See, however, below, 'A Neglected Factor in Greek Naval Strategy.'

[2] Ancient Πεταλία (Strabo, x 1. 2, p. 444).

[3] M. Bérard himself notes the importance of these islands (omitting from his extracts from the 'Sailing Directions' the statement about the scarcity of water), and instances the voyage of Walpole from Sunion to Chalkis which took eight days; during which he took refuge at the islands, but after nine or ten hours was driven into the open sea again by contrary winds (pp. 186–7).

water can be obtained.' On the mainland again is Oropos
Bay, 'where there is anchorage and landing.' There are
shoals eastward of Port Eretri, and 'vessels should keep
rather on the southern shore of the Euripo channel,' but
'north-eastward of these dangers, there is sufficient anchorage open for small vessels in case of necessity, and it can be
approached from the eastward by keeping along the Euboean shore.' Sailing is easy after this (though no anchorage
grounds on either coast are noted) until the Burj channel, the
southern entrance to the outer Euripos port, is reached. The
difficulties of passing 'this narrow and tortuous channel' are
considerable. Once in the outer port, there is anchorage
throughout the central part, if necessary, but only in deep
water 'from twenty to thirty feet soft mud'; there are bays all
round, including the two bays of Aulis. 'On the north-eastern
shore, near the head of the outer port, a plentiful supply of
water which runs from the rocks may be obtained, though it
is not always good for drinking, being impregnated with
vegetable matter previous to entering the sea.' At the Stenó
Pass, between the outer and the inner port, there is a strong
current at about two knots. At the head of the Inner Port
(the bay of Voúrko, which has 'an even mud bottom') are
the strait, the Euripos proper, and the town of Chalkis.
There 'the water is scare, and obtained chiefly from wells
. . . Sailing vessels . . . should only attempt the passage of
the strait at slack water,' for there is strong variation in the
tides and the stream according to the season: 'with southerly
or south-westerly gales the velocity of the tidal stream from
south to north is increased to eight or eight and a half miles
an hour for the first day of the gale; followed, probably on
the second day, by a rush of equal strength southward.' With
its strong and variable tides, Chalkis was not easy to pass,
and with its scarcity of water, not a convenient stopping place.
    Vessels from the north-east, from Macedonia, Thrace,
and the Euxine, would enter the channel of Trikéri between
the northern coast of Euboea and the Gulf of Volo.[1] In the
latter, where there are 'excellent harbours, land-locked from
every wind,'[2] they could always take refuge. It would also

²*Sailing Directions,* ed. 1852, p. 50.
' *Med. Pilot,*³ iv, pp. 326 ff.

be the most convenient place to disembark at, to make the further journey by land, on the principle that 'the route which follows the land as far as possible, and takes to the sea only when the land fails, was the cheapest, easiest and safest.' If, however, ships were to follow the unlikely course of sailing down the channel (called the Talánda, or Atalante Channel, north of the Euripos), they would have in Oreos Bay on the north coast of Euboea, 'excellent anchorage in twenty to five fathoms along its E. and S.E. sides; and as it is protected to the northward by the Argyronisi islands and the main, the sea can have no fetch to endanger.' Further on is Kamaka Bay, which is 'good holding ground and place of shelter.'[1]

The Maliac Gulf has anchoring depths everywhere, the only danger being the miasma with which the winds blowing along the southern part of the Gulf are charged; this would be the second most convenient landing-place for an 'isthmic route.' Beyond it there are many difficulties to be encountered in entering the channel between Cape Licháles and Vromo Limni. Once through this, on the Euboean coast is Gialtra Bay. 'This bay is the only sheltered anchorage on the coast of Euboea, between Euripo and the Licháles Islands, but the water in the central part is rather deep, and no supplies can be procured.' This would not encourage vessels to sail further; if they were at any time blown on to the Euboean shore, they would have no place of shelter within reach.

The coast of the mainland is, however, more favourable. East of Thermopylae the shore between Cape Longos and Cape Arkítza is low and sandy—always an advantage to ancient ships; but beyond the latter point 'the whole western shore of Atalante Bay should have a wide berth.' But Atalante Bay itself forms an excellent shelter. 'It is very capacious, and has good anchorage almost all round, in any depth of water you choose.'[2] Here we have the first good harbour and shelter since the Gulf of Lamia; between it and Chalkis, there are some dangers in sailing, and the only

---

[1]*Sailing Directions*, ed. 1852, p. 51. (This is presumably just west of Oreos Bay; but I cannot find the name Kamaka on any recent map of this district.)
[2]*Ibid.*, p. 52.

harbour is that of Larymna. 'Vessels rounding Cape Kerata should give it a wide berth, as a shoal extends a quarter of a mile N. of it.' Larymna 'is a narrow inlet running south-westward nearly two miles, having from twenty fathoms water at the entrance to four near its head, where there is a stream of drinkable water.' Shoals exist on the N.W. side of the entrance. The water, especially, would be an inestimable advantage on this coast. Further eastward is Port Skroponéri (where were the chief outlets of the Kephissos and the Melas rivers); there is a small islet, called Gátza, just at the entrance, such as was beloved by the Phoenicians; but this was never a frequented port: 'it is a bight running nearly three miles W.S.W., and surrounded by high land: the port does not seem to be resorted to by the natives; there is no village, and the water is deep for ordinary anchorage, being from twenty to fifteen fathoms.' The nature of the country surrounding the port is sufficient to deter men from settling there. Sailing from Atalante to Chalkis, past Cape Gaídaro, sudden squalls and violent storms of wind from either coast were dangers that might be encountered. 'Talanta Channel, N.W. of Cape Gaídaro, is clear of danger at a prudent distance from the coast, which generally is steep-to on either side of the channel. The high range of the Kandili Mountains in Euboea, which reach nearly 4,000 feet above the sea, a little within the coast, extends to a distance of seven miles. The violent gusts of wind which descend from these mountains during the north-east and northerly winds, and also the heavy squalls that may blow from the high land on the opposite side of the channel, should be carefully guarded against in vessels under sail.' No mention is made of the port of Anthedon, though the village of Lukísia is now near the site of that town; so presumably it cannot be very favourable, even as a refuge in time of stormy weather. Between Cape Gaídaro and Chalkis the channel has 'with the exception of the shoals near the lighthouse (just north of the town) anchoring depths all over it, in from seventeen to ten fathoms, mud bottom, sheltered from the westerly winds by Cape Gaídaro, and the shoal which extends nearly two-thirds of a mile north from it; in the winter season it would be advisable to anchor within

about a mile of the town of Euripo.' This would be a good
shelter, but for the fact that 'there is no water to be procured
this side of the bridge (over the Euripo).' This at once puts a
very great obstacle in the way of ancient vessels taking refuge
here at a time when storms rage in the channel to the north-
west.[1]

Along |this |north-eastern coast, there are five routes
leading into the interior. Two are south of Chalkis, from the
harbours of Oropos and Aulis. Both go over quite low hills;
that from Oropos leads through beautiful pine-woods—at
first through the flat and fertile plain at the mouth of the
Asopos to Sykámino, a village situated at the eastern end
of the last gorge through which the river flows, then over the
hills to Tanagra. The way is smooth and not at all rocky, and
goes, by one or two cultivated fields, at some little distance
to the north of the river. The second route, from Aulis,
followed the line of the present railway: it runs from Chalkis
along the sea-shore at the foot of Megálo-Vounó,[2] close by
the two bays, Mikró and Megálo Vathý, then by a cutting
through the low, but very rough and rocky hills that form
the southern spurs of Megálo-Vounó and separate the
narrow stretch of land by the sea-coast from the plain
through which runs the road from Thebes to Chalkis.
These hills too are not difficult, but they do not invite a
crossing: they extend southwards as far as to join the hills
over which goes the road from Oropos, so as to shut out
completely the view of the sea from any town or village of
Boeotia to the west of them. Beyond these hills the road runs
along the fertile plain of Thebes, almost level the whole way
—over only one very gently rising hill, till it joins the high
road from Chalkis.

From Chalkis to Thebes the road goes by a high pass over

---

[1] As an instance of the dangers of the Euripos to ancient ships (and showing how
passenger traffic, if not trade, in ancient as in modern times, kept to 'routes de terre .
maxima et de navigations minima'), it may be noted that the embassy of the Hyper-
boreans to Delos travelled the length of Euboea by land (Hdt. iv 33). Macan indeed
in his note ad loc. says of this route from the centre of the Aegean to the North 'up
through Euboean waters (the Euripos) from Karystos to Malis'; but it is clear that
the journey was through Euboea by land: from the Maliac Gulf διαπορεύεσθαι ἐς
Εὔβοιαν· πόλιν τε ἐς πόλιν πέμπειν, μεχρὶ Καρύστου. τὸ δ' ἀπὸ ταύτης, ἐκλιπεῖν
Ἄνδρον· Καρυστίους γὰρ εἶναι τοὺς κομίζοντας ἐς Τῆνον· Τηνίους δὲ ἐς Δῆλον.
[2] Ancient Mt. Messapion.

Mt. Messapion; the ascent, from the side of Euboea, is extremely steep over ground that is now but sparsely wooded. At nine kilometres from Chalkis the top is reached, then after one short steep bend the descent westwards is straight and very gradual, leading down through cultivated fields to the plain of Thebes.[1] The country is quite open, and all places situated on the western side of the pass look naturally towards the interior, not towards Chalkis and the sea. Mykalessos was situated just below the steep part of the descent to the west of the summit of the pass.

Inland from Anthedon the route is not difficult.[2] North and south of Paralimni rocky mountains descend down to the water's edge; the path, however, does not ascend far, but runs along the south side of the lake to the village of Moríki, then turns southward across the plain to Thebes. To Akraiphnion, and so to Orchomenos across the Kopais, the path is steep and rocky, but nowhere does it reach any great height.

The route from Larymna to Orchomenos is easy (when the Kopais is drained), to Thebes circuitous and difficult. From the small but fertile plain in which Larymna lay, it mounts up the narrow but short valley of a stream (that has its source in the spring called Anchoe), and passes across wide and open moorland covered chiefly with evergreen oak and wild olive, then through a rough valley (Kephalári) along the line of the ancient shafts of the tunnel that was intended to take the waters of the Kopais,[3] till it arrives at the north-eastern extremity of the lake just above the Biniá Katavothra. Thence to Orchomenos, in the days of the Minyans, the road would have gone straight across the ᾿Αθαμάντιον πεδίον[4] and the Kopais. But a traveller to

---

[1] In early times the port of Thebes for Euboea seems to have been Aulis, not Chalkis (Hesiod, *W. & D.* 646–53). There are still traces of an ancient road by Aulis, Frazer, *op. cit.* v, p. 70.

[2] Herakleides, *Descr. Gr.*, 23 (*F.H.G.* ii. p. 257) ὁδὸς πλαγία, ἁμαξήλατος δι' ἀγρῶν πορεία.

[3] For these shafts, and the draining of the lake by the Minyans, see Kambanis, *B.C.H.* xvi (1892) pp. 121 ff., xvii, pp. 322 ff.; Curtius, *Gesamm. Abh.* i, pp. 266 ff.; Noack, *Ath. Mitt.* xix (1894) pp. 410–2; and esp. Philippson, *Der Kopaissee, Zeitschr. d. Berl. Ges. f. Erdkunde*, xxix (1894), pp. 1–90.

[4] That the ᾿Αθαμάντιον πεδίον was the bay at the N.E. end of the Kopais, and not the inlet S.W. of Akraiphnion, as is generally supposed (see Frazer, vol. v, pp. 130–1), is shown by Pausanias (ix 23. 5, 24. 1). He is travelling (by the route here described) from Thebes to Larymna *viâ* Akraiphnion. Arrived at the latter town

Thebes must go first southwards along a rocky path just above the eastern shore of the Kopais, then descend into a stony but in part cultivated valley (the one place along the northern and eastern shores of the Kopais, from Orchomenos to Arkaiphnion, where barren mountains do not descend, abruptly or gradually, right down to the plain),[1] and then turn westwards by a high and very rough path through Kókkino village and round the shoulder of Mt. Ptoon southward again to Karditza, a village situated just north of the ruins of Akraiphnion. It is a full day's journey ἀνδρὶ εὐζώνῳ from Larymna to Karditza. Thence to Thebes the path goes either over low but rocky hills past lake Hylike and then through the Aonian plain, or by the shore of the Kopais round the Sphinx Mountain to join the road from Haliartos to Thebes.

From the small port of Halai on the Euboean Gulf a road goes through Malesína over the low wooded hill called Aëtolimá to Martíno, and thence down the nearly always dry valley of a stream to Larymna. Except by a steep and very rocky path from Martíno to Hyettos and thence to Kopai, Halai has no independent connexion with the interior.

The road to Thebes from Opous, whose harbour was the next port on the Euboean Channel, must have led through Kopai, and thence across the Kopais past Gla to Akraiphnion and the Aonian plain. The first part of the journey lay through all the rocky and mountainous country which lies between the Kopais and the Channel and must at all times have been impossible for wheeled traffic. The northern half of this is well-wooded, and the path winds its way up several magnificent gorges high above the streams which rush down them, past one or two isolated patches where olives are

he says, προελθόντι ἀπὸ τῆς πόλεως ἐν δεξιᾷ is the sanctuary of Apollo Ptoos; ὑπερβαλόντων δὲ τὸ ὅρος τὸ Πτῶον ἐστι .. Λάρυμνα.... ἐξ Ἀκραιφνίου δὲ ἰόντι εὐθεῖαν ἐπὶ λίμνην τὴν Κηφισίδα .. πεδίον καλούμενόν ἐστιν Ἀθαμάντιον ... καὶ διαπλεύσαντί εἰσι Κῶπαι. Going from Akraiphnion to Larymna, you first travel northwards, then turn round sharply to the right over the shoulder of the mountain; if you continue straight on you descend to the Kopais and ultimately arrive at Kopai on the opposite shore. That Pausanias did not himself travel by this way to Kopai is shown by his failure to mention the fortress at Gla which he would have passed (cf. de Ridder, B.C.H. xviii, p. 271, n. 2).

[1] Those belts of green and fertile-looking soil which Mr. Grundy's map, for instance, gives to Kopai and Aspledon, did not exist before the lake was drained.

grown, till it reaches the summit of the range—a flat piece of ground, grassy and intersected with streams, and very marshy—the beginnings of the rivers. Immediately opposite are the actual peaks, sheer cliffs some twenty to thirty feet high. After winding round these, the path descends rapidly through steep valleys and arrives at the head of the small plain in which are the villages of Loutsi and Pávlou. It is a long day's journey from Opous to Pávlou. Thence the way is over fairly level but extremely rough and rocky ground as far as Kopai, with low and bare hills on either side. The path from Hyettos (N.E. of Pávlou) to Orchomenos, before it descends to the Kopais between Mts. Strovíki and Trelloyánni, goes through very similar country. It was in this mountainous district that the always unimportant towns, Korseia, Kyrtones, Hyettos, Olmones and Kopai were situated, each with its own small plain of cultivable ground; the ancient, like the modern, inhabitants must have been almost exclusively shepherds.

There is also a path from Atalante to Loutsi (now more used than the other) which keeps more to the west. It ascends the mountains, on this side covered with soil on which many bushes and trees grow, in a south-easterly direction, and arrives at the top—a long, flat and grassy plain—just north of Kolákas; thence it descends over much more rocky ground, and in parts very steeply, to Loutsi.

From Atalante to Orchomenos, the other supposed centre of trade-routes, the way goes first westwards along the modern high road, then turns south over low and cultivated hills into a valley about one and a half miles long, with a flat surface some 300 yards wide and very regular and steep hills on either side—like a great broad street. At the southern end of this is Hyampolis guarding Phokis against incursions of the Lokrians.[1] Thence the natural road into the interior leads to Parapotámioi, thence to the Corinthian Gulf through Daulis, and so does not touch Boeotia. From Hyampolis to Orchomenos the path bends round to the east of the hill on which Abai stood, and goes over rough and rocky, but no-

---

[1] A slightly shorter path from Atalante leads up a gorge to the S.W. of that town and high over moors and hills—past a spring for the traveller—and down into the valley at the north end of the 'street.'

where high ground, down to Tsamáli, near the ancient
Aspledon.

Along the southern coast of Boeotia and Phokis, for
vessels coming from 'Sicily, Carthage, and the West,' the
harbours are for the most part excellent. It is not difficult to
reach the gulf of Krisa, and once there 'you may anchor
wherever you please within the two small islands; but small
vessels may go inside the low point, where there is good
anchorage from nine to thirteen fathoms, with good holding
ground, perfectly land-locked.'[1]

The west part of Aspra Spitia Bay (Antikyra) 'affords a
well-sheltered and good anchorage in thirteen to sixteen
fathoms of water about two and a half cables from the surrounding shores.'[2]

The Bay of Dómbrena (Thisbe) is equally favourable.
'This magnificent bay is five and a half miles in length east
and west and from about one to one and a half miles in
width. In the middle is Kouveli islet. . . . The shores of
the bay are rocky and irregular, the water is generally deep,
and there are no hidden dangers. . . . The entrance is from
the south, and is fronted by Phonia, Gromboloura, and Mak-
ro, three islands which make a land-locked basin of the interior. . . . Mt. Korombili, of conical form and 2,670 feet high,
rises over the east part of the bay, and serves as a good
guide.'[3]

Lastly, of Livadostro Bay (Kreusis) we are told: 'the Kala
islets lie nearly in the middle of the entrance to Dómbrena
Bay, but are steep-to and not of much importance except for
the space they occupy. East of Dómbrena Bay is port Livadostro, an inlet two miles wide at the entrance; on its west
side the coast rises almost perpendicularly from the sea to
the high land of Mt. Korombili.'[4]

The routes from the interior to this coast are interesting.
That from Lebadeia (Livadiá: which now holds the position
of Orchomenos as chief town in Western Boeotia) to
Antikyra,[5] after passing over cultivated hills and valleys, and

---

[1] *Sailing Directions*, ed. 1852, p. 31.
[2] *Medit. Pilot*,[3] iv, p. 426.   (6th ed. [1929], iii, pp. 58–70.)
[3] *Ibid.* pp. 427–8. Cf. Bérard, i, pp. 430 ff.
[4] *Ibid.* p. 428. Cf. Paus. ix 32. 1 for the violent winds of this gulf.
[5] See Paus. x 5. 5, 36. 5; Frazer, v, pp. 222–33.

some extensive moorland, descends into the wild and narrow valley of the Cleft Way, out into the small plain of Ambrossos (now Distomo).[1] From Distomo the way ascends a little to pass over the hills which shut out the view of the sea from the plain, then descends with astonishing abruptness down a narrow valley southwards to the sea; at the bottom of the valley it turns to the right along the coast to Antikyra. So that the first thing that faced a 'caravan' with goods that had been disembarked at Antikyra was a very difficult climb up a narrow and precipitous valley.

The route from Thebes to the Port of Thisbe (Dómbrena Bay) is curiously like this one, though so much easier. From Thebes to the town of Thisbe is perfectly simple, first westward along the road to the Kopais district, then to the left up the easy valley of the Thespios as far as Thespiai. Here opens out another valley from the north-west coming from Askra and the Valley of the Muses. From Thespiai the road goes down the equally easy valley of the Permessos, till it turns into the plain of Dómbrena just above the village. From here, as from Distomo, the sea is not yet visible; the road after crossing the plain must first rise over the rocky and barren hills and then descend rapidly to the small harbour.[2] Though the bay is large and quite safe, almost everywhere the mountains come right down steeply to the water's edge, so that there is very little room for quays. With the barren hills for its background no one can think of the Bay of Dómbrena as the centre of busy international traffic.

Also typical of Boeotian 'isthmic-routes' is that from Plataia to Kreusis.[3] On the map (followed by Bérard) it looks simple enough: Plataia is but three hours from the coast, and the route is along a river-bed. Yet it is in fact a difficult one: three ridges connect the mountains to the south of the Oëroë with those to the north, and the river cuts its way through these in narrow ravines that leave no room for the path, which has to climb the mountain side. Many mountain

[1] The route from Orchomenos was probably the same, especially as the Sacred Way to Delphi went by Livadiá; but the easier, if longer, road would have been through Chaironeia and Daulis, to join the other at the Schiste.

[2] Paus. ix 32. 2 πλέοντι δὲ ἐκ Κρευσίδος οὐκ ἄνω, παρὰ δὲ αὐτὴν Βοιωτίαν, πόλις ἐστὶν ἐν δεξιᾷ Θίσβη. πρῶτα μὲν ὄρος ἐστὶ πρὸς θαλάσσῃ, τοῦτο δὲ ὑπερβαλόντα πεδίον σε ἐκδέξεται καὶ μετὰ τοῦτο ἄλλο ὄρος· ἐν δὲ ταῖς ὑπωρείαις ἐστὶν ἡ πόλις.

[3] See Skias, Παρνασσός, iv (1900), pp. 114–39, with a map.

D

torrents flow from both south and north to join the Oëroë, and the path must make wide detours round each. It is not till two-and-a-half hours of the journey have passed, but half-an-hour from the coast, that the sea is visible. This is typical, like the routes to the opposite coast to Larymna, Anthedon, Chalkis or Aulis, and Oropos. In addition there is a scarcity of good drinking water along the coasts of the bay. Kreusis did not even belong to Plataia but to Thespiai.[1]

In addition, on this coast were the small towns of Tiphai, Boulis, and Korsiai; but they were the homes of fishermen only, then as now, and did no trade. Communication with the interior was too difficult.[2]

Another point to be remembered is that these valleys, Aigosthena, Kreusis, Thisbe, Antikyra, and Amphissa, are all cut off from one another by high and difficult mountain ranges. Except for precipitous and rocky paths, ₁the only communication between them is by sea (the easy and natural way) or by a devious route up one valley and down the next.[3] This means that each little port has its own *Hinterland* to draw on and nothing more; that there is no possibility of the growth of any one large port, which as a medium of exchange and as a centre of international traffic is essential. Contrast with this the way almost all Attica, east of Mt. Aigaleos, slopes down towards the Peiraeus, and still more, contrast the opposite shore of the Corinthian Gulf, the coast line of Achaia and Elis; here there is a strip of flat land stretching the whole length of the coast, which makes possible a trad-

---

[1]If Plataia ever had a harbour, it was probably that now called H. Vasilios, S.E. of Kreusis, to which a rough path over the mountains S. of the Oëroë leads. The olive groves here and at Kreusis (in the small valleys of arable land) belong now to the inhabitants of Kaparéli, a village not far from Leuktra, not to those of Kókla, the village near Plataia (Skias, *op. cit.* p. 120).

[2]Paus. ix 32. 4; x 37. 2; Frazer v, p. 134. The inhabitants of Tiphai were known as the best seamen in Boeotia: a poor honour, and they made a virtue of necessity. See Skias, *op. cit.* p. 116, n. 2.

[3]Mr. Grundy in his map marks main *straight* roads between Pagai, Aigosthena, Kreusis, Tiphai, Thisbe, Korsiai, Boulis, Antikyra, and Kirrha, all the way along this mountainous coast. Except between Antikyra and Kirrha, where the path is a fairly easy one and goes over some cultivated ground (through Desphina), there is not now, nor ever was, any sort of direct land connexion between these places, other than the roughest of Greek mountain paths. Cf. Paus. x 37. 2, on the way from Antikyra to Boulis—ἐξ Ἀντικύρας δι' ἠπείρου μὲν καὶ εἰ ἀρχήν ἐστιν οὐκ οἶδα· οὕτω δύσβατα ὄρη καὶ τραχέα τὰ μεταξὺ Ἀντικύρας τέ ἐστι καὶ Βουλίδος· ἐς δὲ τὸν λιμένα σταδίων ἐξ Ἀντικύρας ἐστὶν ἑκατόν. The same is not so true of the ports on the north-eastern coast. Oropos, Aulis, Chalkis, and Anthedon are not difficult to connect by road; nor Larymna, Halai, and Opous.

ing-centre like Patras, as well as minor ports such as Akrata, Vostitza, and Katákolo. There is no big port on the northern shore of the Gulf.[1]

Boeotia, then, possesses some routes from the interior to the sea that are easy, some that do not of themselves invite travellers, but at the same time do not afford any very considerable obstacles to their passage if other advantages are present. The journeys, too, by sea up the channels north and south of the Euripos, are attended with difficulties (of which the lack of water is the greatest), but these are not such as could not be overcome by very eager traders; while in the Gulf of Corinth the harbours and bays afford every advantage to the sailor, so long as he avoids the storms of the extreme north-eastern gulf near Kreusis. That is to say, if Boeotia as a whole, lay in the way of trade-routes from west, north, and east, so that for instance, trade from the north to the west would naturally disembark at Larymna or Anthedon or Chalkis (or even at Opous in Lokris), and take to the sea again at Antikyra or Thisbe or Kreusis, then the roads within Boeotia are not sufficiently difficult to discourage such trade. From Chalkis or Anthedon to Thebes and so to the opposite coast, would be especially favourable routes. But if Boeotia does not possess this favourable position, then there is nothing within the country itself to tempt either the inhabitants to the sea, or through-traders to the land. Nearly all the way along its coast mountains or hills slope down to the water's edge and shut out the view of the interior, while the plains are so surrounded by mountains that from nowhere in Boeotia, except mountain-tops and places actually on the coast, is the sea visible.

Relying on Ephoros, Strabo, and Pseudo-Skymnos, as on three independent and equally trustworthy authorities, speaking of 'les manuels de géographie' and an ancient proverb when he means a single worthless compiler, and

---

[1]This is the principal reason why the trade of Livadiá, which used to go to Antikyra (*Medit. Pilot*[3] iii, p. 426), now goes to the Peiraeus since the opening of the railway. It is not so much that the time taken is shorter, as that, once at the Peiraeus, you are already at a centre of exchange. The inhabitants of Antikyra are now all agriculturists or fishermen; and the carefully engineered road which connected it with Distomo, and had more turns and bends in its short but steep course than any other road in Greece, is now falling in ruin; grass grows over it, and a bridge has broken down. The peasants of course prefer the steep mule-track mentioned above.

implying that they state that trade passed through Boeotia
when, at the most, all they say is that foreign goods might
easily have reached Boeotia, M. Bérard has asserted that
Boeotia really is such an isthmus, is situated at an important
junction of trade-routes with ports turned to all points of the
horizon, and by means of this explains the tradition of the
Phoenicians at Thebes, the very centre of this happily-
placed country. But he omits to consider one very important
factor—the island of Euboea and its situation along the
north-eastern coasts of Boeotia and Lokris. Euboea is really
part of the mainland, the channels of Euripo and Atalante
are but two gulfs stretching far into the interior.[1] This
means that on its east coast, the coast that is really open to
the Propontis and to Egypt, Boeotia has not a single harbour.
No more inhospitable, shelterless coast could well be imagined: the mountains everywhere descend right down to the
sea-shore. Owing to the absence of harbours on the east of
Euboea, and the inhospitable nature of the coast, any vessel
from the north and east making for Boeotia finds the way
blocked by Euboea, so that Larymna, Anthedon, or Aulis
can only be reached by a long détour round either extremity
of the island. Traffic from the Hellespont to the West, if it
took an isthmus-route at all, and that not the isthmus of
Corinth, would pass through the northern straits of Euboea,
and land either in the Gulf of Volo or perhaps in the Maliac
Gulf. In either case, the journey thence by land would reach
the Gulf of Corinth at Itéa, and so would go through Phokis,
but would not touch Boeotia.[2] No sailor would round the
extreme north-west point of Euboea, then veer round and
sail south-east till Anthedon or Chalkis was reached, in
order that his goods might then take the caravan-route

[1]Geologically this is also true. Neumann-Partsch, *Physikalische Geographie v.
Griechenland*, pp. 174–6.

[2]The only east coast harbour is Kyme, whence there is a long and circuitous road
to Chalkis. No one who has watched the unloading of ships, by hand labour only,
will imagine that any trader unloaded goods at Kyme, sent 'caravans' across
Euboea, embarked his goods again at Eretria or Chalkis, unloaded them on the
Boeotian shore, sent them across Boeotia, and then re-embarked them at Thisbe or
Antikyra, all in order to avoid sailing as far as the isthmus of Corinth.

How far the Hellespont and the Pontus were open to traffic in the Mycenaean
age, is very doubtful. M. Bérard assumes that the Phoenicians were there before the
Milesians. See Mr. T. W. Allen's remarks on this matter, *J.H.S.* xxx (1910), pp.
308, 319; and Leaf's *Troy*.

through Thebes to Dómbrena or Livadostro. Similarly with vessels from the east and south-east, sailing for the west. Phoenicians indeed from Tyre or Cyprus would not touch Greece at all, but sail along the north coast of Africa. But from the islands of the Aegean and the coast of Asia Minor to Italy and Sicily, trade would pass through Corinth; this is by far the quickest route: to sail first up the Euripos, then cross Boeotia would be waste of time only, and no easier voyage—it was as dangerous to round the headland of Kaphareus as Sounion.[1] And we know as a matter of history that with the growth of the Greek cities in Asia Minor and in Sicily, grew also the importance of Corinth—in the eighth and seventh centuries.

But, while Euboea shuts off from Boeotia the trade of the east, there is one case in which trade might have crossed the eastern plain through Thebes to the west—the trade of Euboea itself, of Chalkis, with its colonies in Italy and Sicily. There is also a second route, a land-route, across Boeotia, that from Phokis and the North to Attica; thence from Attica past Megara and Corinth to the Peloponnese.[2] But the importance of both these routes depends entirely on the importance of the countries or towns at each extremity—of Chalkis and Sicily in the one case, of Phokis and Attica and Megara in the other. But it is worthy of remark in this connexion—M. Bérard habitually ignores such points—of how little importance were Chalkis, Attica, and Megara in the Homeric period. The latter is not even mentioned. Chalkis reached the heyday of its greatness in the seventh and sixth centuries and then declined; Megara flourished about the same time; Athens even later. Had these towns had a large trade in Homeric times, then Kadmean Thebes might have been in some measure 'un carrefour de routes isthmiques,' or of one isthmus-route, from Chalkis to the Corinthian Gulf, and one land-route, from Phokis and the

[1] I would now say this eastern trade *might* pass through Corinth, and that this is by far the quickest *isthmus*-route (if an isthmus-route were taken, that is). See below, pp. 190 ff.

[2] Thucydides (i 13. 5) thought that in early times Corinth was only a link between two continents not between two seas; though according to Cornford (*op. cit.*, p. 33) 'this is a modern view; we naturally think of the isthmus as a *land*-link, "opening up a range of territory"; we travel along it by the railway which takes us from Patras, through Corinth, to Athens.'

north to Attica.[1] How unimportant these 'isthmic routes' were even after the rise of Euboea, can be seen by many instances. Mykalessos, only six miles from the coast, situated on the very line of the traffic between Chalkis and Thebes, but on the *land* side of the pass, counted as an inland town,[2] and in the Peloponnesian war was as little expecting an attack from the sea as if it had been in the very centre of the plain.[3] Plataia, too, only three hours from Kreusis, had no traffic with the sea, and was proportionately proud of the part it took in the battle of Salamis.[4] The route from Anthedon to Thebes is easy; yet scarcely anybody mentions it.[5] It passes by the two lakes, but of Likeri we do not know much more than the ancient name, of Paralimni not even that.[6] As Mr. Frazer says:[7] 'It is strange that ancient history and mythology are almost wholly silent on the subject of these two lakes, one of which at least has good claims to beauty. In their secluded mountains they lay remote from the bustle and traffic of the world, from the caravans of commerce, and the march of armies.' And how much do we hear of Antikyra, the southern port of Orchomenos, or of Abai and Hyampolis, the two towns on the route from Orchomenos to the northern coast? Of all the ports of Boeotia only Oropos appears ever to have been of great importance—as the place to which came traffic for Athens from Thebes by land, and from Euboea and the north by sea.[8]

Add to this, that, though tradition (at least from the fifth

[1]Tradition perhaps supports this view of the comparative unimportance of this land-route in early times. Neither of the two great early invasions from the north into the Peloponnese, the Achaean and the Dorian, is said to have touched Boeotia. When the Boeotians of Thessaly made their conquest, they came for the sake of the land itself; they did not march through it on their way southwards.

[2]ἔνθα Βοιωτῶν ἐν μεσογαίᾳ πόλις Μυκαλησσός ἦν, Paus. i 23. 3. This is said from the point of view of the sailor in the Euripos, which is significant. The language is similar to that used in the sailing hand-books of the time.

[3]Thuc. vii 29. 3 (ἀπροσδοκήτοις μὴ ἄν ποτέ τινας σφίσιν ἀπὸ θαλάσσης τοσοῦτον ἐπαναβάντας ἐπιθέσθαι).

[4]Hdt. viii 1 (ἄπειροι τῆς ναυτικῆς ἐόντες); Thuc. iii 54. 4 (ἤπειρῶται ὄντες).

[5]Pausanias (ix 26. 2) gives a rationalistic form of the Sphinx-legend, according to which she led a pirate-band which landed at Anthedon and ravaged the Thebaid.

[6]Ulrichs (*Reisen*, ii, p. 258) suggested the lake of Harma (from Aelian) and the lake of Hyria (from Ovid). No earlier writer mentions it.

[7]*Paus.* v, p. 62.

[8]See Herakleides, *Descr. Graeciae*, 6 (*F.H.G.* ii, p. 256). So too one might land at Marathon for Athens (*Od.* vii 78–81).

century onwards) placed Phoenicians in Thebes, it has nothing to say of their existence in any of the coast towns; which is strange if they were in Boeotia because of the country's advantages as a commercial centre. For how did Phoenicians rule and trade in Thebes, unless they held also the ports at the extremities of the various isthmic routes? Indeed all the legends of the Boeotian towns suggest that in early times the influence of Thebes spread over the whole of the interior of Eastern Boeotia but that it stopped short of the coast; and similarly, that Orchomenos ruled over the western plain, but not over the coast-towns at its extremities. Theban legend can be traced, that is, in Plataia and Tanagra in the south, at Mykalessos, Harma, Glisas, and the Tenerian plain in the east and north, at Thespiai and the Sphinx mountain in the west. But there is a little or no Theban legend in the coast-towns, Oropos, Hyria,[1] Aulis, Anthedon, Thisbe, Tiphai, Korsiai, and Kreusis; just as there is none in Eleutherai or Erythrai on the Attic border, or in Onchestos and Askra on the west. In the same way the influence of Orchomenos can be seen to have been strong in the western district, in the Kopais plain itself, at Lebadeia, Koroneia, Haliartos, Schoinos (on Lake Hylike), Mt. Ptoon, Akraiphnion, Olmones, Hyettos, and Aspledon. It does not exist either in Halai or Larymna, and is to be seen only faintly in Anthedon, on the northern coast, nor in Antikyra, Ambrossos, or Kirrha on the southern.[2] All of which suggests that the importance of Thebes and Orchomenos at this time was due to the natural wealth of Boeotia itself, not to their being centres of international trade. This wealth was due to the richness of the soil; the agricultural products of Boeotia were proverbial in antiquity.[3] Not well suited to the olive,[4] for except in a few favoured spots like the Bay of Skroponéri, Anthedon, and Dómbrena, the winter is

---

[1]Those legends (of Nykteus and Lykos) which connect Hyria with Thebes suggest rather an early conquest of the latter by the former, than *vice versâ*.

[2]See Roscher's Lexicon, *s.vv.* the eponymous heroes and heroines.

[3]See especially Eur. *Phoen.* 638 ff.; Theophr., *Hist. Plant.* viii 4. 4–5; *Caus. Plant.* iv 9. 1–6; Pliny, *Nat. Hist.* xviii 7. 12 §§ 63, 65–6 (wheat); Herakleides, *Descr. Gr.* 8–9 (vines at Tanagra); Paus. ix 28. 1; Theophr. *Hist. Plant.* ix 10. 3 (the soil of Helikon).

[4]But some mid-European fruit-trees flourish that are unknown in the rest of Greece: Philippson, *Der Kopaissee*, p. 78.

too cold, and, except for the hill slopes, especially by Livadiá, having a soil which is in most parts too heavy for the vine, Boeotia was pre-eminently the country for wheat-growing: it had much of the best corn-land in Greece. The positions of Thebes and Orchomenos gave them naturally the predominance in the eastern and western plain respectively. Both of them, Thebes with the springs of the Dirke and the Ismenos, Orchomenos with those of the river Melas,[1] had abundant supplies of water. The former is in the very centre of the eastern district, the latter commanded the Kopais. Their early importance, in the time of Kadmeans and Minyans, was due to their position as the chief towns in two large agricultural districts; the later importance of Thebes was due to the same cause; while the later comparative insignificance of Orchomenos was due, as Strabo implies,[2] to the flooding of the Kopais plain which destroyed what had been the chief source of the wealth of the Minyan city. We need not look for trade-routes.

NOTE

In the second edition of his work, which was published in 1927, Bérard had a note on this article of mine; in which he says, 'je n'ai jamais répondu à cette critique de ma "théorie," estimant qu' une discussion suppose, de part et d'autre, un minimum de bonne foi.' My lack of good faith consisted, first, in having the impression that Bérard had not visited the interior of Boeotia (not, as he thought, that he had not sailed the coasts)—an impression which, as stated above p. 21, n. 2), was shared by Leaf. I was wrong in this; had Bérard pointed this out earlier, I should, of course, have withdrawn my note. The falsity of the impression in no way weakens my argument. Secondly, he accuses me of suppressing his statement that the Homeric Nisa was on the site of the later Megara when I wrote (p. 37): 'it is worthy of remark in this connexion—M. Bérard habitually ignores such points—of how little importance were Chalkis, Attica and Megara in the Homeric period: the latter is not even

---

[1] Now the Mavropotamos: so-called both in ancient and modern times, according to Mr. Frazer (v, p. 193) 'from the dark colour of its deep clear water, in contrast to the light-coloured and muddy water of the neighbouring Cephissus'—itself called Mavro-Nero; the names are often interchanged.

[2] ix, p. 415.

mentioned.' But even if Nisa is Megara, it was still a place of no importance in Homer; and even if Bérard is right in calling it the port of Kadmean Thebes, that still does not establish an isthmic route, for which other ports on the opposite coast are essential.

Bérard added triumphantly the use of the 'isthmic route' Itea-Salonika in the last war by the Allies on French advice. An isthmic journey to avoid submarines is something different from one by merchants to avoid the sea; and this route does not come near Thebes. As I have said above, merchants from the north and north-east who did want to travel as much as possible by land would (if they did not go through Thrace, Macedonia and Thessaly) disembark in the gulf of Lamia and go up the very steep valley to western Phokis and thence by the equally difficult pass to Amphissa and Krisa; Kadmean Thebes does not come into the picture. Nor did Bérard ever answer the question why Thebes was not an important centre of isthmic routes in classical times.

Quite recently Professor Toynbee (*A Study of History*, i, p. 404) has claimed for Minyan Orchomenos the place given to Kadmean Thebes by Bérard. 'We conjecture that the Minyae were a maritime commercial people who came by sea to the four points on the Continent at which we find them'; which are Orchomenos, Iolkos, Pylos, and the river Axios. 'Orchomenos . . . is situated at the key-point of one of the portages between the Aegean Sea and the Corinthian Gulf. The spur of Mount Acontius, on which the city of Orchomenos stands, commands the passage across the river Cephissus for anybody travelling overland from the Aegean port of Larymna, on the Euripus, to the Corinthian Gulf port of Cirrha, at the head of this bay of Crisa.' But Larymna is in no proper sense an Aegean port; others travelling overland from it might go south of the Kopais, by Haliartos and Lebadeia to Antikyra, or to Thespiai and Thisbe; and how many travellers were there from this obscure port, at which Orchomenos and the Minyans are unknown? What moreover is meant by Orchomenos 'commanding the passage' across the Kephissos? Professor Toynbee would place the Minyans where we find them recorded in place-names; would he place the English in England where the name is similarly preserved?

III

TRADERS AND MANUFACTURERS
IN GREECE[1]

THERE are two errors, in some respects complementary,
to one or other of which all historians some of the time, and
some historians all of the time, are specially liable. The first
is the use of language, of certain words and phrases, appropriate to contemporary history, and the application of them
to the past, in such a way as to mislead the reader and, as
often as not, the writer as well. To take an obvious instance:
we speak of political parties in Athens—a war-party, a peace-
party, a moderate party, Perikles' or Demosthenes' party.
This, of course, can be defended if by party you mean a
group of people holding for a time similar views and no
more. But in modern European history the word party has
come to have a much more precise meaning; a modern
reader naturally has this in mind; and the use of the word
therefore in a history of Greece may be misleading. Similarly,
to take an instance germane to the subject of this paper: the
terms capital and capitalist. It is obviously correct, in a
sense, to speak of capitalists in ancient Athens: a farmer
who owns land and stock is a capitalist; one who has money
to invest in industrial enterprise, who has liquid capital,
is one even more clearly; and Athens was full of such
men. Thucydides alludes to the fact, as a well-known one,
that one of the important results of a settled government is
accumulation of capital.[2] But when we speak of a capitalist
society to-day, more often than not we are thinking not
of the fact that a vast number of people have some capital
however little of their own, but of the very rich and powerful,
who control large industries and widespread banking busi-
nesses, who, by their wealth, directly influence, or so we
think, the policies of states, even, it is asserted, have governments in their pockets. And some writers on ancient history,

[1]A paper read before the West of Scotland branch of the Classical Association of
Scotland in December, 1934.
[2]i 2. 2.

anxious to explain the so long neglected economic causes of political events, have thus written of Greek capitalists: they have said, for instance, that the capitalists of the Peiraeus forced Perikles' hand and the Peloponnesian war was the result—a war, they say, primarily due to economic causes, the significance of which was quite unknown to ancient historians. In doing so they mislead both themselves and their readers; for they have not first stopped to inquire what sort of people these capitalists of the Peiraeus were; it is just this word *capitalist*, with its modern colouring, which may lead to error. It gives the wrong tone to the picture.

To rectify this sort of mistake much has recently been written both by others and by Professor Hasebroek, whose recent book on *Trade and Politics in Ancient Greece*,[1] has created some stir: 'a useful reaction against the fashionable exaggerations of the economic historian.' Hasebroek has a not very difficult task in showing up some of these exaggerations; but in doing so he falls into the second kind of error of which I spoke, a kind which leads to worse misjudgement of the past than does the first. I mean the error of assuming that because a thing was not done in earlier times in the same way as we do it now, it was not done at all; of supposing that before the age of steamships, railways and motor-cars no-one travelled, before the age of printing hardly anyone read a book, that because in antiquity men had not our elaborate facilities both of transport and of international banking, therefore they did, practically, no trade—only a little, of the simplest kind of barter. (Just as you will always find men who travel extensively, but continue to believe that foreigners don't do things that their own countrymen do, because they do them differently.) This seems to me a fundamental error; and it is this, in relation to trade and industry, which I am examining in this paper. As we shall see, Hasebroek falls into absurdity and self-contradiction, just because he knows that ancient capitalists—in trade and manufacture—were in many respects different from modern ones: because, he argues, they were, as capitalists, politically unimportant (in this, as I think, he is right), therefore they were altogether

[1]English translation by L. M. Fraser and D. C. Macgregor: G. Bell and Sons 1933.

unimportant; because we must not speak of 'captains of industry,' 'merchant princes' and 'international financiers,' at least not without qualification or definition, therefore, trade itself was unimportant. It is wrong, he thinks, to speak of Athens, or Corinth, or Miletos, or Syracuse, or Byzantion, as commercial and trading states: all Greek states were predominantly agricultural, with some internal exchange of goods, with relatively little foreign trade: relatively, that is, both to their own agricultural activities, and to modern commercial states.

He insists that in all the numerous colonies settled by the Greeks throughout the Mediterranean and Black Sea areas, land, not trade, was the first consideration: men driven out of the home-lands whether by poverty or by political faction were looking for new land to cultivate overseas. That is true, at least with the exception only of certain *emporia*.[1] He also says that the majority at least of these colonies, especially those prosperous ones in S. Italy and Sicily, remained mainly agricultural. That also may be true. But it is also true that modern colonization, in the Americas and in Australasia, has been of the same type: all were originally agricultural and most are predominantly so still—at least in respect of foreign trade; and we do not say the commerce of these colonies is unimportant because their chief export is in food and raw materials. Or take the importing states of the old world: Hasebroek has to admit of course that Athens imported most of the corn she consumed and almost all her timber. He often makes a point that these were necessities; and somehow or other persuades himself that there is some essential difference between trade in necessities, in articles of primary consumption, and other trade.[2] As if this country did not import especially necessities, including corn and timber; but we are not regarded as any the less a com-

[1] We must remember as well that many of them were founded after trade with the countries in which they were founded was already common, and that this trade obviously in part determined the place of the colonies. See Blakeway, *B.S.A.*, xxxiii (1932–3), 170 ff.; *J.R.S.*, 1935, 129–39.

[2] 'Trade in general' is what he calls this (p. 144); almost, I suppose, trade for its own sake—like a game of tennis, just sending goods backwards and forwards. Similarly, Laistner, in his recently published *History of the Greek World from 479 to 323 B.C.*, writes: 'Commercial treaties, so called, were made to ensure the importation of essential commodities, not to further the growth of commerce as such' (p. 383).

mercial people for that. We might go indeed further: one of Hasebroek's main arguments is that the policy of ancient states was never determined by commercial considerations —neither foreign nor internal policy; yet a country dependent on supplies of *necessities* from abroad would, one might suppose, be more likely to take trade into consideration in its public policy than one which traded in non-essential goods.

Let us take a step further. Athens imported at least twice as much corn as she grew in Attica—probably considerably more on the average, but our evidence is too scanty and unsatisfactory for us to be certain —; at least two-thirds that is of her total consumption was from abroad. She imported all the timber she needed for shipbuilding, and a good deal of that needed for house-building and for furniture. She imported all her iron and bronze for every tool she made, or else the tools themselves. I mention three of the first necessities only. How did she pay for them? For the Greeks were well aware that imports and exports must in the long run, somehow, balance; and we may note in passing that they expressed this truth in what seems at least to be a more natural way than some do to-day—they did not say: we must, alas, buy some of the things we want from others in order that we may make for others what they want; they said: we must work and make things that others will buy in order that other people will work for us in producing the things we want. What then did they make to pay for these necessary imports? To this question we can unfortunately make no very satisfactory answer; but we can make certain things clear enough for the purposes of the present argument.

We know that they exported olives and olive-oil; but we have no idea in what quantities—that is, for what proportion of imports this sufficed. Also that they exported pottery: for this we have fortunately the indubitable evidence of archæology (an aspect of the question completely neglected by Hasebroek)—thousands upon thousands of pieces of Attic pottery have been found in all quarters of the Mediterranean and the Black Sea areas, wherever in fact excavation has taken place, as well as inland in Bulgaria and Serbia and the basins of the Danube and the Rhone. There is indeed a problem here: the greater part of this pottery belongs to the second half of the sixth century B.C. (when Athens finally ousted all her rivals in this trade) and to the fifth century. There was, by all the evidence, a decline in output in the fourth century—the cause for this being quite obscure. (It is not that other centres of manufacture outbid Athens: there is a decline everywhere in the Greek world—it would seem clear that, since men must have plates and cups and dishes and so forth, some other material took the place of earthenware, a material which does not survive the ages: one would suppose glass, as this had long been known, but that we do not hear of its general use in Greece.) However that may be, in the fourth century, some other Attic product must have in part taken the place of pottery as an export to pay for imports—for Athens was still importing corn, timber, and iron and bronze—if anything in greater quantities, per head of the population, than in the fifth century; and there was no longer the tribute of the subject allies to help payment indirectly.

Then there was the silver of the Laurion mines—a source of great wealth to Athens; and here again we have direct evidence of export in the vast numbers of Attic coins found in almost every part of the Mediterranean and the comparative rarity of foreign coins found in Attica[1]—that is, a great surplus of export in silver over import. (Remember that silver was the standard of currency almost everywhere—very few states coined gold.) We should note here that the find of Attic coins in another state does not necessarily imply direct trading with that state. In modern times, even when most countries were on a gold standard, trade is not done by a transference of gold, but by bits of paper—various forms of an I.O.U. An exporter to this country receives a promise to pay in sterling—he may not himself immediately buy goods here with this piece of paper, he may get someone in a third country to accept it, who then buys goods or services here; but ultimately the piece of paper must come back here, because only in this country can the I.O.U. be finally can-

[1]This statement must be made with reserve, till the full description of the coins found in the American excavations in the Agora has been published. (An analytical list up to date has been given in *Hesperia*, v (1936), 123-50.)

celled. But ancient trade was done by means of a transference of silver: a trader in Athens would pay for imports, normally, in Attic coins; but, since all coinage was supposed to be intrinsically worth its nominal value, a drachma to have a drachma's worth of silver in it, and since Attic coins were known to be of exceptional purity, there was no necessity for them to return ultimately to Athens; they would be accepted anywhere; Attic coins are a part of Attic exports and those found abroad will in most cases represent not, like a paper currency, the mere instrument of an exchange of goods, but the actual means of payment of some goods sent to Athens, though not necessarily from the country where the coins were found. It was the same as if Attica had exported bar silver, as gold-producing countries to-day pay for their imports largely with bar gold (whether Athens actually exported silver in bars, as well as in coin, we do not know—I don't know that such a thing is mentioned in any ancient writer).[1] That is why Xenophon, or whoever wrote the tract on *Revenues* which has come down to us under his name, is right when he says, in urging that the state should take a direct part in exploiting the mines of Laurion, that—provided of course the mines are not too soon exhausted—you cannot produce too much silver, as you can of every other product. It is true he was a very poor economist, and explains this truth by the naïve theory that whereas there is a limit to the amount a man will consume in food, or housing, or clothes, there is no limit to everyone's desire for money. Yet in practice he was right. Just as to-day there is, in practice though not in theory, no limit to the market for the one product that we hardly use at all, namely gold, and only too obviously a limit to the market for all the goods we need so badly, so that the gold-producing countries are happy and the food- and coal- and iron- and cotton- and rubber-producing countries sad—so in ancient Athens there was no limit to the market for her silver—with it she could buy what she wanted from abroad, whether the goods or, as for her fleet in the fifth century, the services of others.

[1]Hasebroek says no Greek state had any financial policy in connexion with trade; but Wilamowitz suggested long ago (*Aus Kydathen*, 1880, p. 30) that the reason why Athens preserved the archaic type of her coinage was its international usage—including in its area of circulation barbarian lands as well.

In the absence of any figures for this, as for her other exports, we still cannot definitely say how her imports were paid for. We can be reasonably sure of other exports as well —manufactured goods—and what we call invisible exports —shipping and tourist traffic. But the fact that we have no figures and no exact nor comprehensive description of Athenian trade, is no reason for denying what is obvious— that she must have paid for her imports, and paid for them by exporting goods and services, not as Rome in the republican period by money collected from subject states—at least not in the fourth century, when trade was at least as active as in the fifth and there were no subject states. When Philip for a time held up the trade with the Black Sea by his attacks on Byzantion and Perinthos, there were some 200 vessels waiting to come through the Bosporos to the Aegean.[1] We must remember the statements so frequently made by ancient writers—that goods from all the world were to be had in Athens, that Greek and foreign traders of all kinds were settled in the city and its port (we are told later that good Attic was only to be heard in the country districts): general statements of this kind must always be received with caution, but in this case we can be confident that the general picture, that of a busy, cosmopolitan port, is a correct one. It is in fact the natural sequence. Men begin by trading in necessities, and if this is on a large scale, the facilities of all kinds thereby created lead to a general trade in all sorts of goods.

What, then, was the fashion of this industry and commerce? How was it carried on? Or rather, what were the methods peculiar to the ancient world, those which differed from our own? The principal thing to keep in mind is that big as the total of trade was, every individual industry and every individual transaction was on a small scale. There were no big captains of industry, no big international financiers; and not only no powerfully rich individuals, but no big companies—in fact no companies in our sense of the word at all. This fact can be brought out best if we consider the silver and lead mining industry at Laurion. Initially mining demands a considerable capital—relatively, that is, to other

[1]Didymos, *Comm. Demosth.*, col. 10. 45–50.

industries—owing to the large amount of preliminary work
to be done—in sinking shafts, making galleries, extracting
the metal and smelting, before the product can be sold. The
advantages of united planning and execution of all the
work in one area such as that of Laurion (which is not very
large) are obvious. And all, or nearly all, the mines were the
property of the state, so that there were no difficulties arising
from individual ownership of the surface land in small
parcels; the state could have arranged, whether by its own
officers working the mines itself or by letting to contractors,
for a combined working of the whole area, or at least of large
sections of it. But nothing of the kind was done. On the
contrary the state let out small sections of the area, as
separate mines, to individuals, who could within certain
limits work each his own mine as he wished; and for short
periods only, never more than ten years: a man bought a
lease of a mine for this period; if at the end of it he did not
find it profitable, or not profitable enough (that is, if he
thought he could employ his capital better elsewhere), or
simply if his capital gave out for any cause, he gave up the
work, and the state had to find another lessee. His near
neighbour at another mine might continue his; probably indeed his lease would run from a different date. There was a
very large number of these separate workings, everyone of
them on a small scale: a common price for a lease in the
fourth century was 150 dr. only—that is, 150 days' pay for
unskilled labour; some cost 20 dr. only. This is the sort of
entry we have in the records of the state officials who sold
these leases: 'The following mines were declared as workable
by their present lease-holders, from the list set up in the
archonship of Kallimachos: (1) The mine known as Hermai-
kon at Laurion, marked with a stele, bounded on the N. by
the wall of the estate of Diotimos of Euonymon, on the S.
by the smelting factory of Diotimos of Euonymon, on
the E. by the road from Thorikos to Laurion, and on the W.
by the road from Laurion to Thrasymos: purchaser of the
lease Onetor s. of Arkesilas of Melite; price 150 dr.' And
so forth; dozens of separate transactions in a single year.
This system would seem to entail all manner of disadvantages
—not only those arising from a general absence of planning,

E

but others too: for example, a careful watch had to be kept that one lessee did not run his underground galleries outside his allotted area, whether inadvertently or with evil intent, did not by his method of working, otherwise legitimate, imperil the safety of his neighbour's mine, and so forth. All sorts of elaborate regulations were necessary, which would hinder economical working and which a planned scheme for the whole area would have avoided.

The immediate cause of this was the lack of sufficient capital in the hands of individuals (sufficient to enable or to justify a man in risking it in mining enterprise), and the fact that co-operation of capitalists to form large companies was unknown. But whatever the cause, and I shall say a word about this later, the fact itself is clear; and what is true of mining is true, as far as we can test it, of every other industrial activity. In agriculture, since Solon's time the land had been divided into comparatively small holdings, and the peasant-farmer, who, with his family, worked his own land, was as characteristic of Attica as of most other parts of Greece; a few richer men might have a larger or more fertile, better irrigated, piece of land than most and might have slaves to work it or part of it; many poorer men were glad to serve for hire at harvest and vintage; but the general rule was the αὐτουργός, the man on his own land. This we can at once appreciate, for over the greater part of Europe agriculture is still to-day carried on on the same basis. But in ancient Greece the same was also true of manufacture, even though in this slave labour was common. The cobbler, the carpenter and the joiner, the stone-mason, the potter, the smith, the tanner, would, normally, each own his own shop, which was also his home, and would work himself at his trade, with or without the help of hired labour or of slaves. A factory that employed twenty hands was accounted a large one, far above the average; Demosthenes' father who owned two factories, one with thirty hands (which was also his home)—a cutlery and arms factory—and one with twenty—for furniture-making—was a very rich man. When the state determined on large and expensive building operations, as on the Acropolis and at Eleusis in the fifth century, the rebuilding of the Peiraeus walls in 395–4, again at Eleusis about 330

B.C., how did it proceed? Did it engage one large contractor for each building, as would be done now, who would supply the material, the transport, the tools and the labour? Not at all; there were no large contractors. In the fifth century, through its elected architects (paid, by the way, at the same rate, no more, as the skilled workers) it entered into numerous individual contracts with providers of the various materials, with owners of carts and animals for the transport, and with every one of the skilled workers. We know fortunately a good deal about the methods used, for, as it was public money that was spent on these buildings, accounts were kept, to the last obol, and published; and some have survived. We know for example that, on the Erechtheion, groups of five, six or seven men were engaged in cutting the flutes of each column. In one group are to be found one free man and five slaves—four of them the property of the free man; in another, six free men; in a third, two free and three slaves; and so forth. Another entry is: 'For placing marble blocks 8ft. x 2 x 1, to Phalakros of Paiania, 4 blocks, 40 dr.' —he is a citizen. Another: 'For placing a block 6 ft. x 2 x 1, to Simmias living in Alopeke, 1 block, 7½ dr.'—he is μέτοικος. Another: 'To a carpenter working by the day, for making and placing a strut, 9 days, 9 dr.'—he is a slave (and his name Croesus). Very occasionally the workers are nòt named: e.g. 'to two men for removing scaffolding,' or 'to sawyers working by the day, Radios and his fellow-worker— συνεργός '—Radios was a metoikos and his companion may have been his slave, or perhaps a partner in the business. Still more rare is it to find mention of a contractor— e.g. for a piece of encaustic painting, a contract given to a metoikos, and for him a citizen must find surety that the work will be done. It is the same with the purchases: '2 tal. of lead bought from X, 166 leaves of gold from Y'—the lead being required for fixing the iron clamps that held one stone to another, the gold for decorating the mouldings.

All these craftsmen, citizen, metoikos and slave, work side by side, at the same or similar jobs, and at the same rates of pay; where there are slaves, the owner does not stand by and see that they work. From the point of view of the state, which is engaging their services, each is an individual with whom a

separate contract has been made, though doubtless in practice a man would in offering his services to the architect
tell him that he had two or three slaves also skilled workers
whom he could bring along with him. Those would be the
fortunate ones; other free men worked on their own. Even
more interesting from our present point of view are the
similar records of building at Eleusis in the fourth century.
There, to judge by the remains, which are detailed enough
but cover only a small portion of the work, far more work
was let out to contractors, not to individual craftsmen, and
it is probable that more of the work was done by slave
labour; but here too very small sections of the work were let
to each contractor, just as quite small quantities of material
were ordered from each merchant (who dealt direct with the
state architect, not with contractors for the building):
timber, bricks, stone, pitch, paint, all from different merchants (several of them supplied timber), each supplying
in any one month—the accounting period—material worth
20–50 dr. There were, literally, dozens of such contracts
made every month with merchants, carriers (very expensive
comparatively) and all sorts of persons in the building trade.
So true is it that there were no big men nor big companies
who could undertake the whole or even a fairly large section
of the work required.

Let us turn to commerce and its methods. In passing, I
will say of the internal distributive trade, that the retail shops
were all, as we should expect, small individual affairs, and
that wholesale merchanting, which dealt largely in imported
goods, was also in numerous hands—managed by individuals
who were many of them rich by the Greek standard—'well-
off, as wealth goes with us,' as Solon said to Croesus—but
not really rich: not men with £10,000 a year when the large
majority of their fellows were content with £100–£200—
not what we mean by rich. But the methods of international
trade are more interesting. A man was engaged, let us
suppose, principally in the corn-trade, in buying that is to
say from South Russia, Egypt or Sicily. In some cases he
would own a ship—one ship; that would be his main capital
wealth—corresponding to another man's land or shop—
his savings or his father's savings have been spent in buying

it. In this case, he engages the services of a master-mariner
as captain and of a small crew; otherwise he charters one
owned by the captain. Like everything else, the ships also
are small—a common size for the bigger sort being 500
tons burden. He will naturally want to take goods with him
from Athens to sell abroad, to avoid having to sail with
ballast, for the sake of the round trip, as we say. For that, in
nine cases out of ten, he had to borrow; or if he sailed with
ballast, he borrowed in order to buy the corn at his port of
destination. He normally made the journey himself in the
vessel; sold his goods, if he had any, to wholesale merchants
abroad, bought corn with the proceeds of the sale or with
the borrowed money, and sold that to the wholesalers on his
return to Athens. An isolated transaction, by a man not
accounted poor, but without sufficient capital to finance even
one voyage. He was not a carrier, conveying the goods of
other men; still less was he a company owning a fleet of
vessels; but a single man investing his own and another's
capital in a trading venture.

And that other's capital. This was again an isolated transaction. The merchant got into touch with, if he was not
already known to, a man with money—1,000 or 2,000
drachmae, seldom more—at the moment lying idle. The
capitalist lent the money on the security of the cargo, or both
the cargo and the vessel, for the one voyage; and was paid
back when the voyage was successfully completed—when
the merchant returned to Athens—with interest; generally
twelve per cent. interest, which sounds high, but was not so
really, for it included insurance against loss both of the cargo
and the vessel, at a time when the seas were less safe than
they are now; and when he got his money back, it was again
idle, earning no interest, until he could find someone else
who needed capital—it was in no sense a permanent invest-
ment. There was no regular investing public, though in
general merchants and capitalists would be in personal touch
with one another at the Peiraeus. There were no commercial
banks, no discount houses, whose main business it would be
to finance foreign trade; there was no *creation* of credit
which is the foundation of modern trading methods, no
international finance in that sense: but individuals who lent

their existing surplus capital to other individuals. Sometimes two or three men would join in partnership to lend to a merchant and share the risk; but no companies in this any more than in any other branch of commerce or industry.

There were, of course, banks—or rather bankers; for this again was an individual business. This is, to me at least, the most obscure branch of ancient industry. We know that banking was a risky business—that is, we hear of many failures among bankers; we know also that some bankers acquired very great wealth—much more, that is, than the average well-to-do man; Pasion is the most conspicuous example in Athens. This would suggest that they engaged in much speculative lending, which in some cases was success- ful and profitable above the standard of ordinary lending, in others disastrous. Yet we hear very little of such speculation. At first the bankers were simply money-changers: a not unimportant business when trade was active—for there were hundreds of different currencies; and not only were these based on three or four different standards, but all states did not issue pure coinage. Not only, that is, was there a regular rate of exchange between the Attic drachma and the Corinthian, and between the silver coinage of the great majority of states and the gold coinage of Cyzicus or of Persia and later of Macedonia; but every coin had to be looked at to make sure not only that it was genuine, not forged, but from what state it came—for on that depended its exchange value. But this very necessary help to trade would, one would suppose, bring in a steady enough profit, but be neither very speculative nor exceptionally profitable. The bankers also received deposits, and would lend money to the depositor on that security; but they were not, as far as we know, general lenders on the basis of their deposits—they did not make a regular business of lending to A, B, and C, on their security or prospects money deposited with them by X, Y and Z, which is the modern method. Above all, again to judge by our evidence, they did not invest in mercantile adventure—or rather not their clients' money; they might, of course from time to time, as individuals, invest some of their personal fortune. They did not, that is to say, invite men to deposit their liquid capital with them and invest it for them, pointing out the advantage of their own greater experience and of spreading the risk to the individual client over a number of mercantile transactions. And as it happened, in Athens, not many of them could invest even their private fortune in mortgage on land and houses; for the great majority of the bankers were foreigners, and so could not hold land; they therefore could not foreclose in case of default. So that all mortgage business was done by citizens, and it was always a case again of one individual lending to another. Nor did the bankers, at least before the third century, lend money to the state—the source of so much wealth and power to modern bankers (we know of one insignificant loan by a bank to the state commissioners for the Eleusis buildings, but that is all); there was in fact, no public debt in our sense of the word, in the Greek states of the fifth and fourth century. Some of the bankers, Pasion among them, did however perform one service which was of the first importance to international trade. They had agents abroad; and it was possible for a merchant to deposit money in the bank at home and receive a credit note to the agent, which enabled him to draw money where he wanted it to finance his purchases. This avoided the risk of taking actual coin (or bullion) on the voyage; it was the beginning of the credit-system, of paper-money, without which modern international trading would be impossible. These agents, and others employed by the merchants, would also send word home of profitable markets. Beyond this, we cannot speak for certain of the activities of Greek bankers, though I suspect that they did more than we know of. When therefore we read, as we sometimes do, of Pasion as the Greek Rothschild—well, in one aspect, there is some point in the comparison. He began life as a slave in his master's bank, as it were in the Frankfurt ghetto; he made himself indispensable to his master and was freed, and took over the bank himself; he became immensely rich, and was finally given the citizenship of Athens, as it were a peerage; and the relationship of his son to the Athenian aristocrats, who were ready both to sponge on him and mock him, was not unlike similar relationships in modern times. But the comparison is only good in this social aspect; as a banker, professionally,

Pasion, in spite of his international range, cannot usefully be likened to a Rothschild.

Now it is just in this matter of foreign trade and banking that the difference between ancient and modern practice is greatest—so great that writers like Hasebroek have been led into denying the importance of ancient trade altogether. We can, as I have said, well understand agriculture being carried on mainly on the small farm; by using a little observation as well as imagination we can understand manufacture being carried on in the small shop—for some manufacture, in trades for instance in which personal attention to the individual needs of customers is an advantage, is so carried on in the heart of great cities to-day. But it is difficult to think of international trading—both the transport of goods and the financing of the business—except in the modern way: it must be done on a big scale and regularly—by big ships owned preferably by big companies, who do nothing but this business and who do it regularly, by big merchants who are importers and nothing but importers, on a larger scale, above all by the big bankers. A small boat, of not more than 500 tons burden, chartered by a single merchant in a small way, who loads her with goods which he hopes to sell at various ports, and sails with her and makes his bargains, and buys other goods with the proceeds—that we relegate to Conrad's stories of the South Seas traders: it seems impossible in civilized trading communities. But when we come to think of it, it is not more improbable than the execution of the great building plans by similar means. The actual cost of the Acropolis and Eleusis buildings erected at the inspiration of Perikles, is in this respect significant—to show the scale of the transaction. It approached half a million pounds in our money—several millions in purchasing power—spread over a period of fifteen years, from 447 to 432. There was a committee of amateurs for each building chosen by the populace, with a skilled architect also chosen by the populace, from year to year; as the plans had originally been approved by them. The money also was voted by the populace, as occasion demanded. There were separate contracts made with every quarrier of marble, every merchant in gold and ivory and ebony bought from abroad, every waggoner who transported the marble from Pentelikos to Athens, every stone-mason who put one stone on another, every carver who helped on the columns and worked at the ornamentation of architrave and frieze and coffered ceiling, every man who fixed the marble tiles on the roof, every painter and gilder and bronze worker, every sculptor who did figures for frieze or metope or pediment. And all the numerous accounts resulting from these contracts checked month by month by the Council—500 men chosen by lot who also had all the other business of the state to see to—helped by accountants also chosen by lot, and by popularly elected commissioners. What an absurd system. How could so huge and so elaborate a plan of building be carried out in that way? But fortunately we have the evidence of our own eyes that it was, and not without success—the remains of the buildings are there to witness to this important truth. And in fact we have similar, though not so exact, archaeological evidence of the extent of international trading, which supports and supplements our literary evidence. It is important to emphasize this, for Hasebroek ignores it. It is the evidence of goods and coins found all over the Greek world in places other than those of their origin; and belonging to nearly all periods of Greek history from 2000 B.C. onwards. I cannot describe this evidence in detail—it would take too long, and it has never been properly classified and described from our present point of view;[1] I will mention only two significant pieces of evidence. The latest excavations of the British school at Athens have been conducted at the unimportant sanctuary of Hera at Perachora in the territory of Corinth —not indeed far from that city, but quite away from the ordinary lines of traffic, a small, insignificant place barely mentioned by ancient writers, unknown and unthought of in modern times till this excavation. Yet among the objects

[1] A beginning has been made with Blakeway's very important article already referred to, on Greek trade in the West, in B.S.A. xxxiii. See also his *Demaratus*, in J.R.S. xxv (1935), 129–49. I do not know that any similar work, a classification of the material with a view to the history of commerce, has been done in numismatics. It is badly needed. (Blakeway's early death is a tragedy for learning. He was one of the very few men who have combined a sense of history with a grasp and an understanding of archaeological evidence. Let anyone who is still taken in by Hasebroek's pretentions read his articles, and learn what scholarship means.)

found there are hundreds imported from abroad, in this case mostly from Egypt in the seventh and sixth centuries: all got somehow in the way of trade—they were not presents of an Egyptian Croesus, but Corinthian imports—whether part of a regular trade in Egyptian *objets d'art*, or, as would seem more probable, brought over by merchants with other more important goods, we do not know—for us it does not matter: the trade with Egypt was there, and continuous. Secondly: there is, as everyone knows, an abundance of good building stone almost everywhere in Greece; there is not, I suppose, in Greece proper, and the islands, a town or village more than ten miles from such excellent material to be had for the quarrying and the short transport; most are in much closer proximity. The Greeks used this stone freely; but for their finer buildings, as for their sculpture, they preferred marble, especially island marble. To satisfy their desire for beauty, or if you will for luxury, they transported marble freely, generally by sea, at great expense. (Again we have some evidence from building-records, this time mostly from Delphi; and the cost of transport would be for us out of all proportion to the whole cost of building.) Naturally, for marble is heavy stuff; it had to be very carefully quarried, and carried for the most part in large blocks weighing several tons; and this with no mechanical cranes for loading and unloading, and with slow moving ships, that made not more than six or seven knots in the most favourable weather. If they were prepared to trade in an unwieldy material like marble, as they did freely from the second half of the fifth century onwards, why should we suppose, against all the evidence, that they were not regular traders in more manageable goods?

There is another aspect of Greek trading which I should like to touch on, because Hasebroek repeats yet once more an old but persistent error. He says that persons engaged in trade and industry were despised by the Greeks, looked upon as vulgar persons, that they were in fact illiterate, that at Athens they were practically all foreigners: 'Traders,' he says, 'belonged to the lowest social and economic plane. Any citizen who turned to trade or commerce for a livelihood would have to spend his time among aliens and foreigners;

and he would only do this if he were compelled to.' And a little later: 'There can be no doubt whatever that the industrial life of Athens was in the hands not of its citizens (apart from those of them who had been metics before they were citizens), but of foreigners and aliens.'[1] Now, even if this were true, it would not affect in any way our judgement of the main question—the importance of foreign trade in the Greek world—though Hasebroek seems to think it would; it would only decide the class of persons who carried on the trade. It would affect very. greatly our picture of ancient Athenian society; but that is a very different matter. It would affect the picture of modern European society if all international finance were, as some seem fondly to imagine, in the hands of Jews; but it would not mean that finance is unimportant in the capitalist world. On the contrary the presence of the foreigners in such great numbers in Athens (or other Greek cities) is proof of the extent and importance of trade: men came to Athens because of the opportunities of a profitable employment of their energies in trade. Hasebroek's statements, however, both about the social position of traders and manufacturers, and the part taken by citizens in trade and industry, are profoundly untrue. No greater mistake can be made. In the first place the great majority of the foreigners in Athens were themselves Greeks,[2] from Miletos, Rhodes, Byzantion, Sicily—all over the Greek world: *they* at any rate did not despise trade. Secondly, how can anyone read but the opening pages of the *Republic* and still think (or at least write, to support an argument) that citizens avoided contact with traders and aliens? Kephalos was a foreigner and a cutler; and it is not only the eccentric Sokrates who is friendly with him and his sons, but Plato's aristocratic relations and many others. Why indeed should they not be? They were as good Greeks as themselves, and as well educated and intelligent.[3] The Greeks were not a personally exclusive, stand-offish people, but extremely

[1] p. 27.
[2] Whatever Hasebroek may say to the contrary.
[3] Lucian is often quoted to show the Greek contempt for trade, as though his evidence were without question good for all Greece and for all periods. Yet even he is misunderstood, as a careful reading of the opening chapters of the *Somnium* and of such a passage as *Icaromen*, 30–1, will show.

sociable. Secondly, to say that manufacture (industry in this sense) was mainly in the hands of foreigners is simply to ignore the evidence, which goes to show that while any foreigner was free to have a business, the greater part of industrial production was in the hands of citizens. You will find in Hasebroek, tucked away in a footnote,[1] a reference to these many citizen producers, but he supposes them to have been mostly foreigners who had been given the citizenship and had continued in their business. His evidence for this? That one politician Andokides called another politician Hyperbolos, who was a lampseller, a foreigner. Simple, enviable man, who has never heard of political controversy! And he does not explain to us why the lordly Athenians should grant the citizenship to all these humble folk whom they despised as aliens and tradesmen. We must bear this in mind: all agriculture was done by the citizens, for foreigners, with few exceptions, could not hold land. All mining[2] and quarrying was conducted by citizens, for the same reason. (I am not here concerned with the use of slaves in these industries, who were numerous.) We already have a large proportion of Attic industry exclusively in their hands. Add to that the numerous craftsmen of all sorts, and you get a juster picture of Athens. And for foreign trade: in all the speeches which Demosthenes wrote for mercantile lawsuits (often by the way for a client who was a foreigner— he did not despise him) we find that in the complex of operations which went to make up the whole transaction— lending money, buying goods, voyaging, selling and buying again, and finally selling in Athens—citizens and foreigners are almost invariably mixed together: a citizen and a foreigner join in making a loan to a merchant, two citizens are introduced to a foreign merchant by a common friend for the purpose of a loan, a foreign trader resident abroad always stays with a citizen friend of his when in Athens who will identify his friend to the banker Pasion; citizens sail on the trading vessel with the merchant. It was the usual thing,

---

[1]P. 27, 2: 'No doubt large numbers of the citizens whom we find in industrial occupations were in this category': i.e., had been metics before they were citizens (see above, p. 59).

[2]Two metic mineowners are known, doubtless men with special privileges of ἔγκτησις γῆς.

and passes without comment, just as citizens and metoikoi worked together on a building; and it is remarkable how seldom in these law-court speeches is there any abuse of an opponent as a foreigner (there is plenty of other abuse)— you get it in Lysias in his speech against the corn-dealers who were accused of rigging the market (not uncharacteristic this, for Lysias was himself a foreigner only too anxious to be more patriotic than the Athenians themselves); you get occasional jibes in Demosthenes.

It is true that, on our evidence, the majority of the *merchants* were resident aliens, metoikoi, not citizens (just as the majority of the investors were citizens), though we hear often enough of citizen traders. But that is what we should expect. That is why they came to Athens and settled there, because of the many trading opportunities. We can liken these metoikoi in some ways to the colonies of English and Scottish merchants in Danzig and elsewhere in the seventeenth and eighteenth centuries, or to the Europeans settled in India and China. We do not say that the Chinese are not merchants and manufacturers because the greater part of the international finance and trading is in the hands of the Europeans. We can press the parallel a little further. The Chinese are the landowners, the agriculturists, the manufacturers, the traders for all internal trade and with the foreign settlers, as well as being alone citizens of China with the rights and duties of citizens. So were the Athenians in Attica the only citizens and landowners, and as well farmers, craftsmen and traders—men that is who kept to their old calling; some only would join in the new industry and commerce with the foreigners. There is of course one important difference between the conditions in China and in ancient Athens: in China there is a social barrier between the two elements of the population crossed only occasionally; one gathers that there exists a fine mutual contempt. In Athens there was no such barrier; men were far too sociable, and since nearly all were Greeks there was no difficulty of race or language to create one. The metoikoi were welcomed and protected; they were a privileged class, almost the adopted children of Athena.[1]

[1] Wilamowitz, *Hermes* xxii (1887), 211–59.

In general, what point would the jests of Aristophanes and the serious criticisms of Plato and Aristotle, of the Athenian democracy, what point would they have if the large majority of the citizens belonged, as Hasebroek says, to the *rentier* class, or, if very poor, were enabled to live as soldiers or dicasts by state-pay for their services? Particularly Plato's. His whole argument is that a man can do only one thing well, and that public work is a whole-time affair, for which special training is required: how then can shoe-makers, sculptors, farmers, merchants, architects, engineers, tanners, have either the training or the leisure for it? Plato is not just talking in the air; he has Athens in mind, and Syracuse. Yet many moderns write as though every Athenian could give his whole time to public affairs—just what Plato would have found desirable.

It is worth while considering, very briefly, the reason why industry and commerce was always conducted in small units, or rather one of the reasons—the chief economic cause of it; there are always social causes as well. It was the absence of machinery in manufacture. Consider the position of the modern manufacturer. A new machine is invented by means of which the output of the factory can be increased with but little or no increase in the labour involved and in overhead charges; the cost of the new machine is the only question to be considered, and if trade is prosperous that will be worth paying—the factory is on the way to large scale production with all its attendant advantages—buying raw material on a large scale, for instance, at a cheaper rate. Compare with this the position where all work is done by hand. The Greeks, I may say, were perfectly familiar with the principle of sub-division of labour: Xenophon[1] contrasts the situation in populous communities with that in small ones: in the latter a leather-worker for example makes all kinds of leather-goods, and works at every process in the manufacture himself; in populous places on the other hand, not only are different kinds of leather goods made in different shops, and even, he says, women's shoes made in one and men's in another, but in the same shop workers specialize in different processes—one cuts the leather, another stitches, another fits and so

[1] *Cyroped.* viii 2. 5.

forth; and Aristophanes in the *Peace*[1] has a long list of the various kinds of metal-workers—peace-workers and war-workers; incidentally, they are obviously most of them citizens. Now suppose that in a shoe factory four men working at different processes made up an economic unit; and suppose a man had a shop large enough to hold twelve men —three units working together (he would be accounted quite well-off on this scale); and that he was able to direct the work of all himself. Trade is prosperous and he might extend his business; but for this he had to find (1) an exactly corresponding number of equally skilled workers; (2) a building to hold them; and (3) another overseer. *All* his expenses are increased in the same proportion as his output, even if he is successful in finding these three requisites. He would hesitate to risk such a capital expenditure, even though he felt confident of his market; compared with the modern manufacturer he has to invest a much larger proportion of his capital, and at greater risk; and the expenses for every pair of shoes produced are not less, and the profits no higher, even if all goes well. Of course some men did take this risk, and it paid them: Lysias and his brother for instance—but that was a munition factory working at high pressure during the long years of the Peloponnesian war; Lysias could not revive it after the war was over, when he was a comparatively poor man. And here note a particular risk if, as was the case in all large factories, all or the majority of the workers were slaves. Buying more slaves meant again risking your *capital*, and they must be already skilled or quick learners. And if the owner's judgement was not quite accurate? If he bought his new building and a dozen slaves to work in it, and he found there was only profitable work for half of them? Or if there was a slump? He cannot just dismiss his workmen, as he could hired men; he must go on feeding, clothing and housing them[2]—his expenses, those which correspond to both overhead expenses and wages in modern times, are as heavy as if the factory were fully occupied with work; or he will try to sell them, but almost certainly at a loss—for if he cannot employ them profitably,

[1] 545–9; cf. 296–8, 457–8, 463, and *dramatis personæ*.
[2] Cf. Aristophanes, *Lysistrata*, 1204–5.

presumably no one else can, and no one will be eager to buy. That is one reason why slave labour, common as it was, did not oust the free workman, as we should expect. If we consider just these few factors in ancient industry, we see how natural it was for industry to be conducted almost always on a small scale; why therefore there was practically no really large accumulation of capital in single hands, and why, as a further consequence, there was no large capital to invest either in an industry like mining where it would have been so advantageous, or in international commerce; so that this too remained in the hands of individuals, none of them more than moderately well-to-do.

I have touched thus superficially on this primary cause of small-scale production in the Greek world (and, as I said, there were other causes, especially social ones), for this reason: that, in spite of great differences of time and place, these same conditions, at bottom, obtained not only in Greece in the sixth to the fourth centuries B.C., but in the Hellenistic age, in Rome, and (with the exception of slavery) throughout the Middle Ages and the Renaissance, down almost to modern times: till, that is, the industrial revolution which began in the second half of the eighteenth century. But no one pretends that at no time during that long period and in no place in Europe was industry and foreign commerce important; no one pretends that the trade of Constantinople, Venice, Ragusa, Genoa in the Middle Ages and early Renaissance, that of the Hanseatic towns from the sixteenth century, or that of London from at least the fifteenth century onwards, was insignificant. Yet in denying the possibility of extensive trade in Greece on these *à priori* grounds—because of the 'primitive' methods used—modern writers are equally denying its possibility before the end of the eighteenth century. In passing, I may say that Hasebroek and others also point to difficulties of ancient sailing and the existence of piracy as effectively preventing a regular and active commerce in Greek times; but piracy also was endemic in European waters and elsewhere till the end of the eighteenth century and especially in the great days of Venice and Genoa; and so long as ships were under sail, there were always seasons of little or no regular traffic. Men forget

how recent the modern conditions of industry, commerce
and finance are; and suppose they must be indispensable.
Just as, it seems to me, it is quite obvious that there were
in proportion as many lettered men in fourth-century
Greece as in modern Europe, in spite of the primitive,
indeed absurd, methods of ancient book production, so was
there extensive trade between Greek states like Athens,
Corinth, Miletos, Rhodes, Byzantion, Syracuse, Massalia,
and between them and Egypt, Phoenicia,[1] and the Pontos,
in spite of all the difficulties traders had to contend with:
which were not greater than the difficulties confronting all
traders till the nineteenth century. It is in fact true that
active men have ever been more inclined to get over or get
round obstacles than to remove them; especially if the
obstacles are cherished because men like them for another
reason. (There are still some people who like trees and
hedges along our roads, and do not want them removed in
order that motor-cars may go faster.) Nothing, one would
think, was simpler than printing: it is only making dies of
letters and stamping them on paper; coins were made in that
way in Greece, so why not letters? But the Greeks thought
of many other things, and so produced and read their
books without removing this obstacle. So with their trade.
They carried on in spite of the primitive conditions
and methods—no paper money, difficulties in international
law, no machinery and so neither rapid work nor rapid
travel; frequent wars and much piracy. But these are all
difficulties which men had to deal with till quite modern
times. For we are not attempting to prove that the actual
volume or value of Greek trade was, per head of the population, equal or nearly equal to, that of the modern world.
For one thing we have no figures; what matters is its *importance* to the Greek people, that is the amount of physical and
mental energy they devoted to it, both relatively to other
peoples and other ages, and to other activities, especially
agriculture, of their own. Remember of course that the
clumsier the method adopted, the greater the energy to be

---

[1] The most recent evidence from Syria, from Sir Leonard Woolley's excavations
near Antioch, show an active trade with Athens, in the fifth and fourth centuries;
and we may recall the special privileges given to Sidonian merchants in Athens.

F

expended. It required more, not less, initiative and energy to transport a cargo of pottery and wine and olive-oil from Athens to South Russia—a journey of eight to ten days— and a cargo of corn back again, than it does to do a similar piece of trading with America to-day. Men said then, as we say now: 'We want peace that we may trade again.'[1] Thucydides expressly connects the growth of prosperity in Greece with increased travel by sea, not only with improved agriculture; the Corinthians in urging war with Athens upon the states of the inner Peloponnese mentions first the danger to their trade, as being what was most likely to touch them first —it was not only cities on the coast to which trade was important; the Athenians took steps during the war to hamper their enemies' trade and to protect their own.[2] The products of all the world, we are told, were to be had at the Peiraeus; and Isokrates said that the Peiraeus was the mart of all Greece. These statements may not be literally true; but they show that such ideas were quite familiar to the Greeks, and, together with all our other evidence, literary and archaeological, that the picture of ancient Greece as a world of peasants and politicians, interspersed with an occasional Phoenician trader, is a false one.

[1]Aristophanes, Pac. 341; cf. 999–1005; Av. 1523; Dem. Ol. ii 16.
[2]Thuc. i 1–19; 120. 1; ii 69; iv 53. 3 (Spartan trade with Egypt and Libya).

IV

THE LAW OF CITIZENSHIP AT ATHENS

(a) Two Problems of Athenian Citizenship Law[1]

In his recent interesting article on the decree of Demophilos, 346-5 B.C., which ordered an extraordinary *diapsephisis* to be held throughout Attica,[2] Dr. Aubrey Diller concludes that it 'introduced a great change in the scrutinies in the demes. It made them universal, uniform, and compulsory. All existing members were to be scrutinized at once (Aischin. i 77, 86, 114, ii 182; Dem. lvii; Androtion and Philochoros in Harp. διαψήφισις; Dion. H., *Dein.* 11), and all future members at the time of their admission (Arist. *Ath. Const.* 42). But the great innovation of Demophilos was the appeal, which substituted the formidable γραφὴ ξενίας, with heavy penalties for the unsuccessful appellant in place of the old harmless δίκη, which offered endless opportunities for corruption in its long and devious course before the Forty, the arbitrators, and the private court.' The object of this paper is to re-examine the evidence, first, for Demophilos' decree; second, for the penalty involved in an unsuccessful appeal; but though I argue against Dr. Diller's conclusions throughout, I should say that his insistence on considering the development of the Athenian procedure in citizenship cases is of the first importance, for hitherto most scholars have written as though scarcely any changes took place.

I. THE DECREE OF DEMOPHILOS

An important point is involved in the question whether we have to deal with a law or a decree. Both Dionysios of Halikarnassos in his introduction to his extract from Isaios, *pro Euphileto*, and Libanios in his hypothesis to Demosthenes lvii (Euboulides *v.* Euxitheos), speak of a law (both obvious-

[1]First published in *Classical Philology*, xxix, 1934.
[2]*Proc. Amer. Phil. Assoc.* (1932), pp. 193–205. My references to Lipsius are all to *Das attische Recht* (1915).

ly meaning the same law) governing procedure in the *diapséphisis* and in appeals arising from it; neither mentions Demophilos by name. Dr. Diller rejects this evidence, because what Dionysios and Libanios describe

was only a temporary measure. The scrutiny was to be applied forthwith to all existing demesmen, not merely to new demesmen in the future. This account is confirmed by Aeschines and Demosthenes, both of whom allude to an extraordinary amount of litigation arising from the appeals. It is impossible that such a process should be perpetuated by a standing law.

This I do not follow; there must have been a standing law to make the procedure legal at all; and Dr. Diller himself implies on a later page (202) that it was repeated after 345. He goes on:

On the other hand, the account in the *Constitution (Ath. Const.* 42) does indeed refer to a standing law, authorizing a process to be applied in the future to every candidate for admission to the deme. What is the relation between this law and the decree of Demophilos? It is a logical inference that the decree carried two provisions, the temporary measure attested by the orators and rhetoricians and the standing law attested by Aristotle.

But no single decree could contain both an executive order not yet made legal by an already existing law and a new law. A *graphe paranomon* (and there would have been many ready to bring one in this case) would have upset it at once. New laws were passed in Athens only by an elaborate, established procedure. There must have existed, prior to 346–5, a law enabling an extraordinary general scrutiny to be held when the ecclesia voted for one (by a decree) and settling the procedure, and, prior to the writing of the *Constitution of Athens*, a law establishing the procedure of ordinary annual scrutinies in the demes and of disputes arising from them; both probably, but not necessarily, forming parts of the same law. Compare, for example, the law of Timokrates quoted by Demosthenes xxiv 63, which also provides for present and future cases. Dionysios and Libanios therefore are correct in speaking of a law, not a decree, although, to be quite accurate, they should also have mentioned the decree which was the particular occasion of these speeches. On the other hand, the measure moved by

Demophilos was almost certainly a decree. Aischines' references make it probable; and Demosthenes (lvii 7) expressly terms it one, if the Euxitheos case was tried as a result of this measure, as Dr. Diller believes. The law, therefore, and Demophilos' decree are quite separate, and the latter subsequent to the former, and an application of it.

But it may not have been long after it; and if it were not—if the law, that is, was passed round about 350 B.C.—then Dr. Diller's main contention, that there was a radical change in procedure in citizenship cases about this time, and that this can be seen from a comparison between Isaios xii and Demosthenes lvii, might still stand. This involves us further in a consideration of the dates of these two speeches; for it is essential to Dr. Diller's argument to establish both that the procedure in the two cases was different and that Isaios' case preceded the change in the law and that of Demosthenes was subsequent to it.

The only positive reason for supposing that Isaios xii was not delivered in 345–4 or 344–3 (not 346–5, for the case was delayed)[1] is that the date is too late for Isaios. But, as Wyse points out in his introduction to the speech, it is not too late for a man whose earliest extant work belongs to 389–8,[2] and who 'survived till the rule of Philip.'[3] On the other hand, Dionysios does not say that the speech was made in a case following the general scrutiny of 346–5; he only quotes the law governing all scrutinies, both ordinary and extraordinary, and appeals from them; and some weight must be allowed to this. For in his chapter on Deinarchos[4] he rejects on chronological grounds two speeches which he expressly says belong to cases arising from this scrutiny; had

[1]We need not take too literally the statement in c. 11 that the arbitration lasted two years. All we have to suppose is that the case was carried over from one year (345–4, or 346–5) to the next, and so to a second arbitrator.
[2]We cannot, unfortunately, use in this connection the fact recorded by Harpokration that Isaios wrote a speech πρὸς Βοιωτὸν ἐκ δημοτῶν ἔφεσις. If this was the Boiotos of Dem. xxxix and xl, and if the speech was an attack on Boiotos' citizen rights, then it must have been later than 350–348, the dates of Demosthenes' speeches, in which otherwise it must have been mentioned. But, apart from the possibility of another Boiotos, it may be, as Diller says (p. 201, n. 10), a speech in defence of someone against Boiotos as accuser, like Dem. πρὸς Εὐβουλίδην (only in that case it is not, or should not be, subsequent to Demosthenes' speeches; for it would then be in answer to Mantitheos).
[3]Dion. Hal. Isae. 1.
[4]xi 655.

he thought the Euphiletos case was one of these, he might
easily have said so, and used the fact to give a more precise
date to Isaios. As, however, most scholars suppose that the
case did arise from a general scrutiny in all the demes,
whether that of 346–5 or an earlier one, we must consider
the consequences of this view; that is, if there had been, in
the fourth century, no earlier general scrutiny, then Isaios
xii belongs to 345 or 344.

On the same assumption, Demosthenes lvii belongs also
to the same period, 346–5 or 345–4.[1] The reasons for
supposing that it is earlier, and therefore that there had been
earlier extraordinary general scrutinies, are many of the facts
revealed in the speech. Euxitheos, the appellant, was the
son of Nikarete by her second marriage; she herself was the
daughter of Damostratos by his second marriage; her half-
brother died in Sicily in 413 at the latest, leaving three
children, of whom the eldest, Euxitheos' first cousin, was
alive when the case was tried—over seventy, therefore, in
345. Her half-sister had a son who died on service, therefore
over twenty, at Abydos in 387 (37–38). The appellant's
father was taken prisoner, perhaps when adult, as we are
told nothing to the contrary, but perhaps as a child, during
the Decelean War, in 405 at the latest (18). When, however, we remember that Euxitheos himself must have been
thirty-five or older at the time of the trial, for he had held a
priesthood and the demarchy (46, 63), that his mother may
have been well over thirty when he was born (as it was her
second marriage and Euxitheos need not have been the
eldest of the five children of this marriage) and so may have
been born as early as 420, her half-brother and sister being
considerably older (born 440–435), and that grandnephews
of her were of age at the time of the trial (39, 43)—remembering all this, it will be seen that 346–5 is by no means an
impossible date, and, remembering Euxitheos' age at the
time of the trial, that a much earlier date is unlikely. But an
earlier date is obviously not excluded; we must reckon with
the possibility that, if there were general scrutinies before

[1]Diller (p. 194, n. 2) says it must belong to this period because of its 'overwhelming affinities' with the evidence of Aischines and the Atthidographers. But
any extraordinary general scrutiny would have produced the same sort of excitement and a similar crop of lawsuits and slanders.

346–5, Demosthenes lvii may be earlier than Isaios xii.[1] It is clearly dangerous to base an argument on the assumption that it must be later.

If, however, it should be assumed that, because we hear of none, no other extraordinary general scrutiny took place within, say, a generation before 346,[2] then both Isaios xii (if we suppose, for the moment, that the case arose from such a scrutiny) and Demosthenes lvii belong to the same series of trials. Dr. Diller argues that this is impossible because the procedure is quite different in the two cases. The former had been before an arbitrator before it came to the dicastery. That means that it was in form a *dike*, a private suit, and one which came within the jurisdiction of the Forty; for Dr. Diller believes, with Bonner against Lipsius, that only cases coming first before the Forty were remitted to the arbitrators —a difficult problem in which at present I incline to think he is right.[3] In Demosthenes lvii, on the other hand, there is no mention of arbitration; and, like Dr. Diller, I find it hard to believe, with Wyse (p. 717), that no weight need be attached to this, because if the arbitration had gone against him, Euxitheos would naturally have suppressed all reference to it; I think it more natural, to judge from the rest of the speech, that he would have referred to it as another instance of his enemy's chicanery and cunning. If this is correct, and if only cases within the jurisdiction of the Forty were remitted to arbitrators, then Euxitheos' case had not been taken by the Forty; and it is natural to suppose that it had been taken by the thesmothetai, who, at the date of the *Constitution of*

---

[1] The question of Demosthenes' authorship of the Euboulides speech need not be discussed, as it is in any case a genuine speech of the period.

[2] If Euxitheos' case is 346, as Dr. Diller thinks, there had clearly been no other since his father returned from his enslavement abroad, *ca.* 400–395 (18, 41); or it would have been mentioned in the course of the speech.

[3] Ar. *Ath. Const.* 53, 58. 2; Bonner, *Class. Phil.*, II (1907), 407–18; Lipsius 225–28, 981. I may point out one mistake made by Bonner (pp. 410, 417). Pischinger had instanced Lysias xxiii as a citizenship case which had nevertheless been before an arbitrator, though it must have been dealt with by the thesmothetai; Bonner replies that there is no mention of arbitration in the speech. True, but it is implied; as Bonner says, τοὺς τῇ Ἱπποθωντίδι δικάζοντας are the Forty, or rather the Hippothontid section of them; and all cases dealt with by the Forty were sent to arbitration. The answer to Pischinger is that this is not a citizenship case: this dispute between the speaker and Pankleon is not the case for which Lysias made the speech; its nature is not given, but it was clearly a *dike*, a claim for damages, which, had Pankleon been, as he claimed, possessed of Plataean right and enrolled among the Dekeleeis, would have come before the Forty and an arbitrator.

Athens, dealt with 'those voted out of their demes' (59. 4). But the *Constitution* is later than both cases; Demosthenes lvii, therefore, which conforms to the procedure there indicated, is later than Isaios xii, and probably enough belongs to 346–5. In that case, however, Dr. Diller must be right in supposing that Isaios xii cannot have been spoken in a trial arising from a general scrutiny in all the demes, but from one in the deme Erchia alone (a scrutiny like that in the deme Halimous when the roll of citizens was lost [Dem. lvii 26]);[1] for, as we have seen, there can hardly have been a general scrutiny within a generation preceding the case against Euxitheos. In this, then, I think Dr. Diller is right, though we cannot yet be certain.

A smaller matter is Dr. Diller's argument that whereas in Euxitheos' case the appellant spoke last, in Euphiletos' case he spoke first. This, however, depends entirely on the future tense ἀξιώσουσι in Isai. xii 8; which may easily be parallel to ὁ νῦν ὑμᾶς ἀξιώσων (viii 11), where the opposing side had certainly spoken first (see Wyse, *ad loc.*). It is, by the way, an advantage to the defence to speak last, especially in this kind of case, whatever Aischines may say.[2]

In conformity with these there is, according to Dr. Diller, another difference in procedure: In cases that had been before an arbitrator, no new evidence could be brought in the dicastery, no surprise could be sprung on either side; but Euxitheos does bring new evidence once (lvii 14) and offers it often elsewhere. The difference may be admitted; but its importance must not be exaggerated. The offering of new evidence (εἰ ὑμεῖς βούλεσθε, ὦ ἄνδρες) is, as Lipsius says (pp. 836–37), mainly a rhetorical device; and where such evidence is apparently brought, we cannot be at all sure that its nature had not already been made plain at the *anakrisis*. (I believe the frequent formula, 'I hear my opponents will argue,' just as much as 'my accusers have argued,' is neither intelligent anticipation nor later insertion on publication, but

---

[1] Or the case may have arisen from one of the annual scrutinies in the demes, of entrants at the age of eighteen. Euphiletos is quite young, and his elder brother speaks on his behalf. (The statement in 12 that he had been first legally enrolled, then struck out, is not decisive against this.)

[2] It is worth noting the change of tone in Aischines from i 77 to ii 182. In the latter he is defendant.

a reference back to the *anakrisis*.) This is, in fact, the most obscure and difficult problem in Athenian procedure: What arrangements were made, in *graphai* and all other cases which had not been before arbitrators, for making each side acquainted with the general line of evidence to be offered by the other before the dicastery? Some arrangement must have been made; defendants could not have been expected to meet charges of which they knew nothing but the barest outline. It would take me too far from the present subject to go into the matter here;[1] I will only note that in Euxitheos' case it is the defence that is entitled to bring apparently new evidence. In this, and the fact that he spoke last, the defendant is favoured.

When, however, Dr. Diller goes on to argue, on the basis of these details of procedure, that by the time of Demosthenes lvii, the trial of an ἔφεσις ἐκ δημοτῶν was practically equivalent to that of a *graphe xenias* ('the great innovation was the appeal,[2] which substituted the formidable γραφὴ ξενίας, with heavy penalties for the unsuccessful appellant, in place of the old harmless δίκη'), I can find no grounds for believing him. Both classes of trial came before the thesmothetai; but there the resemblance ends. Aristotle, in his classification of the jurisdiction of the thesmothetai, mentions various γραφαί and εὔθυναι, then εἰσὶ δὲ καὶ γραφαὶ πρὸς αὐτοὺς ὧν παράστασις τίθεται, ξενίας καὶ δωροξενίας, and many others; then εἰσάγουσι δὲ καὶ τὰς δοκιμασίας ταῖς ἀρχαῖς ἁπάσαις καὶ τοὺς ἀπεψηφισμένους ὑπὸ τῶν δημοτῶν καὶ τὰς καταγνώσεις τὰς ἐκ τῆς βουλῆς finally εἰσάγουσι δὲ καὶ δίκας ἰδίας (59. 2–5). If he distinguishes trials of appeal from the demes from all *dikai*, he distinguishes them no less from all *graphai*, including the sub-section ὧν παράστασις τίθεται, which includes γραφαὶ ξενίας. The *dokimasiai*, for example (which are also cases of appeal: *Ath. Const.* 55. 2 *ad fin.*), were certainly not *graphai* in the ordinary sense of the word. The differ-

---

[1] See Bonner, *Evidence in Athenian Courts* (1905), pp. 48–52, and Calhoun's excellent article in *Class. Phil.*, xiv (1919), 338–50; in which, however, I do not feel that all the difficulties are removed.

[2] Dr. Diller adds a note here: 'This view is confirmed by the language in Dem. lvii 6, which reads as if the appeal was a novel device recently instituted.' I can see nothing in the language even to support the view in any way; and there had certainly been *epheseis* of a similar, if not identical, nature for a long time (e.g., Dem. lvii 60 and below, p. 81).

ences are vital. First, in a *graphe* the prosecutor introduces the case to the magistrate, and summons the defendant to appear; and the latter must appear under pain of a verdict against him *in contumaciam*; nobody is compelled to prosecute, and to avoid malicious prosecution the prosecutor must, under penalty of a fine, carry his case through to the end; in the particular class of cases to which the *graphe xenias* belongs, he has to pay a special court fee as well. In an ἔφεσις ἐκ δημοτῶν, it is the appellant (the real defendant in the case) who introduces the case, and summons[1] the prosecutors to appear, who must obey the summons;[2] he, as it were, calls upon them to 'show cause' why his name should not be restored to the deme list; and he may drop the case and accept expulsion from citizenship at any time. The initiative, that is, in the two cases, is on opposite sides. Second, any citizen could institute a *graphe xenias*; in an ἔφεσις ἐκ δημοτῶν the parties belonged to the same deme—the 'prosecutors' who must answer the summons being representatives of the deme; although of course other actions might arise out of appeals from deme scrutinies, even against non-members, as for slander, bribery, or false witness.[3] In fact, ἔφεσις ἐκ δημοτῶν has closer analogies to a *diadikasia* than to any other class of trial except the *dokimasia* of a magistrate, with which Aristotle groups it; where no charge of malpractice was being tried, but only the question as to whether or not the chosen candidate had the necessary qualifications. For, third, and most important, the nature of the charge in an *ephesis* is different from that in a *graphe xenias*; in the former, whether after an extraordinary

---

[1] Προσκαλεῖσθαι certainly; Diller is wrong to read προκαλεῖσθαι (p. 196, 4). See Usener *ad* Dion. H., p. 617.

[2] Whether the prosecutor is technically the deme as a whole, which appoints ξυνήγοροι to represent it, or the demarch, as Euboulides. In either case they can be called οἱ κατήγοροι (Isai. xii 7; Dem. lvii; *Ath. Const.* 42. 1).

[3] It is doubtless cases like this which explain the titles κατὰ Κηρύκων and κατὰ Μοσχίωνος, which Dionysios says (*Dein.* 11) were speeches delivered in cases arising out of ἐφέσεις ἐκ δημοτῶν (assuming the titles to be correct); there is no need, on this evidence, to suppose Dionysios to have had 'a poor understanding indeed of the whole matter' (Diller, p. 202).

An action for bribery could have been brought against Timarchos and Leukonides, if we could believe what Aischines tells us (i 114–5). Diller (p. 194) speaks of the original action of Philotades, rejected by his deme Kydathenaion, as being against Timarchos of Sphettos, who asserted that Philotades was a freedman of his. Of course the action was against the deme; Timarchos was the principal witness and the cause of the whole trouble.

THE LAW OF CITIZENSHIP

scrutiny (in one or in all the demes) or after the annual scrutiny of those entering the deme for the first time at the age of eighteen, the jury had to decide only whether the appellant was of legitimate Athenian birth, and there need be no question of fraud or dishonesty on either side; in a *graphe xenias*, the charge was one of fraudulent usurpation of citizen rights, a very different matter.

It will at once be objected: How, then, could the penalty for failure of the appellant in the first case, of the defendant in the second, be the same—slavery and confiscation of property? This brings me to the second part of my paper.

2. THE PENALTY FOR UNSUCCESSFUL APPEAL

Ὅταν δ'ἐγγράφωνται διαψηφίζονται περὶ αὐτῶν ὀμόσαντες οἱ δημόται, ... εἰ ἐλεύ-θερός ἐστι καὶ γέγονε κατὰ τοὺς νόμους. ἔπειτ' ἂν μὲν ἀποψηφίσωνται μὴ εἶναι ἐλεύθερον, ὁ μὲν ἐφίησιν εἰς τὸ δικαστήριον, οἱ δὲ δημόται κατηγόρους αἱροῦνται πέντε ἄνδρας ἐξ αὐτῶν, κἂν μὲν μὴ δόξῃ δικαίως ἐγγράφεσθαι, πωλεῖ τοῦτον ἡ πόλις, ἐὰν δὲ νικήσῃ, τοῖς δημόταις ἐπάναγκες ἐγγράφειν (*Ath. Const.* 42. 1).

Thus Aristotle on the regular, annual scrutinies; everyone has observed that the procedure and penalty are the same in the case of extraordinary scrutinies as well, which he has not occasion specifically to mention. Everyone has observed, too, that in the second sentence, with the words μὴ εἶναι ἐλεύ-θερον, he has telescoped the two phrases of the first sentence, ἐλεύθερός ἐστι καὶ γέγονε κατὰ τοὺς νόμους; for a citizen must not only be a free man, but both his parents must be citizens, and they must be legally married.[1] It is pointed out, however (e.g., by Sandys, Wyse, Lipsius, and others), that ἐλεύθερος is often used loosely to mean 'citizen' as opposed to all other persons, to foreign but free as well as to slaves; and that has been felt to be a sufficient explanation, though when Aristotle is quoting a law he ought not to use words loosely.[2]

But the explanation is not sufficient; for we are still left with an anomaly, one which I at least cannot stomach, though as far as I know no one else minds it. It is this: In

---

[1] This last point, whether a man whose parents were Athenian but not married had citizen rights, is, as a matter of fact, disputed. I believe Müller (*Jahrb. für klass. Phil.*, xxv [1899], 732 ff.) and Wyse (pp. 280–82) to be right, that he had not, against Lipsius (pp. 475, 506). But the point is not important here.

[2] Photiades (Ἀθηνᾶ xxxviii [1926], pp. 5–7) thinks that Aristotle is using the word in its strict sense, and that he omits to mention appeal in the second case; but he does not go farther than this.

nine cases out of ten, if not in every case, when a boy was presented to his deme and rejected as illegitimate on the ground that one of his parents was foreign or that they had not been married, there can have been no possible fraud by the boy himself. Yet we are told that if his father appealed (for even this could not be the boy's responsibility) and lost his case, a perfectly innocent youth, of free birth, but by the fault of his parents, if of anyone, illegitimate, was condemned to the severest penalty—enslaved for the rest of his life. His parents might be dead, and an elder brother or an uncle appeal in all innocence; but there was no hope for the boy. I cannot believe it.

This is being sentimental? The Athenians did not in fact show 'their usual gentleness' in their citizenship laws? Very well; but the anomaly does not end there. If there was any deceit in the case (there may have been none, for the father may have been himself misled by his wife's father or guardian when he married), but if there was any, it was the father's, who introduces the boy; he is trying to palm off an illegitimate son (or someone else's, some rich foreigner's son) as legitimate, as a true Athenian; and he gets off scot-free—there is no punishment for him. Is this to be believed?

Contrast the case when the boy was really a slave. Here, if he is sold, he suffers no loss of status; he is not even punished, legally, only transferred from one master to another. Of course, there is harshness here too, but only of the kind that is inevitable in a slave-owning society. A slave could only be freed by a formal, legal process—naturally, so that he could henceforth be recognized by the state as a free man; the legal process was his protection. But the corollary of that is that without the formality he is still a slave; if he only secures his freedom through his owner palming him off as his legitimate son, he reverts to his original status on the fraud being discovered. And the owner, the father, who is primarily or wholly guilty, does in this case suffer; his slave, his own property, is taken away from him, confiscated, and sold to another; he loses both son and slave. Not a very severe punishment, I own; but sufficiently deterrent, and I do not consider that Athenian laws were all of them harsh.

I suggest therefore, and confidently, that the words μὴ

εἶναι ἐλεύθερον in the law quoted by Aristotle are to be taken literally, that the second sentence in the passage quoted above does refer only to cases where a slave was passed off as a legitimate Athenian; and that Aristotle makes no further reference to the other class of cases when on appeal it was decided that the boy was illegitimate but free, either through carelessness (and there is carelessness enough in the *Constitution of Athens*) or because no punishment followed; the boy remained free but an alien. If the father was shown guilty of fraud, he could be proceeded against on another charge— for instance, for perjury; but this particular jury had only to decide whether his father or his mother was foreign, or had not been legally married; just as in a *dokimasia* the jury had only to decide on qualifications for office, and there was no further penalty for one disqualified, though again a prosecution might follow if fraud was suspected. But this omission by Aristotle has deceived all the later writers, Plutarch, Dionysios, Libanios, the lexicographers, and the moderns.

Now take the analogous case when a man was rejected at an extraordinary scrutiny after exercising citizen rights for some years; the class of case of which Aristotle says nothing, but for which the later writers make the same statement as to punishment for unsuccessful appeal which they make for the cases arising from the annual scrutiny. Clearly, here too a man might be justly rejected as illegitimate yet be innocent of fraud; for the decision might be based on new facts about his parents coming to light. Take the case of Euxitheos. In considering all these Athenian trials, of which we possess only a speech on one side and do not even know the verdict, it is our duty to read between the lines, to try to find what the opposing case was, even though we can never reach certainty and great mistakes can be (and have been) made. It is clear that Euxitheos had a very strong case: his father Thoukritos had been recognized on his return from slavery abroad, in spite of his foreign accent, by the majority of his kinsmen as the true son of Thoukritides of Halimous; no objection had been raised to him at a special scrutiny held when the register of citizens was lost; his wife was the daughter of Damostratos of Melite, and the marriage was performed with the proper ceremonies; no objection had been

raised to either of them or to Euxitheos himself, when the
latter was entered in the deme at the age of eighteen; and
none to Euxitheos when he was elected priest of Herakles.
Of all this, even though we have not the documents,[1] it is·
reasonable to suppose that the evidence was good. The weak
points in his case are really two only. The first is his parents'
marriage; for Nikarete had been married before to one Protomachos who left her for a rich heiress. Protomachos, as was
doubtless usual, if not compulsory, in such cases, saw to it
that Nikarete was properly provided for when he left her—
in fact, married to Thoukritos with her brother's consent (her
father being dead); but his action was obviously open to
attack, and Euxitheos has to be very careful in explaining it
(41, 46)—a story that Euxitheos was not really the son of
Thoukritos, or was born before his parents' marriage (i.e.,
that Protomachos divorced Nikarete for adultery), at once
suggests itself. The second weak point is his casual reference
to his demarchy at the end of the speech (63), and his unpopularity due to his strict sense of justice: why has he not
mentioned it before as evidence for his legitimacy? His
election to the post must have been quite recent, and probably disputed for the very reasons that later led to his rejection from the deme. What were these reasons? They must
have been considerable, for all that Euxitheos says; Euboulides could not simply have said 'Euxitheos' mother once
nursed Kleinias and sold ribbons ·in the agora, so he cannot
be an Athenian true-born.' Probably some new facts had
come to light suggesting or proving either that the real
Thoukritos had never returned from abroad, that it was a
case of mistaken identity, or that he and Nikarete had not
been married; most probably Euboulides would assert both;[2]
but something like this would explain the sudden rejection of
a man who had for years enjoyed all the rights of citizenship.
For it is not necessary to believe any of Euxitheos' stories
about the way the vote was taken in the deme and other

[1]When we have got documents, they are often illuminating of the way advocates
make use of them. Cf. e.g., Dem. lix 59–61 (below, p. 81, n. 2).

[2]Doubtless some of Euxitheos' kin were against him; including, I suspect, that
Nikostratos whom he asserts (probably quite unjustly) to have been a foreigner
foisted on the deme by Euboulides and his set (59); for Nikostratos was a name used
in his father's family (21). The same Nikostratos who was accused of bribery at this
time (Aischin. ii 86)?

happenings there (cc. 9–14, 57–65)[1] to see not only that
he had a strong case, but that, even if his opponent's case
was stronger (say, if his father were proved not to have been
the real Thoukritos), he at any rate had not been guilty of
fraud (unless he had all along known the facts), especially,
as he points out (chap. 48), in view of the fact that no *graphe
xenias* has been brought against him all these years, and that
his foreign or illegitimate birth had not been discovered
until the accident of the ecclesia's decree ordering an extraordinary scrutiny in every deme.

If, then, he was innocent of fraud, of all malpractice, it
would have been as unjust to condemn him to slavery
because his non-Athenian birth was held to be proved, as
any boy of eighteen; and even more surprising, for it would
have been a penalty to which any Athenian might become
liable however innocent, and legislators would presumably
have thought of this. (Cf. Aischines' words, οἱ ἠτυχηκότες
τῶν πολιτῶν, quoted by Demosthenes [xviii 132].) Was
Euxitheos, if he lost his case, liable to enslavement? He
speaks in his exordium of the importance of the issue to him
and of the shame involved if he fail—which may mean anything. In his peroration (full of the exaggeration of conventional sentimentalism to be found in law courts all over the
world) he speaks of his passion to have his mother and himself buried in the family vault, to remain a member of the
state, to keep his kin; rather than lose all that he would kill
himself. Not a word about slavery. A candid reader, who had
not yet been told that enslavement was the penalty of failure,
would certainly not guess it from the speech. I do not believe
it was. I think, in fact, that there was no punishment involved
in the case at all, only a verdict as to fact: Was Euxitheos a
legitimate son of Athenian parents, and himself a citizen, or
not? If not, then his status is that of an alien. The case is
similar to those involving claims to titles and political privileges and entailed estates in some modern countries. In
England and in Scotland a man can claim to be the rightful
holder of a peerage against the present holder, putting in
perhaps evidence of a marriage of which he is the eldest son,

[1] At the same time we may feel glad that Thucydides of Halimous, with his
foreign connexions, lived two generations earlier.

or one of which he is the legitimate descendant, and if he
wins his suit the present holder loses the dignity of a peer and
with it the political privileges and the entailed property;[1]
but he is not punished. Such a result meant a severer loss in
Athens—loss of citizenship and therefore of all title to
property in land and houses. But there is no essential difference in kind between Athenian and modern law in this class
of case. Nor do I believe that, if enslavement had been the
penalty for unsuccessful appeal, so many appeals would have
been made, particularly at a time of popular excitement over
the number of false entries in the registers (Dem. lvii 2–3;
Aischin. i 77: which, untruthful as it is, as Dem. lvii shows,
at least proves the frequency of appeals).[2]

I maintain, then, that in trials that are ἐφέσεις ἐκ δημοτῶν
not only was enslavement not a penalty for unsuccessful
appeal, but that there was no penalty, except in the case
where it was decided that the appellant was a slave; and that
in that case the penalty (loss of the slave) fell, as we should
expect, on the man who had introduced him to the deme.[3]

Let us consider other cases, similar or analogous. It is
unfortunate that in the only other trial which is in nearly all
respects similar to that of Euxitheos, namely, that of Euphiletos, we have only a fragment of a speech; we can only say
that in that fragment there is no mention of enslavement, and
(as I think) its tone is against the idea that enslavement was

[1] The law of entail has recently been altered, and in Scotland at least the law of
'negative prescription' (twenty years in this case) would obtain against a claim to
the land. But the principle is the same. Cf. for example, the story of the Macdonald
baronetcy recalled in *The Times* of June 16, 1935, in the obituary notice of Lady
Macdonald.

[2] It has long been recognized that Plutarch's account of the thousands sold as
slaves after the extraordinary general scrutiny of 445–4 B.C. (*Per.* 37) is untrue. The
figure (which comes from Philochorus, frag. 90, who says nothing of enslavement)
is itself quite unreliable; Plutarch is applying the law of *Ath. Const.* 42. 1 (and
misunderstanding that, as I am arguing here) to the fifth century; and his statement
implies that everyone who was rejected in his deme appealed. I believe myself that
the only lawsuits in 445–4 were *graphai xenias*, held before the *xenodikai*, a special
board probably instituted for this occasion, and not long afterwards abolished (see
Körte, *Hermes*, lxviii. [1933], 238–42).

[3] In the 'Law of the Demotionidai' (*IG*, ii², 1237; see Wade-Gery, *Class. Quart.*,
xxv, 129–43), which, as Diller points out, has many points of analogy with the
citizenship law here discussed, there was a penalty for unsuccessful appeal—1,000 dr.
—and also one (100 dr.) imposed on the member who introduced a rejected candidate at the scrutiny of the *phratria*, whether there was an appeal or not. This at an
extraordinary scrutiny. For ordinary scrutinies in future, the parent or those who
vouched for him were in certain circumstances liable to a fine. See also below, pp. 81–2.

the penalty. In Isaios viii 43 the speaker argues that his opponent in persuading the jury that their mother is a foreigner 'is putting us to the risk of losing not only our property, but our citizen-status as well,' as they were born after Eukleides; not of losing their status as free men, or anything about confiscation of property, only citizenship and the inheritance which is in dispute; even so it was serious enough, and (with exaggeration) ὄνειδος ἕξομεν διότι ἠμφεσ-βητήθημεν.[1] Similarly, when Boiotos, son of Mantias, brought a suit against his father to compel him to introduce him into the phratry ('to show cause' why he should not be introduced), and subsequently into the deme, his citizenship was involved in the question of his legitimacy (both his parents were Athenian; their marriage was doubted), but not his freedom (Dem. xxxix 2; xl 10); the same with Phrastor's son by Neaira's daughter, whom the genos rejected—he brought a suit against the genos (again 'to show cause'), but retired from it rather than take the oath that the boy's mother was Athenian;[2] the boy did not thereby become a slave (Dem. lix 59–61). These cases in which *gene* and *phratriai* are involved are interesting for the light they throw on Athenian social structure. They were not official divisions of the state, and membership in them was not compulsory for a citizen, though, to judge from the orators, it was normal; but rejection by his genos or phratry would obviously weaken a man's claim to citizenship. Hence their 'laws,' while of their own making, must be in harmony with those of the state; and a man could compel them to act according to their laws by a suit in the state law-courts;[3] while at the same time a false statement to secure entry to a phratry or a genos would be punishable by the state—just as in modern countries baptism is not compulsory but can be demanded, and a false entry in a church

---

[1] Cf. ἡ αἰσχύνη in Dem. lvii 1. There is no mention in Aischines either of anyone being sold as a slave as a result of the appeals; but not much can be made of his silence.

[2] So the prosecutor asserts; the documentary evidence that he brings only refers to the rejection by the genos.

[3] It would be interesting to know whether the state would enforce payment of a fine such as that imposed by the 'law of the Demotionidai.' I imagine not. A man could leave the phratry, or allow his child to be rejected, rather than pay the fine; running the risk of this fact being brought up against him later, e.g., when his son was to enter the deme or his daughter to be betrothed.

G

register is a statutory offence.[1] But Dr. Diller's view that the phratry and genos scrutinies are earlier than the deme scrutinies and than the body of law in connexion with the latter seems singularly perverse. The state must have had some means of resolving disputes as to citizenship which first arose in a deme, and this must have been by appeals to the dicasteries in some form.

Now take certain *graphai* relating to the law of citizenship:

If a man betroth a foreign woman to an Athenian ὡς ἑαυτῷ προσήκουσαν, he shall lose his citizen rights and his property be confiscated, and the informer shall have one third of the value of the latter; the information to be laid before the Thesmothetai by any citizen possessed of full rights, as in the case of *graphai xenias* [law *ap.* *Dem.* lix 52].

If an alien marry a citizen woman (and live with her as his wife) by any device or means whatsoever, an information may be laid against him before the Thesmothetai by any citizen possessed of full rights; if he be convicted, he shall be sold, himself and his property; and the informer shall have one third of the value. And if an alien woman marry a citizen, the same law shall apply, and the citizen who marries her shall be fined a thousand drachmae [*ibid.* 16].

These two laws are in all respects analogous to that of *xenia*; they both concern prosecutions for fraud, and for a more serious offence than nominating a boy who is not legitimate for entry to a deme; an offence of an altogether different character from that of the innocent boy who is nominated to the deme, or that of a man such as Euxitheos. Yet in none of these cases is a citizen reduced to slavery. In the first he is disfranchised and his property is confiscated; in the second and third the fraudulent alien is sold (and doubtless in many cases he was bought by friends who sent him out of Attica a free man), the citizen woman is unpunished, the citizen man fined. And he is fined only if he connived at the fraud; there is no suggestion that Phrastor would have been fined because

---

[1] Cf. the very interesting law quoted from Krateros by Harpokration *s.v.* ναυτοδίκαι: ἐὰν δέ τις ἐξ ἀμφοῖν ξένοιν γεγονὼς φρατρίζῃ, διώκειν εἶναι τῷ βουλομένῳ Ἀθηναίων, οἷς δίκαι εἰσί, λαγχάνειν δὲ τῇ ἔνῃ καὶ νέᾳ πρὸς τοὺς ναυτοδίκας (see Lipsius 86–88). The *nautodikai* in Aristophanes' day had charge of trials for *xenia*, as well as for commercial offences, both of which a hundred years later were in the hands of the thesmothetai; the fact that one foreign parent is allowed shows that the law is either earlier than 451–0 or belongs to the period before 403 when Perikles' law was in abeyance, and, if the latter, that Perikles' law had been formally abrogated; and it shows both that the phratry's law must conform to the state's, and state protection of the phratry's rights.

he was misled into thinking Neaira's daughter to be legitimate (Dem. lix 53). And the alien woman who married a citizen is so punished only if she was aware of the fraud—if, in fact, the fraud was hers; it is not suggested that Neaira's daughter was in danger, but Stephanos, who had betrothed her to Phrastor. Above all, no punishment of the children if Neaira were convicted; if they are hers, they will be struck off the roll of citizens, nothing more (124).

Lastly, the *graphe xenias* proper, that is, prosecution by any citizen of a man for knowingly and fraudulently exercising citizen rights though an alien. There seem to be only two or three definite references in classical authors to the penalty in case of conviction: Lysias xiii 60, ἀγωνισάμενον τῆς ξενίας τὰ ἔσχατα παθεῖν, which does not necessarily mean slavery, for Demosthenes describes the loss of civil rights and confiscation which threatened Stephanos (lix 53) as ταῖς ἐσχάταις ζημίαις περιπεσεῖν; Isaios iii 37, ξενίας φεύγων ... παρὰ τέτταρας ψήφους μέτεσχε τῆς πόλεως; and Dem. *Epist.* iii 29, ὡς δοῦλον ἐλαυνόμενον καὶ γραφὴν ξενίας φεύγοντα καὶ μικροῦ πραθέντα. Only one definite allusion to enslavement as the punishment even for this offence occurs, and that in a Demosthenic letter which may well not be genuine; and if it is genuine, it may mean that Pytheas was accused not merely of foreign birth but of being a slave (so that the case would be of the class analogous to that mentioned by Aristotle; see above, p. 76). So that I doubt it here too. The penalty may have been disfranchisement and confiscation of goods; and there must at least have been some provision made for cases where men in all innocence were acting as citizens, and there was no scrutiny about to be held in their demes; if, for example, the doubts about Euxitheos' birth had arisen when there was to be no general scrutiny.[1]

I believe, then, that the later writers, the rhetoricians and the lexicographers, were all misled by Aristotle's omission to distinguish the results of an unsuccessful appeal in two quite different types of cases, and by the deceptive affinity be-

---

[1] The γραφὴ ὑποβολῆς, once mentioned in a lexicon (see Lipsius 717), with the same punishment as for *xenia*, was probably an action against a parent for introducing a supposititious son to his phratry.

tween appeals from the demes and the various *graphai* for infractions of the citizenship laws—by the penalty inflicted on foreigners for fraudulent marriage with citizens, and perhaps for fraudulent exercise of citizen rights in general. Two instances of this misunderstanding by late writers are especially interesting: Suidas, *s.v.* ἀποψηφισθέντα, gives the usual account, that those rejected on appeal were sold as slaves, and quotes Dem. xviii 132 (τὸν ἀποψηφισθέντ᾽ Ἀντιφῶντα), though it is clear from Demosthenes himself that Antiphon was not a slave;[1] and Schol. Dem. xxiv 131, where Demosthenes speaks only of detention in prison of those who, convicted of *xenia*, are about to prosecute a witness at the trial for perjury and so upset the previous verdict,[2] and the scholiast makes only the conventional and not pertinent comment that men prosecuted for *xenia* must remain in prison until the trial and are sold as slaves if convicted (though as these are cases of *xenia*, enslavement may in fact have been the punishment).

We know very little of the development of Attic law in these cases. I agree with Dr. Diller that Aristotle's use of the word διαψηφισμός in connection with the expulsion of large numbers of the tyrants' adherents in 510 is probably an anachronism; and in any case the voting did not take place in the demes, which had not then been instituted;[3] though I see no reason for doubting either the expulsion or the alleged

[1] Antiphon, after rejection by his deme, may not have appealed; so this case cannot be taken in support of my main contention. It only proves the conventional and misleading comment of lexicographers. I do, in fact, believe that all who appealed and failed are included in Aischines' οἱ ἠτυχηκότες τῶν πολιτῶν and in Hypereides' ἀπεψηφισμένοι (frag. 29).

[2] Or, it may be, of those who, convicted of alien birth, are about to be prosecuted for perjury, i.e., for knowingly and fraudulently exercising citizen rights. If the usual interpretation of Dem. xxiv 131 is correct, that the defendant is about to prosecute, then some special provision must have been made whereby a man in prison could institute a prosecution before a magistrate and summon the other party. If my suggestion is right, that it refers to a further prosecution of the original defendant for perjury, then that would be evidence that even in a *graphe xenias* only status, not further punishment, was involved, unless fraud or perjury at the trial were also proved.

[3] 'Diapsephisis ... Angewandt wurde dieses Verfahren schon bei der allgemeinen Prüfung des Bürgerstandes nach dem Sturze der Peisistratiden, die man offenbar in Verbindung mit der Einrichtung der Demen und der Anlegung der Bürgerbücher vornahm'—Busolt-Swoboda, *Gr. Staatskunde*, ii, 949. Surely not. This expulsion was an oligarchic measure, taken by Isagoras, before Kleisthenes' legislation. Kleisthenes restored them.

reason—impure birth.[1] In 445–4 there was a *diapsephisis*; but we have no accurate knowledge of the procedure in trials arising from it—only that they were probably in the hands of the specially appointed board of *xenodikai*.[2] But we may well believe that already in the fifth century appeal to a dicastery from the vote of the deme was usual in the case of the annual scrutinies, and can be confident that a regular procedure was instituted in the legislation of 403 B.C. In the fourth century it seems probable that at first the Forty had charge of the appeals (which then were remitted to arbitrators before trial), later the thesmothetai; if Lipsius (pp. 87–88) is correct in supposing that mercantile cases first came before the thesmothetai at some time between 355 and 342, the board of *nautodikai* being then abolished, it may be that appeals from the demes were transferred to them at the same time (for *graphai xenias* were at some time transferred to them from the *nautodikai*, who originally had charge of them); in that case the change will have been made before 346, say about 350 B.C. But the change was only a formal one, giving perhaps greater importance to the trials; the appeal remained a trial of fact, and essentially different from a prosecution for fraudulent usurpation of citizen rights and privileges. The *phratriai* and *gene*, not being official bodies, could make each its own law, which might vary in strictness (necessity of a full vote in case of doubt, etc.);[3] but all would conform in general with the law of the state, and be modelled on it.

NOTE

In an answer to this paper[4] Dr. Diller argued first, that a *decree* instituting new regulations (as opposed to a νόμος) was possible provided it did not conflict with any existing law, not only if an existing law allowed it, and that there was much confusion, both verbally and in practice, between a decree and law. It is possible that I have exaggerated the strictness of Attic procedure in legislation; but even so, it

---

[1] Still less is there any reason to suppose that the account is not from the *Atthis,* because Plutarch omits mention of it in *Sol.* 29 (Diller, p. 203).

[2] Above, p. 80, n. 2.

[3] Andok. i 127; Isai. vii 16–7; viii 19.

[4] *Class. Phil.* xxx, 1935, pp. 302–11.

leaves my main argument untouched—that the change in the procedure in citizenship cases, whether brought about by a new law or by Demophilos' decree, was only a formal one, and consisted chiefly in their transference to the thesmothetai. Secondly, he insists that there had been no general scrutiny previous to that of 346 in the fourth century, and probably not in the fifth. But in regard to the fourth century I agree with him; when I say 'there had been appeals from scrutinies before 346' (above, p. 73, n. 2), I do not refer to general scrutinies. There must have been some regulation for appeals from special scrutinies, as from that in the Halimous deme when the register was lost. Thirdly, he says that 'the issue in the appeal and the γραφὴ ξενίας was exactly the same; and this was of course the chief reason for associating the two processes.' But they are not associated by anything except that the Thesmothetai presided at both kinds of trials; in the long list of cases which came before the thesmothetai Aristotle distinguishes them very clearly. My main objections to the current view Dr. Diller only briefly refers to in a footnote (p. 308, n. 34).

(*b*) THE CITIZENSHIP LAW OF 451–0 AND THE διαψήφισις OF 445–4[1]

In the *Cambridge Ancient History* this problem is discussed by three different scholars, Mr. Tod, Mr. Walker and Prof. Adcock (pp. 5, 102–3, 167–8); they agree in connecting the passing of the law and the scrutiny closely, and in regarding the former as motived only by the selfishness of a demos determined to keep its privileges to itself. Indeed Prof. Adcock says that the scrutiny was nothing but the retrospective enforcement of the law, and Mr. Walker says that, as a *preliminary* to the distribution of Psammetichos' corn, the list of citizens was revised. This seems to me all wrong. The idea of kinship as the basis of membership of the state was fundamental throughout Greece, and in this respect the nationality of the mother was as important as that of the father; it was not confined to Athens or to democracies. As there was, in fact, so much intercourse between the different

---

[1]First published in the *Journal of Hellenic Studies*, l, 1930.

cities, and barriers to trade and change of domicile had broken down, there had been in practice, inevitably, some intermarriage (how much at Athens we do not know—certainly chiefly among the Few); but the law of 451 was an attempt to restore what was regarded as normal by the Many; it was in accordance with average sentiment. And that, next to this, the chief motive was a fear lest the population would continue increasing and eventually make the constitution unworkable, we need not doubt. The constitution *was* only workable within a certain limit of numbers, and it is Aristotle, no friend of the democracy, who says that this was the motive of the law.[1] (Mr. Walker says we must be on our guard against thinking of the measure as undemocratic 'in the ancient sense of the term. . . . To the Greeks democracy meant, not the overthrow of privilege, but merely the extension of its area.' Exactly; and this law did not extend, but narrowed the area, and was therefore undemocratic in the ancient sense of the word, as in the modern—or rather would have been, had not the feeling for kinship pulled in the other direction.) Professor Adcock sums up: 'This narrow policy was a grievous error. The limit of Athenian greatness was the limit of her devoted citizens, and this action is a great reproach on the statecraft of Pericles, a denial of Athens' past, and a menace to Athens' future.' That one of the chief causes (though not the only one) of Athens' failure to unite Greece was an insufficient man-power, and that this in turn was caused largely by her citizen-ship laws is true. But that should not make us forget that, had the numbers of her citizens risen rapidly to 60,000, 80,000, 100,000 (mainly concentrated in the towns), the whole constitution and manner of public life would have changed, as they did at Rome. Athens could not have re-

---

[1]We must, however, remember that the admission as citizens of the children of citizen men and foreign women would not as such increase the population, unless there were citizens who refused to marry at all because they could not marry foreigners. Only a corresponding admission of the children of citizen women and foreign men would do this. Indeed one may suppose that one of the motives in 451 was a fear that citizens' daughters would not get married, as it almost certainly was in 403, when, after the war, there were so many more women than men among the citizen population (Xen. *Mem.* ii 2–6; Isocr. xiv 51; cf. Dem. lix 112–3). It was the refusal of Athens (here again like every other Greek city) to naturalize the metics, even though settled for many generations, that more than anything else prevented an abnormal increase in the population.

mained true to her ἦθος; and we should recognize, not only that a determination to remain true to her past was a natural one, but that, however much she might have gained by a more generous decision, she would also have lost much, and the world would have lost with her. Impracticable, absurd her institutions may have been; but there is something precious (and certainly unique) in conditions that will produce an Aristophanes and a Demosthenes.

Secondly, this citizenship law was not made retrospective in 451, as the cases of Kimon and of Thucydides or Oloros show (and the analogy of 403 would suggest), and there is no reason for supposing any retrospective measure, nor any measure at all except a decree ordering a scrutiny in every deme in 445. Owing to the very considerable increase of the foreign population (not all of it with metic rights) since 479, to the growth of the towns and the migration thither of poor citizens as well as foreigners free and slave, and to the fact that a citizen did not change his deme with his domicile, a large number of persons, aided by the muddle caused by this rapid development, had got themselves or their children or other people's children fraudulently enrolled as citizens, many very likely after news had come that there was to be a gift of corn from Egypt; all claimed their share, and in consequence of the scandal a universal scrutiny was ordered. This is not to deny that selfishness was a powerful motive with many voters in 451, and there was doubtless much malice, backbiting, blackmail, lying and uncharitableness in 445, and much injustice done. Men's characters are various. But the object of the διαψήφισις was to investigate charges of fraud, and to secure that the law was obeyed.

V

THE POSITION OF WOMEN IN ATHENS IN THE FIFTH AND FOURTH CENTURIES B.C.[1]

It is a commonplace that, whereas in the Aegean age and in Homer the position of women was a noble one, in Athens of the classical period it was ignoble. For example:

The best woman, according to the Athenian definition, is she of whom 'least is said for either good or harm.' . . . In this respect the Athenians were far less liberal than Sparta and other Grecian states.[2]

γυναῖκας, ἃς ἐβόσκομεν κατ' οἶκον, a passage expressive of the contempt felt by the cultured Greeks for their wives.[3]

The position of Athenian women [in the time of Aristophanes] precluded the possibility of comedy in the highest sense.[4]

In Menander's hands the individualizing of female character and the freeing of the female will have gone but a little way: women were emerging from a state hardly above slavery, and his women are mentally without distinction.[5]

In scena sua mulieribus primas partes dudum tribuerat Euripides novi aevi antesignanus, a comico eam ob causam saepe derisus: ipse iam comicus iis primas tribuit . . . non iam, ut patrum aetate, tacere primum videbatur mulierum officium, non de iis tacere, in artis praesertim operibus, prima laus.[6]

Women of the respectable class were condemned to comparative seclusion. They enjoyed far less freedom in fourth-century Athens than in the Homeric age.[7]

And so forth. It will be admitted that these passages fairly give the prevailing view on the position of women in Athens; that this view is almost universally held (I know of one contradiction—a sentence in an article in the *Manchester Guardian*[8]—and one important modification, by Dr. Botsford, to

[1]First published in *Classical Philology*, xx, 1925.
[2]Tucker, *Life in Ancient Athens*, p. 51.
[3]Starkie on Aristoph. *Vesp.* 313, quoting *Lysistr.* 260–1.
[4]Rennie, *Acharnians of Aristoph.*, p. 9.
[5]Neil, *Knights of Aristophanes*, p. xiv.
[6]Van Leeuwen, Arist. *Thesm.* p. ii.
[7]E. M. Walker, *Greek History*, p. 78.
[8]An article by J. S. Blake-Reed on the tombs of the Kerameikos: 'Damasistrate and her husband clasp hands at parting. A child and a kinswoman stand beside the

which I shall come later); and that it is expressed confidently, as on a matter which admits of no doubt, about which there is no conflict of evidence and which is well known to everyone. This paper is not an attempt to prove that this view is untrue; but that there is a conflict of evidence; that much that is relevant is ignored and other evidence misunderstood and misapplied; that is, that the confidence in the prevailing view is quite unjustified.

This view, then, is that legally, socially, and in general estimation women occupied a low place in Athens in the fifth and fourth centuries, lower than in most other Greek—especially Dorian—cities of the time, lower than in Homeric and in Aegean society and than in Rome, and of course much lower than in our own enlightened age. It will be agreed that these three aspects—the legal, the social, and that of general estimation—must be kept distinct. The women of France, for instance, in the matter of property and of political rights, are in an inferior position to those of England, but no one would suggest that they are socially less free or held in less honour.[1] A resident alien in Athens and other Greek states had few rights, but he was free and had honour where honour was due. Slaves had no rights at all; but socially there was a nearer approach to equality between them and their masters than between rich and poor in England to-day, as can be seen from Aristophanes and Menander. Further, the *Arabian Nights* gives us a picture of a society where women have (practically) no legal rights and are socially confined, yet are the equals of men; for there love, and especially the comic side of being in love, is almost the only thing that matters, and (as in no other book that I

chair, but husband and wife have no eyes save for each other, and the calm intensity of their parting gaze answers all questionings as to the position of the wife and mother in Attic Society' (*Manchester Guardian*, Feb. 23, 1922). See also Matthias, ap: *B.P.W.* 1894, p. 1288, and *Jahrb. f. Philol.* cxlvii. (1893), 261–76. Zimmern's view may also be called a modification of current opinion (*Greek Commonwealth* [3rd ed.], pp. 333 ff.). J. D. Beazley also has since written in a different strain; see below, p. 94, n. 2.

[1]A future historian may put a black mark against *us*, if he relies (as he would) on Dr. Johnson: 'Sir, I question if in Paris such a company as is sitting round this table could be got together in less than half a year. They talk in France of the felicity of men and women living together: the truth is; that there the men are not higher than the women, they know no more than the women do, and they are not held down in their conversation by the presence of women' (1778, *aetat.* 69). And compare Boswell on the 'degree of intelligence which is to be desired in a female companion.'

know) men and women are equal, and very much alike, in
this important part of life. And in fact the prevailing, and
surely correct, view about the women of Homer is based not
on the external details of their life, for after all Penelope
weaves, Nausicaa washes clothes, and even glorious Helen
works at her loom, but, rightly, on the part they play in the
story, the way their characters are studied, the interest shown
in them. But in Athens, we are told, women were powerless
in law, scarcely stirred from the rooms in which they were
locked, and were systematically treated with contempt.

Now there is a certain inconsistency in the expressions of
the prevailing view, which is worth examining, as it at once
suggests that our confidence should be modified. It has often
been observed how great an interest is shown by the Athenian vase-painters of the late Fine Period in family life; but
this period is that between 470 and 430 B.C., the period of
Kimon and Perikles when women are generally thought to
have been of least account, the period that closes with the
Funeral Speech; and these vases were made chiefly for the
Athenian market.[1] To Van Leeuwen, as to many, Euripides
is the rebel, and the herald of a new age; but of what age?
Presumably of the fourth century; but others, such as Neil
and Walker, assert the seclusion of women then; and I know
of no general evidence pointing to any difference between the
fourth and fifth centuries in this respect; we do not find—
as we surely should—writers pointing out, whether for
praise or blame, that women who in our fathers' time were
slaves now are free. Aristophanes, of course, laughs at
Euripides for making women talkative; but also for doing
the same disservice to their husbands, making them different
from Marathon men; so that does not help us.

Further: 'Euripides gave the first place on his stage to
women.' True, but surely not more than Sophocles and
Aeschylus had done? 'It was no longer thought, as in their
fathers' time, that to be silent was the first duty of women;
nor that to say nothing about them was the highest merit of a
work of art.' Do, then, Clytemnestra and Antigone say

[1] See especially Pottier, *Catalogue des vases antiques du Louvre*, iii, 1041–2; and
cf. Buschor, *Greek Vase-painting* (Eng. transl.), pp. 150–1, Fig. 154, a figure on a
jug in Oxford of about 430 B.C., 'she is the vehicle of a wonderful feeling'; see also
pp. 146–7.

nothing? Are their creators silent about them? In a fine passage on Euripides' women, Van Leeuwen writes:

Veras [denique in scena exhibuit mulieres, non νευρόσπαστα aliqua sexum muliebrem ementita; eum mulieribus illic vindicavit locum, quem in ipsa vita assignavit iis natura, denegarunt saepe viri; ita eas pinxit ut viros—non probos potissimum viros, sed viros—ante eum pinxerant alii. Et hoc ipsum in eius arte improbabat Aristophanes; qui facile tulisset si tragicus contemtim de mulieribus nonnunquam esset locutus, ceteroquin in operibus suis eas neglegens.[1]

But who were the others who had depicted men as Euripides did women? Who were the poets admired by Aristophanes who occasionally expressed contempt for women, and were otherwise silent about them? Certainly neither of the two great Athenians. I am not denying that Euripides may have raised questions then new to tragedy.[2] But I am speaking of the general attitude of the three poets; and if the attitude of Euripides is significant in a discussion of the position of women at Athens, that of Aeschylus and Sophocles is not less so. There is, in fact, no literature, no art of any country, in which women are more prominent, more important, more carefully studied and with more interest, than in the tragedy, sculpture, and painting of fifth-century Athens.

Professor Gardner says:

No one can read the account of Nausicaa's reception of Odysseus without feeling that dignity and self-possession such as she displays could not exist in a maiden brought up in seclusion and trained only in the labours of the loom.[3]

That is as may be; but what of Deianira? 'The heroine of the *Trachiniae* has been recognised by general consent as one of the most delicately beautiful creations in literature,' wrote Jebb;[4] who, naturally, compared her with Nausikaa. Is it not, in fact, true that if the position of woman had precluded the possibility of the highest comedy, it would also have precluded the highest tragedy, seeing that both are repre-

[1]Ed. *Thesmoph.*, p. vi.
[2]Doubtless Wilamowitz is in general right when he says (*Herakles* [1889], p. 10, quoted by Van Leeuwen, ed. *Ran.* iii, 1): *Es muss geradezu gesagt werden dass Euripides das weib und die durch das verhältniss der geschlechter enstehenden sittlichen conflicte für die poesie entdeckt hat.* Yet this ignores the *Agamemnon*.
[3]Gardner and Jevons, *Manual of Greek Antiquities*, p. 341.
[4]Ed. *Trach.*, p. xxxi; he contrasts the Deianira *furenti similis ac torvum intuens*, the 'Armenian tigress,' of the Roman Seneca, pp. xliii–xliv.

sentations of life? Or rather, just as you can have some high comedy without women (or without men, for that matter) —most of the *Wasps* is high comedy of the best—so you might have some tragedy, for example, *Prometheus* or *Julius Caesar*; but very little, very restricted in range? What is the explanation of this? We are told the tragedians got their women from the great characters of the epic, just as their plots are from that source. They did not derive other things, not the religious views they expressed, nor their politics, nor their male characters; these, Orestes, Odysseus, Kreon, Theseus, are—in so far as they are not universal—Athenians of the fifth century; but their women are Homeric. I like to think of Sophocles—no feminist reformer, certainly— sitting down to write a tragedy; he is a master-poet and observer, but he has led a purely masculine life; he has met no women except his mother, his wife (occasionally), and his sisters (yet more rarely), together with a few passing *filles de joie*; and he treats them with contempt, in his case doubtless a good-natured contempt. What should we expect? An *Ajax* but with no Tekmessa; an *Oedipus* with very little of Jocasta; a *Creon*, with, perhaps, an Ismene, but certainly not *Antigone*. He might have gone so far as to write an *Alcestis*, as a pretty story of proper feminine obedience. But there would have been no Attic tragedy. We have, as it happens, many references in Homer to the story of the house of Atreus which was such a favourite at Athens; but it is an interesting fact that in the epic it is Aigisthos, not Clytemnestra, who is the dominant figure and kills Agamemnon; and Orestes, with no help from Elektra, who takes vengeance on Aigisthos —a very masculine tragedy. How different is the story as all three Athenians tell it.[1]

When we make statements about the position of women in the Homeric age or in Minoan Crete as confident as those we make about Athens, we are relying, rightly, on the imaginative literature of the period in one case, on the art in the other.[2] We have evidence of both kinds for Athens of the fifth century, and in far greater quantity. We have three

[1]We may note also that the story of Antigone is probably of Attic origin (Jebb Introd., *init.*).
[2]Also on the importance of goddesses; but this holds for Athens as well.

poets—of very different temperaments—instead of one; we have sculpture, and hundreds, nay thousands, of painted vases. Yet this evidence is regularly ignored. Homer's Andromache, like Hektor, is proof of epic feeling; but for Athens only Jason and Kreon, not Antigone and Medea, are evidence. We may trust the paintings and the statuettes of Crete, but the Dresden Athena and the Sosandra of Kalamis mean nothing—that statue which Lucian so much admired for the grace of its pose, the comely arrangement and order of the drapery, the modest courtesy of its expression, the noble, scarcely visible smile, the foot just made for the dance, the pretty ankle, καὶ ἄλλα μυρία.[1] But even if we regard Attic tragedy and temple sculpture as remote from Attic life, as I think we cannot do, but if we do, we still have the innumerable vases and the sculptured tombs, which, if anything, give us a picture of contemporary Athens.[2] They tell the same tale as tragedy. We can observe in them as in life, as indeed we might expect, that there are two sexes, and neither creates more interest, is more prominent, than the other. Imagine a student, especially favoured of Heaven, to come to the study of Homer, say, Sappho, Alkman Simonides, and the three tragedians, and of Attic vases and sculpture, without having read anything that scholars have written about ancient life; would he suppose that there was anything remarkable about the position of women in Athens, except perhaps the special honour paid to them? Could he imagine that they were kept locked up and despised? 'Ah,' will be the answer, 'that only shows the dangers of half-knowledge; wait till he comes to Thucydides and Aristotle.' But at least there is a conflict of evidence, something that challenges thought and demands explanation? There is a puzzle?

[1] *Imag.* 6; *Dial. Meretr.* iii. 2. It is noteworthy that Lucian, in describing his ideal of feminine beauty, takes details from five different statues, the Aphrodite of Knidos, Aphrodite of the Gardens, Pheidias' Lemnian Athena and Amazon, and the Sosandra—all of which are Athenian. Kalamis and Praxiteles are the essentially Attic sculptors. It is the Dorian schools of Argos and Sikyon which are almost exclusively masculine.

[2] 'The Attic tombstones and their tranquil representations of women with their maids, mothers with their children, young warriors and unaged men, which . . . silently confute the peculiar belief that the people whose poets created an unrivalled line of noble mothers, wives, maidens, and viragos, had a low opinion of womanhood' (Beazley, *C.A.H.*, v, p. 442).

As I said, there is one scholar, the late Dr. Botsford, who was not satisfied with just repeating what others have said before him. But he did not carry his view to its logical conclusion, and so left himself in what seems to me a quite obviously untenable position; in such a way, however, as to show the difficulty in the prevailing view. He took Aeschylus—as well as the vase paintings—as evidence not only for the important part played by women in contemporary life, but also for the freedom of movement which they clearly enjoyed; and he instanced Isodike and Elpinike, the wife and the sister of Kimon, as historical examples. He did not adopt the theory that Elpinike assumed the Spartan manners of her brother (indeed that genial soldier was very un-Spartan in his way of life); nor does any ancient writer appear to have thought of this clever explanation, nor indeed to have considered that any explanation was necessary. But he still suffered from the burden of the Funeral Speech, and the excerpts of Stobaios; so he supposed a decline in the succeeding generation after the comparative freedom of a century and a half since Solon; he states that women were secluded in the Periklean age, and that a revolt against this begins again in Euripides, in the *Medea*, for example.[1] But this results in a paradoxical view of Greek social history. The Funeral Speech (always assuming the sentiment in it to be Perikles' own, not Thucydides') belongs to the winter of 431–430; let us take January 1, 430, as the fatal day. The *Oresteia* was exhibited in the spring of 457, the *Medea* in 431. Only twenty-six years, then, of unquestioned seclusion? And Perikles must have been not so much hammering at a nail that had long been securely fastened in the wall as attempting to drive one back that was new, yet already threatened to come out. Moreover, Sophocles is as good evidence as Aeschylus; no change in the attitude toward women (except, of course, one individual to the writer, but irrelevant to the present question), nor any in the freedom with which they come and go on the stage, is observable in

[1] *Hellenic History*, pp. 132, 219 ff., 286 ff., 332, 408 f. Some other writers have of course taken the dramatists as evidence, among them Mahaffy (*Social Life in Greece*² [1875], pp. 152-3, 185 ff., etc.). But that did not prevent him talking of 'the really Asiatic jealousy with which women of the higher classes were locked up in imperial Athens, and the contempt with which they were systematically treated.'

him. The *Antigone* appeared in 442 or 441, at a time that
we may take, I suppose, to be the very acme of Athenian
greatness, when the Parthenon was nearing completion,
Pheidias was engaged on his Athena, the empire was at
peace, and Perikles supreme; and Antigone is worthy of her
age. Ismene, most timid of women, tries her best to dissuade her sister; but she never uses the one argument
which, according to the rules we have laid down for the
conduct of Greek maidens, should have been the first
to occur to her and immediately conclusive—she does
not censure Antigone (and herself) for appearing outside
the *gynaikonitis* and still more for proposing to walk through
the streets of Thebes. Neither does Medea hurry indoors
when the stranger Aigeus appears, and the latter—a perfectly respectable Athenian—does not seem to expect her to.
But we would get into hopeless confusion if we tried to find
changes in the position of women in Athens—in the social
freedom they enjoyed, that is, and the estimation in which
they were held—from the evidence of Attic tragedy.
Neither do the vases and the sculpture of the fifth century
lend any support to such a view; and we may add that the
scandal that gathered round Perikles' name implied an
equal degree of social freedom in the women of his generation to that enjoyed by Elpinike.[1]

So far I have been trying to show that there exists a great
variety of evidence which is consistently ignored, but is
strictly relevant and of the greatest importance, and I will
repeat in passing that even if we do for fifth-century Athens
what we have no right to do and would not think of doing
for any other country or period, namely, ignore its imaginative literature (so far as it suits our theories) as being
remote from life, even if we do this, we still have to account
for the vases and tombstones which tell the same story. I
now come to evidence of another kind, which is generally
supposed to establish, not merely to support, the prevalent
view, and which I consider to be generally misapplied.
There are numerous passages, numerously quoted, in Attic

[1]E.g., Plut. *Per.* xiii 9 (from a contemporary source, a comic poet or Stesim-
brotos: see xiii 11). It is worth while noting what Xenophon does say about the
gynaikonitis and its bolts and bars (*Oec.* ix. 5).

tragedies and comedies, expressive of the general sentiment, 'a woman's sphere is the home' or 'a good wife obeys her husband' (not a sentiment, by the way, very foreign to our own or any other time); others again of the type, 'a wife is a necessary evil.' Dozens of these were collected with great industry by Stobaios; they have been re-collected by modern writers with equal industry and used with greater folly, for at least Stobaios did not build on them a fanciful history. Indeed he could not; for he was fond of collecting into contiguous chapters passages of opposite meaning from the same writers: 'that it is good to be a farmer,' 'that it is bad to be a farmer'; 'that it is good to have children,' 'that children are a nuisance'; and so forth; and if anyone likes to read that 'the best thing in life a man can have is a sympathetic wife' or 'there is nothing so intimate, when you come to think of it, as a man and wife,' he will find such impeccable sentiments as frequent in the *Florilegium* as in the most approved writers of other ages. But what is the value of passages thus divorced from their context, dead fragments torn from the living organism of which they were once a part? Isolate in the same way sentences from modern writers and you will see the effect; such as this from *Diana of the Crossways:*

> [If a woman gets into a divorce court] let her escape unmangled, it will pass in the record that she did once publicly run, and some old dogs will persist in thinking her cunninger than the virtuous, which never put themselves in such positions, but ply the distaff at home;

and

> men desire to have a still woman, who can make a constant society of her pins and needles.

Women, were then, equally in the nineteenth century confined to their homes and domestic occupations; respectable women did not go abroad. There was murmuring, indeed, even then, as in Athens in the time of Euripides; *Diana* again:

> Were the walls beaten down . . . she owns that the multitude of the timorous would yearn in shivering affright for the old prison-nest, according to the sage prognostic of men; but the flying of a valiant few would form a vanguard, etc.

H

The future historian of England will also decide, as Professor Gardner does for Athens, that there 'marriages were entered into from motives of prudence rather than of sentiment,'[1] and to prove this he will quote:

About thirty years ago, Miss Maria Ward, of Huntingdon, with only seven thousand pounds, had the good luck to captivate Sir Thomas Bertram, of Mansfield Park, in the county of Northampton, and to be thereby raised to the rank of a baronet's lady, with all the comforts and consequences of a handsome house and large income. All Huntingdon exclaimed on the greatness of the match, and her uncle, the lawyer, himself, allowed her to be at least three thousand pounds short of any equitable claim to it.

And in a footnote he will add: 'Compare the sentiments of the typical English country gentleman, Mr. John Dashwood, in *Sense and Sensibility, passim.*' He will be particularly glad to find also this quotation from *The Country House*:

It was not often that a letter demanding decision or involving responsibility came to her hands past the kind and just censorship of Horace Pendyce; many matters were under her control, but were not so to speak connected with the outside world.

Ignoring the innumerable occasions in novels when wives do in fact open their own letters, the historian will write:

Nothing shows more clearly the great difference between ancient and modern ideas as to the treatment of women. It was not customary for them to see their own letters until their husbands had first read them and decided that they might; and even Galsworthy, who was accounted an enlightened man in advance of his age, considered this to be not only proper, but kind.

That is after all what we do: in Attic tragedy women come and go from their houses at will[2] and play an important and

---

[1]*Op. cit.*, p. 343. Cf. p. 353: 'The Athenian married not for affection, nor to gain a companion, but to secure a trustworthy guardian of his house and goods,' etc. Yet even Simonides of Amorgos, whom we are fond of quoting, wrote

θάλλει δ' ὑπ' αὐτῆς κἀπαέξεται βίος,
φίλη δὲ σὺν φιλεῦντι γηράσκει πόσει.

Cf. Plat. *Legg.* viii 840D: ὅταν δ' εἰς τοῦτο ἡλικίας ἔλθωσι, συνδυασθέντες ἄρρην θηλείᾳ κατὰ χάριν καὶ θήλεια ἄρρενι, τὸν λοιπὸν χρόνον ὁσίως καὶ δικαίως ζῶσιν ἐμμένοντες βεβαίως ταῖς πρώταις τῆς φιλίας ὁμολογίαις. And why are *Ethica Nic.* viii 1162 a16–29 and Plut. *Sol.* 20 never quoted?

[2]And in the Old Comedy; but I do not like to base theories on this, for anything may happen in Aristophanes. The Boeotian and Megarian arrive safely in Athens in wartime in the *Acharnians*, and leave again; Lampito without difficulty keeps her appointment at Athens in *Lysistrata*. Yet some evidence may be had from the latter play, for the point is actually raised (ll. 13 ff.); but there is nothing about the

public part; but because there is a fragment of Euripides,

ἔνδον μένουσαν τὴν γυναῖκ' εἶναι χρεὼν
ἐσθλήν, θύρασι δ' ἀξίαν τοῦ μηδενός,

we say that 'he is convinced that their honour and happiness
are best secured by seclusion and self-effacement,' and, on
what evidence I know not, that in his description of Andromache he has given us his conception of a model wife.[1]
Because Menander made one of his characters say,

πέρας γὰρ αὔλιος θύρα
ἐλευθέρᾳ γυναικὶ νενόμιστ' οἰκίας,[2]

no woman ever went outside her house. Modesty, σωφροσύνη,
we are told, was all that was required of women, as though
σωφροσύνη were not the cardinal Greek virtue, for men and
women alike. Besides, modesty is a feminine virtue now, as
will be seen from the following: 'No nice girl ever *wants* to
marry a man,' as I once read in a novel whose name I have
forgotten—a *fragmentum adespotum*; 'Mrs. Egerton com-
forted Viola by assuring her that love came gradually with
nice women, and that the nicer they were the more gradually
it came';[3] or, to quote *Mansfield Park* again:

I *had*, Fanny, as I think my behaviour must have shown, formed a
very favourable opinion of you from the period of my return to
England. I had thought you peculiarly free from wilfulness of temper,

impropriety of their going out nor of bolts and bars, but only of occupations which
are not peculiar to Athenian women. Neither is Blepyros shocked at Praxagora's
absence in *Ecclesiazusae*, only annoyed that she has taken his clothes and, not
unnaturally, suspicious (ll. 323 ff., esp. 348–50). Van Leeuwen's note on the
Lysistrata passage is characteristic: ignoring the actual reasons given by Kalonike
he just writes *mulieres decebat* τὸ οἰκουρεῖν, with the usual quotation of a fragment
(this time from Epicharmos).
　There is another point about the plot of the *Lysistrata* which is, I think, significant, though I will not build any argument upon it: the revolt of the women
brings their husbands to terms at once; there is no question of the latter finding
consolation in the arms of *hetairai*, nor of their being content with the society of
their own sex. This is what we should expect if Athenian society was, in the main,
of the normal European type, not otherwise. See ll. 725, 957, 1092; and Wilamowitz'
curiously mistaken note on this last.
　[1]Fr. 521; Haigh, *Tragic Drama*, pp. 279–80.
　[2]Fr. 238. It is interesting and characteristic that this line and a half is all that is
quoted in modern handbooks, though even Stobaios preserved five:

τοὺς τῆς γαμετῆς ὅρους ὑπερβαίνεις, γύναι,
τὴν αὔλιον· πέρας γὰρ αὔλιος θύρα
ἐλευθέρᾳ γυναικὶ νενόμιστ' οἰκίας,
τὸ δ'.ἐπιδιώκειν εἴς τε τὴν ὁδὸν τρέχειν
ἔτι λοιδορουμένην, κυνός ἐστ' ἔργον, Ῥόδη.

The last two lines at least should have warned us that the passage comes from a
play, and had at one time some dramatic propriety.
　[3]Phyllis Bottome, *The Kingfisher* (1922), chap. xxv.

self-conceit, and every tendency to that independence of spirit, which prevails so much in modern days, even in young women, and which in young women is offensive and disgusting beyond all common offence.

It is not difficult to recognize dramatic character in passages from books of our own time, when the whole books are known, just as we can guard ourselves against taking language too literally, and do not conclude from the existence of a women's corner in the newspaper that it necessarily follows that their interests are confined to subjects treated there, nor from the 'Ladies' Enclosure' at Lord's that at the headquarters of cricket women are admitted indeed to the ἀγῶνες but excluded from the sight of men; it is more difficult to be on our guard in dealing with ancient writings and fragments from them. But we have no right to suppose sententiousness in the place of dramatic propriety; to think that Euripides and Menander, any more than Jane Austen or Mr. Galsworthy, were not building up characters, but only felt inspired to add their quota to man's proud store of knowledge as to the proper conduct and destiny of women. I shall not be believed, I know; I shall be told I am reading into the Greek a meaning which the author never intended; but that seems to me at least more intelligent than to suppose that such lines had no meaning at all. If you glance at the chapters of Stobaios in which he has collected excerpts on marriage (that it is good to marry, that it is not good to marry, and that it is sometimes good and sometimes bad—such is his simple philosophy), if you look through these passges you will find that two, from Euripides, are as follows:

> ζηλῶ δ᾽ ἀγάμους ἀτέκνους τε βροτῶν·
> μιᾷ γὰρ ψυχή, τῆς ὑπεραλγεῖν
> μέτριον ἄχθος·

and

> οὔποτε φήσω γάμον εὐφραίνειν
> πλέον ἢ λυπεῖν.

But these passages, though of much the same character, are never quoted by us, as the rest are, to prove the Athenian contempt for marriage. And no wonder, for we have their context. They come from the *Alcestis*.

It will be argued: 'Well, there may be some truth in what

you say; but what of those passages in which men most
certainly spoke their real opinions? What, for example, of
Perikles and Aristotle? And, secondly, what of Menander
and the New Comedy?' I might answer the first question
simply by asking 'What of Napoleon and Schopenhauer for
the nineteenth century?' But it will be well to go into the
matter in more detail; and I will begin with an analogy.
The word ἀπράγμων is frequently used by Attic writers,
especially by Aristophanes and Plato, but also by others, and
always in a complimentary sense, as of a quiet, sensible
man, who does not meddle overmuch in politics.[1] But if you
look up Liddell and Scott[2] on this word, you find, *after* many
references to these writers, the sentence: 'But at Athens
such a man was regarded as one who shirked his public
duties, whence Perikles says, τὸν μηδὲν τῶνδε μετέχοντα οὐκ
ἀπράγμονα ἀλλ' ἀχρεῖον νομίζομεν.' A single argumentative
sentence (or rather two, for Perikles returns to the charge
in his second speech),[3] which in any case means 'We
do not give him the flattering name of ἀπράγμων but ἀχρεῖος,'
is taken as representing the whole of Athenian thought on
the matter, as though Aristophanes and the others (who
include Demosthenes) were Spartans or Englishmen. So
with the famous paragraph in this same Funeral Speech.
Perikles says:

If I must speak of women's special virtue, I will put the whole
matter in a nutshell: great is their glory who can live up to the nature
that Providence has given to women, and hers especially who is least
talked of amongst men either for good or for evil.

I do not say that this means nothing; on the contrary, it is of
great historical and psychological interest—note how Perikles speaks with the confidence which all men assume when
talking on this subject; note also the contradiction involved
in saying that her fame is great who is quite unknown. But
what is its significance compared with the fact that Antigone,
Alkestis, Hekabe, are heroines of the Attic stage? That you
cannot read an Attic tragedy without finding women who

---

[1] Or of a state which does not aggressively interfere with its neighbours. It is a
great deal more than 'almost a term of praise in conservative writers' (Shorey, *Class.
Phil.* [1920], p. 300).
[2] (Eighth edition.)
[3] Thuc. ii 40. 2, 63. 3.

are far from being unknown among men? What does it matter that Xenophon thought that girls up to the age of fifteen should be trained to see and hear as little as possible and ask as few questions as possible (and then be married and at once put into a position of great responsibility at the head of a large household)—on which we base our view that Athenian women had no intellectual education[1]—when we gather from the *Thesmophoriazusae* that they at least knew all about Euripides, from the *Lysistrata* that they were well up in politics, and from the *Ecclesiazusae* that they had the usual popular knowledge of the latest social theories? Women were at least educated enough to be corrupted by sophists and poets, just like men.[2] So I am not much concerned when I read:

How little and seldom they went out is clear from the account which we have that after the battle of Chaeroneia the women stood trembling in the doorways, asking passers-by as to the fate of their husbands and fathers and sons. Even at such a crisis they did not venture out into the street; yet the orator Lycurgus calls their conduct unworthy of the city and themselves;

especially when I look up Lykourgos and find that what that would-be Spartan objected to was not the appearance at the street-doors, but the mourning and wailing: *that* was unworthy of themselves and of Athens.[3]

Lest it may appear that I am straining the evidence, I will take a similar case which makes against the general theory I am advancing. Plato believed more thoroughly than has any other political theorist in the essential similarity of the sexes, and the claim of women to equal rights and duties with men; it was as absurd, he said, to divide the world into men and women for the purpose of public affairs or of education or of anything other than the begetting and bearing of children as it would be to divide it into the bald and the not-bald. He also says, in that description of the democratic state for which so much was borrowed from contemporary Athens, that such is the passion for liberty and equal-

---

[1] *Oec.* vii 5; cf. *Companion to Greek Studies*, p. 599.
[2] Plat. *Gorg.* 502D; cf. *Legg.* 658D.
[3] Lykourg. *c. Leocr.* 40; Gardner, *op. cit.*, p. 349. Diodoros, on the other hand (xiii 55. 4), and Plutarch (*Mor.* 598C) are quite orthodox; and anyone who wishes may quote against me Plautus, *Epid.* 210-5.

ity that not only has the second-rate man equal influence with
the first-rate, but foreigner is equal to citizen, slave to free,
women to men; all are equal, even animals to human beings.
This passage is not of no account; indeed, it should be taken
into consideration when we say glibly that Athens was less
liberal in its treatment of women than other Greek cities,
especially as in a manner it receives the support of Aristotle.[1]
But if I were to build up an argument and say: 'You see,
women were in practice equal to men, and the Socratic circle
in particular thought they ought to be made equal in law';
I might be met by this just reply: 'Do not rely on men's
theories, but their actions, nor on single passages but the
whole tenor of their writings. Read through all the dialogues
of Plato, and where else will you find so purely masculine a
society depicted? For the Socratic circle as he depicts it,
with the one most notable exception of Diotima, women do
not count.' That seems to me to be true, and far more significant than any collection of passages that state that women
have as much right to exist as men. It is as masculine a
society as that of the σοφοί and their pupils of Oxford and
Cambridge in the days when there were no women's colleges
and Fellows were forbidden to marry.

But the argument is double-edged. If Perikles said that
women's only virtue was to be least spoken of among men
either for good or for evil, that is, if this sentiment is rightly
attributed to him (as I believe—he had a taste for paradox)
and is not Thucydides' own, remember that these words
were spoken by the man who was living with and was
devotedly attached to the woman who was most talked about
in Athens both for good and for evil—Aspasia, the Hera to
his Zeus, the Deianira to his Herakles, the mistress of his
household, and the hostess to that circle of men and women
who were the acquaintance of Perikles.[2] If Simonides ever

---

[1] Plat. *Rep.* viii 563 A–D; *Pol.* vii (v) 1313 *b* 32; cf. viii (vi), 1319 *b* 27.

[2] I am aware that the importance of Aspasia has been disputed by scholars such as
Wilamowitz (*Arist. u. Athen*, ii, 99, 35) and Busolt (*Griech. Gesch.*, iii, 1, 505–13);
who deny that she was interested in intellectual things and that men brought their
wives to her house (they wouldn't, not to a *hetaira*). The steps of the argument are
as follows: (1) all Plutarch's information about Aspasia comes ultimately from
Aischines Sokratikos; (2) Aischines' dialogue *Aspasia* was a romantic and unhistorical work; therefore (3) the information is not true. The premises are themselves ineffectual: the first is a doubtful statement; and as to the second, if the *Aspasia*

uttered a similar sentiment—he probably did—we can reply to him, 'My dear Sir, you have also written a poem called *Danaë*, which you cannot now prevent us reading'; and if Pheidias, as he may have done, said that women were ugly creatures, we may look at the sculpture from the Parthenon, and be content to smile.

It has been suggested, indeed, that the exceptional education and the social position which Aspasia enjoyed were both due to the fact that she was a foreigner and a *hetaira*. It would not, I think, be worth while referring to the remarkable view that the Athenians confined their contempt for women to those of their own class and city, while having a regard for vagrant foreigners, were it not that it has found its way, for our astonishment, into Verrall's *Four Plays of Euripides*. It is only in a passing allusion, it does not affect his argument; for that great man was the last person to use facile theories about other men's sentiments to explain what he felt to be difficulties. It will be remembered that he argues that the *Helena* was written for private performance in the house of a woman named Eido, the prototype of the Theonoë of the play, who was the daughter of a chemist or doctor named Proteas; a resident at Athens, but probably a foreigner. Eido's wisdom, 'that is to say, her intellectual gifts and

was like other Socratic dialogues, it was μίμησις, a representation of life, as Aristotle says (*Poet.* 1447 *b* 11); therefore Aischines thought it true to life to make Aspasia do and say such and such things, and Athenian men and women to discuss matters with her. There is also a second argument (Busolt, *op. cit.*, pp. 513-4): another Socratic, Antisthenes, said that Perikles was much in love with Aspasia; therefore he contradicts Aischines; therefore Aspasia had no mind, and Perikles did not also admire her. Even if Aischines' picture is unhistorical in respect of these two real persons, yet it is meant to be true of Athenian life in general, and that is sufficient for my purpose.

The evidence of the greatness of Aspasia is in fact like that for Perikles (Plut. *Per.* xvi, 1): the Socratics supply the direct, the comedians the indirect evidence for it, calling her Hera, Omphale, etc.

We need not even doubt that his contemporaries (at least his friends) spoke of Perikles as 'married' to Aspasia, even though their son was a νόθος. Aristotle says that Peisistratos 'married' Timonassa of Argos as his second wife, though he refers to his Athenian wife as ἡ γαμετή ('*Aθπ.* xvii 3) and Thucydides distinguishes the children of the first marriage as γνήσιοι (vi 55. 1); so Hdt. v 94. Sandys (on '*Aθπ. loc. cit.*) absurdly supposes that Peisistratos was still living with his first wife when he married Timonassa. Perikles, remember, divorced his wife before living with Aspasia.

Others take the opposite view of Aspasia but argue in a similar way. Willrich, for example, in his new book *Perikles* will have his hero spotless; Aspasia must therefore be spotless too: she had never been a *hetaira*. His reason is simply that Perikles would not have married her, or associated with her, if she had been.

literary tastes, is expressly traced to the mother's side.' So, says Verrall, her mother was

probably an accomplished *hetaera*, a word for which we may be content to have no English equivalent, but which described a condition perfectly honest according to the notions of the fifth century B.C., the condition indeed of most women who took part in what we call 'society.'[1]

Poor woman; if Proteas was not an Athenian, she might at least have been his wife. The fallacy is partly due to the supposition that we have no English equivalent for the word *hetaira*; but we have, or rather a European one—*demi-mondaine*, a word that properly describes Aspasia and many another less gifted and less fortunate woman; the fact that Aspasia managed to get clear of her half of the world makes no difference. Substitute that word and read 'her mother was probably an accomplished *demi-mondaine*,' and one sees at once that it was improbable. Euripides, remember, according to Verrall, is complimenting her daughter. The whole idea of a specially educated, specially privileged *hetaira*-class is fantastic: one imagines schools at Miletos and elsewhere (Miletos, by the way, was an Ionian town where we should expect an oriental seclusion[2]) for the education of girls who were to make their way at Athens, and in Athens no 'Select Establishments for the Daughters of Gentlemen,' but 'Academies for Young Ladies in which are taught Geometry, Dialectic and Deportment, whereby the Daughters of Foreigners may learn how to captivate the fancy and secure the lasting affection and esteem of the leading members of the Nobility and Gentry. No Athenians need apply.'

To return to the main theme: We come to Aristotle. That philosopher was a consistent believer in the inferiority of the female sex; it is a view which enters into his physiology and biology, his political and ethical, and his æsthetic theories. He does not say that women ought to be and in fact are confined to their homes, that they ought not and do not ever mix in society, that they are negligible beings, to be ignored or despised;[3] only that they are, intellectually and morally,

[1] P. 84.   [2] Especially at Miletos (Hdt. i 146).
[3] He did believe, though half-heartedly, in γυναικονόμοι, as in παιδονόμοι, to protect as to oversee women (Pol. vi (iv). 15. 3. p. 1299 *a* 22, *b* 19). But he says that such an institution is not to be found, either in democratic or in oligarchic states,

inferior to men. In this, as far as I can see, he is not peculiarly
Greek, still less peculiarly Attic; in all ages, I suppose, we
should find, if we were as honest and as outspoken as the
Greeks, that the majority of men believed in their own
superiority. Now Aristotle's expression of this view is
interesting. In the *Politics* he is at great pains to distinguish
between the rule of a master over his servants (the rule of
superior over inferior), that of a parent over his children, and
'citizen rule,' πολιτικὴ ἀρχή, the rule over persons free
and equal, and to place the rule of husband over wife in the
last category.[1] There is indeed an important distinction; for
whereas among citizens a man rules and is ruled in turn,
the rule of husband over wife is permanent. But it is at least
worthy of notice that Aristotle should, in any sense, put
women in the class of the 'free and equal.' But he is even
more interesting in the *Poetics;* as we should expect, both on
general grounds and because he is dealing with Attic
tragedy. He is speaking of Character in tragedy, in which

there are four points to aim at. First and foremost, that they shall be
good. . . . Each type of personage has his own goodness; for a woman
has hers, and a slave his, though the former's is perhaps less than a
man's, and the latter's is wholly inferior. The second point is to make
them appropriate. The Character before us may be, say, manly; but it
is not appropriate in a female character to be manly, or clever.[2] The
third is to make them like the reality, which is not the same thing as
their being good and appropriate, in our sense of the term. . . . We
have an instance . . . of the incongruous and unbefitting . . . in the
speech of Melanippe. . . . The right thing, however, is in the Characters just as in the incidents of the play to endeavour always after the
necessary or the probable.[3]

But if Aristotle in the words ἴσως τούτων τὸ μὲν χεῖρον
is, as all now suppose, simply expressing the typical Greek
view (as opposed, that is to say, to the Roman or the modern
view), and if, moreover, he was living in a society where this

but in aristocratic (vi (iv). p. 1300 *a* 4, viii (vi). p. 1322 *b* 37; cf. vii (v). p. 1310 *a*
25); that is, in dream-states only. He does also say that it is an inevitable accompani-
ment of poverty that women will go about in public (ἐξιέναι: *Pol.* vi (iv). p. 1300
a 6).

[1]*Pol.* i. p. 1259 *b* 1, 1255 *b* 20.

[2]'What you call cleverness is not at all necessary in a girl.'—Trollope, *Framley
Parsonage*, chap. xl.

[3]*Poet.* 1454 *a* 16 ff.

view was put most vigorously into practice, where women had in fact no chance of showing character of any kind save in domestic wrangling, why does he only notice the incongruity of Melanippe's speech? Why not the far greater incongruity, unfemininity, unlikeness to life, of all the women of Attic tragedy—all but a few, Chrysothemis, Ismene, Andromache, and, if you will, Alkestis? Melanippe's speech is objected to apparently because it was a good politician's or lawyer's speech, and women were not public speakers. But Antigone—not one speech, but everything she does and says? 'The right thing is always to endeavour after the necessary and the probable.' How was Antigone a probable character in such an Athens as we suppose Aristotle to have known? We expect at least that he would have explained that this kind of improbability was inevitable, without it there would be no tragedy, though we could have wished it ἔξω τοῦ δράματος. Indeed, there is no sense in which we can say that the 'goodness' of Antigone is inferior to the 'goodness' of Oedipus. Great observer as he was, Aristotle, as we know, was ever inclined to make his facts fit into his theories of the universe; and this instance is no exception. But here his cautious 'perhaps'[1]—a caution rare with him in general and not found in his other declarations of the inferiority of females—may be a sign that he was half-conscious of being up against facts that he could neither explain nor get rid of.

But we can go farther. The male, says Aristotle, is by nature superior, and the female inferior; and the former rules, and the latter is ruled; this principle, of necessity, extends to all mankind. But we have something else equally, if not more significant. We, when we wish to contrast our own practice with that of other peoples, speak—I do not profess to say with what justice—of an oriental treatment of women; we say, for instance, that Athenians treated their wives with a truly oriental contempt. It is surprising, but Aristotle uses much the same language: it is characteristic of barbarians, he says, that women are there treated as slaves. (I say surprising, because this passage is not quoted in our treatises on the subject, though it is from no remote book,

[1] Or 'doubtless'; but 'doubtless' implies a doubt.

but from the opening pages of the *Politics*).[1] Plato says the same,[2] so does Plutarch.[3] I am not saying that Plato and Aristotle are correct in thus contrasting Greek and barbarian; but only that when they come across this phenomenon their feelings about it and their language are similar to our own. Newman in his note on the passage from the *Politics* quotes two English writers on the Fuegians and the Montenegrins, to illustrate both the sentiment and the language.

It might be thought that Aristotle would have been more at home with the plays of Menander than with Attic tragedy, for in Menander's hands, as I have already quoted, 'the individualizing of female character and the freeing of the female will have gone but a little way: . . . his women are mentally without distinction.' Well, there have been many surprising things said about Menander, this not the least, considered as the judgement of so good a scholar as Neil; I find it difficult to believe that anyone should find Glykera, Pamphile, and Chrysis undistinguished. But take it as true, there are yet two things to be noted. In the first place, Menander will have altogether deserted the tradition of the fifth century, not of Euripides only, not of tragedy only, but of comedy—think of characters like Clytemnestra, Medea, and Lysistrate in connexion with the phrases 'the individualizing of the female character and the freeing of the

---

[1] *Pol.* i. p. 1252 *b* 5.

[2] *Legg.* vii 805D–E. This passage is particularly interesting, for he goes on: ἢ καθάπερ ἡμεῖς ἅπαντές τε οἱ περὶ τὸν τόπον ἐκεῖνον; νῦν γὰρ δὴ τό γε παρ' ἡμῖν ὧδέ ἐστιν περὶ τούτων γιγνόμενον· εἴς τινα μίαν οἴκησιν συμφορήσαντες, τὸ λεγόμενον, πάντα χρήματα, παρέδομεν ταῖς γυναιξὶν διαταμιεύειν τε καὶ κερκίδων ἄρχειν καὶ πάσης ταλασίας· with which he contrasts the Spartan halfway house to his own system of identical upbringing for both sexes. There is nothing here, of course, of women not mixing in society, of being confined to their houses; only their business in life, their work is domestic, and quite separate from men's, and this Plato would alter. His language is very like Meredith's (above p. 97), with the same implication. Aristotle (*Pol.* viii (vi) 1323 *a* 5) asserts that among the poorest classes in Greece, the women worked like slaves; which we can well believe.

[3] *Lucull.* xviii. 3. Monimè, the Ionian wife of Mithridates, καὶ παρὰ τὸν ἄλλον χρόνον ἀνιαρῶς εἶχε καὶ ἀπεθρήνει τὴν τοῦ σώματος εὐμορφίαν, ὡς δεσπότην μὲν ἀντ' ἀνδρὸς αὐτῇ, φρουρὰν δὲ βαρβάρων ἀντὶ γάμου καὶ οἴκου προξενήσασαν, πόρρω δέ που τῆς Ἑλλάδος ἀπῳκισμένη τοῖς ἐλπισθεῖσιν ἀγαθοῖς ὄναρ σύνεστι, τῶν δ' ἀληθινῶν ἐκείνων ἀπεστέρηται. Is not this the language of any European? Though I will not base any argument on a later author, such as Plutarch, although he draws so much from classical sources, and his views on the proper relation between husbands and wives are as sound as Aristotle's, if more gracefully expressed (*Mor.* 139C, 140D, 142D, etc.). Cf. also Athenaios xiii 556B.

female will.' Secondly, if his women are mentally without
distinction, so most certainly are his men. His plays are not
one-sided, ill-balanced things, with real men but shadowy
women; whatever else they may be, they are admirably
proportioned. I am sure Neil did not feel any lack of balance;
but he had the ready idea to hand, 'Women were emerging
from a state hardly above slavery,' and he uses it to solve a
difficulty. Had he not, had he thought out some independent
explanation, would he not have noticed that Menander's
women are very like his men, and have added their joint
lack of character as another item in the puzzle of Menander's
reputation in antiquity? If you think it a puzzle; I do not.[1]

I will recapitulate the argument of one of Menander's
plays, the *Epitrepontes*, the best preserved. Pamphile, the
daughter of a well-to-do citizen, some ten months before the
play opens, on the occasion of one of those nocturnal festivals
from which modern parents would be so careful to guard
their daughters, but which Attic freedom allowed, had had
an adventure with a youth inflamed with wine, with the
result usual for the prelude to a romantic comedy. In the
darkness neither had seen the other's features, but Pamphile
managed to get hold of a ring worn by him. Four months
later Pamphile marries a young man named Charisios; and
·five months afterward, during her husband's absence
abroad, she gives birth to the child she had conceived at the
midnight festival. She had told no one of her adventure but
her old nurse, neither Charisios nor her father; and now,
fearful of discovery, she exposes the child, which is found,
and ultimately adopted by a charcoal-burner, Syriskos.
But Charisios later hears of the event and in an outburst of

---

[1]In fact Neil was writing before the discovery of the greater part of our Menander;
and was presumably arguing, like so many, from Terence and Plautus. It is rather
the rashness of the judgement that should be noted.

One may compare Xenophon's Ischomachos and his wife. 'Perhaps the most
remarkable blot in Xenophon's sketch is the total absence of any intellectual
requirements on the part of the woman,' says Mahaffy (*op. cit.*, p. 279). But it is
not at all remarkable; there is nothing intellectual about Ischomachos either and
naturally he does not demand anything of the sort in his wife. He is simply the
'economic man,' seeking how to make his estate pay best; and he requires an
economic wife. He is to make the money, she to spend it (a division of labour
which many might be glad to adopt). Xenophon is supposed to give us a complete
picture of the ideal Athenian wife; as if Xenophon gives a complete picture of
anything. As well call his Socrates complete.

anger leaves Pamphile for the society of some companions of his youth and a flute-girl and tries to drown his sorrow and forget his love for his wife by drinking and merrymaking. But he cannot drive his love from his heart, and refuses to have anything to do with the flute-girl; conduct at which she is much hurt.

Smikrines, Pamphile's father, highly indignant at this treatment of his daughter by Charisios, and ignorant of her story, also anxious for the dowry which she brought to her husband, comes to visit her in great anger and tries to induce her to return to him and get a divorce, and so save at once her honour and his money. She, as devoted to Charisios as he to her, and knowing the true cause of his conduct, refuses and defends her husband. Charisios, by a fortunate chance, overhears this conversation, and is more than ever moved by his love for her because of her tenderness toward him; and when it is proved to him that the child adopted by Syriskos is his own and he is thus convicted of the very crime he had been charging against his wife, he suffers a complete revulsion of feeling:

Dearest Pamphile, what tender words were yours! what a wife I have lost by my folly! I am the sinner; I am the father of a bastard child, and I showed no whit of forgiveness to her in her same distress, brute and merciless as I was. I so noble, so wise, so spotless! She so gentle to me, I so harsh to her.[1]

It all ends happily, of course; the foundling is the child of both Pamphile and Charisios; and only Smikrines is disappointed of his anger.

Now such a story is intelligible and pleasurable to us, because, granted the preliminary facts, the conduct and sentiments of the characters—the jealousy of Charisios, the steadfastness of Pamphile, their mutual affection, the indignation of old Smikrines, the kind-heartedness of Habrotonon —are such as we can understand and share; they are not indeed modern, but universal; the treatment is modern and therefore particularly delightful. But they could not have been intelligible, they could scarcely have been possible, in an Athens where there was no kind of equality between the sexes, where there were no marriages of affection and hus-

[1] Ll. 524–47.

bands regarded their wives with contempt—naturally, since the best women were dolls—and where, as we are solemnly assured, it was usual and respectable for a married man to have a mistress and the ideal wife tolerated her presence and brought up his bastard children.[1] It makes one impatient to have to point out anything so obvious; but what else can one do?

Some years ago there was published a book called *Antimachus of Colophon*, or *Women in Greek Poetry*, by E. F. M. Benecke,[2] which dealt with the position of women considered from the point of view of sentiment. It received the blessing of Jebb and of the Cambridge *Companion to Greek Studies*,[3] and it has the great merit of bringing the whole argument to its logical conclusion. If, he argued, men and women never met, love between them was impossible; if men despised women, romantic sentiment on the part of the former at least was unthinkable; therefore there was no romantic sentiment in Greece between men and women. The logic of this we may admit,[4] and as it did not occur to Benecke to doubt his premises, he sought only to establish his conclusions. Need I say that he performed this task by the by now familiar process of quoting fragments—especially from that branch of Athenian literature of which we know least—the Middle Comedy? He found, indeed, many jokes, culled by Athenaios, at the expense of marriage, some good, some bad; such as 'I don't so much blame a man for marrying once, he has had no experience; but a man who does it a second time deserves no pity';[5] 'how happy must grasshoppers be, where

---

[1] Cf. Jebb on *Trach.* 447 ff.: 'The meaning is not merely that Iole's relation to Heracles was excused by the omnipotence of Eros. Concubinage [παλλακία] was not merely tolerated by Attic opinion, but, in some measure, protected [Lys. i 31; Isocr. viii 39]. Its relation to the life of the family is illustrated by the *Andromache* of Euripides, for though Andromache is Trojan, and Hermione Spartan, the sentiments are Athenian [see ll. 226, 938–42].' How easily sentiments in tragedy become Athenian when they suit the current view! Yet the *Agamemnon*, if not common sense, might have warned us against this long ago. Athenaios understood classical Greek sentiment well enough (xiii. 556B).

[2] Sonnenschein, 1896.

[3] Pp. 616–7.

[4] Always bearing in mind, however, the society of the *Arabian Nights*, where the sexes are segregated, but love, romantic or otherwise, is common.

[5] Both Euboulos (Kock, ii 205) and Aristophon (*ibid.*, p. 277) thought of this. So, of course, did Dr. Johnson, in a witty form.

the females are dumb';[1] 'how much better to have a mistress than a wife; the latter with the law behind her can treat you with contempt and remain your wife; but a mistress knows she must please you or find another lover';[2]

A: Do you know he's married?

B: Married, you say? and only last week I left him alive and walking about.[3]

I need hardly say that such jests are not confined to the Middle Comedy. You also find sentimental lines of the kind, 'It is nice when husband and wife are at one,' and one would have supposed that if Athenian sentimentality and Athenian humour (both in success and in failure) about marriage was much like our own, it was evidence, so far, that their general ideas about that institution were also similar.[4] But Benecke thought not only that Greek and modern ideas were as the poles apart—that went without saying—but that we could trace a change of sentiment, to the advantage of marriage and the romantic passion, in the course of the fourth century; and that this change was largely due to the poem called *Lyde*, by Antimachos of Kolophon, written about 400 B.C., a work and poet about which we know less than we do about the majority of lost Greek poems and their authors. In the Middle Comedy—of which we know so little—we are told, love was felt only for *hetairai* and was not of an elevated kind; in the New, love as we understand it, romantic love, began to come into its own.[5] Antimachos, we read, was responsible for this. Before him you do not find in Greek poetry any man in love with a woman. Aristophanes makes Aeschylus say:

οὐδ' οἶδ' οὐδεὶς ἥντιν' ἐρῶσαν πώποτ' ἐποίησα γυναῖκα.[6]

[1]Xenarchos (*ibid.*, p. 473).   [2]Amphis (*ibid.*, p. 236).
[3]Antiphanes (*ibid.*, p. 108).
[4]The modern equivalent of this humour being: *faute de mieux on se couche avec sa femme*.
[5]It is hardly necessary to say that advice not to marry can be found in Menander as in Antiphanes (e.g., Kock, iii 22), and abuse of *hetairai* in the Middle Comedy. We may also compare Mommsen on Roman comedy (*Hist. of Rome*, [II [1894,] 154-5): 'In the endless abundance of cudgelling and in the lash ever suspended over the backs of the slaves we recognize very clearly the household-government inculcated by Cato, just as we recognize the Catonian opposition to women in the never-ending disparagement of wives.'
[6]*Ran.* 1044. Athenaios, by the way, probably relying on Hermesianax, regarded Lyde simply as one of many courtesans famous in literature, like Mimnermos' Nanno (xiii, 597A, 598A, B), from whom Benecke thought sharply to distinguish her.

It was not, says Benecke, necessary for him to repudiate the charge of bringing men in love on the stage; the thing was unknown. Some years ago I saw a play by Brieux the moral of which—if one may speak of the moral of so excellent a comedy—was that a man is no better off, not more free from petty tyranny, with a mistress than with a wife; it depended for its point on a general assumption that, as Amphis said, he is freer unmarried. I can imagine that in some future age, if some of our own epigrams on marriage are preserved, and some reference to the story of Brieux' comedy, and perhaps a romantic novel of the 1920's ending in a happy marriage, the historian will write:

A great change of sentiment seems to have taken place in Europe in the early years of the twentieth century; before then marriage was the subject for mocking laughter [see Oscar Wilde, fr. 126, Shaw, fr. 55, etc.], afterward for romance. The change may have been in part due to a lost comedy by Brieux, which appeared about 1910; though we may see how great a gulf is fixed between ancient and modern sentiment by the fact that that writer only recommended marriage on very low grounds, because a man was no better off with a mistress.

This is not a whit more fantastic than Benecke's house of cards. No love before Antimachos! One may suggest that there is a certain famous chorus in the *Antigone* beginning

ἔρως ἀνίκατε μαχάν,

written forty years before the *Lyde* appeared, and by a greater poet; Deianira says she will forgive Herakles his infidelity because it is the same passion which dominates mortal and immortal, men and women alike; Euripides wrote a speech over which the men of Abdera went mad,

O Love, high monarch over gods and men;

there is that most romantic of all stories, how Achilles conquered the Amazons, and fell in love with the princess Penthesileia at the moment of her death at his hands; there are some lovely lines in the *Agamemnon* describing Menelaos' home in the absence of Helen. But I am afraid the reader will object that the lightest whisper of the name of Helen is an undue stressing of the obvious. I think so too; and several times while I have been writing this paper I have been

I

inclined to tear it up, content with a comfortable dogmatism of my own.

I am not, of course, imagining for a moment that I have exhausted my subject. I have, for instance, said nothing of the evidence of the orators; but I have said enough. I have not mentioned Latin comedy either, of set purpose. For in any dispute about Greek life in which its evidence is brought forward, it is possible for either side to say, that is Roman, not Greek. I might for example quote the lines from *Heautontimorumenus* (381–395) about true love between one man and one woman that no calamity can dissolve, unlike the affairs of *hetairai*, and the following scene (short as it is) between Clinia and Antiphila (398–409), and 1.885 of the same play,

gaudere adeo coepit quasi qui cupiunt nuptias.

But it would lead to excessive disputation. I know there is some evidence which seems to support the prevailing view, or rather some aspects of it. Every country has its own conventions and customs, and Athens had hers: one gathers from the first speech of Lysias and elsewhere, for example, that it was a common thing for a man to invite a friend to dinner, at which his wife would not be present; there are no women in the glimpses of social life at Athens which Plato gives us; it would be difficult to imagine a modern comedy in the subject of the *Clouds* or the *Wasps*, in which the wives of Strepsiades and Philokleon did not play a prominent part (they are both mentioned, remember, but do not appear). One might recall other similar instances. But it has not been my intention to examine, however briefly, all the evidence. Let me repeat that all that I have tried to do is to prove that the matter is doubtful, that there is a problem to be solved. I do indeed believe that it is certainly wrong to speak of 'Attic contempt' for women; and also that there is no reason to suppose that in the matter of the social consequence and freedom of women Athens was different from other Greek cities, or the classical from the Homeric age—ancient writers seem to be unconscious of any such difference except in the special matter of the athletic training which girls received at Sparta. But, for the rest, I consider it very doubtful if Greek theory and practice differed fundamentally from the average, say, prevailing in mediæval and modern Europe. When Theognis said, 'I hate a woman who gads about and neglects her home,' I think he expressed a sentiment common to most people of all ages; and at least there were gadabouts for him to disapprove of. After all, a great deal of Greek literature deals with the relations between the sexes in one form or another; and it would have died long ago if Greek sentiments had been radically opposed to ours. And, if the view which now obtains is correct, I would emphasize certain paradoxes: first and foremost, that in that case Attic tragedy and art are in one most important respect remote from Attic life—a phenomenon surely unique in history; that it was the lover of Aspasia who is thought particularly to have despised women; that it is when you come to the inner shrine, the intimate secrets of the platonic philosophy, that you meet Diotima; and that it was this unromantic people of Greece who created and preserved the story of Helen.

THUCYDIDES

VI

'THE GREATEST WAR IN GREEK HISTORY'

Ἐλπίσας μέγαν⸌τε ἔσεσθαι καὶ ἀξιολογώτατον τῶν προγεγενημένων.

ALL historians of Greece and all editors of Thucydides have commented on his estimate of the importance of the Peloponnesian War; and their comments can be divided, roughly, into two classes. There are kindly persons who say, in a patronizing way, that it was natural for Thucydides to magnify the importance of his theme; it is a pardonable error, a human failing; many writers have been thus guilty. Others, of a franker temper, straightway condemn him for his faulty judgement. All alike agree in thinking that judgement manifestly wrong.

All agree too, that this can be easily shown by a comparison, one of the comparisons that Thucydides himself makes, with the Persian Wars. Macan has expressed this view most forcibly and most clearly, both in 1895 in his edition of Herodotus, and in 1927 in the *Cambridge Ancient History*. In the former he is discussing the place of the battle of Marathon in the later Athenian tradition:

'The personal views of Thucydides upon the Persian wars were plainly as follows. The importance of the Persian wars as a whole had been not a little overrated, but of the two wars the repulse of Xerxes was vastly the greater achievement. The first of these two propositions is a direct and adverse criticism upon the views which partly inspired and partly were in turn promoted by the work of Herodotus. The second proposition was presumably a protest against the view current in the anti-imperial, anti-Periklean, anti-democratic, or at least anti-nautical sections or strata of Athenian society. Thucydides magnifies his own subject at the expense of the wars of Hellene and Barbarian, ludicrously missing the oecumenical significance and wantonly compressing the duration and magnitude of the Herodotean theme. But it cannot be said that, upon the low level to which he proposes to reduce the duel with the Barbarians (and 'consequently the great work in which its memory and *raison d'être* were enshrined for ever), Thucydides misconceives the proportionate importance of the two Persian wars. . . . In all this Thucydides reiterates, *mutatis mutandis*, the Herodotean analogy; but the mutation involves the diminution of Marathon almost to a vanishing point. For Thucydides himself the battle of Marathon is little more than a chronological expression (i 18. 1; cf. vi 59. 4). How completely, or at least how coldly, Thucydides separates himself from the apotheosis of the *Marathonomachae* which had long been consummated at Athens, is shown by his remark . . . upon the Athenian custom in regard to citizens slain in battle, and the exception in favour of the men in Marathon (ii 34. 5). The passage . . . betrays no great warmth in the historian's own heart at mention of the name which Aristophanes was wont to send thrilling through the theatre, sure of his effect. . . . The work of Thucydides from beginning to end is a superb apology for Perikles, both in what it records and what it omits.

'It is thus inferentially the Periklean view of the Persian wars which is dominant in the work of Thucydides: a view proper enough to the statesman who practically abandoned the "eastern question" in order to develop Athens at the expense of Hellas: the abortive "peace of Kallias," passed over by Thucydides in discreet silence, being the chief contribution of Perikles to the solution of that question, which at any rate he succeeded in shelving.[1] From this standpoint the war which was to decide the question of primacy, hegemony, prostasy in Hellas, was far the most important war which ever had been, or well could be: and that is exactly the view taken by Thucydides of the war which he deliberately chose as the subject for an everlasting memorial.'[2]

So in 1927 Macan could write of Thucydides' 'ludicrous depreciation of the historical importance of the Persian wars'; and suggests that his theory of a single twenty-seven years' war 'is a reasoned conviction, but it betrays a bias to magnify his office, and has somewhat the air of a sophistic thesis.'[3] (Yet everyone has accepted it since.)

[1] I do not know in what sense the peace of Kallias can be called abortive. There are many who have held that it is fictitious (as to which, see *J.H.S.* l, 1930, p. 105); but, if it was not fictitious, it was very effective. Thucydides, of course, makes a direct reference to the most important of its provisions (viii 56. 4); and the omission of it in his fragmentary account of the Pentekontaëteia is not more remarkable than the omission of the Periklean foundations of Thurioi and Amphipolis. (That the peace restricted the activities of the Athenian fleet—east of Phaselis—as well as that of the Persian, as observed, not very accurately, by Vlachos, *Hellas and Hellenism*, 1936, p. 105, is probably true. Vlachos, pp. 293–4, has a correct idea of what the Peloponnesian war meant to Thucydides.)

[2] *Herodotus, Books iv–vi*, vol. 2, p. 184 ff. Cf. also *Books vii–ix*, vol. 2, p. 17 ff. which give a rather juster view.

[3] *C.A.H.* v. p. 413.

R. Harder in a recent article speaks of Thucydides' *Vergangenheitsblindheit* and his attack on Herodotus in the same tone as Macan (and can think the *Menexenus* speech to be a serious attempt by Plato to restore the glory of the Persian wars and the idea of a Greece united to fight the barbarian).[1] What is more important, even Ehrenberg would seem to share Macan's view (though he is not directly referring to the opening paragraphs of Thucydides), when he writes:

das Herabsinken des Ereignisses von 490 zu einem fast nur noch chronologischen Punkte (Thuc. i 18. 1; vi 59. 4); . . . die leise aber recht spürbare Kritik, die Thukydides den Perikles an der Apotheose der Marathonkämpfer üben lässt (ii 34. 5).[2]

I cannot myself see any criticism or coldness in Thucydides' words (not Perikles'), ii 34. 5: τιθέασιν οὖν ἐς τὸ δημόσιον σῆμα, ὅ ἐστιν ἐπὶ τοῦ καλλίστου προαστείου τῆς πόλεως καὶ αἰεὶ ἐν αὐτῷ θάπτουσι τοὺς ἐκ τῶν πολέμων πλήν γε τοὺς ἐν Μαραθῶνι· ἐκείνων δὲ διαπρεπῆ τὴν ἀρετὴν κρίναντες αὐτοῦ καὶ τὸν τάφον ἐποίησαν.[3] He was not the man to think it necessary to send a thrill through his readers (who were not Athenians only) at every mention of Marathon.[4] Nor do I understand why to regard the battle as marking an epoch (as one might regard 732, 1453, or 1815) is to detract from its fame or its importance. But there is no doubt that Thucydides did regard the Peloponnesian war as the most important in Greek history; and fortunately he has clearly stated his reasons. Since those reasons have seldom been examined, and there are many who think he was simply magnifying his own subject and depreciating Herodotus, and even, like R. Cohen, that the Peloponnesian war was an insignificant event and would always

---

[1] *Neue Jahrb.* x, 1934, 492–501.

[2] *Ost und West* (1935), p. 122.

[3] If at all, I should be more inclined to read a criticism in ii 36 (which is from Perikles' speech). Is ii 34. 5 just a wrong reference in Ehrenberg?

[4] Aristophanes was not, either, in reality. It should not be, though it constantly is, ignored that his *Marathonomachai* are the fiercely pro-war, anti-Spartan, spy-hunting Acharnians; are the natural supporters of Kleon—

  ὦ γέροντες ἡλιασταί, φράτερες τριωβόλου,
  οὓς ἐγὼ βόσκω·κεκραγὼς καὶ δίκαια κἄδικα,
  παραβοηθεῖθ', ὡς ὑπ' ἀνδρῶν τύπτομαι ξυνωμοτῶν.

                                                            (*Equit.* 255–7);
and are waspish dicasts as well as singers of the old songs of Phrynichos.
  Hypereides' *Epitaphios* too is as curt about Marathon as Perikles.

have been thought so, had a Thucydides not written about it,[1] it is worth while seeing what he meant, and what he implies.

The whole argument of his introduction, cc. 1–23, apart from a good deal of matter brought in for its own sake, because he was interested in the past, is in support of his statement. At the beginning of the war, he says, the combatants were at the height of their power and prosperity; and practically all Greece, and some foreign peoples as well, were involved. In the earliest period of Greek history, according to such evidence as we have, the country was unsettled and poor; and though wars, or rather neighbourly quarrels, were frequent, they were on a small scale and were not destructive. The Trojan war was the first effort of a united Greece; and it really was on a big scale—we must not be sceptical about this (10. 1–2); but the numbers involved were not as great as those of the present day; and of those who were involved only a small part were fighting at any one time. (Here we must admit a slight inconsequence: Thucydides reckons the Greek forces at, say, 60–80,000 strong (10. 4), which is actually larger by far than any overseas expeditionary force of the fifth century.) The cause was poverty rather than a small population. Then there was a long period of disturbance, followed by the colonization of the Mediterranean shores. After this came a great increase in prosperity owing to use of the sea, made possible by the growth of strong navies; but these navies were, relatively to those of our own day, not big before the Persian wars, and not very big even then. So all wars were small affairs, neighbour against neighbour, except, to some degree, the Lelantine; the prosperity of Ionia was stayed by the Persian advance by land and sea; and the tyrants, though prosperous, were each

---

[1] *L'Hellénisation du monde antique* (Paris, 1934), p. 245. Tarn would seem to agree with him (*J.H.S.* lv, p. 255). It is interesting to compare this view with that of Dionysios of Halikarnassos, that it was an unpleasant event and therefore should have been left unrecorded (*Epist. ad Pomp.* 767). In the premiss at least he approaches nearer Thucydides' own point of view than do the moderns.

There are some moderns who think the Hellenization of the East brought about by Alexander *more* important than earlier Greek history; that is the spreading of a civilization more important than the civilization itself. This is perhaps not surprising in an age when many think means of communication of greater value than what there is to communicate. But to belittle Greece in order to praise the spread of Greek culture seems very perverse.

of them intent on his own security and did not combine. Nothing was done as a joint effort of all Greece. The Persian war was such an effort, and against Xerxes the states were united under Spartan leadership; later Sparta and Athens shared the leadership, at first in peace, then at variance with each other; and these quarrels had the effect of giving each side experience and big armaments ready for this war. Athens, in particular, was very powerful and wealthy. Past achievements are always exaggerated (most people have no historical sense) and this war was really the biggest (though I know there is a tendency too to think a present war always the biggest), as its events prove. I have done my best to narrate those events accurately (c. 22). The biggest of the previous wars was the Persian, which was over in two land and two sea-battles, quickly; but in this war—what disasters! a wholesale destruction of men and cities, such as to make reports of past events seem credible after all.

That is Thucydides' argument: of past wars the Trojan lasted a long time, but not so many men were engaged in it, it was discontinuous, and only a few cities were destroyed; in the Persian, large numbers were engaged, but it lasted but a short time. But the Peloponnesian war lasted, almost continuously, for twenty-seven years; and all Greek states, and some other peoples besides, became involved in it. What does he mean by this? It is the argument of a man who regarded war not as an occasion for glory, not as nothing more than a means of deciding some important question (whether, for example, Greek or Persian was to prevail), but as an evil. The Peloponnesian war did more material and moral harm than any other had done; it threatened to destroy Greek civilization altogether, and Thucydides, when he died, could not have been confident that it had not destroyed it, that there would be any such revival as that of the fourth and third centuries. Hence what is relevant is, exactly, the scale of the war—the number of states and peoples engaged in it, victims of it, its duration, and its intensity—the amount of material and moral damage done. It was the greatest κίνησις that had ever been.

Thucydides, that is, meant just what we mean when we call the last war the greatest in history, or, more simply, the

Great War: we are thinking of the number of men involved and killed, the amount of destruction, the moral as well as the material loss—the fabric of society nearly broken, both intellect and virtue weakened or abused. It is a reasonable judgement; and it does not in the least imply that we are unaware of the importance to European history of past wars against the Turks, the Moors, the Arabs, or, for that matter, of the Greeks against the Persians. Nor was Thucydides unconscious of the importance, nor yet of the romance of Marathon and Thermopylai; when he likens the fighting on Pylos to Leonidas' last stand, he says it is 'to compare small things with great' (iv 36. 3). He knew well enough that the Peloponnesian war would decide the problem of the hegemony of Greece, nay, something much more important than that—the question whether *any* state would be strong enough to exercise a hegemony and impose some unity on the Greek people; he knew that that problem was the principal cause of the war, and was solved by it, in the negative. But he knew too that a war fought on that scale, with such intensity, and over so long a period, at once became more serious than any particular problem it was called upon to solve. That is why he lays so much stress on certain incidents which had very little influence on the military result of the war—on the victory of Athens or of her enemies—but were symptomatic of the evils generated by it: the struggle for Plataia, the Corcyrean sedition, the conquest of Melos; Plataia particularly. A small state, for which all Greeks (except the envious Thebans) and especially all Athenians must feel, at least at times, a sentimental regard; a gallant, romantic state; the neutrality of its territory guaranteed by all. The first fighting of the war is on this neutral ground; it is a treacherous attempt to seize the city under the usual cover of an invitation from within; its failure is followed by an equally treacherous and bloodthirsty killing of disarmed prisoners by the gallant Plataeans. The siege is prolonged, the defenders showing every sort of courage and determination; Athens cannot help, for strategy is more important than gratitude. When at last the remnant, reduced to the last extremity, must surrender, the Spartans expressly stipulate for a surrender on terms, in order that in the event of a peace on the basis of the *status quo ante bellum*, Plataia need not be given back because it had voluntarily gone over to the Peloponnesian cause. This piece of sophistical casuistry cannot however be immediately maintained; the prisoners who had 'surrendered' are treated as men captured at the sword's point; and men who in a happier age would have been allowed to march out with all the honours of war, are treated to the mockery of a trial and mercilessly killed, because justice must be done; because men responsible for the treacherous execution of the Thebans four years before must pay the just penalty. Βίαιος διδάσκαλος ὁ πόλεμος. Of course the Persian wars were productive of less misery than the Peloponnesian; of course Marathon is scarcely worth a mention. To call Thucydides' history of the great tragedy 'from beginning to end a superb apology for Perikles' is to me one of the strangest misjudgements ever made by a sensible man. Even in detail Macan cannot keep his head: he instances as something specially ludicrous in Thucydides that in ii 16. 1, he 'for his own purposes makes more of the removal of the country-folk in 431 B.C.!'[1] As if the deliberate sacrifice in the Peloponnesian war of all that they had built up in the country, year after year, did not in effect mean more to the Athenians than their sudden retreat in 480, followed almost immediately by successful re-occupation.

Thucydides was not alone among the Greeks in looking upon war as an evil. Herodotus, if with less profound appreciation, would have agreed with his judgement; and his wisest editor in attacking Thucydides shows a want of understanding as well of his favourite author. In recording (vi 98) the earthquake on Delos,[2] Herodotus writes: 'This was a portent to mankind of the coming evils; in the reigns of Darius, Xerxes, and Artaxerxes, Greece suffered more

[1] Than of their leaving Attica in 480. *Herodotus vii–ix*, vol. 2, p. 19, n. 3.

[2] What a lot of folly, by the way, has been written about this, and the discrepancy between Herodotus and Thucydides: champions of one, champions of the other, down to How and Wells' 'there was probably one in 462'! Earthquakes are not all of the same intensity; they vary from the most destructive to shocks that are barely perceptible by a few persons or the finest instruments. Some people on Delos felt a shock in 432, and proudly said they were the first who had ever felt one there; others answered that there had been one in 490. To suppose that Thucydides is contradicting Herodotus is idle; all we can say is that Herodotus is so emphatic that he may be contradicting, not of course Thucydides, but the report of the earthquake of 432.

evils, whether at the hands of the barbarian or through
internal wars, then in twenty generations before them.' Not a
portent of the glorious victory of Greece over the Barbarian,
of light over darkness, of the saving of civilization and the
preservation of Europe; but of evil. We moderns can only
see the glory[1]; but Herodotus and Thucydides saw things
differently: Αὖται δὲ αἱ νέες ἀρχὴ κακῶν ἐγένοντο Ἕλλησί τε
καὶ βαρβάροισι.[2] Ἥδε ἡ ἡμέρα τοῖς Ἕλλησι μεγάλων κακῶν
ἄρξει. So did the Greeks in general. The Greek dislike
of war, their sincere, if helpless, protests against it,
from Hesiod (Aspis 237–269) and Herodotus and Pindar
down to the last fine words of Agelaos the Aetolian at Naupaktos—'we Greeks must stop fighting each other, or we
shall soon be unable to call even our quarrels our own,'[3] are
as much part of Greek history as the continual wars themselves. In that great sea of words that form the *Speeches* of
Isocrates, the one thing that makes them, in part, readable
is the sincerity of his protest against the endless fighting;
and his plea for a crusade against the 'national' enemy is
based much more on a desire to remove the disturbing
elements from Greece, to unite all his countrymen in peace
among themselves, than to obtain for them military glory
in the East. There are many misleading statements in that
popular book (popular with scholars), Zimmern's *Greek
Commonwealth*; none more misleading than this on war: 'To
understand its normal place in city state society we must
forget all that we have ever heard or read about either its
wickedness or its romance. To the early Greeks, as to many
of the Balkan highlanders to-day, it did not seem either
wicked or romantic, but was simply an exciting and not
unusual way of spending some weeks in early summer, a
traditional part of the national economy and of the citizen's
public service.'[4]   οὐδεὶς γὰρ οὕτω ἀνόητός ἐστι ὅστις πόλεμον

---

[1]It is not perhaps surprising that Macan should have written what he did in 1895;
it is more so that he should have retained his opinion after 1918.
[2]It was characteristic of the humane Herodotus to add καί βαρβάροισι.
  Deffner, *Die Rede bei Herodot.* (for which see below, p. 169 ff), p. 63, agrees,
and quotes the well-known passage, i 87, and also iii 21 and iv 119; but not v 97,
nor vi 98, the most impressive of them all. Thucydides has similar passages illus-
trating the ordinary Greek view—ii 8. 1, 65. 2, iv 20. 2, 62. 2-4.
[3]Cf. Hermokrates at Gela, Thuc. iv 64. 2.
[4]P. 245.

πρὸ εἰρήνης αἱρέεται· ἐν μὲν γὰρ τῇ οἱ παῖδες τοὺς πατέρας θάπτουσι,‘ ἐν δὲ τῷ οἱ πατέρες τοὺς παῖδας.

I am not suggesting that Thucydides, or Herodotus, was a pacifist, in the sense of one who believes that all wrongs, and all causes of friction between states, can be removed by peaceful means, or, if this is impossible, should be left alone. For that there is no evidence; and I doubt whether Herodotus ever put such a question to himself. Nor was either of them blind to what is worthy of enduring fame in war, to the courage, selfless devotion, discipline and intelligence that are displayed. Still less do I believe that they had practical and moral ends in view in writing their histories, that they wanted simply to show that wars are disastrous; I do not think Thucydides set out to condemn the imperialistic policy of Perikles which directly caused the war, any more than to compose an apologia. The aim of each of them was a scientific one: to record what had happened. But it is necessary to be accurate about what Thucydides had in mind when he stressed the importance of his theme.

VII

THUCYDIDES AND SPHAKTERIA[1]

PROFESSOR V. WILAMOWITZ-MOELLENDORF has recently published a paper in which he argues, firstly, that the very remarkable topographical errors in Thucydides' account of the Pylos and Sphakteria campaign, shown so clearly in Grundy's and Burrows' articles in the *Hellenic Journal*, can only be accounted for on the supposition that he had none but Athenian sources of information, and secondly, that as later —after 421—he had access to Peloponnesian sources, his account of this campaign was written before 421; we have, therefore, an early example of Attic prose comparable with the oligarchic *Constitution of Athens*.[2] Now seeing that the incident of the campaign which interested the contemporary Greeks most was the surrender of the Spartans, and that Thucydides goes out of his way, *more Herodoteo* rather, to give an anecdote (with explanation) to illustrate this interest, it would be sufficiently remarkable if he had not been to the trouble of getting the Spartan version of the affair; the more especially as Spartan sources were easily available in the prisoners themselves, who seem to have received at Athens the common treatment of that time, compounded of cruelty and freedom, which is so foreign to our own method, and to whom Thucydides could have had ready access.[3] It is therefore worth while seeing if there is any reason for supposing Wilamowitz' view to be true.

It will be remembered that the two most notable errors are the absence of any reference to the lagoon of Osmín Agá, and the statement that the Spartans intended blocking up the entrances to the harbour because these were quite narrow, giving room for but two ships to enter abreast

---

[1] First published in the *Classical Quarterly*, xvii, 1923.
[2] *Sitzungsber. d. preuss. Akad. d. Wiss.*, 1921, pp. 306 sqq.; Grundy, *J.H.S.*, 1896 (map); Burrows, *J.H.S.*, 1896 and 1898 (photographs). Both Grundy and Burrows also assumed purely Athenian sources.
[3] Thuc. iv 40. 2, 41. 1; Ar. *Eq.* 393–4, 468–9; *Nub.* 184–6; Plut. *Nic.* 9; Thuc. vi 89. 2.

between Sphakteria and Pylos, and but eight or nine between Sphakteria and 'the other mainland' (c. 8. 5–6); while the topographical details in the account of the fighting both at Pylos and on the island are remarkably accurate. But the first error (if it is one) is not explicable on the assumption of an Athenian source; for every Athenian on Pylos when he looked inland and towards the enemy would have the lagoon spread out before him, and the whole plan of defence must have been dictated by its presence. It is the much easier explanation of Grundy and Burrows that the lagoon, as is *a priori* probable, was deeper in the fifth century than now, was connected with the main bay of Navarino by a passage possible for triremes, and was therefore but part of the harbour of Pylos, and that part in which a fleet would anchor to protect itself from the storms which disturb the waters of the bay.

As to the second error, Grundy supposed that the Spartans did block the northern entrance to the bay and the assumed passage from the bay to the 'inner harbour' just mentioned; and that Thucydides (ignorant of the ground) misunderstood his informant. The difficulty of this view was pointed out by Burrows. *He* supposed that the *Athenian* fleet sailed in by the northern and southern entrances, two and eight or nine abreast respectively; and that Thucydides (though present at the Sphakteria fighting) misunderstood his informant. The difficulty of this view was pointed out by Grundy. Wilamowitz holds that Thucydides' informants were Athenians on Pylos who had no eye for topography, who had not been on Sphakteria and feared lest the Spartans should block the entrances. From Pylos they could not see the southern entrance, the highest point of Sphakteria intervening. (Yet they gave very detailed measurements, eight or nine ships abreast.) In truth the Spartans never had such intentions; and Thucydides only heard of it from the Athenians. These men had often to drink brackish water on Pylos (26. 2); so they told Thucydides it was the same with the Spartans in the island (26. 4); though why it should be so often assumed that the ancients argued in this fashion I do not know; and these men might have as easily come to the opposite conclusion, for there was also a fresh-water spring on Pylos, 26. 2; perhaps they did, and this is why Thucydides mentions the spring on Sphakteria, 31. 2.[1] I suppose, though I cannot find that he says so explicitly, that Wilamowitz believes Thucydides to have had two sets of informants— one for Pylos and the topography of the whole district, another for the fighting on Sphakteria (which includes Demosthenes); in this he closely follows Grundy.[2] It is here that we are landed in our principal difficulty. Demosthenes himself, according to Wilamowitz and others, told Thucydides of his plans and their successful execution; yet he either confined his topographical information to the wrong views he held while occupying Pylos or failed to correct the information given by another. The Athenians in general, who had at least passed the southern entrance on their first arrival at Pylos, who had entered by it when they attacked the Peloponnesian fleet, who sent two ships daily to cruise round the island and kept such watch as might be to prevent food being taken to the enemy, who had themselves such difficulty in finding anchorage and landing-ground (14. 1, 5, 23. 2, 26. 3, 30. 2), these Athenians must have known far more about the width of the passage, the depth of the water, and the strength of the currents than the majority of the Peloponnesians. Of course there were ignorant and also stupid Athenians. But you cannot argue that such an error arose because the informants were Athenians (only ignorant) and then build up a theory on this basis. It is too like the argument of the cabman in *Sylvia Scarlett*:

'What did the driver look like, missie?' one of the men asked.

Sylvia described him vaguely as rather fat, a description which would have equally suited any of the present company. . . .

'I wonder if it 'ud be Bill?' said one of the cabmen. . . . 'I reckon it's Bill. Did you notice if the gentleman as drove you had a swelling behind his ear?'

'I didn't notice,' said Sylvia.

'About the size of a largish potato?' the theorist pressed encouragingly.

[1]Wilamowitz says 'er hat also widersprechende Angaben nicht ausgeglichen.' There is, however, no contradiction; his words in 31. 2 are περὶ τὸ ὕδωρ, and, as far as he knew, this water may have been as brackish as he says it was in 26. 4. In fact, the spring on Sphakteria is now fresh.

[2]It is curious that he writes 'von der Arbeit von Grundy ist nur die Karte verwendbar.'

'I am afraid I didn't notice,' said Sylvia.

'It must be Bill,' the theorist decided. 'Anyone wouldn't notice that swelling in the dark, especially if Bill had his collar turned up.'

'He did have his collar turned up,' Arthur put in.

'There you are,' said the theorist. 'What did I tell you? Of course it's Bill.'

The world of cabmen or of scholars? or just the world?[1]

There are one or two minor points: Wilamowitz remarks that we are told no details of the position of the main Peloponnesian camp (but the Athenians on Pylos could have given Thucydides an even better idea of that than the Peloponnesians themselves), nor the names of any of their commanders, except Thrasymelidas, the leader of the naval attack on Pylos (11. 2). In this case he supposes some prisoners may have been taken. Did some Athenian at once ask a prisoner the name of their commander, and his father's name and status, in order to tell the historian? And what of the commanders on Sphakteria, not Styphon only who was taken prisoner, but his two predecessors (38. 1)? It was an Athenian invention, says Wilamowitz, that the Spartans intended to block the entrances; but what of their other intention, to get timber from Asine for engines with which to attack the walls (13. 1)? How did Thucydides learn that?

Wilamowitz holds that the account of the last fight on Sphakteria is one of those which are truthful indeed, 'aber den nachdenkenden Leser zu einem ganz anderen historischen Urteil führt. . . . Wir hören von einer schweren Niederlage der Spartaner, durch die das Prestige ihres Heeres und Staates eine Einbusse erleidet, die kaum durch den Sieg bei Mantineia nach Jahren ausgeglichen wird. So hat es auch Thukydides angesehen, ganz mit den Augen der Athener, die ihm von ihrem Siege erzählten.' In reality, it was a heroic fight ('von Soldaten höchsten Ranges mit einem Haufen Miliz'— πολλοῖς κώνωψι μαχομένων) worthy to be placed beside Thermopylai. So Grundy also wrote: 'Even

[1]Schwartz (Das Geschichtswerk des Thukydides, pp. 290 ff.) thinks Thucydides' mistake about the southern entrance to the Bay of Navarino to be due to his using a Peloponnesian source (in addition to Demosthenes). Pylos had long been deserted and was unknown, and the Peloponnesian fleet had entered the bay by the northern entrance. Thucydides' informant, quite ignorant of the topography, told him of the Spartan intention to block the entrances, in order to justify the great mistake of sending troops to the island. There is nothing like trying all hypotheses.

in Thucydides' narrative the Athenians and their allies seem like a pack of yelping hounds around a dying lion within whose reach they dare not venture.' *Even in Thucydides' narrative:* a remarkable judgement. In the first place, let it be remembered that what surprised the Greek world (which was ignorant of the circumstances) was simply the surrender of men whose age-long tradition it was to die rather than surrender: 'come back with your shield or on it'; and that taken purely as a military achievement, the fight put up by the Spartans was no more than would be expected from almost any body of Greek hoplites against light-armed troops—and certainly no more heroic than the fight of the Athenians under Nikias on the retreat from Syracuse, nor more remarkable than much of the fighting of the Ten Thousand. Still it was a memorable achievement, one of Sparta's greatest. But can anyone read Thucydides' narrative without seeing that this is his judgement too? that his chief thought was to explain the Spartan defeat to his contemporaries, by insisting on the overwhelming numerical superiority of the Athenians, by giving so detailed a description of their heroic resistance and of the slowly growing confidence of their assailants—by actually pointing out the similarity of their position to that of Leonidas at Thermopylai (36. 3)? Can anyone fail to see that much of the narrative is from accounts given by the Spartan soldiers themselves: c. 34. 2–3 for instance, not so much because it redounds to their credit, explains their defeat, as because it is written from their point of view? γενομένης δὲ τῆς βοῆς ἅμα τῇ ἐπιδρομῇ ἔκπληξίς τε ἐνέπεσεν ἀνθρώποις ἀήθεσι τοιαύτης μάχης καὶ ὁ κονιορτὸς τῆς ὕλης νεωστὶ κεκαυμένης ἐχώρει πολὺς ἄνω, ἄπορόν τε ἦν ἰδεῖν τὰ πρὸ αὑτοῦ ὑπὸ τῶν τοξευμάτων καὶ λίθων ἀπὸ πολλῶν ἀνθρώπων μετὰ τοῦ κονιορτοῦ ἅμα φερομένων. τό τε ἔργον ἐνταῦθα χαλεπὸν τοῖς Λακεδαιμονίοις καθίστατο· οὔτε γὰρ οἱ πῖλοι ἔστεγον τὰ τοξεύματα, δοράτιά τε ἐναπεκέκλαστο βαλλομένων, εἶχόν τε οὐδὲν σφίσιν αὐτοῖς χρήσασθαι ἀποκεκλημένοι μὲν τῇ ὄψει τοῦ προορᾶν, ὑπὸ δὲ τῆς μείζονος βοῆς τῶν πολεμίων τὰ ἐν αὑτοῖς παραγγελλόμενα οὐκ ἐσακούοντες, κινδύνου τε πανταχόθεν περιεστῶτος καὶ οὐκ ἔχοντες ἐλπίδα καθ' ὅτι χρὴ ἀμυνομένους σωθῆναι. Apparently many can; but they must have been remarkable men, these Athenian informants of Thucydides.

K

The Athenian hoplites themselves play almost no part in the fighting; such glory as the victors achieve, belongs to the light-armed, Lemnians, Imbrians, Messenians. There have doubtless been men in history who have done justice to their enemies; there have perhaps been men who have done justice to their allies. But surely there have never been any who so entirely effaced themselves as the Athenians who told Thucydides of their glorious victory on the island.

It seems to me then clear, both on grounds of general probability and from the narrative itself, that Thucydides wrote his account of the campaign only after as much inquiry as possible both from Athenians who had taken part in it and from the Spartan prisoners (one can almost imagine his first question 'what were you doing on the island at all?' and some caustic reply about armchair strategists at home).[1] This does not prove that this part of the history was not written before 421, for the most natural time for Thucydides to inquire among the Spartans would be soon after their arrival in Athens, and before his own departure for good in the spring of 424. But it means that there is no proof that it was, not even a slight balance of evidence; and there is at least one sentence which, to my mind, makes it almost certain that the narrative was not in its final form till some years later. On the naval attack on Pylos Thucydides makes the not very profound comment: ἐς τοῦτό τε περιέστη ἡ τύχη ὥστε 'Αθηναίους μὲν ἐκ γῆς τε καὶ ταύτης Λακωνικῆς ἀμύνεσθαι ἐκείνους ἐπιπλέοντας, Λακεδαιμονίους δὲ ἐκ νεῶν τε καὶ ἐς τὴν ἑαυτῶν πολεμίαν οὖσαν ἐπ' 'Αθηναίους ἀποβαίνειν· ἐπὶ πολὺ γὰρ ἐποίει τῆς δόξης ἐν τῷ τότε τοῖς μὲν ἠπειρώταις μάλιστα εἶναι καὶ τὰ πεζὰ κρατίστοις, τοῖς δὲ θαλασσίοις τε καὶ ταῖς ναυσὶ πλεῖστον προύχειν (12. 3). Wilamowitz notices this last sentence, but only to comment on the archaic use of ποιεῖν. But could Thucydides have written ἐν τῷ τότε in this connexion before 421?[2] Must it not have been written some years afterwards when Sparta was as prominent on sea as on land? at least after Notion? Of course the narrative may have been revised, though Wilamowitz does not think so—'Geschrieben ist

---

[1] I do not now think the occupation of the island so wrongly conceived, though it turned out badly: see below, p. 200.

[2] Cf. also 21. 3 Κλέων ἀνὴρ δημαγωγὸς κατ' ἐκεῖνον τὸν χρόνον (just as in iii 36. 6).

alles vor dem Nikiasfrieden und ist auch so geblieben.' But it is unlikely to have been revised only in order to add this sentence.[1]

It may be said that my argument does not help to answer the question how Thucydides came to make his mistakes in topography. That is so; but there are some questions in ancient history which are at present unanswerable, and this seems to be one of them. The least unlikely solution I think is one somewhat similar to Dr. Grundy's, namely that the Spartans intended to block up the northern passage between Sphakteria and Pylos and that between the bay and the inner harbour, but that Thucydides, who had got a fairly complete account of the fighting from his Athenian and Spartan sources in 425–4, only learnt this explanation later in Sparta itself (on his asking again, how came the men to be on the island), failed to understand its significance owing to his ignorance of the ground, and was unable to collate this new information with the help of his original informants. But I have no confidence in this. For it is clear from 14. 1, καθ' ἑκάτερον ἔσπλουν ὥρμησαν, that Thucydides himself, so far as he had a picture in his mind, thought of the Bay of Navarino as the harbour, for the lagoon has only one entrance. εὐρυχωρία (13. 3) might mean the Bay or the open sea; but more naturally the latter. For Thucydides (if he had any picture in his mind) must have mentioned the Bay. He may have completely misunderstood his sources; but his description of Sphakteria in 8. 6, τόν τε λιμένα παρατείνουσα καὶ ἐγγὺς ἐπικειμένη ἐχυρὸν ποιεῖ shows that he had a very fair idea of the position.[2]

---

[1] Cf. Herbst, *Philologus*, 38, p. 532; Grundy, *Thucydides and the History of his Age*, pp. 476–7.

[2] Bury wrote (*Greek Historians*, p. 85): 'it is easy to see that . . . he received information from Spartans as well as from Athenians about the episode of Pylos and Sphacteria.' P. 86, 1: 'My view is that he first wrote the story from information supplied by eye-witnesses who gave him a general, though partly inaccurate, idea of the place, and that he afterwards tested it on the spot and probably added local touches, but omitted to revise the errors of distance.' This view only adds to our difficulties.

VIII

THUCYDIDES AND THE BATTLE OF MANTINEIA

In *B.S.A.* xxii (1916–18) Professor Woodhouse first published his explanation of what really took place at the battle of Mantineia in 418, and of the foolish mistakes made by Thucydides; he has now restated it in more elaborate form;[1] and since he has in no way changed his views, in spite of Kromayer's criticism,[2] his book deserves a detailed consideration. For Professor Woodhouse does not leave us in doubts about his meaning: according to him Thucydides' 'entire narrative of this campaign, a narrative at first blush so minute, so painstaking and so straightforward, is revealed by dispassionate analysis as simply a tissue of incoherences, irrelevancies, and even downright absurdities' (p. 18); Thucydides' explanation of a military phenomenon is 'nothing but a fatuous delusion and stark nonsense' (p. 79); 'he had no eye for country, no instinct for the decisive elements of a terrain' (p. 65); he can make a general give an order that 'was a physical impossibility,' 'a demonstrable absurdity' (pp. 86–7); and so forth. It is true that he also pays the usual lip-service, that he can say that 'the scientific quality of Thucydides as a military historian . . . is, of course, not here primarily in point' (p. 19), and that these simple results of his inquiry 'sink into insignificance when weighed in the scales against those other excellences upon which the world's verdict of Thucydides' unapproachable supremacy securely rests' (p. viii); that he can, to suit his argument, quote from other passages in the history as though their authority was unquestioned, and even say, to prove a point, 'Thucydides is not to be supposed to have written in a fashion so slipshod, or with caprice so outrageous' (p. 94). But if one who had been a soldier and a general, and who sets out expressly to write a military history, is

---

[1] *King Agis of Sparta and his Campaign in Arkadia in* 418 B.C. Oxford; 1933.
[2] *Antike Schlachtfelder,* iv, pp. 207 ff.

capable of blunders of this kind, it is clear that his authority is worthless unless supported by more trustworthy evidence; and that we have in consequence hardly anything on which to base a reliable narrative of the Peloponnesian war. Which is a matter of some importance.

Professor Woodhouse prefaces his argument, by a translation of Book v 61–75; and an examination of this at once reveals some interesting points. 65. 1 'one of the older men . . . bawled out to Agis'; 65. 4 'what Agis was after, was the making those fellows on the hill, the Argeians and the Confederates, come down from their perch'; 73. 3 'the Athenians got quietly away with whole skins,' the Mantineians and the picked Argive corps 'turned and ran for it.' This sort of picturesque writing is entirely foreign to Thucydides; the colouring is wrong. Professor Woodhouse adopts it to get the reader at once into the desired mood, to make him ready to adopt his view that the Confederates were foolish and cowardly men; yet it is a singularly illogical mistranslation, for it is part of his principal argument that Thucydides did not share that view.[1] The next instances are of another kind: they are intended to make the narrative appear foolish: 71. 3 'to fill the gap thus made, order after order he sent down' to the two polemarchs. But the imperfect παρήγγελλεν no more means 'order after order' than διέφθειρον in 72. 3 means 'repeatedly destroyed,' or ἀπῆγεν in 65. 3 'repeatedly led away.' In this last case Professor Woodhouse falls into the opposite error and translates 'suddenly led away,' because that helps his argument.

68. 2 ἐκ μέντοι τοιοῦδε λογισμοῦ ἔξεστί τῳ σκοπεῖν τὸ Λακεδαιμονίων τότε παραγενόμενον πλῆθος: 'from the following computation, however, any one can see the number of Lacedaemonians that day in the field.' With this translation it is easy enough to point out the inconsistency of saying that the secrecy that involved all Spartan military arrangements prevented their numbers being known, and of then adding a calculation which gives an exact figure; and the inconsistency is not removed by the suggestion (in itself possible enough) that this whole chapter on the num-

---

[1]With the same general object, Professor Woodhouse emends 69. 1 to ⟨αἱ⟩ παραινέσεις, so that he may translate '*the usual* heartening words.'

bers engaged was a later addition, a footnote, by Thucydides. But it should not be necessary to point out that τις does not mean 'any one', and that Jowett's translation of ἔξεστί τῳ σκοπεῖν 'give some idea of' is correct (or, if you like, 'give a picture of'). This translation Professor Woodhouse calls 'the worst in the world,' 'meant to save the face of Thucydides'; and contrasts it with Jowett's translation of τὸ σαφὲς σκοπεῖν, i 22. 4, 'to have present to their minds the exact facts'; as though τὸ σαφὲς made no difference to the exactness of the picture. Yet Professor Woodhouse himself, by correctly translating ἐπὶ πᾶν, 68. 3, 'over all,' 'in the general run,' and not 'the mathematical average,' shows that a rough estimate of the Lacedaemonian forces, and not an exact figure, is all that Thucydides professes to give, and that there is therefore no inconsistency.

71. 1 (on the tendency of Greek armies in attack to edge to the right) 'the men feel *nervous*, and so each man *squeezes* his exposed side as close as ever he can to the shield of the file on his right. . . . The file-leader of the right wing is primarily *to blame* for this deflection, he being bent on edging away continually with his exposed side from the enemy in his front; and by reason of the like *nervousness* the rest follow his lead.' The words I have italicized are all exaggerations of the Greek.

There is yet further exaggeration in Professor Woodhouse's comment (p. 78), when he writes of 'an overmastering impulse of fear'; and 'such impulse . . . plainly cannot have worked with the same intensity in each man, but with every gradation of effect throughout the phalanx, until, growing by what it fed on, and as it were by reciprocal contagion, it must soon have bid fair to burst the bonds of discipline and bring about the disruption of the whole array.' So this notion is 'a fatuous delusion and stark nonsense.' Well, Thucydides had served in hoplite ranks, and should have known; and in fact there is no difficulty, if his words are taken in their natural meaning. Professor Woodhouse indeed says 'it is idle to water down this reiterated φόβος to something innocuous'; but we can say of a modern army that it advanced under cover of a wood *for fear* of the enemy's artillery, or that infantry advance in open formation, taking every advantage of shell-holes and other cover, *for fear* of the enemy's machine-guns, without meaning by this that the men were in a state of disorderly panic.[1] Greek infantry advanced in close formation, as close as possible, but not so close that a man had not elbow room to use spear and sword; the file-leader on the right extremity will try to outflank the enemy's left so as to turn inwards to strike; the man next him on the left will keep close to him (but not squeeze up to him) to prevent a gap which would be to his own immediate danger, as well as to that of the whole line. Professor Woodhouse argues that all such movement to the right was known and under control. Of course it was (at least, more or less under control, according to the varying discipline of armies); but does Thucydides say it was not? He knew it well enough, having commanded hoplites; and on this occasion the whole of Agis' actions imply that it was. There is no sort of contradiction. Professor Woodhouse's own explanation is that the Greek infantryman's shield, held across his body, prevented him from walking straight forward, *made* him walk sideways, like a crab; 'not directly towards the shield, but, as it were, parallel to it'; and further that this 'inclination to the right put the individual hoplite into exactly the correct position for immediate effective application of his weight at the moment of impact.' I should have thought that as the enemy was also advancing crablike to *his* right, the two sides would have slipped away from each other; and in any case a Greek battle was not so simply 'a matter of brawn, . . . a steady thrust with the whole weight of the file behind it—a literal shoving of the enemy off the ground on which he stood' (did the back rows *push* the men in front?), as Professor Woodhouse supposes. It was not a scrummage. The men all used their weapons, and had their right arms free.

66. 2 μάλιστα δὴ Λακεδαιμόνιοι ἐς ὃ ἐμέμνηντο ἐν τούτῳ τῷ καιρῷ ἐξεπλάγησαν (διὰ βραχείας γὰρ μελλήσεως ἡ παρασκευὴ

---

[1] Similarly δείσας just below does not mean 'in dismay,' or 'to his horror.' If it is necessary to show that this is as true in Greek as in English, I would refer Professor Woodhouse to the use of φοβεῖσθαι and δεῖσαι in Thuc. iii 78. 1-2, in a context where he will also learn something of the quality of one of the Athenian commanders at Mantineia.

αὐτοῖς ἐγίγνετο), καὶ εὐθὺς ὑπὸ σπουδῆς καθίσταντο ἐς κόσμον τὸν ἑαυτῶν:[1]

'never within living memory had the Lakedaimonians been so taken aback as at this crisis—they must, of course, make their dispositions for action with hardly a moment to spare. Instantly therefore they set about deployment in quick time into their own formation.' There is a real difficulty here— the only one in these chapters.[2] It lies in ἐξεπλάγησαν— not because we must believe, on the facts, that the Lacedaemonians were not dumbfounded; but because the next sentence suggests they were not—as Stahl says: quae enim causa subsequitur, ea non probat perturbatos esse Lacedaemonios, sed non perturbatos. Γάρ must either explain the fact (e.g., 'for they had not expected to see the enemy then or there'), or justify the statement (e.g. 'there was much confusion as they drew up in line'). Our text does neither; and I cannot believe that Thucydides or any one else would say: 'never had they been so thunderstruck—for they had only a short while to make their preparations—and immediately and quickly fell into their regular line.' Professor Woodhouse's 'must,' 'of course,' 'therefore' obscure, but do not remove the difficulties. Stahl must be right in thinking there is a lacuna, to be filled in some such way as: ἐν τούτῳ τῷ καιρῷ ⟨ἐξαναγκασθέντες εὐθὺς ἐκ πορείας μάχεσθαι οὐδ᾽ ὥς⟩ ἐξεπλάγησαν.

Even so, the Lacedaemonian army and its commander were taken by surprise; and this Professor Woodhouse asserts to be untrue, impossible, nonsense. We are come to the core of the matter. The Central Arcadian plain is roughly of the figure of eight, with Mantineia in the northern half, Tegea in the southern; about eleven miles separate the two cities; the 'waist', the gap between the hills now called Mýtika and Kapnístra, is at its narrowest less than a mile and a half wide, and not four miles south of Mantineia.[3]

[1]This is Hude's punctuation, adopted by Woodhouse. The more usual is with stop or colon after ἐξεπλάγησαν, and no parenthesis.

[2]Except perhaps in the use of ἐμπειρία, 72. 2, which in no way affects the present argument.

[3]For a full description of the plain, with its climatic and other physical characteristics, see Philippson, Der Peloponnes, pp. 90 ff., 493 ff.; Fougères, Mantinée, cc. ii–v; and Kromayer, Antike Schlachtfelder i, 29–46, with plates 1 and 4. Maps: Philippson, Fougères, Kromayer (to vol. iv as well as to vol. i), Loring, J.H.S. xv, pl. 1, and the Greek staff map 1:100,000, Tripolis sheet. My map has been made from this last and from Philippson.

The whole plain is of alluvial soil, level, with a slight but
steady fall from south to north, so that a small stream, the
Zanovistas, flows from Tegea into Mantineian territory,
though much the larger volume of water in the Tegeatis
(the river Sarandapótamos) flows away to the east. All the
water either soaks through the soil, or finds an outlet underground by katavothrai. It is universally assumed, and it
may well be true, though there is no direct evidence on the
matter, that Agis on his first advance into Mantineian territory marched through the Mýtika-Kapnístra gap, and
encamped somewhere, probably on the western edge of the
plain, not two miles south of Mantineia; and that the Confederate position, 'steep and hard to come at,' was on the lower
spurs of Mt. Alesion, just east of Mantineia (or, as I should
prefer to suppose, extending from these spurs to the next
hill to the south-east, Stavromýti, and so covering the most
important of the routes from Árgos).[1] The Lacedaemonian
army (made up of a full levy of Lacedaemonians, Tegeans,
and the rest of Arcadia except Mantineia and Orchomenos)
outnumbered the Confederates; but both sides might expect
reinforcements, sooner or later—Agis from his northern
allies, Corinth, Boeotia, Phokis and Lokris, who would
however take some time to collect their forces and must
come through hostile territory; the Confederates expected
some further help from Athens (who had so far sent only
1,000 hoplites and 300 cavalry), and were hoping as
well that the 3,000 Eleans, who had gone off in a huff,
would soon return. Both armies therefore had some reason
for delay, and both some reason for forcing the issue; but on
the Spartan side (apart from the personal desire of Agis to
recover his reputation) the balance of argument was in
favour of immediate action; and as well, the season was far
advanced (it was already September), and a victory was
necessary, not a stalemate, to break up the dangerous

[1]The reason why I do not feel sure of these positions for the two armies, is that,
if Mantineia was walled, as it certainly was in 385 (Xen. *Hell.* v 2. 4–7), though the
French excavators found no traces of a wall earlier than that of 371 B.C., there
seems but little purpose in the Confederates leaving the protection of the walls to
take up a position next door; if it was not walled, then they were leaving Agis free
to destroy the city as well as to lay waste the land. There is therefore a possibility
that Agis did not advance through the gap, and that the allies were waiting for him
on Kapnistra. But there are difficulties in the way of this too. (See below, p. 140
n. 1, and 154); and the doubt does not much affect the present argument.

coalition. Agis therefore at once led his troops against the enemy; but suddenly, before engaging, withdrew them and marched back to Tegea. Whether this was due to some sudden impulse, when he realized the strength of the enemy's position, as Thucydides says, or was part of some deep-laid scheme, as Professor Woodhouse asserts so confidently, does not for the moment matter. With regard to the former theory we must remember how difficult it was for heavy-armed troops to keep any sort of order on rough and steep ground, and how weak the phalanx became as soon as it lost its cohesion. Nikostratos, one of the two Athenian commanders at Mantineia, had learnt it earlier to his cost.[1] That was one reason too why the Confederates did not now at once pursue Agis, who withdrew in good order. Professor Woodhouse does not appreciate this; yet, to take another instance from this same battlefield, even the wide trench behind which Philopoimen placed his troops in 207, though it had a gentle slope and there was no water in it and no scrub or bush, upset the order of the Spartan phalanx when it crossed it to attack, and Philopoimen had reckoned on this.[2]

Agis had to find some means for inducing the Confederates to offer battle; ravaging the land had not been enough, for the plain of Mantineia grows mostly corn, and that had long been gathered. He thought of the old plan of diverting the water of the Tegeatis. Professor Woodhouse laughs at the idea, but through insufficient study of the land. It would, he says, have been useless to divert the water unless the katavothrai in Mantineian territory (along the western border of the plain) were also blocked. Perhaps Agis intended to do this on his second incursion (as Kromayer suggests)? But Thucydides says nothing of this; he therefore misunderstood the operation. Even so, this would only be a gap in his knowledge or his narrative, not an absurdity. But in fact the situation was quite different. The katavothrai in the plain of Mantineia are insufficient even to take the water of the Zanovistas and the small streams rising east

[1]Thuc. iv 129.
[2]Polyb. xi 15. 7, 16. 1–5; cf. Aristotle *Pol.* v 2. 12 (1303 *b.* 12): ὥσπερ γὰρ ἐν τοῖς πολέμοις αἱ διαβάσεις τῶν ὀχετῶν καὶ τῶν πάνυ σμικρῶν διασπῶσι τὰς φάλαγγας, οὕτως ἔοικε πᾶσα διαφορὰ ποιεῖν διάστασιν.

and north-east of Mantineia; some parts of the plain in the
west are permanent marsh land; almost all of it is under
water in the winter and in some years it does not dry throughout the summer.[1] Far less then were the katavothrai capable
of taking the waters of the Sarandapótamos as well. Conditions must have been better in antiquity, otherwise the town
of Mantineia would not have been built in the plain;[2] but not
so much better that the Mantineians could afford, even if
they kept their katavothrai clear, to laugh at the efforts of the
Tegeans to flood their land. For it had long been a source of
quarrelling between the two cities. Agis then will have begun
diverting the water of the Sarandapótamos into the Zanovistas, by breaking down the dams in the old channel between
the two streams.[3] The effect of this would be inconsiderable
for many days, even after the beginning of the rainy season,
which was then nearly due;[4] it would not even be visible immediately though it would ultimately be disastrous for both
the autumn and the spring sowing of corn. Agis then will not
have expected his enemy at once to leave the strong position
they had taken. In fact they did so at once, not because of
the danger from the water, but in over-confidence, because
they thought Agis was avoiding battle once more. Is it any
wonder that the Spartans were surprised to find them ready
for battle next morning?[5]

But Professor Woodhouse has another argument. There
was no surprise, because all possible movements of the
Confederates were visible to Agis. They must either be still
on the Alesion ridge (on which it is assumed that the

[1] Philippson, pp. 99, 107–9.
[2] At the present time all the villages in the old territory of Mantineia lie on the
slopes of the surrounding hills, none in the plain, unlike the villages of the Tegeatis.
The synoecism of Mantineia in the fifth century must have followed some more or
less permanent agreement with Tegea about the waters.
Philippson holds that there has been some rise in the level of the plain, and
hence a change in the working of the katavothrai, since antiquity (pp. 107, 494).
On the archaeological evidence Fougères denies this for the site of Mantineia itself
(p. 35, n. 1).
[3] See point marked A on map for the probable line of this channel according to
Fougères. Agis did not of course have to dig the channel; it had long been used
for the same purpose by the Tegeans, whenever they would annoy their neighbour,
and dammed when there was agreement.
[4] It begins about mid-September: Fougères, p. 26.
[5] Kromayer makes this point, about the time it would take the flooding even to
begin its work. But Professor Woodhouse ignores it, so it must be stated afresh.
Jowett's note on 66. 2, quoted by him with scorn on p. 52, is in fact sound.

Confederates had been posted), or have left it; and if the
latter, then they must either have withdrawn within the
walls of Mantineia or be down in the plain. But that they
had left Alesion 'was matter of immediate and infallible
observation'; for the ridge 'was, and is, and must always
have been, visible from every part of the plain, so that
nothing could balk the observation or mar its accuracy.'
But that is not true, for Agis had withdrawn to Tegea (it
was essential to his plan to get well away from the enemy,
not to be within *their* sight, obviously waiting for them), and
movements on Alesion are not visible from there, especially,
may we say, towards the evening; unless he had left observation posts on Mýtika and Kapnístra heights.[1] Moreover
Professor Woodhouse forgets two things: the Pelagos wood,
and the time of day. As to the first, I am not disposed
to attach much importance to it, for its extent and
density and therefore its significance for this campaign
are all very uncertain; but Professor Woodhouse may
not shelter himself behind this, for he knows all about
the wood and especially blames Thucydides for ignoring so
cardinal a feature of the locality. Pausanias says that beyond
the sanctuary of Poseidon, that is a mile or so on the road
from Mantineia to Tegea, 'you meet a region full of oak-
trees, and the road goes through the oaks'; and again that
this wood, at a point thirty stades from Mantineia, that is,
level with the Mýtika gap, stretched westwards as far as
the road to Pallantion.[2] That is all; neither Xenophon nor
Polybios mentions it in their accounts of the campaigns of
362 and 207 B.C.; though Professor Woodhouse, following
Kromayer, believes that the attempt by Epaminondas to
surprise the city of Mantineia by a cavalry attack was made

---

[1] This seems to me a real difficulty, though not one noticed by Professor Woodhouse. If Agis had on his first march got within a mile or so of Mantineia, he
presumably drove off Mantineian posts on these heights and occupied them himself.
In that case he would have known the enemy movements, at least during daylight.
If on the other hand he did not penetrate so far (see above, p. 137, n.), then presumably
the Mantineian outposts remained, and would have reported at once that Agis was
not retreating, but was encamped in front of Tegea. This is difficult to believe.
Professor Woodhouse however does believe it (p. 54, n. 17), and combines his belief
with the view that Agis penetrated far beyond the gap, and stayed in the northern
plain three or even four days (p. 156). We must, I think, assume that the Spartan
outposts were on these heights, and allow for night-movements.

[2] Paus. viii 10. 1, 11. 1, 5–8.

possible by the screen afforded by the forest, and in 207
Machanidas must have marched through it to reach his
position before the battle and fought with his back to it.[1]
Obviously we know nothing about the size and condition of
the forest in the fifth century. It may well, with the decline of
population and therefore of cultivation, have increased in
extent and density by the second century A.D. But if it was
as important as Professor Woodhouse says, then clearly it
concealed the movements of the Confederates from Agis.
They marched down from the hills, probably in the dusk,
and through the wood; by the time they have covered five
miles or a little more, they are past the Mýtika-Kapnístra
line, and by next morning they deploy in the plain south of
this line, ready for battle, barely five miles from Tegea itself;
where Agis sees them, on his way back to his camp of the
day before. If the wood did not play an important part, then
they had marched by night. Is it any wonder that Agis was
surprised?

Impossible, says Professor Woodhouse; for the battle
took place on Mantineian territory, the boundary of which
with Tegea was at the Mýtika gap, at its southern end, and
there are only two lines on which an army on the defensive
can take up position: at the gap, and immediately in front
of the town of Mantineia; in each case the flanks of a defending force are protected by hills which jut out into the plain.
They were not at the gap, south of the forest, for there they
would have been wholly visible to the Spartans and could
have caused no surprise (though as Professor Woodhouse is
certain that there was no surprise, and none ever intended,
he is hardly entitled to the argument); therefore they were
just in front of the town.

Here is indeed a flimsy tissue of argument. First there is
no evidence that the frontiers of Mantineia and Tegea were
at the gap, though this is generally believed. The evidence
adduced is that of Pausanias, who mentions two roads going

[1] Xen. *Hell.* vii 5. 14–7; Polyb. ix 8; xi 11–8. The latter's account of the
attempted surprise in 362 is so short (only a note, to compare it with Hannibal's
march on Rome) that the absence of any topographical detail need not surprise; and
it follows the inaccurate Ephoros (Diod. xv 84–7), instead of Xenophon (Kromayer,
i, pp. 42–4, hardly makes the difference clear). But his narrative of the battle of
207 B.C. is very full, and with much attention to topography; yet he says nothing
of the wood.

across the plain southward from Mantineia, the eastern to Tegea, the western to Pallantion; on the former he mentions an altar which marks the boundary, but gives no measurements of distance, on the latter he mentions the grave of Epaminondas thirty stades from Mantineia, and one stade further on a sanctuary of Zeus Charmon.[1] Now it is often Pausanias' habit to describe the objects of interest on a road as far as the frontier, and then take up another road; and he probably does so here. But that would only show that this sanctuary of Zeus was the last matter of interest on the road, not that it was at the frontier. And even if it was, there is no reason to believe that the frontier in Pausanias' day was the same as in the fifth or fourth century B.C. Secondly, there is almost as little reason for supposing that the battle was actually fought on Mantineian soil. True, Thucydides says the Mantineian contingent held the right wing, ὅτι ἐν τῇ ἐκείνων τὸ ἔργον ἐγίγνετο; but clearly this cannot be pressed —or are we to suppose that if the army advanced a yard across the border, at once a dispute might arise and whole units in the line change places?

Thirdly, with the numbers for the Confederate army, some 11,000 men, given by Professor Woodhouse, neither of the two defensive positions allowed by him has any particular value. For an army as large as that which fought against Epaminondas in 362, 22–25,000,[2] they have; for such an army would occupy a space about two miles wide, the distance between Mýtika and Kapnístra at the southern end (and also between the hill slopes immediately south of Mantineia), and it was therefore reasonably safe from attack on either flank, at least by hoplite forces. Hence the Mýtika position was a good one for the allies to adopt against the superior numbers of Epaminondas.[3] But neither position

---

[1] Paus. viii 10. 1–12. 1.   [2] See Kromayer, i, 114–23.

[3] Actually, Epaminondas, by a stroke of genius, used the protection of the hills to defeat the enemy. He attacked in column the enemy's right wing, with but a shield of cavalry on his left, trusting that success here would decide the issue of the day (see Kromayer, i, 55 ff.; I cannot by the way accept his modification of his original view given in vol. iv, 317–23, if I understand it aright). The great danger to this would be if his column were attacked on both flanks. But his left was protected by the hills on which the enemy's right rested for *their* protection; against an attack from the right his troops were specially prepared, and as well protected by a large force of light cavalry, those who afterwards came into conflict with the Athenians (cf. Xen. 5. 23–5).

would be of special value, even to a force on the defensive, if
it numbered only 11,000. I would myself suppose the
numbers of the Confederate forces to be rather larger than
that,[1] but not so large as to make these positions safe for
them. Besides, and lastly, the Confederates were not on the
defensive, but pursuing, ready, perhaps foolishly ready, to
fight if they should meet the enemy.[2] The latter, they
thought, might have withdrawn altogether, in which case
the original plan of a march on Tegea would presumably be
carried out; but he might be in front of Tegea, only three or
four miles distant, so they must be ready for battle in the
morning.

But in that case, asks Professor Woodhouse finally, if the
Spartans were taken by surprise, why did the Confederates
not take advantage of it, by attacking at once, before the
enemy was ready? But they did ($\dot{\epsilon}\nu\tau\acute{o}\nu\omega_{S}$ $\kappa\alpha\grave{\iota}$ $\dot{o}\rho\gamma\hat{\eta}$ $\chi\omega\rho o\hat{\upsilon}\nu\tau\epsilon_{S}$),[3]
or rather attempted to, and were only foiled by the speed
with which the experienced Lacedaemonians were able to
form into line. Even so they gained an initial tactical advantage which might have been decisive; for Agis had not time
to deploy his troops sufficiently far to the left to guard
against being there outflanked (in spite of his superior numbers), and to meet this danger he had to make a gap in his
line. Professor Woodhouse cannot imagine a surprise
except as an actual collision, as between two persons meeting
at a corner; and so supposes that if the Lacedaemonians
were surprised they must have been within a few hundred
yards of the opposing forces (of this, more in a moment), and
the latter all ready to the last man, spears in hand, shield on
arm, helmeted and greaved, at the moment of advance—the
zero hour come, as we say; and naturally therefore argues
that the deliberate way in which the Confederates listen to
little speeches before they advance is inconsistent with any
idea of making use of the momentary confusion in the other
side. But they had not been especially planning a surprise;
and when we are told that they were suddenly seen to be

---

[1] Because of Thucydides' words, 74. 1, $\dot{\eta}$ $\mu\acute{\alpha}\chi\eta$ . . . $\pi\lambda\epsilon\acute{\iota}\sigma\tau ov$ $\chi\rho\acute{o}\nu ov$ $\mu\epsilon\gamma\acute{\iota}\sigma\tau\eta$ $\delta\grave{\eta}$
$\tau\hat{\omega}\nu$ $\dot{E}\lambda\lambda\eta\nu\iota\kappa\hat{\omega}\nu$ $\kappa\alpha\grave{\iota}$ $\dot{\upsilon}\pi\grave{o}$ $\dot{\alpha}\xi\iota o\lambda o\gamma\omega\tau\acute{\alpha}\tau\omega\nu$ $\pi\acute{o}\lambda\epsilon\omega\nu$ $\xi\upsilon\nu\epsilon\lambda\theta o\hat{\upsilon}\sigma\alpha$.

[2] $\mathring{\eta}\nu$ $\pi\epsilon\rho\iota\tau\acute{\upsilon}\chi\omega\sigma\iota\nu$, 66. 1; which Professor Woodhouse unnecessarily alters to
$\mathring{\eta}\nu\pi\epsilon\rho$ $\tau\acute{\upsilon}\chi\omega\sigma\iota\nu$, 'if fight there was to be.'

[3] 70. 1.

ἐν τάξει ἤδη πάντες, this means no more than that they were now in line instead of in column, with every unit in its place; not that every individual was ready to advance. The speeches were naturally given at the last moment, when men were making the final adjustments to their equipment (or does Professor Woodhouse not believe that any speeches were made?); but the final adjustments must be made; the advance must be in good order. There might still be time to take advantage of an enemy that was still in column when it first came on the field. Surprise consists in striking a blow not within a given number of minutes, but before the enemy is ready; and that depends on the degree of his un-readiness. One country can surprise another by an unex-pected mobilization and may strike before the latter is ready, even though the blow is not actually delivered for three or four days. Seeing that Professor Woodhouse makes great fun of those poor scholars who have spoken of the Lacedaemonians' deployment as the work of a few moments only, he might have remembered this.

We can now consider the last serious objection to Thucy-dides' story. After pointing out that this deployment of the Lacedaemonian army would take some time (and that there-fore there can have been no surprise), Professor Woodhouse declares that the order given by Agis to the polemarchs in command of two of his battalions to leave their position in the front line on the right of the Lacedaemonian centre,[1] and move across behind the rest of the centre in order to fill the gap caused by the movement of the left wing, was 'a physical impossibility,' 'a demonstrable absurdity;' 'it was absolutely out of all question for them to reach the gap in the line with their battalions before it could be penetrated by the Argeian select corps.' The Confederates 'charged with con-spicuous ardour, so that the few hundred yards of ground originally separating the two armies must have been covered in a time to be measured not in minutes, but in seconds. In the very crisis and article of the charge, to transfer from the right of the advancing phalanx to the left some two thousand heavy-armed men, moving them with formation unbroken

---

[1] I agree with him that these two battalions were on the right centre, not on the ex-treme right wing of the whole of Agis' army. This seems to me certain.

over several hundred yards of ground, behind and across the
rear of a considerable portion of the army, which in the
meantime continued its own steady onward march—how
could that be within the bounds of human accomplishment?
. . . What a miracle of manœuvring! Well might the two
unfortunate Polemarchs stand aghast at this staggering
demand. The orders of Agis, couched in this form—and
this and none other, be it remembered, is the form in which,
under the voucher of Thucydides, they have actually
descended to us—must have seemed but the wild freak
of a lunatic.' Yet the Polemarchs were afterwards tried at
Sparta for cowardice in face of the enemy, and condemned.
And, we may add, 'the scientific quality of Thucydides as a
military historian is, of course, not here primarily in point.'

Yet all this pother arises from nothing more than this:
that Professor Woodhouse has never asked himself the simple question—what was the distance that separated the two
armies when the Lacedaemonians first began their deployment, and how long would it be before that distance would
be covered by them as they approached each other? He
assumes that it was but a few hundred yards, the time to be
reckoned in seconds rather than in minutes (and it must be
admitted, surprising as it is, that he is not alone in this).[1]
Of course there is no reason for this; of course we must
assume a distance of at least one to two miles (two miles
would take well over half an hour, perhaps three-quarters of
an hour for one of the armies to cover, and at least half that
time for the two to meet if both started simultaneously and
marched at equal speed). Can we imagine Agis deliberately,
knowing exactly where the enemy was to be found, to have
marched in column obliquely across the front of that enemy,
with his unshielded side exposed, and to have deployed when
within seconds' distance of attack? And the Confederates
making speeches while he did it? 'This is the way battles are

---

[1] Lenschau, in his review of Professor Woodhouse's book (*Phil. Woch.* 1934,
p. 494) half sees this difficulty; but in general he supports him.
It may be observed that for heavy armed men, a rapid march such as that of the
Confederate left wing would cover perhaps 100 yards in a minute. The Lacedaemonians advanced more slowly, and started later. If then the distance between the two
armies was but five hundred yards, it would take at least four minutes for them to
meet, more likely five; the time, that is, to be reckoned in minutes rather than in
seconds. Herodotus' account of the charge at Marathon has its modern parallels.

fought on paper,' writes Professor Woodhouse (justly enough) of Henderson's account of this manœuvre.

With this simple and last observation the frail structure of Professor Woodhouse's criticism of Thucydides collapses. It is based partly on an insufficient study of the locality in relation to the problems involved, partly on a misunderstanding of what Thucydides says and on discoveries (as that Agis' purpose in retreating was to induce the Confederates to come down into the plain) that are already in the narrative he is condemning. And the superstructure is as flimsy as the foundations. It is characteristic of most of such criticisms of ancient writers that they not only rush to the opposite extreme—as here that 'from beginning to end Agis is portrayed as a bungler' by Thucydides (which is in fact very far from the truth), whereas in reality he was one of the ablest commanders that Greece produced, and on this occasion acted 'from first to last with unfaltering energy and rare exclusiveness of purpose upon a reasoned and clearly conceived plan' (for Professor Woodhouse everything that Agis does is both brilliant and sound, and all that the Confederates have to do is to fall into every trap he lays)—but also that the reconstruction is even more improbable than the original story even as that is misinterpreted. Professor Woodhouse, after accepting the account of the previous campaign in the Argolid (Thuc. v 57–60) which certainly does not look like the work of a resolute commander, reconstructs the Mantineia campaign as follows: Agis, with an army considerably larger than that of the enemy and of vastly superior quality and enjoying all the advantages of single and intelligent command, invaded the territory of Mantineia and pitched camp within a couple of miles of the city. The enemy having occupied a strong position on the slopes of Mount Alesion opposite, he spent two, three, perhaps four days laying waste a land from which almost everything of value had been removed, without attempting an attack on the city itself which lay there undefended before him. The enemy obstinately clung to his position; whereupon Agis made a feint attack with the object of inducing in them such overweening confidence that they will leave it and offer battle, and withdrew rapidly into the Tegeatis, eight or nine miles back and still (according to Professor Woodhouse) in view from Mantineia. The Confederates, hitherto led by 'prudent and sagacious men,' with a 'highly intelligent method of conducting the defence' and occupying a 'perfect' position on Alesion, men who would not 'wantonly throw away even the most trifling advantage of position,' at once comply with Agis' wishes, and offer battle on conditions such that a defeat was 'all but a foregone conclusion.' They do more; they *are* overweeningly confident, so they do not pursue an enemy they so foolishly suppose to be in flight; but move only a mile or so to the west, to a position that differs from their last in one respect and one respect only, that instead of being impregnable, it will lead to certain defeat. More than this even: in 207 B.C. there existed a trench running from near Alesion across the plain to the katavothrai in the west, cut for the purpose of drainage, sufficiently wide and deep for Philopoimen in that year to use it for defence against Machanidas and post his men behind it;[1] Professor Woodhouse thinks this was probably in existence in the fifth century; so the Confederates make use of it, but to place their army *in front* of it, so as to hinder a retreat and make not only defeat but destruction certain.[2] They do all this quite openly, neither intending nor achieving any surprise.

Agis was equally open. Next morning his army returned to the Mantiniké, through the extensive forest, from which it emerged, marching in column, quite close to the enemy, and deployed to the left, quickly but tranquilly, to within a few hundred yards of the enemy, who looked on as tranquilly. But Agis, unlike the opposing generals, had dark designs in his heart. His intelligence service was such that he knew already not only that the Mantineians and their immediate allies would form the right wing of the enemy, the Argives and their allies the centre, and the Athenians and their cavalry the left, but the numbers of each unit and

---

[1]See above, p. 138.

[2]It is owing to Thucydides' 'failure to notice the two main topographical features of the area of manœuvre,' the Pelagos Wood and this trench, that Professor Woodhouse convicts him of 'possessing no eye for country, no instinct for the decisive elements of a terrain'; yet the extent and density and therefore the importance of the one, and the very existence of the other, are alike uncertain; and neither may have had anything to do with the battle.

therefore the length of line they would severally occupy; and that the 1,000 picked Argive troops would be next the Mantineians, the rest of the Argives to their left. He knew also the relative quality of all the troops opposing him as accurately as Professor Woodhouse, that the 1000 Argives would be the best,[1] next the Mantineians, and the rest of the Argives, the Cleoneans and Orneatae the worst—mere untrained militia. He had devised a well-thought-out scheme. Other generals have been known to attack the weakest point in the opposing line with their own best troops, hoping by a quick victory there to decide the whole battle, and for that taking the risk, if the numbers and general quality of the two armies are equal, of exposing their own weak points to the best troops of the enemy; also to weaken or withdraw a line a short way to encourage an enemy attack. But Agis was cleverer than that,[2] even though with a larger and much better trained force he had no need to take any risk: he would not only attack the Argive militia with his own Spartans, but oppose to the 1,000 picked troops not a relatively weak regiment, not a thin line, but nothing at all; he would order his left wing to march further to the left to oppose the Mantineians, so as to make a gap in his line into which the thousand, the best trained troops of the enemy, would inevitably rush, and marching straight through it, look in vain for an enemy, waving their swords in the air and hitting *nothing*; a complete loss to the Confederate side. Once the Mantineians had been induced to outflank the left wing and the thousand to charge into the gap, 'the Confederates were tactically defeated before ever a blow was struck; the subsequent struggle becoming simply the unfolding of a series of events, a sort of crescendo of surprises, that lay implicit in this its first element, as flower and fruit lie hidden in the germ.'

[1] Actually there is no evidence of the quality of these picked troops except that of this battle, which does not flatter them. They had had a longer and more intensive training than the rest of the Argives, but that is all. The Athenians, including their commanders, were by far the most experienced troops in the Confederate army.

[2] Professor Woodhouse makes great play with the fact that Agis' battle-order had been pre-determined by him, with 'careful and minute precision,' and the order of march that morning arranged with this object in view. Of course; who ever doubted it? Certainly not Thucydides, who gives every credit to Agis (Ἄγιδος ἕκαστα ἐξηγουμένου, 66. 2).

True, there was a slight risk: the thousand might wheel
to the left and attack the left flank of the Spartan regiments
of the centre, though these, with their shield side towards the
Argives, 'were reasonably safeguarded.'[1] But Agis could
guard against that, nothing easier: he could make another
gap in his line. He had ordered the commanders of the two
regiments on the right of the Spartan centre to halt when the
rest advanced, move over behind the advancing troops to the
left of the centre and be ready either to prevent the thousand
attacking the centre's left, or crush them if they marched
straight through. The new gap thus made in the Lacedaemonian line would be filled by the centre's natural movement
to the right as they advanced, and by the right wing (far
outflanking the Confederate left) closing in. All this in the
seconds which elapsed before the opposing forces engaged!
The movement which in Thucydides is 'a physical impossibility' becomes in Professor Woodhouse 'well within the
competence' of the two regiments, though it is nothing but
an elaboration of Thucydides' own account.[2] In the former,
even as misunderstood, Agis had at least the excuse that his
order to the polemarchs was to meet a great and sudden
danger on his other wing; in Professor Woodhouse it was
carefully thought out by a subtle brain—in fact 'the wild freak

[1] Even if the thousand had wheeled round and attacked the Spartan line, which
was about eight deep, in flank and rear? They would at least, one would suppose,
have checked the Spartan advance. But Professor Woodhouse is not consistent here;
he admits that the 'daring tactics of the Spartan king grazed the very edge of
disaster,' and that, if the Argives had so attacked, he was 'in a position truly
desperate,' 'for some sickening moments' (owing to the insubordination of the
polemarchs) 'the king stood on the brink of a hideous abyss of national disaster and
personal ruin.' Yet it is wrong to suggest any element of luck in his victory.

[2] He has not envisaged the movement. True, on his theory, the two regiments
are saved about a quarter of the distance they would have had to cover according to
Thucydides; but the manœuvre would have been more complex: in Thucydides,
to turn left, and march in column towards the gap, then turn right and face the
gap in line; in Professor Woodhouse, to turn left and march in column, and then
to deploy into line to the left, to be able to attack the advancing Argives. This move
would have taken at least as long as the other.

If he had been content to suggest that Agis' order to the polemarchs was given
in the conditions described by Thucydides, but with just this modification, that
they were meant to take the Argives in flank or prevent a flank attack on the
Spartan centre, there would be little to quarrel with; though it would have remained
but a guess, and it would have been important to add that Thucydides, had he
heard of the order in this form, would have at once understood it. For Professor
Woodhouse himself quotes from Thucydides both a sentence on the value of such
surprise (which is worth all the long quotation from Clausewitz), and an instance
of its successful application, by Demosthenes at Olpai (v 9. 8; iii 107 ff.).

of a lunatic,' becomes that much more dangerous thing, a madman's careful and calculated cunning.

And the insubordination of the polemarchs? In Thucydides they disobey a sudden order in the middle of an advance; according to Professor Woodhouse one given before the battle, part of a scheme that must have been communicated to all the higher officers. What becomes of Spartan discipline? How would the lower ranks be likely to behave, if officers commanding regiments could be so deliberately insubordinate? Professor Woodhouse suggests that the two men were political and personal enemies of Agis. Very likely; but how much more natural becomes their conduct, if they received an order altogether unexpected, certainly risky (even if Agis was right to take the risk), when already on the march and nearing the enemy, if they hesitated for a moment, suspecting some malign motive in the king, perhaps each waiting for the other to begin, and it was at once too late to transmit the orders down the line. It may even actually have been too late when the order reached them; we cannot be certain that the verdict given against them at Sparta was strictly just.

Professor Woodhouse allows himself a last fling. The Argive thousand were not only induced to enter the gap in the line and so render themselves harmless, but were carefully shepherded to a part of the field where they would also be least harmed—because 'recruited from the wealthier families of Argos, the men in the ranks of the thousand were, to say the least, no convinced democrats; so that it is not surprising to find them, only six months later, intriguing with the Spartans for the subversion of the discredited Argeian democracy'; and the wizard Agis foresaw all this, and arranged that they should be handled as gently as possible.[1] 'We are as good as told in so many words [by Thucydides], that in the debâcle the Argeian select corps was dealt with tenderly, whereas the Mantineians having sown the wind were compelled to reap the whirlwind. Diodoros also has preserved a morsel of evidence to the same

[1]This is of course inconsistent with the view that the two polemarchs had been ordered across for the express purpose of crushing these Argives; as pointed out by Cary, *C.R.* 1933, p. 240.

effect,[1] in his account of the advice proffered to Agis by a
certain Pharax . . .—not to drive the vanquished Argeians to
desperation, but to open for them a way of honourable withdrawal from the field.' All that Thucydides says is that the
Mantineian loss was heavy, the Argive light; all that Diodoros
gives is a foolish little story, so typical of the *civilian*
Ephoros, of advice not to waste lives in attacking desperate
men. For Professor Woodhouse this is 'clear and positive
tradition,' that the Argives were purposely allowed to escape.
It is besides by no means to be taken for granted that the
select Argive thousand were an aristocratic corps; they were
a standing force, specially trained—but as likely for the
defence of the democracy as for anything else. Thucydides
does not tell us it was they who upset the constitution and
intrigued with Sparta six months later. Aristotle indeed says
that the γνώριμοι had won glory at Mantineia;[2] but this is
just as likely to have occurred in the fighting of the main
Argive force, if they resisted valiantly when most of their
fellows fled.

Professor Woodhouse's attack on Thucydides' narrative
fails. It fails because he misunderstands that narrative in
general and in detail, because for difficulties, both real and
imaginary, he seeks not for a simple but an involved solution, and because his own reconstruction entirely fails to
work. Besides, once we desert Thucydides, it is so fatally
easy to make up a different story. For example: 'It is clear, if
we are not bemused by a superstitious reverence for every
word in Thucydides,[3] that there must have been in authority
on the Confederate side a man who combined in a rare degree
a cool head and a daring spirit. We may guess with confidence that this was Nikostratos the Athenian.[4] He knew, none
better, what a desperate task had been entrusted to the
army. They had just been rescued from an impossible

[1]xii 79.
[2]*Pol.* v 3. 5 (1304 *a*, 25). But he can use οἱ γνώριμοι simply of hoplites, as in
c. 2. 8 (1303 *a*, 8); so he may mean the select thousand; and Plutarch (*Alkib.* 15)
says it was οἱ χίλιοι who overthrew the democracy.
[3]Or, *wenn wir Thukydides zu lesen verstehen*: see below p. 157, *ad fin.*
[4]Nikostratos had in fact proved his coolness and daring, as well as a great intelligence, by his conduct at Kerkyra (Thuc. iii 75–8). He had had one severe defeat,
due to a too intrepid spirit (iv 129; cf. also iv 53–4). No one would suppose this
from Professor Woodhouse's narrative.

position in the Argolid by a timely truce; but the politicians, with a fatal self-confidence, had at once denounced that, and ordered the army into the field once more against the same greatly superior forces of the enemy. By a rapid move he secured Orchomenos, and so was free from immediate danger in the rear. But the formidable northern allies of Sparta would soon be in the field, and meanwhile he must face the Lacedaemonian army already his equal in numbers and probably his superior in quality. He must endeavour to engage and defeat the latter before the reinforcements arrived from the north. His plan was brilliant: he sent the Elean forces away in the direction of home, as a ruse to mislead the Spartans, with orders to go sufficiently far for the ruse to succeed but to return to the plain—to the Mantiniké or the Tegeatis as circumstances later dictated— to take the enemy by surprise. (Thucydides' account, that the Eleans went off in anger after a quarrel, is a poor attempt to disguise his utter failure to understand this move.)[1] Meanwhile, with his weakened forces, he must hold out in a defensive position; which he chose well, and stayed there while the enemy fruitlessly ravaged the fields. Agis attempted or feigned to attempt an attack, but the position was too strong, and he returned nearer to his base at Tegea. But news had now come that the northern allies of Sparta were on the move, and might be expected very soon. The Confederates would be caught again between two forces. Nikostratos moved down to the plain in pursuit of the Lacedaemonians, trusting the Eleans, after indeed a difficult march, to arrive in time, and hoping still for further help from Athens. So well planned were his movements that he almost caught the Lacedaemonians unprepared for battle; only the excellence of their discipline saved them. In the battle itself, his daring and resource were equally conspicuous. For the Eleans were not yet in sight, and he was now dangerously outnumbered. He risked—he had to take a risk —thinning his line in order to send the Mantineians far out to the right to attack the enemy's left in flank. The manœuvre succeeded. To prevent his own attack being held up by this

[1] Or, *wer Thukydides nicht so versteht, der hat seines Geistes nicht einen Hauch verspürt;* see below, p. 158, *init.*

move, Agis had to order his left wing out to face the Mantineians, and thus made a gap in his line. Into this gap,
Nikostratos ordered the select Argive corps to charge and
take the Spartan centre in flank. But, as has so often happened in battles, the triumphant Argives turned to the easier
and, as it must have seemed, more decisive task of helping
the Mantineians destroy the left wing of the Lacedaemonians.
This allowed Agis (to whose coolness at the moment also a
tribute must be given) to use the full force of his centre and
right against the remaining Confederate forces, now outnumbered by nearly two to one. They fought well,[1] but the balance
was too heavily weighed against them. The centre gave, and
the Athenians on the left found themselves surrounded on
three sides, in a position from which only the small but
gallant cavalry force saved them; Nikostratos himself fell,
bravely fighting, and with him his colleague Laches. Even so,
the Spartans, though masters of the field, could not follow up
their victory; resistance had been too strong (for the Thucydidean statement that they willingly relinquished victory
when it was in their grasp should deceive no one). The
great anti-Spartan alliance was still in being, and with the
arrival, too late for the day of battle, of the Eleans and Athenian reinforcements, the army was not broken. But the vola-
tile politicians of Argos, too confident a fortnight before,
were now too fearful; and allowed themselves to be jockeyed
out of power and a peace to be made with Sparta.' And so on.
It is a good parlour game; but it is not to be taken seriously,
and does not affect the authority of Thucydides.[2]

Professor Woodhouse will doubtless seize on certain

[1]It is characteristic of Professor Woodhouse that he accepts without question the
one statement in Thucydides which should perhaps be used with caution: that the
Confederate centre gave way at once before the Spartan attack. It is the rarest of
things for men to be fair to allies in defeat; and though Thucydides was prepared
for bias, he may not here have allowed sufficiently for it. Even a fair-minded and
level-headed Athenian in the ranks at Mantineia may well have thought the centre
gave way all too easily, when he found himself so desperately fighting with the
enemy on three sides of him; and the victorious Mantineians were probably in no
mood to allow for the much harder task set the Argives and Cleonaeans.

[2]Cf. the wise words of Kromayer on the Spartan army at this time (*Klio* iii, 192,
n. 5): 'wir wissen von der Heeresverfassung Spartas im Jahre 418 nichts, als was in
Thukydides steht. Hier durch Conjecturen oder Verwerfung der thukydideischen
Nachrichten eine Uebereinstimmung mit den späteren Perioden herstellen zu
wollen, heisst den Ast absägen, auf dem man sitzt.' So also E. Ufer in Kromayer u.
Veith, *Schlachtfelder* iv, p. 108–9 (on Plataia).

suggestions in this paper (as that the Confederates made use of a night march and so surprised the Lacedaemonians), and point out that this is not in Thucydides, and must not be used by me who defend his authority. But Thucydides asserts, or implies, a surprise, and therefore must have had *in his own mind* the thought that the confederate advance was covered by something—the wood, or high ground, or darkness. And that there are defects, serious defects, in his narrative of Mantineia, as throughout his history, no one would deny. The chief of these is, as Professor Woodhouse points out, the paucity of topographical information. Another is that we are told very little of plans on the Confederate side, nothing for instance of the effect of the expected arrival of Sparta's northern allies, nor of any outposts on the hills to watch the enemy; and still less of the political situation in Athens, what caused them to send such a small force originally, and only small reinforcements.[1] But Kromayer's judgement of Caesar and Polybius is, to say the least, as true of Thucydides: 'Irrtümer und Entstellungen mag man bei Cäsar und Polybios finden, logische und militarische Torheiten und Unmöglichkeiten wie bei den anderen genannten [Livy and Plutarch] wird man vergebens suchen. Wo die moderne Kritik sie entdeckt zu haben glaubt, liegt der Fehler bei ihr.' We must, moreover, remember two characteristics of Thucydides. First, that he does not let us into the secret of his sources: he never tells us of what incidents he was an eye-witness or what speeches he had himself heard, nor what battlefields he afterwards visited; nor the number and quality of his informants. We are in his hands, as we are not in those of the more candid Herodotus. With the latter, we are sometimes (not always) entitled and able to suggest a probable reconstruction, not only because he so obviously knows little of (for example) military affairs, but because he lets us see behind his own narrative. It is quite different with Thucydides; fortunate indeed it is that reconstruction is not there necessary. Secondly, Thucydides will not invent; he will say

---

[1] See Henderson, *Peloponnesian War*, 332–4. Perhaps keeping a large force at home as a check to the Boeotians?

We are not told either why the Spartans, hurrying to the aid of Tegea, go by the longer route by Orestheion. It may have been the quicker for an army, as well as ensuring an earlier contact with the Arcadian allies.

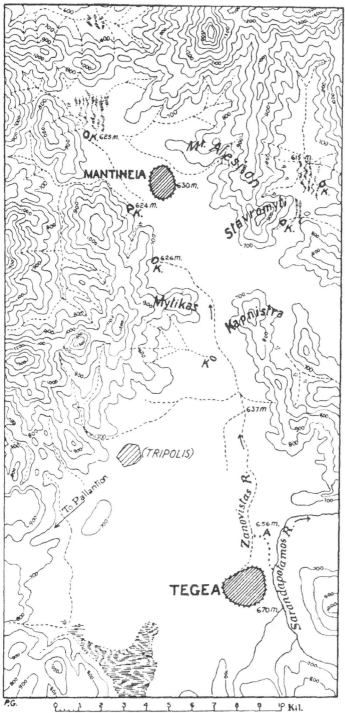

A = *Possible line of channel from the Sarandapolamos R. to the
Zanovistas R., (Fougères).*   **K.** = *Katavothres*

only what he knows or thinks he knows on reliable information. He had clearly never seen the site of the battle of Mantineia; he had heard, perhaps often, of the difficulties over the water which had caused enmity between the two neighbour cities, but did not know their exact nature. He had not got good information about the Confederate commanders' plans. He is therefore vague; for he will not invent details,[1] will not guess how things 'must have been' according to his own judgement. Sometimes we know things which he did not, for an obvious example we know the site of a battle, and can so far supplement his narrative; sometimes we can correct a mistake. But there are no absurdities to remove; and where we have no extra knowledge, it is idle to guess. And in this case Thucydides has been careful not only not to invent, but to indicate that his information was incomplete: he expresses doubts on some points; he will not give the numbers of the combatants, because he could not trust what he had been told; and in his summary of the whole affair he shows his usual care—καὶ ἡ μὲν μάχη τοιαύτη κ α ὶ ὅτι ἐγγύτατα τούτων ἐγένετο. There is no pretence that the narrative is in all respects complete.

There is a curious similarity in some details between the battles of Mantineia and Plataia: in both there is insubordination by Spartan officers, in both manœuvring of troops which results not in improvement but in great danger; in both the ultimate victory is unreservedly attributed to the steadiness of the Lacedaemonian hoplites. The narratives of both have received a similar treatment at the hands of Professor Woodhouse—misguided criticism and an unsuccessful, nay fantastic reconstruction. The criticism in each case is based initially on a profound, a fundamental error: that the accounts of both Herodotus and Thucydides are 'deeply tinged by Athenian malice.' Herodotus indeed can give a perhaps malicious (but not envious) story; but it does not affect his judgement. Thucydides doubtless heard malicious stories, which he suppresses; his judgement too is unaffected. But some people are born colour-blind; and they can never be made to see.

[1] Contrast Polybios, who sometimes lands us into greater difficulties than ever Thucydides does, by giving topographical details, learnt from others, of places he had not seen: e.g., of the Kynoskephalai campaign, xviii 12.

IX

THE SPEECHES IN THUCYDIDES

THERE is this apparent advantage in the dogmatic announcement that Thucydides' speeches are free inventions, that it saves further thought; they may be ignored by the historian of the Peloponnesian war, as those of Dionysios or Livy are in early Roman history. Yet a moment's reflexion will show that the economy is more apparent than real. For those historians who have been most dogmatic in announcing that the speeches are inventions, have yet made full use of them: Beloch, Schwartz, Wilamowitz; not an uncritical use, but their own pictures both of the characters of certain of the speakers, as Kleon, Nikias, Alkibiades, and of the arguments used on such occasions, are in fact inspired by these speeches, as Mommsen's picture of Coriolanus, for example, is not inspired by the speech Dionysios puts into his mouth.[1] We are therefore in practice left with a theory in the air, devoid of application and therefore of meaning.

This has not at all hindered its dogmatic assertion; in fact, it has helped it—for had its logical consequences been properly drawn, historians would probably have been a little more careful in making it. It is certainly the prevailing view, expressed timidly by some, boldly by others, that the speeches do not in any sense give, even approximately, the content of those actually spoken; though there are some who have taken a more reasoned view, as Busolt did, and Blass. Let us examine in some detail the arguments recently put forward by one of the most notable exponents of the 'free invention' theory: they are clearly expressed and, I think, expose more than one fallacy. In a review of Taeger's

[1]For a recent example, see Laistner's *History of the Greek World from 479–323 B.C.*; who uses phrases such as 'the speech put in Perikles' mouth' on several occasions (e.g., pp. 77. 4, 85. 1, 124–5), and so presumably rejects their authenticity, yet uses them as historical on pp. 74, 128, and elsewhere. Similarly it is not unusual for a scholar, fearful of seeming to doubt that the *Iliad* must be separated from the *Odyssey* by at least a century (and a restless century), and that parts of each are much younger than the rest, because this would be 'unscientific,' yet cheerfully to use all of both poems as evidence for a single culture. For a recent example of this see Erdmann's *Die Ehe im alten Griechenland* (Munich, 1934), pp. 2–11.

Thukydides, who had said that the speeches were not expressions of Thucydides' own ideas, but 'treue Wiedergabe fremder Gedanken,' Schwartz writes as follows:[1] 'Damit setzt sich der Verfasser zunächst in Widerspruch zu dem Urteil des gesamten Altertums, das es für eine unwürdige Unterschätzung von Thukydides' historiographische Kunst gehalten haben würde, wollte man in ihnen nicht seine eigenen Erzeugnisse, sondern mehr oder minder getreue Abklatsche der wirklich gehaltenen Reden sehen. Er setzt sich ferner in Widerspruch zu Thukydides selbst. In der berühmten, immer wieder missverstandenen Stelle i 22. 1 ist zunächst auf den Potentialis, dann auf τά δέοντα, "das was die Situation verlangte," das nötige Gewicht zu legen; daraus allein geht schon hervor, dass Thukydides an nichts weniger dachte als daran, durch authentische Wiedergabe der wirklich gehaltenen Reden genau den Stand der "Weltanschauung" zu fixieren, auf dem die Redenden in dem Moment, wo sie in seiner Darstellung auftreten, angelangt sind. . . . Und dann die entscheidenden Worte ἐχομένωι ὅτι ἐγγύτατα τῆς ξυμπάσης γνώμης τῶν ἀληθῶς λεχθέντων: ἡ ξύμπασα γνώμη heisst nicht "der Gesamtsinn," sondern "die Willensrichtung im ganzen," der praktische Zweck der Rede, und τὰ ἀληθῶς λεχθέντα meint nicht den authentischen Wortlaut, sondern dass die Redner nur in solchen Situationen auftreten sollten, in denen sie wirklich gesprochen hatten. Auch dies Program zielt, wie das meiste in i 26–22, gegen Herodot, der in einer Rede des Korinthers Sokles die Geschichte der Kypseliden einlegt oder die Athener und Tegeaten sich mit Anführung von "neuen und alten Taten" um die Ehrenstellung auf dem linken Flügel streiten lässt und was dergleichen mehr ist. Es versteht sich von selbst, dass Thukydides sowohl "den Gesamtzweck" als die Tatsache, dass eine Rede gehalten war, in weitestem Sinne verstand: dass die attische Gesandtschaft, die in Sparta, ohne dazu beauftragt zu sein, die attische Politik verteidigt, eine Fiktion ist, sagt Thukydides für den, der ihn zu lesen versteht, deutlich genug, und wer in dem Epitaphios und der letzten Periklesrede statt der γνώμη des historischen Perikles nicht den Perikles und das

[1]*Gnomon*, ii (1926), 65–82.

perikleische Athen erkennt, wie sie Thukydides nach dem letzten Zusammenbruch erschienen, der hat seines Geistes nicht einen Hauch verspürt,' etc. (pp. 79–80).

Consider first what exactly is the effect of this view. We may believe, in most cases, that the debates referred to actually took place, and that the general tendency of the speeches, their practical aims, were as Thucydides records: we may believe, for example, that the Corinthians urged on the war and that Archidamos was for delay; that a debate took place in Athens over the fate of Mytilene and that Kleon was for exemplary punishment, others against it; that Alkibiades was urgent for the Sicilian expedition, Nikias against it; and so on. Even within these limits we must not be simpletons: we must understand of course that when Thucydides says that Athenian delegates were at Sparta on other business and requested permission to address the assembly on the question of war and peace, he is saying quite plainly that there were no Athenians there and that no Athenian speech was made. τῶν δὲ Ἀθηναίων ἔτυχε γὰρ πρεσβεία πρότερον ἐν τῇ Λακεδαίμονι περὶ ἄλλων παροῦσα . . . προσελθόντες οὖν τοῖς Λακεδαιμονίοις ἔφασαν βούλεσθαι καὶ αὐτοὶ ἐς τὸ πλῆθος αὐτῶν εἰπεῖν, εἴ τι μὴ ἀποκωλύοι. οἱ δὲ ἐκέλευον τε παριέναι, καὶ παρελθόντες οἱ Ἀθηναῖοι ἔλεγον τοιάδε (and 87. 5, after the conference is ended, καὶ οἱ μὲν ἀπεχώρησαν ἐπ' οἴκου διαπραξάμενοι ταῦτα, καὶ οἱ Ἀθηναίων πρέσβεις ὕστερον ἐφ' ἅπερ ἦλθον χρηματίσαντες). That means, to the select who can read Thucydides: 'there were no Athenian delegates there, so I am going to give in the form of a speech by an Athenian delegate the best sort of argument that might have been used to dissuade the Spartans from going to war.'[1] This common-sense allowance made, we may believe in general that the debates Thucydides refers to took place; but beyond that the speeches are pure invention. There was a debate about Mytilene, but we do not know more about the speeches made on the second day

[1] It may surprise some, but modern historians sometimes express themselves in the same way. At the Conference in London to discuss the Hoover plan on July 17, 1931, 'The Greek view was expounded to the experts, in the first place, by M. Venizelos, who happened to be in England when the Conference opened' (*Survey of International Affairs*, 1931, p. 350, n. 1). This clearly means that Venizelos was still in Greece, and did not address the conference.

than about those of the first (iii 36. 2); and Thucydides gives his idea not of the arguments actually used, even in the most general way (not even, that is to say, 'I will sum up all the arguments used by all the advocates for extreme measures in one speech which I give to their leader'), but of the general principles, which might have or ought to have guided the voting on either side. Such speeches *may* be in character, may preserve the ἦθος of a Kleon or an Alkibiades, as speeches in Sophocles and Euripides do; but they are not more historical than those. That is what many later historians did—invented speeches to give themselves a chance of fine writing, as Dionysios when he attributes a speech to Coriolanus which is no more historical than Shakespeare's. Thucydides' speeches may indeed be judged to be better than Dionysios', more true to life, less rhetorical, but only in the sense that Euripides' speeches are better than Seneca's in *his* tragedies, Shakespeare's than fustian; they are not historically truer (except, I suppose, in so far as Thucydides being a contemporary of the events he narrates will give a truer sort of speech). Moreover, this is both how ancient critics understood the matter and how Thucydides himself describes it. Take Thucydides' own words first.

There is one phrase which at first sign seems to support Schwartz' view—ὡς ἂν ἐδόκουν μοι[1], contrasted with the οὐδ' ὡς ἐμοί ἐδόκει just below where Thucydides is describing his method of relating events: the speeches are given as I thought, the events are not, but by a strict canon of accuracy. That, however, he was not intending thus directly and bluntly, without more ado, to contrast his methods in dealing with speeches and with actions, is shown partly by the different shade of emphasis in the two phrases ('not as *I* thought'—he is here thinking not of his own practice in recording speeches, but of others' practice in recording events), partly by the rest of the sentence. According to Schwartz, ἡ ξύμπασα γνώμη means not 'the general sense,' but 'the practical aim,'[2] and τὰ ἀληθῶς λεχθέντα not 'what was actually said,' but that the speakers will only be introduced on such occasions as those on which they did speak;

---

[1] μοι CG, Dion. Hal.: ἐμοί ABEFM (acc. to Hude).
[2] What was the 'practical aim' of the Funeral Speech?

and this only 'in the widest sense.' That is, we may believe that Kleon intervened in the Mytilenean debate; and Thucydides was not so clumsy as to make Alkibiades a leading speaker in 431. Not more than that. But how can τὰ ἀληθῶς λεχθέντα mean anything except 'what was actually said,' just as in the phrase τὴν ἀκρίβειαν αὐτὴν τῶν λεχθέν-των, which he had written immediately before? and if the whole phrase means no more than 'the practical aim of speeches delivered' (in the widest sense, including, as in the case of the Athenians at Sparta, speeches not delivered), what is the meaning of ἐχομένῳ ὅτι ἐγγύτατα? Where was the difficulty? There was no difficulty before 425 in knowing what speeches had been delivered, and very little afterwards. To what must he 'keep as closely as possible,' if not to the real content of what was said? Dionysios had no such difficulty. The natural, and therefore the proper, translation of the whole sentence is: 'the speeches have been composed as I thought the speakers would express what they had to express (not, 'the ideal arguments') on the several occasions, by keeping as close as possible to the general sense of what was actually said.' Only thus do we give any meaning to words which imply that Thucydides was meeting with difficulties, and did his best to get over them.

But this is to go against the unanimous verdict of antiquity. Aristotle and Plutarch, when they cite the very few fragments of Perikles' oratory that had been preserved, do not think of quoting from his speeches in Thucydides; and Dionysios throughout discusses the speeches as Thucydides' own compositions. This is true; but it is because they are all thinking not of historical content, but of literary style; and no one has ever doubted that the style, the literary art of the speeches is Thucydides' own.[1] Dionysios had a very poor idea of the duty of a historian, as witness his criticism of Thucydides for choosing so depressing a theme as the Peloponnesian war for his subject; and that he should misunderstand, in everything, Thucydides' historical methods is only what we should expect. To say that a

[1] It is curious that Plutarch should add to the few extant phrases of Perikles, 'and some decrees' (*Per.* 8, 5); for the wording of the decrees was certainly not characteristic of his oratorical style. It can only be a passing pedantry, because they were introduced by the words Περικλῆς εἶπε.

modern view of the speeches contradicts that of Dionysios detracts nothing from its value. But he was, in some ways, a good, or at least a shrewd, literary critic; and he is in reality only thinking of Thucydides as a literary artist.[1] Every historian of merit can be considered from two quite different aspects, as artist and as observer of events or investigator into evidence (that is, as scientist). As observer and investigator he may have one value, as artist, in a history of literature, he has another. Dionysios is thinking only of Thucydides' place in the world of letters (in the narrowest sense), and naturally considers the speeches from that point of view, as specimens of Thucydides' style. That does not prevent us from considering them from the other point of view as well, as documents. Dionysios equally treats Thucydides' description of a battle or of the Corcyrean sedition as specimens of style; and indeed would not have much minded if that too had all been made up, invented by the historian, written ὡς αὐτῷ ἐδόκει, with just the proviso that the battle and the sedition had taken place and had so resulted. We do not believe that; we do not believe that the account of Mantineia is a set-piece, a picture of how Thucydides thought a pitched battle ought to have been fought. And we are not obliged to follow Dionysios' opinion about the speeches either. Never can there have been two men, both professed historians, with such different theories of the way to write history than Thucydides and Dionysios; and if Thucydides could have anticipated the latter's criticism of him as a historian, and known how typical it was to be of his age, he would have gone up to Herodotus and apologized for suggesting that he too did not have one desire, and one desire only, to write 'wie es eigentlich geschehen ist.'[2]

[1] So are those moderns who have objected to some speeches as upsetting the balance of the composition; see, for example, Schwartz (*Das Geschichtswerk des Thukydides*, 102 ff.) and Adcock (*C.A.H.* v, 482–3) on the Athenian speech at Sparta. It is curious that it should be just this speech that should be regarded as inartistic, and that some should think the whole episode a fiction. Was Thucydides so bad an artist? Not according to Schwartz, who thinks the arrangement of the speeches at this conference so bad that it is due not to Thucydides himself, but to the editor. Such a view needs no answer; and even on the 'free invention' basis, it has been sufficiently answered by Pohlenz, *Göttingische Nachrichten*, 1919, 95 ff., and by Deffner, *Die Rede bei Herodot*, 97.

[2] Schwartz himself wrote as follows about Dionysios in 1903 (Pauly-Wissowa, v, p. 936): 'Alles in allem ist die römische Archäologie ein genauer Kommentar zu seinem theoretischen Ausführungen über Historiographie, auch darin, dass sie

M

How little these later writers were concerned with content, how exclusively they devoted their attention to style and arrangement, can be seen from their treatment of the orators. They take perfunctory note of the occasion of a speech, or of the law involved; beyond that they are not interested in the historical and legal issues. There were a few antiquarians left who were interested, whose comments have been scrappily preserved in the *lexica*; there were no historians. That is why almost all the documents, the νόμοι and ψηφίσματα, μαρτυρίαι and προκλήσεις, are missing from our manuscripts (all of them from some manuscripts, most of them from all)—even where it is difficult to appraise the argument of the speaker without them, even though the skill of the speaker in dealing with the evidence would, one would have thought, have interested the reader and the critic. They are not in the speaker's own words, they do not illustrate his 'style'; so they can be omitted. Dionysios' commentary on the twelfth speech of Isaios illustrates this well: he is only interested in τὰ εἰκότα; though even these cannot be properly appreciated without the evidence. If Thucydides had in fact included verbatim reports of speeches in his history, there would have been a danger that they would not have been preserved—unless they had been of value for the history of oratory.[1]

In the same number of *Gnomon* in which Schwartz' article here referred to appeared, was a review by L. Curtius of Johansen's *Phidias and the Parthenon Sculptures* (pp. 15–28). In the course of this he points out, not only that no one man could have made models for all the sculpture, or even for the whole of one section of it (metopes, frieze or pediments), not only that we can perceive the hands of different artists within each section, even sometimes in the

praktisch die Vermutung bestätigt, welche jedem bei der Lektüre des Briefes an Pompeius sich aufdrängen muss, dass Dionysios von dem, was die antike Historiographie wollte und konnte, auch nicht die ersten Elemente begriffen hat.'

[1] From another point of view one can observe this dominating interest in literary style in a curious example: Plutarch in his life of Demosthenes gives instances, recorded in the superficial biographers of the third century, of the orator's wit; he does not give one from Demosthenes' own speeches (not, for example, the delightful description of Aischines in *F.L.* 314). It was not that he had not read them (as probably he had not read Cicero's); but they were no longer historical documents, not even documents for the speaker's own life; they were only illustrious models of style, and Plutarch had been brought up so to regard them.

frieze on the same slab, and that we know from the Erechtheion building accounts that separate figures were made by
different (and to us otherwise unknown) artists; but also
that even if these sculptors had full-size models before them,
it is the man who translates them into marble who is the
real artist—witness the difference between his work and
that of the copyist of the Roman age. To say that Pheidias
planned the whole is to say very little. 'War er bis in jede
Einzelheit durchgearbeitet, so dass der ihn übersetzende
Gehilfe den Anhalt für jede Form hatte, dann muss durch
den Fries ein jede Figur gleichmässig erfüllender Stil durch-
gehen. Die Entscheidung kann nur gefällt werden, wenn
man sich von der herrschenden Vorstellung frei macht, als
bestünde ein Kunstwerk irgendwie in einer Idee, einem
Gefühl oder einer allgemeinen Anweisung. Ebenso wie ein
Gedicht erst mit seiner gesprochenen oder geschriebenen
Wortfolge da ist und nicht vorher, so ist auch ein Werk der
bildenden Kunst erst mit der präzisen gezeichneten, gemal-
ten oder gemeisselten Einzelform gegeben. Diese bestimmt
das Werk, nicht allgemein "Gewand," sondern jede besondere
Falte mit ihrem Verlauf, ihrer Brechung, ihrer Höhe und
Tiefe, nicht allgemein "Körper," sondern die Einzelfläche
seiner Modellierung. Entweder bestimmte Phidias durch
seine Zeichnung nicht nur die generelle Züge der Kom-
position, sondern auch jede Einzelform der von ihm durch-
gearbeiteten Figuren—und dann können am Fries keine
wesentlichen Stilunterschiede auftauchen, oder solche
tauchen auf und dann kann Phidias nur die leitende Idee
des Frieses gegeben haben, dieser selber aber ist das Werk
einzelner selbstständiger zusammenwirkender Meister,
nicht Gehilfen.' That is both important and, within limits,
true. I say, within limits, because it is not the whole truth
about the Parthenon sculptures and it obscures part of the
truth. For not only is there a unity of design throughout, but
that design, especially in the frieze and the east pediment,
is itself a work of the highest genius (the east pediment is the
only truly successful pedimental sculpture known, the only
instance in which the artist has made the shape of his frame
serve his design instead of dominating it, not used a more or
less conventional design subservient to the frame). It may

be true that 'von Phidias selber ist an den Giebeln nicht ein Fältchen nachzuweisen'; it must be true if the pediment-figures were all sculptured between 438 and 432 and if Pheidias left Athens for good in 438 (which is by no means certain). But the genius shown in the design remains; and as for the different 'styles' observable in the figures, there is a profounder truth in the wise words of Beazley: the frieze is 'so homogeneous throughout that the sculptors must all have worked to a design and followed it closely, and that design not a mere sketch but carried out in considerable detail'; and in general: 'in spite of all differences from one part to another, it is possible to speak of a style of the Parthenon: this style can be recognized in other works as well, but to say that it is nothing more than the Attic style of the third quarter of the fifth century is no explanation: styles of this grandeur do not grow up, they are created by great men: and Pheidias has a better claim to be considered the true begetter of the style than Alcamenes, or Agoracritus, or an unknown.'[1] In fact the more sculptors we must suppose at work, and the better artists they were and the closer together they worked, the greater must have been the influence of the designer, the master; or there would be no unity. The Parthenon is not just the happy result of some first-rate craftsmen and artists, masons and sculptors and painters, working together—a sort of community building.[2]

However, that is by the way. What Curtius says about a work of art in general is true: no verses, no poet; no drawing or painting, no painter. That is why we know scarcely anything of Polygnotos, Apollodoros or Apelles *as artists*, why, as I have said in another essay in this book, it is not only rash but idle to 'reconstruct' the comedies of a Diphilos or a

---

[1] *Camb. Anc. Hist.* v, 438–9.

[2] 'That a single artist controlled the entire creation with the unifying power of a dominating mind and will, is both probable and unprovable' (Rhys Carpenter, *Hesperia*, i, p. 22). It is certain. We must remember that on the Erechtheion not only were the different figures of the frieze allotted to several sculptors, but the work on the columns and walls and ceiling was also so given to numbers of named craftsmen. This does not mean that there was no designer of the whole building and that this designer was not the master-artist. Work on columns and work on the sculpture of the frieze are not, of course, the same thing; but we must be careful in our use of these facts known to us from inscriptions.

Philemon. In that sense, the speeches of Thucydides are his own, not Kleon's, not Alkibiades', not 'the Corinthians'; before he wrote them down, they did not exist. The words make the speeches, and the words are Thucydides'. But when we have said that, we have not said everything. Artists work in different ways, and some of them possess two different values; Canaletto, for example, among painters. He has his place in the history of art for the aesthetic value of his work, his sense of design and composition, of tone and colour, and so forth; but because he chose to make his pictures by painting contemporary Venice (that was his method of getting a satisfactory, pleasing design), he also has a quite different value to the historian—an accidental value so far as his artistic powers are concerned, but none the less real: his pictures are historical documents of architecture. So it is, only even more obviously, with writers: some are, as we say, imaginative writers, others deal with facts, in a scientific manner. That Thucydides is also a great literary artist does not (no one has ever supposed that it does, except in the speeches) detract from his historical value. His account of the retreat from Syracuse is a masterpiece of art; it is his own; it did not exist before he wrote it; but it also has independent value, as a truthful record of events. So when we have stated that his speeches are his own, that Aristotle and Dionysios and Plutarch regarded them as his own, we have stated a truth, but (for the historian) not the whole truth. We have then, and not before, to ask ourselves the question: have they a historical content? are they based on speeches actually delivered, and delivered in the circumstances recorded by the author? And if so, can this historical content be analysed? And we must further remember, that if we answer these questions in the affirmative, we are not, in essentials, contradicting the opinion of antiquity—even where that opinion, as in the case of Dionysios, is of very little value.

Consider first the difference in the record in the two cases of speeches and actions. In both it was difficult to get at the truth (χαλεπὸν τὴν ἀκρίβειαν αὐτὴν τῶν λεχθέντων διαμνημονεῦσαι, and ἐπιπόνως ηὑρίσκετο); but for different reasons. In the case of actions, men did not always tell the same story about the same thing; they were biased, and their memories differed; and no man can see the whole of one action, so that even of those actions at which Thucydides himself was present the record must be supplemented by the memories of others. But the more men he could question, the more complete and the more accurate would be his record—he would learn more details and different aspects of the same details: he was not content with chance information nor with nothing but his own view (οὐδ᾽ ὡς ἐμοὶ ἐδόκει). With the speeches, on the other hand, though all present heard the whole of what was said (including, in some cases, Thucydides himself), yet none would remember more than the general drift of the argument, or perhaps some sentence which stamped itself on the memory;[1] and though it would be an advantage to confirm one man's record by another's, it would not be, as with actions, to learn further details or a different aspect; almost all accounts would be equally defective and defective in the same way. Thucydides had therefore either to confine himself to a brief statement of the general argument used, or to rewrite the speech. And he must rewrite in his own [style. The actual words used it was impossible to recover; and had he attempted to write in the different styles of the several speakers (supposing him to have possessed this mimetic gift), that would have been to falsify the evidence; it would have been to pretend that a speech of Kleon's was reproducing his actual words, or nearly his actual words, when such a thing was impossible. Thucydides will make no such pretence; and his preface and summary to every speech are therefore ἔλεξε τοιάδε, τοιαῦτα μὲν εἶπεν, not τάδε and ταῦτα. When he is recording a treaty, an armistice, in the actual words used which could be found on the inscriptional record, he uses ἥδε and αὕτη, etc. (iv 117. 3, 119. 3; v 17. 2, 20. 1, 22. 3, 24. 2, 46. 5, 48. 1). It is in every way characteristic of Herodotus, who, when he records speeches, is a story-teller rather than a historian, that, whether in the dialogue of a story (as that of Atys and Adrastos) or in the speeches at a political conference, he

---

[1] It is quite *possible*, for example, that ἀνδρῶν ἐπιφανῶν πᾶσα γῆ τάφος was a sentence actually spoken by Perikles.

uses τάδε and ταῦτα, as a story-teller should.[1] Thucydides' τοιάδε, in contrast to Herodotus' τάδε, gives us more, not less confidence in the historical content of his speeches, just as his use of τοιάδε on these occasions and of ἥδε to introduce the terms of a treaty makes it clear that he is not pretending to record the actual words of the speaker.[2]

Before we attempt further analysis of the speeches, it will be as well to refer briefly to certain objective arguments that have been used to prove that they must all be free inventions: I mean arguments of this kind—that the reference to the possibilities of ἐπιτειχισμός in Attica and of revolts of subject states in the speech of the Corinthians at Sparta cannot have been written before 413 when Dekeleia was taken and the allies began to revolt (so that the content of the speech is not only Thucydides' own, but was only written in the light of later events), or that Perikles' speech in book i is a detailed answer to that of the Corinthians which he had not heard. Only a brief reference is necessary, because most of these arguments defeat themselves, and their weakness has been already exposed (see, for example, Adcock in *Cambridge Ancient History*, v, p. 482). As if nobody had ever thought of ἐπιτειχισμός before 413, and the possibility of a revolt of the Athenian allies had not always been present! As if Greek diplomacy was not the most open thing in the world, so that people in Athens would know all about both official and general opinion in

[1]That is, if he uses any pronoun. Of the 250 cases of direct speech in his history he does not use τοιάδε in more than a dozen or so; and that he does not mean anything special by it, he shows by generally writing ταῦτα as its correlative (i 60, iii 145, vii 5, etc.), or by writing both τοιάδε and τάδε in the course of the same dialogue (iii 134, vi 68–9). Only once may the use of τοιάδε be significant, vii 168. 3, to describe the letter the Corcyreans *might* have sent to Xerxes in certain eventualities. Once he has τάδε καὶ λόγου τοιοῦδε ἐχόμενα (after a previous τάδε in the same story) with ταῦτα as its correlative (vii 135–6).

That Herodotus should also always use τάδε when recording inscriptions is natural, but not significant.

[2]Nikias' dispatch from Sicily (vii 11–5), though it was a written document, is reported as δηλοῦσαν τοιάδε; and its style is Thucydidean. This is what we should expect. There is no reason to suppose it was preserved among the state 'archives,' like copies of treaties and laws; and Thucydides only professes to give a report of what was read out to the assembly; he is relying, that is, on men's memories (including, of course, those among Nikias' companions in Sicily whom he interviewed and who might have known the gist of what he wrote). It is on all fours with the speeches.

Corinth and the Peloponnese![1] I will only discuss one of these arguments, which is advanced by Schwartz in the article already referred to; it shows how far a man can be misled in detail by a false general theory. Thucydides says that Hermokrates recommended that the Syracusans should advance with their whole fleet to Tarentum before the Athenians left Kerkyra, and attack them there: either the enemy will be frightened and give up the expedition altogether, or they will be certainly defeated, before ever they reach Sicily. No such proposal was ever made by Hermokrates, in Schwartz' opinion: 'Hermokrates' Gedanke, den Athenern eine Flotte entgegenzuschicken, soll mit dem Bericht über die glückliche Ueberfahrt der attischen Expedition (vi 44) kontrastieren und zeigen, wie leicht es gewesen wäre, sie zu vernichten und welcher Gefahr sie zunächst entging; um so stärker tritt der Leichtsinn des Unternehmens hervor und um so tragischer wirkt nachher die Peripetie.' In fact, if the proposal had been carried out, it would, almost certainly, have resulted in an early and decisive end to the war, but in Athens' favour. Hermokrates of course puts forward the best case he can, with considerable exaggeration: he ignores the time necessary to get a Sicilian fleet ready, during which the Athenians would have arrived off Italy; the Syracusans will have an excellent base in a friendly Tarentum (a by no means certain event: Tarentum did not like the Athenian expedition, but they might not have liked a Syracusan fleet any the better; they certainly did nothing later to help them); the Athenians would be sailing across the open sea and would be in disorder, and they would have only uninhabited coasts to put into (another exaggeration). But what could the Athenians have wished for more than a naval battle off Tarentum? Their scouts (vi 42. 2), if not many another, would have told them of the approach of the Syracusan fleet as it made its way along the coasts of Sicily and Italy; they would have been all ready for it, even if they had not reached Italy before. Their fleet was unimpaired, full of confidence, easily

[1] There is no reason to suppose that Hermokrates could not have heard in Syracuse that Nikias was a reluctant commander (vi 34. 6). How quickly such news got about can be seen from the reluctance of the Spartans to speak too openly in the Athenian ecclesia (iv 22. 3).

the best fleet in the Mediterranean at that time; it, in fact, easily defeated the Syracusans in the first encounters, even after the latter had had plenty of time in which to make their preparations. If the enemy refused to give battle, or broke it off successfully and retired into Tarentum, they could continue their journey along the coast to Rhegion; for they were not dependent for their immediate supplies on regular communications with Athens, but on what they had brought with them (44. 1) and on a friendly reception in some part of Italy and Sicily—the Syracusans, if they were to sail as far as Tarentum being dependent in the same way. Syracuse would have been left to a large extent defenceless; and her influence in Sicily would have disappeared. If anything can be certain about an unfulfilled project, this proposal of Hermokrates would have been fatal to his country, and soon fatal. A stroke of good luck, the very daring of the plan, might just have brought victory, with the odds heavily against it. That is the most that can be said for it. And that this is not only a correct judgement based on the facts that we know, but would have been Thucydides' too, can be seen from his own words in book ii, when he says that the Sicilian expedition was not ill-judged from the military point of view, and that its failure was mainly due to political rivalries at home (65. 11): nothing whatever there about 'der Leichtsinn des Unternehmens'; and political rivalries had not yet affected the efficiency of the Athenian fleet when it first arrived off Italy. Schwartz has completely misunderstood the situation; and, it being what it was, what possible motive could Thucydides have had to put this proposal into Hermokrates' mouth, if it had never in fact been made?

Another argument of a similar kind should be referred to, because it was used by so good a historian as Eduard Meyer,[1] and has recently been supported by August Deffner in his excellent work, *Die Rede bei Herodot and ihre Weiterbildung bei Thukydides*.[2] It is that Perikles' third speech (ii 60–4), giving as it does a justification of his policy, must be Thucydides' own summing-up of the situation and of that policy, because it is inserted 'an einer von Thukydides ganz

---

[1] *Forschungen*, ii, p. 390.
[2] Diss. München, 1933, p. 101.

frei gewählten Stelle'—for the meeting of the ecclesia which
Perikles calls is without any historical importance and
'nichts weiter zu tun hatte als seine Argumente und Ver-
teidigung anzuhören.' What does this exactly mean? Are we
to suppose that no such meeting of the ecclesia took place?
The Athenians had sent an embassy to Sparta to treat for
peace; they were τῇ γνώμῃ ἄποροι καθεστηκότες; attacks
were made on Perikles from all sides. He defeated the
advocates of peace, though not all the attacks on himself; he
revived the spirits of the people; and no more 'defeatist'
embassies were sent to Sparta. It was a signal instance of that
remarkable power of his by which καὶ δεδιότας αὖ ἀλόγως
αὐτοὺς ἀντικαθίστη πάλιν ἐπὶ τὸ θαρσεῖν. There was hardly a
more important assembly throughout the whole war; it is
certainly historical. Dionysios objected to the speech on
other grounds: that Perikles, in the dangerous position in
which he then found himself, ought to have spoken
λόγους ταπεινοὺς καὶ παραιτητικούς, not ἐπιτιμητικούς, and that
the most commonplace writers know that a speaker should
not praise himself before dicasteries and ecclesiae; that is
what Thucydides should have avoided if he was a historian
anxious τὴν ἀλήθειαν μιμεῖσθαι.[1] A truthful historian, in
Dionysios' view, would compose a speech suitable to the
speaker and the occasion; and by 'suitable' he meant a
speech of the most general character suited to any speaker
of the type and any occasion of the type. That is the principle
on which he composed his own speeches in his *Roman History*, and many other historians from the fourth century B.C. onwards did the same. Thucydides had other ideas of his duty.

---

[1] *De Thuc.* 922–8. His criticism of the Melian dialogue is of the same type: so
many of the sentiments attributed to the Athenians are 'unworthy of Athens'—
only Persians and pirates would talk like that (906–15). More to the point is his
objection to the sentence ii 60. 6, in which Perikles *explains* the advantages to the
city of his special virtues; this does look more like a summary by Thucydides
himself (cf. i 138. 3).

I am not clear what Schadewaldt (*Die Geschichtschreibung des Thukydides*, p. 17)
means when he writes: 'vernehmlich durch die Niederlage der athenischen Gesandten
in Kamarina (vi 78–88) wird representativ das Versagen der zurückbleibenden
Feldherrn dargestellt.' That Thucydides invents the otherwise unknown Euphemos
as the Athenian speaker, as he invents the speech, to explain their diplomatic defeat?
Certainly not Nikias, and probably not Lamachos, would have been the most
suitable delegate of the Athenians. And in fact, there was no *Niederlage* of Athens
here: the help of Kamarina was more important, morally and militarily, to Syracuse
than to Athens; and if the latter could secure her neutrality, as she did in effect,
she had got the better in the diplomatic battle.

He heard some of the speeches himself; which, he does not tell us, any more than he tells us at which events of the war he was present or which battlefields he had visited. There is another group of speeches which he either could not have heard (as those of Archidamos and Sthenelaidas at the Spartan assembly, after all foreign delegates had withdrawn) or probably did not hear (as those of the Corinthian and the Athenian delegates at this same conference), but the general content of which he could at once have learned and noted. Between these two groups there is no great difference from our point of view: Thucydides could have written memoranda about them, as about all contemporary events, while his own and other men's memories were fresh. In addition, there are those speeches the general purport of which would soon be known everywhere, even though Thucydides may not have been early in contact with anyone who heard them: for example, the Corinthian speech at the Peloponnesian congress (i 120-4), and the Mytilenean speech at Olympia (iii 9-14). This whole class comprises all speeches in the Athenian assembly up to and including that of the Spartan delegates after their men had been cut off in Sphakteria (iv 17-20),[1] the first debate at Sparta (i 68-86), the Corinthian speech at the allies' congress in Sparta, the Plataean-Peloponnesian negotiations (ii 71-3), of which he might have heard from Athenians and Plataeans who escaped from the town, and the Mytilenean speech, besides the short addresses of Athenian commanders to their men before 424, and the lively little dialogue in Amphilochia (iii 113), which he may have heard himself. After 424 we cannot be sure that he either heard any speech or was in immediate contact with men who had heard any, this being of course particularly true of speeches delivered in Athens. These form a second class of speeches; and to them belong as well the speeches of the Plataeans and the Thebans after the fall of Plataia (iii 53-67) and the speech of Hermokrates at the conference of Gela (iv 58-64), as well as many short

---

[1]We do not of course know of any single speech whether Thucydides heard it himself or no, for he may have been away on a military campaign. He was not a prominent politician, so presumably had had military experience before his strategia in 424—perhaps, as has often been suggested, with Demosthenes in Aitolia and Akarnania; and iv 105. 1 suggests that he had spent some time in Thrace.

speeches, as of Peloponnesian commanders to their troops—
for it is clear that it must have been long before he could
have heard any accurate reports of these. But it is not
sufficient just to leave the problem there. Schwartz points
out that in the speeches everything is generalized, that they
have nothing of the momentary effect of a real speech, as
have the fragments, for example, of Perikles' oratory preserved in men's minds and recorded by Aristotle and others.[1]
This is in general true, though there are phrases and
sentences which may well be accurate records of the spoken
word;[2] but it does not follow that the speeches 'keine, auch
nur annähernde Wiedergabe der wirklich gehaltenen sind.'
On the contrary, this fact, like the purely Thucydidean
literary style, should increase our confidence; for it shows
that he is making no attempt to compose a life-like speech,
as a story-teller, a novelist would do. To take a simple case:
suppose that Thucydides had been present at Delion and,
as a member of Hippokrates' staff, as his A.D.C. (if I may
put it so), had gone round with him and listened to him
addressing the troops (iv 94, ἐπιπαριὼν τὸ στρατόπεδον τῶν
Ἀθηναίων παρεκελεύετό τε καὶ ἔλεγε τοιάδε); and suppose that
he had a good memory, and wished to give a single summary of many short addresses in direct speech but not
pretending to record the actual words: how, from the
point of view of literary style and arrangement, could he
have done it, except in the way he has? What in fact are we
to think of these commanders' speeches? That they did not
address their troops before battle—not even Nikias when
his army was in desperate straits (vii 61–4, and 77)? Or
only that Thucydides took no trouble to find out what was
said, because at least in such cases it was easy to invent? Yet
he recorded small details about some of these addresses
which we must suppose to be true: of Hippokrates, that he
had no time to pass along more than half the line of troops
before the enemy attacked (iv 96. 1); of Nikias that he tried
by raising his voice to reach the ears of every single man
(vii 76). If men could remember such things and inform

[1] *Gnomon*, ii, p. 82.
[2] See above, p. 166, n. 1; and ἐγὼ μὲν ὁ αὐτός εἰμι καὶ οὐκ ἐξίσταμαι· ὑμεῖς δὲ
μεταβάλλετε, and other such sentences, may record the speaker's own words.

Thucydides, they could remember the gist of what was said.

These two speeches, that of Hippokrates and the last of Nikias', are explicitly each a summary of several; so are vii 66–8, delivered by Gylippos and a plurality of Syracusan generals, and ii 87, the Peloponnesian admirals to their men before the second battle against Phormion. An even clearer case is the Plataean speech iii 53–9, for we are given the names of the *two* men who made it. Whether, when we are told οἱ Κορίνθιοι, οἱ ᾿Αθηναῖοι 'spoke as follows,' we are to suppose that only the leader or that every member of the delegation spoke (as is possible, considering the Greek passion for talking, and that Philip of Macedon had to listen to speeches from every member of an embassy of ten), we do not know. In one case, v 61. 2, the former alternative is suggested (ἔλεγον οἱ ᾿Αθηναῖοι ᾿Αλκιβιάδου πρεσβευτοῦ παρόντος); but, from our point of view, it is unimportant whether such impersonal speeches are the summaries of one or of several; for the question of their historical content is not thereby affected. Similarly, it is possible (though I do not think in this case that it is at all necessary to suppose it) that Kleon's speech in the Mytilenean debate contains matter from his first speech of the day before, which is briefly referred to. We must not be misled by our own use of direct speech and inverted commas. For us this can only mean the reporting of the spoken word.[1] Not so in Greek; it is a question of style. Grant that Thucydides made immediate notes of a speech that he had heard, though he had no verbatim report, and that later as full an account of the speech as possible was what he wanted for his history: he must, as we have seen, write in his own style—he must not

---

[1]Yet the method is sometimes adopted by modern historians, even though with a somewhat different aim, as by Mr. Collis in his excellent *Siamese White* (London, 1935). Compare with one another these two sentences from the *Notes* at the end of the book: 'The transcriptions of conversations are taken verbatim from the original, except that in some cases indirect has been turned into direct speech' (the 'original', being the Davenport Papers, the reliability of which is itself dependent on the memory and good faith of the writer); and 'the remarks which I suppose Phaulkon to make to the Barcalong in 1680 on the necessities of the situation are, of course, without direct warrant. But that he formulated about that time such a policy is certain enough' (pp. 307 and 313). Thucydides (I believe) always had some direct warrant; and 'about that time' is less exact than he was; but, with this modification, Mr. Collis' words well illustrate what was meant by ὡς ἂν ἐδόκει μοι τότε τὰ δέοντα μάλιστ' εἰπεῖν. The difference between the ancient and the modern writer is that the modern gives his sources, both for events and for speeches, in every case.

fake the oratory of the speaker; but was he to give it all, several pages of it, in *oratio obliqua*? Even Thucydides, supposing he had himself liked the idea, would have shrunk from the added obscurity.[1] And would it have made any difference to its authenticity if he had? We have in fact some short speeches in oblique oration which are in all other respects similar to others in the direct—the commanders' addresses before the battle of Mantineia (v 69), and additional exhortations by Nikias before the last battle at Syracuse (vii 69. 2–3): are they any more authentic? Similarly, in the narrative of Alkidas' naval expedition across the Aegean to help Mytilene (iii 29–31): Teutiaplos' advice is given as a short speech, the others in oblique oration. Are we to reject the first as unhistorical, and accept the second? It is no use saying that we should accept the advice but reject the speech, for the speech, with the exception of one γνώμη at the end, is nothing but the advice.

Amongst the speeches of our second category (those which Thucydides can neither himself have heard nor had immediately reported to him) are some for which we must suppose a particularly long interval before he could get any particular information of them, and then perhaps at second or third hand: these include the Plataean and Theban speeches before the Spartan judges, Hermokrates' speech at Gela, and the conference at Melos. Only a few Thebans and Spartans could have told him at first hand of the first two, only the Athenian delegates of the last; and a good many years must have elapsed before he could get first-hand information about the Gela conference. This is not true, in the same degree, of the debates in Athens about the Sicilian expedition, nor of those in Syracuse after the expedition had sailed. Very many people had heard them, and Thucydides could have got into touch with some. He succeeded (how, we do not know) in getting other accurate information from Syracuse about the events of 415–3. He could therefore have got information about the debates held there as well. Now there is a considerable difference of tone between those speeches about which he only got information late and as

---

[1] viii 76 gives us quite a long abstract of speech in oratio obliqua; but for this book and its relation to our problem, see below.

likely as not at second or third-hand and all the rest: the former are much more generalized, less actual, less vivid. The two speeches of Hermokrates are easily contrasted; the Theban speech demanding the execution of the Plataeans brings out well the spirit of hatred that had been sharpened by the events of 431, but it leaves a feeling of unreality; and the most generalized of all is that of the Plataeans appealing for their lives. This really might be, if taken by itself, nothing but the historian's own idea of how the most moving appeal should have been made—that is one reason why Dionysios admired it so much. Are we to suppose it is that and nothing more? Thucydides had been at pains to discover and record the names of the two Plataeans who spoke on behalf of their countrymen; is it to be supposed he took no trouble to find out what they said? He must have had just as great difficulty in discovering the name of the obscure Teutiaplos of Elis who, he says, advised Alkidas to attack the Athenians at Mytilene; did he learn only the name and not the advice? Or is the name too an invention, and Teutiaplos' plan and that of the Ionian exiles who wanted Alkidas to capture some city on the Asia Minor coast as a base of operations nothing but Thucydides' own conception of the possibilities of the situation? In that case, what becomes of his credibility as a historian? Are the plans of Demosthenes at Pylos and the opposition to them of Eurymedon and Sophokles (iv 3), or at least those of the three Athenian generals in Sicily (vi 47–9), any more reliable? How Thucydides went to work to get his information, who were the persons he consulted and cross-questioned, and, especially, when, how long after each event, did he consult them—these are things he will not tell us. 'He seeks truth as diligently and relentlessly as a modern antiquary who has no object for concealment or exaggeration. But his aim is a different one. He is not going to provide material for his readers to work upon. He is going to do the whole work himself—to be the one judge of truth, and as such to give his results in artistic and final form, no evidence produced and no source quoted.'[1] But that he was able, in some way, to get obscure and difficult information is proved both

[1]Murray, *Ancient Greek Literature*, p. 187.

by the success of his history as a whole, and by particular instances—for example, he saw and transcribed copies of the ephemeral and, one would suppose, secret treaties between the Spartan commanders and Tissaphernes (viii 18, 37, 58).[1] But it is obvious that some of the information, especially about speeches delivered long before, will have been less adequate than the rest. The difference in tone between what we may call the 'remote' speeches and the others, particularly those which Thucydides probably heard himself—including those of Perikles and Kleon—is marked; but this does not suggest that they are all alike free compositions, but that Thucydides had found especial difficulty in securing accurate information about the former, yet for good reasons particularly wanted to emphasize their importance.[2]

There are no speeches in book viii, only brief summaries; and only the Melian conference and a very large number of brief summaries in what many consider the unfinished part of book v. There are three possible reasons for this (leaving out the fantastic idea that towards the end of his life Thucydides repented of the method of writing which he had followed for so many years): it may be because he composed his speeches (as free compositions) after he had finished a big block of narrative and inserted them in appropriate places (appropriate artistically and, if possible, historically too) and died before he had done this for these sections. It may be that he did not think any of the speeches which he says were delivered significant enough to be given at length, significant, that is, for his purpose, for his picture of the conduct of the war; there are very many occasions throughout his work on which he contents himself with the briefest of summaries of words spoken, even where the actual result of the debate was important, and he himself may have been

[1] It was conjectured by Kirchhoff that Alkibiades was Thucydides' informant. If so, he was, for once, reliable; and he could equally well have informed him of the great debates in Athens about the expedition to Sicily, of the commanders' plans when the expedition arrived, and of his own speech at Sparta.

[2] What these reasons were in the case of the Plataean and Theban speeches has been indicated in an earlier essay (p. 121).

Busolt recognized this difference of tone in the speeches, and particularly mentions the Melian debate in this connexion (*Gr. Gesch.* iii, p. 673, with n. 3). But he does not go into greater detail.

present or been immediately informed (cf. ii 73–4, iii 86, iv 106). Thirdly, it may be that he thought he had not sufficient material, not enough reliable evidence of what was actually said, and as a conscientious historian would not invent.

With regard to book v (from c. 26 on) I think the second reason the correct one. It is difficult to believe that a section of the *History* which includes both the Mantineian and the Melian campaigns is unfinished. It is clear that, even though Thucydides wrote his 'second preface' after 404, he must have been making notes, and very full notes, at the time of the events themselves; the narrative of the Mantineian campaign is as detailed and as finished as that of any episode in the war (and yet it contains no speech), and must have been in the main composed soon after the event (except on the hypothesis that it too is not authentic, but the historian's own conception of how the campaign should have been conducted); and I see no reason to suppose that the whole of book v, from c. 27 to the end was not substantially in the form in which we have it before books vi and vii were completed—that is, we should not suppose it to be a later insertion put in when Thucydides at last realized the series of events from 431 to 404 as forming a single whole, and to be unfinished. Therefore, though the period 421–17 is preeminently one of conference and debate, and many of them —more than twenty—are briefly recorded by Thucydides between chapters 27 and 82 of book v, he did not think any of them, not even Alkibiades' speech at Argos which was the immediate cause of the march into Arcadia (61. 2), of sufficient significance to be worth reporting at length.[1]

[1]On the problem of Thucydides' first conception of the series of events as one, which is generally misunderstood, see my note in *J.H.S.* 50, 1930, pp. 107–8. It largely turns on the interpretation of iv 48. 5, the end of the *stasis* in Corcyra ὅσα γε κατὰ τὸν πόλεμον τόνδε. I see no reason to suppose that this qualifying phrase was written with reference to the renewal of *stasis* in 411; it may well have been written soon after 421, and have meant only to guard against the assumption that internal peace at Corcyra was assured—'quarrels may break out again at any moment.' Nor do I believe that even if this passage was written after 411 (and it may well have been—a good deal of book iv was at least revised later: see the essay on Sphakteria, above, p. 130), the use of the phrase ὁ πόλεμος ὅδε for the Archidamian war means that Thucydides had not yet thought of the whole struggle as one; it is a purely formal distinction. Even in the passage in which he argues for the unity of conception of the whole twenty-seven years (clearly against some critics who were objecting to his calling the period 421 to 415 (or 413) war-years), he writes ξὺν τῷ πρώτῳ πολέμῳ τῷ δεκέτει καὶ τῇ μετ᾽ αὐτὸν ὑπόπτῳ ἀνοκωχῇ καὶ τῷ ὕστερον ἐξ αὐτῆς πολέμῳ εὑρήσει τις τοσαῦτα ἔτη.

N

The problem of book viii is simpler. It is certainly unfinished; and it is hard to believe that Thucydides, if he was
going to give in detail the story of the revolution in Athens,
would not have recorded some speeches at length, if he
could—that of Antiphon, for example, of Alkibiades at
Samos (c. 81. 2), those at the institution of the modified
democracy (c. 97). Why could he not? Because he composed
his speeches last and did not live to finish this section, or
because he knew he had not enough material? Little as we
know of his methods of composition, we know one thing of
the first importance: that he was as conscientious as a man
could be in collecting and sifting his material, that he
would not overlook any opportunity of gathering fresh evidence, in a hurry to get his book finished; and that, as the
war went on and on and memories of its earlier years were
becoming fainter and less intelligible to the new generation
that was caught in its grip, he was revising what he had
already written, and perhaps enlarging his aim and scope by
the use of official documents. He died not earlier than 403,
and his last piece of connected narrative (what a pity his
editor did not preserve his notes of the subsequent period!)
was of the year 411; he was, so to speak, at least eight years
behind his schedule. Now, however conscientious he was,
however much he travelled about in his search for material,
he must, while the war was still on, have had much time on
his hands. Why did he not employ it in composing the
speeches of 411? especially that of Antiphon? He will have
known the main facts of Antiphon's activities and of his
trial very soon after the events (he will have met some of the
fugitive oligarchs); he knew the man. He could have composed an excellent speech, such as the orator 'might have
made,' true to his ἦθος and to the occasion. He had plenty
of time between 411 and his return to Athens (when he
would be busy with other work). What other cause can we
reasonably suppose for his silence than that he felt in this
case the difficulty of 'keeping as close as possible to the
general sense of what was actually said'? That he waited
therefore till his return to Athens to test men's recollections;
and perhaps then found that they were unreliable. Of all the
various views that have been held about the composition of

Thucydides' history, I think that perhaps the most mistaken is that which holds that all or most of the speeches were written after the war was over. If they are free compositions, they were exercises admirably suited to employ his long leisure hours. But if they are not, if he was as careful in collecting the evidence of what was said as of what was done, we can understand why there are no speeches in book viii. And in any case, at whatever stage in the composition of the *History* Thucydides wrote his complete speeches, what are the summaries, given in *oratio obliqua*, in book viii? the record of what, as he was told, had been the arguments used, or his own brief notes of the kind of speech he wanted to compose, quite freely, later? Does anyone really doubt that they are the former? That we have in fact a true kernel, τὴν ξυμπᾶσαν γνώμην τῶν ἀληθῶς λεχθέντων?

Considerable confusion of thought has arisen in this question by a subconscious belief that Thucydides' skill as an artist is in some way incompatible, in the speeches, with his truthfulness as a historian; or at least by a refusal properly to analyse all the issues involved. Let me take a minor point first. A typical opinion is thus expressed by Lavagnini:[1] 'Così essi servono in realtà ad esporre quella che è nella mente dello storico la analisi della situazione, e gli offrono il modo di esprimere in forma indiretta le sue riflessioni, senza spezzare con introduzione di elemento soggettivo e personale la obiettività del racconto.' This should mean, in general, that Thucydides was a dishonest man who pretended to an objectivity which was not there, and in particular that the speeches represent his own reflexions. Yet Lavagnini cannot quite mean this last. The two speeches of Perikles to the ecclesia might represent Thucydides' own views (if he was so disingenuous as to express them by this method); but obviously Kleon's does not; and if Nikias' speech on the Sicilian expedition does, then Alkibiades' cannot; if Archidamos' at the Spartan conference, then not the Corinthians' nor Sthenelaidas'; above all, if the Funeral Speech, then not the Corinthian at Sparta nor the Mytilenean at Olympia. In fact when Thucydides wished to express his own views, he does so frankly, as on

[1] *Saggio sulla storiografia greca* (Bari, 1933), p. 53.

Kleon's 'mad promise,'[1] on the effects of the Corcyrean sedition—this really an 'analysis of the situation'—on Nikias, on the modified democracy of 411, and on Perikles' estimate of the military situation. The last is particularly interesting: Thucydides attributes to Perikles two speeches in which he gives reasons for his confidence in a final victory; he adds (ii 65. 5–13) 'Perikles was right in his confidence.' Does that mean 'I am right in my estimate of the military possibilities which I have put into the mouth of Perikles'? Actually Lavagnini and the rest would agree that Thucydides attributes to Kleon not his own opinions, but such as Kleon might, if true to himself, have uttered; and this is to say that Thucydides is, as an artist, being objective (however untruthful as a historian), not hiding his personality under another's mask. However, every speech in Thucydides could be true to the character of the speakers and proper to the occasion (that is, not expressive of his own opinions, nor even of his own idea of how such and such opinions—not his own—could be most persuasively expressed, but how they would have been expressed by those speakers on those occasions), and still be 'free inventions,' without historical validity. It only, so far, proves his skill as an artist to show that 'this is very true to the ἦθος of Nikias, not simply the author putting forth his own view'; it says nothing of historical content. For this a comparison with Herodotus will be of value.[2]

---

[1]Biased as Thucydides often shows himself against Kleon, this is not an instance of it. The promise *was* mad: no sane commander will make boasts of what he will achieve within a short specified period of time.

[2]It is worth while insisting, however, on the obscurity of thought, or of expression, shown by many writers. Deffner, for example (p. 41), says that the object of the speeches in Herodotus is to give his own appreciation of events; and that in this he is most like Thucydides. As he goes on to say that Herodotus only once sums up expressly to give his own judgement (vii 139), that normally, like Thucydides, he uses speeches for this purpose, he should mean that the speeches express the author's own view. But apart from the numerous cases in which opposite views are expressed in the course of debate (as between Artabanos and Xerxes), when Deffner thinks that Herodotus' own view is that of one side or the other, what is the author's *judgement* that is expressed in the conference with Gelon (vii 157–62), or in that at Athens after Salamis when Mardonios tried to seduce the Athenians from the Greek cause (viii 140–4)? That, in this latter instance, the Athenians showed unshaken patriotism? Presumably; but that is a judgement on their *action* in rejecting the overtures, *based on* their reply, not expressed in it. Herodotus will emphasize their patriotism by the speech he attributes to them? Of course; but he would equally be doing this, if he were reporting verbally a speech actually delivered; so that the problem of authenticity is left unsolved.

'Die bisherigen Beobachtungen haben ganz deutlich gezeigt,' says Deffner (p. 32), 'dass Herodot die direkte Rede stets in einem ganz bestimmten kompositionellen Zusammenhang mit der Darstellung bringt. Es waren fast immer bedeutende Ereignisse oder gefährliche Unternehmungen, auf die durch die Einschaltung solcher Ruhepunkte die Aufmerksamkeit hingelenkt werden sollte. Der Situation nach war die Darstellung gerade an einer Stelle angelangt, an der eine Wendung des Schicksals oder die Auflösung einer vorausgehende Spannung oder der Umschlag von Ruhe in Bewegung eintrat.' And he goes on to show that Thucydides, more or less closely, follows this principle, or rather that his method is a more formal application of it, with little of Herodotus' variety. In both historians the choice of occasions for speeches is determined by the principle that these occasions shall be 'historisch bedeutsam und kompositionell wirksam' (p. 100). Deffner shows we are given certain patterns: before a war, first the discussion whether war should be waged at all, then of the strategic problems (as in Hdt. vii 8–11 and 49, Thuc. i 68–86 and Perikles' speech, 140–4), the speech before the decisive engagement (Xerxes and Demaratos before Thermopylai, Miltiades before Marathon, Themistokles before Salamis), often in Herodotus a speech to mark the pause after the battle (as viii 140–4), and a parallelism between the discussions that take place in the opposing camps (as before Salamis, and in Thucydides vi).[1] But what exactly does this

However, the question whether Herodotus uses any of his speeches to express his own views is one which need not now detain us. Everyone thinks he sees the author in Solon's talk with Croesus, in Artabanos and Demaratos (see Deffner, pp. 60–1) and elsewhere. I do not myself agree; I think Herodotus was far too good an artist to intrude his personality in this way. This does not mean that he may not in fact have agreed with some opinion expressed by Solon or Artabanos; only that it is not his object to give the 'right' view, but the view contrary to that of his confident and likeable Croesus, his boastful and foolish Xerxes. His method is dramatic, not didactic. Deffner (p. 64) notes that in his account of the Persian debate on the best form of government (iii 80–3), Herodotus does not give his own opinion: 'er kommt wie so oft zu keinem Ergebnis, sondern überlässt dem Leser die Entscheidung.' Just so; but it is true throughout. He knew how to let his words tell their own story. He has no need of puppet-characters.

[1]But Deffner, p. 94, exaggerates the 'strenge Parallelität' between Thuc. vi 9–24 and 33–41: that 9–14, 16–18 correspond to 33–34, 36–40 ('sich streng in These und Antithese gegenüberstellen'), and 20–24 to 41 (which 'den Ausgleich zwischen den beiden, die Synthese, herstellt'). Apart from the difference in length between the members of this last pair, they are not parallel in content. Nikias' speech is another warning, the Syracusan general's is in effect support for Hermokrates. If there is

amount to? I do not of course suppose that Herodotus is reporting words actually spoken; but supposing he were, or that he thought he was (that is, that he had informants whom he believed), where else could he 'insert' his speeches? Did not the debate in the Persian court (on this supposition) take place just when Herodotus says it did? Did not Miltiades persuade Kallimachos, and Themistokles Eurybiades, before Marathon and Salamis? How else could military plans be discussed except first whether war was to be declared and then the strategic problems involved? If Herodotus and Thucydides had had nothing but written, authentic records on which to work, if they had eschewed all other evidence, the general plan of their histories—the position in them of the speeches—would still have been the same. Herodotus thought it historically true that Miltiades, as the author of the decree that the Athenian army should march out to Marathon and of the plan to attack the enemy just when that attack took place, was also the moral author of the victory; and that his plans were carried out, not because he was a commander-in-chief with full powers, but because while at Marathon he persuaded, by speech, Kallimachos and his fellow strategoi. He may have made up the speech entirely out of his own head; but that is a different thing from saying that he 'inserts' a speech, at a dramatic moment, to direct the reader's attention, *durch solche Ruhepunkte*, to an important event or a dangerous undertaking.[1] Of course the

any parallel to c. 41 on the Athenian side it is c. 25, with 26. 1, corresponding to the last sentence of 41. But what is the value of establishing this sort of correspondence? Deffner's argument may be good enough against Pohlenz' view (*Gött. Nachr.* 1919, p. 124) that Nikias' second speech was 'composed' before the cc. 9–18; but that is all. The correspondence proves nothing either way about historical validity.

Similarly we must be on our guard against the view that Thucydides, any more than Herodotus, followed any fixed principle of antithetical speeches. Where opposing speeches were each of them significant (and, I would add, where he felt he had sufficient material), he would give both—Corinthians and Corcyreans, Kleon and Diodotos, Thebans and Plataeans, Hermokrates and Euphemos; where, though many contrasting speeches were delivered, only one was significant, he would give that, with only a brief reference to the rest, as in the debates at Athens, i 139. 2–144 and ii 60–5, and at Gela, iv 58–64. He would give three speeches, if he thought right, as in vi 9–24, or four as at the conference at Sparta. He has no fixed 'artistic' scheme; his method is governed by historical considerations.

[1] We may disbelieve Herodotus, if we like, and argue that the whole plan of campaign had been agreed upon before the troops left Athens; but that has nothing to do with the question of Herodotus' purpose in giving Miltiades' speech. It only touches his general credibility on military matters, just as when we disbelieve him about the Persian cavalry at Marathon, or (to take a certainty) about Kallimachos' position as polemarch.

occasions of great speeches in both Herodotus and Thucydides are *historisch bedeutsam*—that only shows they were good historians; of course they were *compositionell wirksam*—they were good artists as well, men who knew how to handle their material.

And what is meant by calling the speeches *Ruhepunkte?* Miltiades' speech at Marathon does not mark a pause; still less Themistokles' at Salamis; nor indeed any of the big political speeches—they indicate action. Only reflexions, such as those of Xerxes as his army crossed the Hellespont —at the dramatic moment of the crossing from Asia to Europe—could be so described. And in Thucydides all the speeches, with one exception, the *Epitaphios*, perhaps also the Theban-Plataean *agon* (iii 53–67), are part of the action, and a very energetic part of it. Is Kleon's speech in the Mytilene debate put there to give the reader a pause for reflexion? or the conference at Sparta, or Perikles' speech urging the Athenians to resist the Peloponnesian demands, or the debate before the expedition to Sicily? On purely formal grounds we can distinguish as Thucydides did, between words spoken and deeds done. But when we are thinking of the actions of the war as a whole, the speeches are as much a part of them as the battles. Still stranger is the comparison of them with the choral songs of tragedy, marking a pause in the drama.[1] We may at least ask, which choruses—those of Aeschylus' *Suppliants* or of *Iphigenia in Aulis?* And if we mean Sophocles, his odes mark a pause in the action, and may, in a superficial and prosaic way, be said to give the 'reflexions' of the poet. But what have they to do with speeches that are calls to action, vigorous and successful calls? It is not in the odes of Greek tragedy that we look for the rhetoric which is to be found in poetry and prose alike.[2] Oratory played a larger part in determining the course of events in Greece than in other countries. Nikias feared that his despatches from Syracuse might fail of their effect κατὰ τὴν τοῦ λέγειν ἀδυνασίαν of the messengers (vii 8. 2). A general would still to-day, in such a crisis, send an officer back to tell the government the truth and would

[1] As Bury, *Ancient Greek Historians*, p. 112.
[2] And even if the speeches did mark pauses in the action, that would not mean they are not authentic. The Catalogue of the forces before Syracuse definitely marks a pause before the climax; but it is not a free invention.

choose for the purpose a man who could express himself clearly and forcibly; but in Nikias' case the message had to be delivered at a meeting of the ecclesia.

It is possible enough to point out similarities between Herodotus and Thucydides in the treatment of speeches: between the opening chapters of book vii of the former and i 68–86 of the latter; between viii 104–44 and i 32–43; even perhaps to regard, with Deffner, the Theban-Plataean debate as Thucydides' development of a form suggested by Herodotus ix 26–7 (the Aeginetan-Athenian *agon* before Plataia). But these similarities are as nothing compared with the differences. I am not here thinking so much of the differences in content, though these are remarkable enough —that Herodotus could believe that world events are determined by a monarch's dream, and that he had a trustworthy account of what that dream had been; that the Athenians and Tegeatans had made those formal speeches before taking up their positions at Plataia, or that Sosikles included the detailed history of the Corinthian *tyrannis* in his speech at Sparta. That Thucydides rejected this kind of thing might show only that he had better political insight, and a greater sense of reality than his predecessor. It is the difference in manner which is here so significant. Herodotus is vivid, dramatic: Ἐν σοὶ νῦν, Καλλίμαχε, ἐστὶ ἢ καταδουλῶσαι Ἀθήνας ἢ ἐλευθέρας ποιήσαντα μνημόσυνα λιπέσθαι ἐς τὸν ἄπαντα ἀνθρώπων βίον οἷα οὐδὲ Ἁρμόδιός τε καὶ Ἀριστογείτων. Ἀρτάβανε, πατρὸς εἶς τοῦ ἐμοῦ ἀδελφεός· τοῦτό σε ῥύσεται μηδένα ἄξιον μισθὸν λαβεῖν ἐπέων ματαίων. Σὺ εἰ μενέεις αὐτοῦ καὶ μένων ἔσεαι ἀνὴρ ἀγαθός· εἰ δὲ μή, ἀνατρέψεις τὴν Ἑλλάδα· τὸ πᾶν γὰρ ἡμῖν τοῦ πολέμου φέρουσι αἱ νέες. ἀλλ' ἐμοὶ πείθεο. Οἷον ἐφθέγξαο ἔπος. Thucydides is generalized. It is perverse that this should have been regarded as evidence that his speeches are his own invention. The opposite is of course the case. It is Herodotus with his vivid manner, as vivid in his political, historical speeches as in the dialogue of his stories, who is writing as the story-teller would, as the ποιητής, in the manner of Homer.[1]

[1] Many scholars have noted that Herodotus writes often in the tradition of Homer and the early Milesian tales. I believe that he (perhaps the authors of these tales as well) was also influenced by the method of the Oriental story-teller: not only the matter of many of his stories, but the treatment too (especially his ταῦτα δὲ εἶπας καὶ ἐποίεε, and the like) are in the manner of *The Arabian Nights*.

As has been said, he hardly distinguishes in his own mind between the duties of the story-teller and the historian. What Thucydides criticized in him and would not imitate, was not merely his light-hearted treatment of great political and military events—he himself being a profounder political thinker, and possessed of better judgement and experience of war—but his method of reporting, his story-teller's air of giving an eye-witness's account of conversations between Xerxes and Artabanos, between Themistokles and Eurybiades, equally with those between Kandaules and Gyges or Kleisthenes and his daughter's suitors. Hence the much greater variety of treatment in Herodotus. This Thucydides rejected, for his aim was a different one.[1]

I have argued that Thucydides put himself to the trouble of getting evidence of the words spoken as of the deeds done. This does not affect his position as a literary artist. To collect and sift and test evidence, to decide what events are significant and what are not—and hence to select what actions and what speeches are to be recorded and at what length— is the work of the historian as scientist; to present them in an intelligible manner, and so that the reader receives the impression intended by the author, is the work of the artist. That Thucydides was, in some degree, carrying on and developing the tradition of Herodotean historiography (or at least of books vii–ix of Herodotus), with its use of the direct speech, is true. That he was aware of the tragic contrast between the ideal Athens of the Funeral Speech and the real Athens during the pestilence, between the cynically triumphant city of 416 and the disaster that was to follow; that he was consciously contrasting the Funeral Speech with the realism of the other Athenian speeches— that delivered at Sparta, Perikles' other two, Kleon's, the delegates at Melos, Alkibiades—and more subtly the differ-

---

[1] It is a curious thing, but perhaps the only occasion on which Herodotus deserts his normal method and writes formal speeches which, in spite of the difference of matter, show some resemblance to those of Thucydides, is the Persian debate on the best constitution; it is also almost the only group of speeches (among the historical speeches, apart from the tales), of which we can be confident not only that the style is Herodotus, but that the matter is quite foreign to the supposed speakers: that it is not Persian, but Greek, and not of the end of the sixth, but of the second half of the fifth century. Yet it is the one occasion on which Herodotus emphasizes that he is recording the substance of what was really said.

ent degrees and quality of realism in these speeches—the gay, confident cynicism of the Athenians at Sparta, the brutality and force of Kleon, the bald statement of the doctrine of might at Melos (there was no longer need for argument), the ambitious imperialism of Alkibiades, all contrasted with the ideas of the man who felt that the union of half Greece under Athenian leadership was a noble aim, and that Athens was worthy to be the leader (or that he would make her worthy), but would not hide from himself that this, like all empire, involved a tyranny of the strong over the weak: all this is also true.[1] But it does not follow that Thucydides made up the Funeral Speech, or any of the others, and inserted it, to point the contrast. It can mean that Thucydides the artist knew how to handle his material. He thought the contrast between Perikles praising Athens as he desired her to be—'so that none could complain of being ruled by a city unworthy of empire'—and Perikles having to persuade the ecclesia to particular policies, and between him and other Athenian imperialists, was significant; we need not doubt that he used his materials to bring out this significant contrast without concocting them, just as we do not doubt that the attack on Melos immediately preceded that on Sicily,[2] nor the tragic end of the finest armament that ever left

[1]The contrast between Perikles and Kleon is especially clearly brought out, for the latter adopts many of Perikles' own words (iii 37. 2, τυραννίδα ἔχετε τὴν ἀρχήν; 38. 1, ἐγὼ μὲν οὖν ὁ αὐτός εἰμι τῇ γνώμῃ, and 40. 4, ἐκ τοῦ ἀκινδύνου ἀνδραγαθίζεσθαι—all from ii 61. 2, 63. 1-2). Kleon wearing the mantle of Perikles, and no ape, but as forceful and persuasive—that, says Thucydides, is one of the results of imperialism and war.

Many objections have been made to the Athenian speech at Sparta, none I think of weight. An objection that I have long felt is that its insouciance seems purposely provocative: for both the reminders to Sparta of her unpopularity (76. 1, 77. 6), and the bland βουλεύεσθε οὖν βραδέως (78, 1), addressed to a notoriously slow-moving people who had just been taunted with their slowness (μέχρι μὲν οὖν τοῦδε ὡρίσθω ὑμῖν ἡ βραδύτης), seem exquisitely designed to produce the result which followed, to sting the stupid Sthenelaidas into making the speech he did make; a result which Archidamos (καὶ τὸ βραδὺ καὶ μέλλον, ὃ μέμφονται μάλιστα ἡμῶν, μὴ αἰσχύνεσθε, 84. 1; καὶ ὡς ἡμᾶς πρέπει βουλεύεσθαι ἀδικουμένους μηδεὶς διδασκέτω, ἀλλὰ τοὺς μέλλοντας ἀδικεῖν μᾶλλον πρέπει πολὺν χρόνον βουλεύεσθαι 86. 4) tried to avoid. There would have been nothing surprising in itself if it had been meant to be provocative; the Megarian decree was certainly so, and the Athenian attitude was 'if we must have war, it suits us to have it at once.' But Thucydides clearly did not think so (72. 1). This fact also shows that one explanation of the difficulty 'this shows that such a speech was not given,' will not help.

[2]Or do we doubt it? Here is a fine example of confused thought—Laistner, The Greek World from 479 to 323 B.C., pp. 124-5: 'The conviction that this episode (the destruction of Melos) was the most illuminating, as it was the worst, example of the excesses to which unrestrained imperialism could give rise, led Thucydides to

Greek shores. The course of events may itself be dramatic, and the truthful historian will make this clear.

Equally is it true that Thucydides' understanding of events increased, his picture of their relative significance became clearer as the war progressed. It is obvious, for example, that earlier Athenian contacts with the west became much more significant after the Sicilian expedition, and that Thucydides would look with a fresh eye on some earlier actions and speeches which at the time had seemed unimportant. It may be true (though I do not think the truth is so simple) that, as Jaeger puts it, in the *History* as we have it, 'vom ersten Buch an wird das sizilische Unternehmen von Thukydides vorbereitet,' and 'kein Zweifel, dass Thukydides diese Vorstufen erst am Ende des Krieges, als er den sizilischen Feldzug schrieb, in sein Werk eingefügt hat',[1] if by that we mean that in the light of later events he went over his material again and made use of some that he had omitted, or emphasized what he had before neglected; that he would try to get more information (from Sicilian sources, in this case) on these events, and that above all he would realize, as he may not have done at the time, the importance of the conference at Gela and the part there played by Hermokrates, and would find out as much as he could about it. But that is a very different thing from saying the speech he attributes to Hermokrates is nothing but his own free invention, the sort of thing that one who later opposed Athens successfully 'ought to have said' in 424. There is no more reason to suppose that than that he invented the earlier Athenian expeditions to Sicily, the importance of which also he probably had not forseeen.

The Epitaphios is a good test case. Many have thought of it as indeed a Funeral Speech, but by Thucydides and

present in the form of dramatic dialogue the arguments for and against the doctrine that right is might. Nor is it accidental that the artist has juxtaposed the fate of Melos with the unprecedented disaster that within three years befell the Athenians.' Why 'the artist has juxtaposed,' and not the historian? It was 'not accidental' because an artist wanted a dramatic contrast? Are we then to conclude that Professor Laistner does not believe that the overthrow of Melos took place in the winter of 416–5 immediately before the first preparations for the Syracusan expedition; that he thinks the juxtaposition as unhistorical as the dialogue? Not at all; he has just previously recorded the episode, places it in 416, and relies entirely on Thucydides as his authority.

[1] *Paideia*, p. 502.

over the grave of Athens, written after 404, a speech 'auf die mit dem Falle Athens für alle Ewigkeit zu Grabe getragenen Ideale.'[1] To which Beloch objected 'aber in dem Augenblicke, wo diese Ideale so völligen Schiffbruch gelitten hatten, würde er den Zeitgenossen als blutige Ironie erschienen sein, und so hat Thukydides doch sicher nicht gemeint, so wenig er auch für die demokratischen Ideale begeistert war.'[2] A possible, but anyhow an insufficient answer. Thucydides says that Perikles made the funeral speech over those who had fallen in the first year of the war. If this is not true, I see no reason to believe any other simple statement in Thucydides. If it is true (and no amount of 'wer nur einen Hauch' and 'wer nur griechisch kann' will persuade me that it is not), Thucydides will have heard it and have made notes of it; in finally composing it, he will have kept as close as possible to the general sense of what was actually said. Why should we doubt it? Perikles was the great architect of that Athens which nearly all the rest of Greece feared and envied; he knew that his whole policy might lead to war on a grand scale. He took that risk; more than any other single man he was responsible that the war broke out when it did. He felt confident that, barring the unforeseeable, Athens would be victorious, his Athens, the great centre for which he had laboured so much. The first year of what would in any case be a long war was just over, and the course of events had been exactly as he had planned; his confidence in victory seemed justified. What better occasion could occur on which to remind his countrymen of the ideals for which they were fighting? Whether Thucy-

---

[1] Meyer, *Forschungen*, ii, p. 282.

[2] *Gr. Gesch.*[2] iii 2, p. 12. We should also bear in mind what Wilamowitz said of the *Apologia* (*Platon*, ii, p. 50): 'If Plato wished to defend the memory of Socrates, and to prove his condemnation unjust, he had to reckon with the judges reading the book, and also the other disciples of Socrates. He was bound, then, to take, at least as a foundation, the thoughts that Socrates really uttered, and to avoid carefully anything that Socrates could not have said.' We can add that Thucydides was professedly a historian. Dionysios of course thought of the *Apologia* purely as Plato's own composition (*Ars rhet.*, 295–8; *de Dem.*, 1026).

When was iii 82–3 written, which is explicitly Thucydides' own reflexion? After the democratic restoration of 403? It makes the conduct of that event all the more admirable; for there are always, once violence has been used, so many wrongs to set right, so many precautions to be taken to prevent a recurrence of what you think to be evil. Even in the hands of honesty and intelligence; and in any other hands the precautions become distrust, never ending, and setting wrongs right becomes revenge, never ending also.

dides shared his belief in these ideals, it would be difficult to say. He certainly regarded the war as an immense disaster; he had no great admiration for the democratic constitution of Athens. His clear statement of the true motives of the war seems to show that he did not think that the war could have been avoided by less provocative action on Perikles' part in 433 and 432; but whether he thought that, as the Athenian empire made war at some time inevitable, that in itself condemned the imperial policy, or agreed with Perikles that the ideal Athens was worth this risk, we shall never know. What we do know is that he would not, so far as is possible for a man, have allowed his opinion to colour his narrative, whether of things done or of words spoken. That at the end of the war he may have been wiser after the event than during its course is naturally true; he was but human. But this appears frankly in his own words (ii 65), not in a speech. Even if there is more of Thucydides' own thought in the Epitaphios than I would allow, it is still certainly meant as an objective picture of Periklean policy, not a vehicle for the expression of his own views, whether in 430 or 415 or 403. Different as they are in so many ways, Thucydides and Herodotus have this at least in common: neither makes use of author's puppets.

I have not been able to see A. Grosskinsky's *Das Programm des Thukydides* (Berlin, 1936), which is an analysis of i 22. Mr. J. E. Powell in a review (*C.R.*, 1936, pp. 174–5) gives an interpretation of i 22. 1 with which I agree; but insists on the incompatibility of Thucydides' theory and practice; and continues: 'we must guard against supposing that he was necessarily as conscious as ourselves of the gulf between theory and practice; but it is more natural that such a programme was formulated before than after the speeches themselves were created' (Grosskinsky arguing for a late date, about 404, for the writing of cc. 20–22). With this proposition I would in general agree; but I think Thucydides was far more successful in his aim to 'keep as closely as possible to the general sense of what was actually said' than Mr. Powell (I imagine) would allow. Pohlenz too has a similar interpretation of i 22 (*Gött. Nachr.*, 1919); but his analysis of the speeches is as different from mine, in method and result, as it could well be.

X

A FORGOTTEN FACTOR OF GREEK NAVAL STRATEGY[1]

IT is a common-place of most scholars, followed enthusiastically by writers of text-books, that Greek sailors did not like the sea; they went from island to island, or crept along the coast. Rarely did they leave the sight of land, and then only the most venturesome; and they did not sail by night. I don't know that I have seen it stated in so many words, but it is implied that the close relations between Miletos and Sybaris were maintained by voyages across the Aegean to Corinth (e.g.: 'Corinth becomes the centre of exchange with Italy: it pays better to break cargo at the isthmus than to sail round the stormy coasts of the Peloponnese'[2]), thence (but in Milesian or foreign ships?) through the gulf, up the north-west coast to Kerkyra, hurriedly and anxiously across to Otranto, then, following every curve of the coast, past Tarentum and Metapontum, to their goal. If goods must go further, as so many did to Etruria, they took another isthmus-route overland to Laos or Skidros, thence along the coast again, even as far as Massalia and Emporiai. I was correcting an examination paper the other day in which candidates were asked to mark trade-routes on a map: some of them marked a route from Peiraeus to Kyrene *via* Rhodes, Phaselis, the Syrian coasts and Egypt, and another *via* Corinth and the coast route to Sicily, to Selinus, Carthage, and the Syrtes; the sea-route from Athens to the Hellespont was shown as by the Euripos, the Thessalian coast, every curve of the Chalcidic peninsula, and the coast of Thrace. I did not know whether to deduct marks; for this is certainly what they are taught. Yet it clearly does not.

---

[1] First published in *Journal of Hellenic Studies*, liii, 1933.

[2] Rostovtzeff, *History of the Ancient World*, i. p. 201. Thucydides regarded the isthmus as a land-bridge between North Greece and the Peloponnese, as we do, not between two seas: οἰκοῦντες γὰρ τὴν πόλιν οἱ Κορίνθιοι ἐπὶ τοῦ ἰσθμοῦ αἰεὶ δή ποτε ἐμπόριον εἶχον, τῶν Ἑλλήνων τὸ πάλαι κατὰ γῆν τὰ πλείω ἢ κατὰ θάλασσάν, τῶν τε ἐντὸς Πελοποννήσου καὶ τῶν ἔξω διὰ τῆς ἐκείνων παρ' ἀλλήλους ἐπιμισγόντων, χρήμασί τε δυνατοὶ ἦσαν, κ.τ.λ. (i 13. 5).

give the whole picture of Greek marine commerce.[1] If it
did, Corinth, Sikyon and Kerkyra would soon have had a
monopoly of trade with the west; but in fact Chalkis and
Eretria, Miletos, Samos, Phokaia, later Athens and Rhodes,
did as much; and it is certain that they were none of them
dependent on Corinth for the privilege. Moreover, further
west, Massalia was founded, not by Kyme or Elea or
Syracuse, as would be expected on the isthmus-theory, but
from Phokaia; and trade was maintained by the Straits of
Messene and Corsica. Samos traded direct with Spain; and,
we may be sure, their vessels did not hug the coast of Africa,
dependent on the goodwill of the Carthaginians. If we look at
recorded cases, we can see that trading vessels sailed direct
from Egypt to Rhodes and Athens, and from Sicily to
Athens:[2] on the former voyage vessels did not necessarily
put in at Rhodes between Egypt and Peiraeus;[3] and in the
Zenothemis case we read that a voyage was begun direct
from Syracuse to Peiraeus, and when two or three days out
at sea, at night-time, an attempt was made to scuttle the
ship, which however managed to reach Kephallenia; thence
it went to Athens, and, obviously, not by Corinth.[4] When
Herodotus[5] gives the length and breadth of the Euxine,
though inaccurately, the correct inference is that the Greeks
sailed, when necessary, direct from Byzantion or Sinope to
Tauris, from Odessos to Phasis; and by night as well as by
day.[6] We can be certain that Milesian vessels did in fact sail
to Sybaris round the stormy south coast of the Peloponnese,
and across the Ionian sea; that Corinth and Athens traded

[1] A character in one of the stories in Karkavitsas' book Λόγια τῆς Πλώρης says:
δὲν εἴμαστε Μαυροθαλασσῖτες, νὰ πᾶμ ετὴν ἄκρη ἄκρη· Γαλάξειδιῶτες μᾶς λέν.
[2] Dem. lvi, xxxii.
[3] Dem. lvi 9. Cf. Thuc. vi 13. 2, τῷ Σικελικῷ διά πελάγους.
[4] Dem. xxxii 5–8. The agreement cited in xxxv 10–12 is for a voyage from
Peiraeus to Mende or Skione and the Bosporos, thence by the west coast to Borys-
thenes, and a return direct to Peiraeus.
[5] iv 86.
[6] Thuc. ii 97 also shows that night voyaging was common. But it is unnecessary
to multiply instances; the fact that some knowledge of the stars was necessary for
the skilled seaman is sufficient proof. It is only necessary to stress the fact. And that
trading by sea in winter was avoided if possible was due, not so much to the fear
of bad weather, as to the difficulty of sailing on cloudy nights, and even cloudy
days, with no stars or sun as guide, and no compass. Of course, some sailing in
winter was done: cf. Thuc. iii 16. 2, and I.G. i², 63 (the heralds of the new τάξις
φόρου must be back in Athens by December); and no fuss is made of it.

direct with Etruria, not *via* Sybaris, and that Phokaian vessels were to be seen in Massalia, and Massaliots in the East. Syracusan merchants were to be found in Phoenicia.[1] In fact it is clear from the nature of all bottomry-loans that we know of, that there was no breaking of a journey for the goods to go by an 'isthmic route' and resume on another ship; for they cover insurance for both cargo and vessel, and for the one vessel only.

On the other hand, the Athenian fleet on its way to Syracuse did sail first to Kerkyra and hugged the shores of Italy; the fleet to Egypt touched at Cyprus and perhaps at Phaselis, as well as at Rhodes; and the fighting in Phoenicia (Erechtheid inscription) may have been in the course of sailing along the coast towards Egypt. What was the reason for this variety in practice? It was due to a radical difference between warships and merchantmen; and when this has been analysed we shall be in a position to understand as well one of the chief factors in Greek naval strategy. The merchantman was built to carry heavy loads, and went under sail. Its crew were comparatively few in number, we do not know how many for any class of ship, and in addition to the crew there were usually the cargo-owner, the master and owner of the ship, and the ship's captain, with, presumably, their personal servants.[2] In a ship under sail, carrying heavy cargo, it was easy to carry as well food and water for all persons on board for many days. A journey from Athens, Miletos or Rhodes to S. Italy and Sicily, without a break for revictualling, was possible enough; or from Athens and Rhodes to Egypt, Kyrene to Gytheion or Peiraeus, Byzantion to Phasis; sailing both night and day. Contrast the conditions of the trireme: it was propelled by oars. Men (especially, if you like, free men) cannot row more than a few hours continuously, nor more than a certain number in every twenty-four, in ordinary circumstances (a forced journey, like that of the ship that took the second decree to Mytilene, gives the extreme of endurance). Secondly, the trireme,

---

[1] Xen. *Hell.* iii 4. 1.

[2] All of these 'passengers' and the crew could, in case of shipwreck, take to the ship's one λέμβος (Dem. xxxii). Ordinary passengers, however, sometimes had little chance of safety: Dem. xxxiv 10, when thirty were drowned, the master and the crew saved.

unlike the galleys of Roman and later times, was built for speed, as lightly as possible and to carry as few passengers as possible; the development of naval tactics by Athens in the fifth century increased this tendency: there were forty 'passengers' *plus* the officers in the Chian ships at Lade; in the later Athenian vessels only ten and the officers, and the ships were even lighter built. But the whole number of persons on board was round about 200; for so many it was impossible to carry more than at most a day or two's supply of food[1] and, especially, of water (rowing in the Mediterranean summer is thirsty work, however abstemious the Greeks were); it was at all times desirable to carry as little deadweight as possible. There was not normally room for sleeping on board (contrast Thuc. iii 49. 3), perhaps no means of cooking for the whole crew. All this meant that on an ordinary journey the trireme would not travel for more than twelve hours a day at most, and must if possible put in to land once every twenty-four hours to renew its supply of food and water (of the latter, at least), to give the rowers proper rest and sleep, and to cook a meal.[2] That is why the triremes, unlike the merchantmen, hugged the coast. Troopships and horse-transports suffered from similar limitations. Even when, as on the Syracusan expedition, special ships with a corn-supply and bakers accompanied the fleet (Thuc. vi 44. 1), a landing would be necessary for the baking if the food was to be consumed *en route*; actually it was intended as an emergency supply once the armament reached Sicily.

This involved yet another condition in war-time, that the shore into which they were compelled so frequently to put, should be friendly or benevolently neutral, or at least not occupied by the enemy. Consider Thucydides' description of the voyage to Sicily, remembering that the larger the armament the greater the difficulty of finding food: the

---

[1] Three days' supply just before a battle was taken in by the Corinthians (Thuc. i 48. 1) in rather old-fashioned ships in 432 (49. 1).

[2] See in particular Xen. *Hell.* vi 2. 27–30, Iphikrates' expedition round the Peloponnese; keeping in mind that Xenophon was a landsman. Also, Thuc. iv 30. 2.

For the importance of the water-supply for all ships, see *Stadiasmus Maris Graeci* (*Geogr. Gr. Min*, i, 427 ff.), which gives directions where water was to be found; Plut. *Quaest. Gr.* 54; and Athen. v 208A: all quoted by Cary and Warmington, *Ancient Explorers*, 6–8.

O

whole armament is collected and reviewed at allied Kerkyra, and divided into three divisions, ἵνα μήτε ἅμα πλέοντες ἀπορῶσιν ὕδατος καὶ λιμένων καὶ τῶν ἐπιτηδείων ἐν ταῖς καταγωγαῖς, πρός τε τἆλλα εὐκοσμότεροι . . . ὦσιν, κ.τ.λ. (42. 1). They sailed across to C. Otranto, then along the Italian coast, τῶν μὲν πόλεων οὐ δεχομένων αὐτοὺς ἀγορᾷ οὐδὲ ἄστει, ὕδατι δὲ καὶ ὅρμῳ, Τάραντος δὲ καὶ Λοκρῶν οὐδὲ τούτοις, ἕως ἀφίκοντο ἐς Ῥήγιον τῆς Ἰταλίας ἀκρωτήριον. καὶ ἐνταῦθα ἤδη ἠθροίζοντο, καὶ ἔξω τῆς πόλεως, ὡς αὐτοὺς ἔσω οὐκ ἐδέχοντο, στρατόπεδόν τε κατεσκευάσαντο ἐν τῷ τῆς Ἀρτέμιδος ἱερῷ, οὗ αὐτοῖς καὶ ἀγορὰν παρεῖχον, καὶ τὰς ναῦς ἀνελκύσαντες ἡσύχασαν (44. 2-3).[1] Such were the difficulties of a naval expedition abroad: they were able in places to land for water (the prime necessity) and to anchor for rest; some cities would not allow even this; the most friendly allowed them to land and set up a camp, and from there to buy food; an ally would have offered entry into the town as well with all the facilities for lodging and purchase. Similarly, Apollodoros son of Pasion doubtless exaggerated the dangers and discomforts that he had so patriotically undergone; but he correctly describes the conditions of naval warfare, when he says that, *the shore being hostile*, his ship could not put in for the evening meal, and his men went supperless and sleepless the whole night.[2]

That is to say, a Greek fleet had an extremely narrow range of action; it must be within easy reach, a few hours' journey, of a suitable friendly shore—a shore that is, that has not only an abundance of food and water, especially the latter, but on which a regular encampment can be made, where men can land, cook, sleep, and embark again at any time. A fleet is, of course, always to some extent tied to its base; no fleet, however strong at sea, can live long without the land; it must be able from time to time to renew supplies of food and, now, fuel, and to do repairs; but in the days of the great sailing-ships and in modern times, a fleet can be at sea for days and cover great distances, pursuing or avoiding the enemy. A Greek fleet of triremes had every day, so to speak, to have a base of some kind within easy reach. On a distant expedition, it was almost more dependent on a friend-

[1] Cf. Hermokrates' words, Thuc. vi 34. 4.
[2] Dem. l (c. *Polyclem*), 22. Cf. also, 47 (landing for a meal).

ly shore than an army on a friendly country: land troops can
more easily forage for themselves; the only advantage to the
fleet being that it could, within limits, choose its own place
for landing. The trireme, in fact, was not built for the open
sea. It was built for speed, therefore as lightly as possible,
but for speed in manœuvre, in actual battle, not for voyaging;
for tactics, that is, not for strategy.   Hence for a battle
even tackle was left on shore, as at Plemmyrion and Aigos-
potamoi. Conditions of supply making it anyhow impossible
for the ships to be long away from shore, the naval architects
concentrated all their skill in building light vessels that
could be easily handled in battle, but were unfit, comparatively, for the open sea. Rowing is in any case not a
reasonable method of travel by sea. Tarn is right in saying
a trireme was more like 'a glorified racing eight' than a
ship;[1] and racing eights are not built for voyages.

This characteristic of the trireme, the unsuitability of its
build for long sea-voyages, its dependence on the land for
almost daily supplies, has been noted by scholars who have
given special attention to the subject, by Tarn[2] and Köster,[3]
for example, though their accounts have not received sufficient recognition from historians; and the latter has shown
the distinction between the Greek merchant vessel and the
trireme noted above.[4] But the proper application of the
principle to Greek naval strategy has, as far as I know, been
missed. Take first the Persian War. The Greeks gave up the
idea of holding the pass of Tempe, we are told, because it
could be turned: certainly an insufficient excuse for the
retreat. The Greek army, in full force, could have held all
the passes, certainly long enough to have secured the loyalty
of Thessaly.[5] But for the navy conditions were different. It

[1]*Hellenistic Military and Naval Developments*, 1930, p. 124.
[2]*Op. cit.*, and 'The Greek Warship,' *J.H.S.* 1905, pp. 137, 204.
[3]*Das Antike Seewesen*, Berlin, 1923, and in Kromayer u. Veith, *Heerwesen u.
Kriegführung*, Munich, 1928 (in Müller's *Handbuch*). Indeed both Köster and Tarn
somewhat exaggerate the unseaworthiness of the trireme, its helplessness in bad
weather, for example. We seldom hear of Athenian fleets destroyed by storm; after
Arginusai the undamaged vessels survived well enough. For their purpose, voyage
along a friendly coast and battle, they were well designed.
[4]*Seewesen*, pp. 186–7. He also (p. 143) has much of interest about Greek sailing,
pointing out, as is unfortunately still necessary, that it is not true that they could
only sail with a following wind. See also p. 81, on the Homeric sailor.
[5]See however H. D. Westlake in *J.H.S.* lvi, 1936, 12–24, who analyses in detail
the political situation in Thessaly, and attributes the Greek retreat to the medism
of the Aleuadai.

must be there if it was to prevent the Persian fleet sailing south and capturing passes in the rear of the Greek army; but there was scarcely a tenable position for it. Between the mouth of the Peneios and C. Sepias (or whatever was the S.E. point of Magnesia), the whole line of the eastern shore of Ossa, Pelion and Magnesia is inhospitable to ships, exposed to the N.E. winds, and offering no landing anywhere for a large number of men, and though well supplied with water, very ill supplied with food;[1] the land round the mouth of the Peneios itself offers a sandy shore and easy landing and room for encampment, but there was no town there, and supplies would have had to come through Tempe; Persian land troops, coming down by the E. coast, E. and then S. of Olympos, would have cut off the fleet from its supplies and from contact with the army, even without forcing the pass of Tempe. If we add to this the tactical position, that the Greek fleet would have been compelled to engage the enemy in the open waters, where their slower speed[2] and inferior numbers would have exposed them to the greatest disadvantage, and that, in the event of defeat, they had no retreat but to their base at the Peneios mouth, and would have been entirely cut off, we can see why the Greek commanders chose rather to lose Thessaly than risk the whole cause with so little prospect of victory, and when defeat would have been decisive.

At Artemision the whole position was superior: tactically, because they could fight in more enclosed waters, and strategically, because Euboea formed a good base, and the N. coast good landing ground, and they could, in case of need, retreat down the Atalante channel to Chalkis or further, *provided that the shores were friendly*. It is said often enough that after the fall of Thermopylai the fleet retreated as well because to remain N. of Euboea was useless; but

---

[1] The Greek fleet might, as a matter of fact, have been stationed at Artemision with the army in Thessaly, if it could have been sure of holding the enemy fleet; for the latter could do nothing between Tempe and the Gulf of Pagasai to hamper the Greek army. But in the event of defeat at sea, the army would have been lost.

[2] Although all good writers since Grote have recognized the technical superiority of the Persian ships, it is too often forgotten, and needs emphasizing once more. The position at Artemision, and still more at Salamis, was the same as in the concluding battles of the Syracusan expedition: the better ships and seamen were at a disadvantage in narrow waters.

this is only half the truth: it retreated because its position would have become untenable. With Xerxes in possession of the coast of Opuntian Lokris, and then of Chalkis and Euboea, the fleet at Artemision was as much cut off from its base as if it had been a land force; or, at least, it would have been compelled to sail out eastwards, towards the open sea and across the Persian front, and then down the barren east coast of Euboea. The fleet must be near its base; with the Persians occupying on land first Lokris, then Boeotia and Attica, it was forced back to Salamis or the Isthmus.[1] Similarly on the Persian side: it is wrong to argue with, for example, Wace,[2] that Aphetai cannot have been within the Gulf of Pagasai or at its entrance, because 'if the Persians could enter the Gulf, they would have passed the Greeks at Artemision and have outflanked Leonidas at Thermopylai.' They could not do that unless at the same time they had secured the shore behind Themistokles and Leonidas, as later they might have landed at Argos to turn the position at the Isthmus, if Argos was really friendly. Otherwise they might have as easily outflanked the Greeks by sailing down the east coast of Euboea. But the Persian army and fleet moved together even more for the sake of the latter than the former.[3]

I am not supposing that this explains all the difficulties in the story of the Artemision–Thermopylai fighting. These consist in the action of the Phocians, and the fact that a Spartan king was sent to guard the passes with a considerable, yet manifestly inadequate, force. There are two passes by which Central Greece can be reached from the Spercheios valley, the one by Thermopylai and Elateia, the other in a southerly direction (as the railway and a road in modern

---

[1] Köster, *Seewesen*, p. 211, and in Kromayer-Veith, p. 167, rightly calls the Greek position *unhaltbar* after the fall of Thermopylai, but without explaining why. Kromayer (*ibid.*, p. 149) followed the usual view in calling it *gegendstandlos*, as did Grote (iv, p. 170). Köster, *Seewesen*, p. 140, touches on strategy as affected by the build of the trireme, but misses the main point.

[2] 'Topography of Pelion, etc.,' *J.H.S.* 1906, p. 146.

[3] For further consideration of the details of the strategy before the fighting at Artemision, see Köster, *Stud. z. Gesch. d. antiken Seewesens, Klio*, Beih. 32, 1934, 60–8, 91–5, 97–113. If the Persians seriously contemplated taking the Greeks in the rear by circumnavigating Euboea, they underestimated the difficulties of supply, as well, probably, as the inhospitable nature of the coast. The manœuvre may have been intended only to frighten the enemy.

times) towards Doris and the western end of the Phocian plain, and thence by Amphissa to Delphi. This latter route appears to have been of quite secondary importance, in both Greek and Roman times (note that, if Herodotus is right, the Phocian defence against Thessalian inroads is at Thermopylai); but it must have been known, and in all probability the 'flight' of the Phocians before Hydarnes was nothing more than a retreat of outposts and a concentration to defend this pass, under the mistaken impression that it was here that the Persian turning movement was to be attempted. By the time the enemy was through Thermopylai and on the road to Elateia the Phocians were cut off from their allies and surrendered. But the numbers at Thermopylai, considerable but insufficient, are unexplained. It may be that a bad blunder was committed, and it was thought the force would be sufficient. It may be, as Kromayer supposes, that the Greeks never intended anything but a delaying action (as, he says, they had intended at Tempe too), to hold the Persians while the defence at the Isthmus was completed, and that everything except the cutting-off of Leonidas and some of his troops went according to plan.[1] It may be that the boundless optimism and energy of Themistokles had persuaded them that a decisive victory could be obtained at sea, if Thermopylai were held for but a short time, and therefore the whole fleet was put into action, though only small land-forces. But it seems more probable that Herodotus' account is near the truth, that the mistake was due to dissension among the allies, some being for action at Ther-

[1] A great deal of folly has been written by historians, from Herodotus to Beloch, about the action of Leonidas. Here at least there should be no difficulty. He found his position was turned, and it was his duty to extricate his army by a quick retreat. He at once sent back his troops; but a retreat, with the enemy in pursuit, does not consist only in a quick march with your back to the enemy. Leonidas had to keep some troops, and those the most reliable, to cover the retreat, to face the enemy. He chose that duty for himself, and his Spartans, Thebans and Thespians, running the risk, an unavoidable risk, of being cut off. That was the action of a good soldier and a brave man, which Leonidas was. F. Miltner now argues as well that Leonidas had to hold the Persians till the Greek fleet was safely through the Euripos, a very probable view (*Klio*, 1935, 228–41).

Kromayer also suggests that the Greeks would have defended the Kithairon-Parnes line, either north or south of the mountain-range, if they had had sufficient troops at their disposal, as they had next year, but not in 480, when so many men were on board ship. But practically the whole of the Peloponnesian army, and probably the Boeotian as well, was available. It was not the Greek habit to defend mountain passes.

mopylai, others for the Isthmus. We are familiar enough
with instances, at all periods of history, of disputes within
governments as to whether an expedition shall be sent—
some vehemently in favour, others as strongly against, with
the result that a compromise is reached and the expedition
starts, but an inadequate one. (Just as, I imagine, after fierce
debate among the directors of our railway companies, it was
decided that fresh bread should be served in restaurant-cars,
provided that there be not enough of it.) Even so, it is
difficult to understand the absence of any Athenian force at
Thermopylai. A large proportion of their men were at sea,
much larger than in any subsequent campaign; but not all
of them; and no one can accuse them of lack of enthusiasm.
Perhaps Themistokles persuaded his countrymen to concentrate all their energies on the fleet, and would not risk his
land-forces on so inadequately-found an expedition as that
to Thermopylai.[1]

However that may be, Xerxes occupied Phokis, Boeotia,
Attica. Then, and not till then, when the coast was in
friendly hands, could the Persian fleet sail round and be
ready to engage the Greeks at Salamis; without Phaleron as
a new base they would have been helpless. Once there the
question was, whose food-supply would last the longer?
The large Persian host, in a foreign country, with an immense line of communications, now in a land not rich in
foodstuffs and probably in part denuded of what it had,
must have been in difficulties. But how much more serious
the position of the Greeks! The whole allied fleet within the
straits of Salamis, the Athenian land-forces and large
numbers of refugee non-combatants on the island, and all
dependent, once the enemy chose to block the entrances
to the bay, on the food-supply of a barren island and what
the Athenians had managed to bring with them from Attica.[2]
It must have been only a matter of days before they would
have been compelled to surrender, or make their way out
into the open sea where the Persians would have all the
advantage in the fighting. No wonder the majority of the

[1] Were there perhaps many land-troops detached to guard the coast of Attica and
S. Euboea to prevent a Persian landing?
[2] Herodotus had heard something of this: viii 68. 7.

allied commanders were for retreat to the Isthmus; no wonder they urged against Themistokles the soldier's plea that military considerations were being sacrificed to political (not that political considerations were to be ignored: the Athenian and Aeginetan sailors might have suffered in morale if their families were in the hands of the enemy). Themistokles was risking everything for the sake of the tactical advantage of the straits. Artemision had persuaded him that the Greeks could win if they fought in those narrow waters, and only so; but the advantage was of no value if the Persians refused to attack. By giving false information, he induced them first to divide their forces, then to enter the straits. Why they did so, whether from over-confidence, or because the difficulties of supply were much more serious than we are told, because they *could* not wait for the Greeks either to surrender or attack, we shall never know. The event justified Themistokles. But it was a desperate gamble; and we can only be astonished at the man who, by his insistence and energy, the force of his personality, could impose his will on his colleagues, when all the military arguments but one were against him.

To get back to my immediate subject, the limitations of the trireme, its dependence on nearby land, and the conse-quences of this. We can see more clearly how important for Athens in the Peloponnesian War was the neutrality or friendship of Argos, and the possession of Kythera and Pylos: an expedition round the Peloponnese, communication with Naupaktos, became comparatively easy.[1] We can see why, to support the attack on Pylos, the Spartans landed troops on Sphakteria, φοβούμενοι μὴ ἐξ αὐτῆς τὸν πόλεμον σφίσι ποιῶνται: without the island the Athenians had no good base, Zakynthos, which was the base for the allied fleet in the Navarino campaign, being much too far off for triremes; and we know what difficulties, even after their complete victory over the Spartan fleet, the Athenians experienced in the blockade through having no friendly shore near at hand.[2] We can understand too why neither Demosthenes'

---

[1] Cf. Xen. *Hell.* vi 2. 27–30, cited above, p. 193, n. 2.

[2] Köster (in Kromayer-Veith, pp. 196–7) notes the necessity of a nearby base in foreign expeditions, and quotes the case of Demetrios Poliorketes before Rhodes, and then the similar considerations which induced the Duke of Parma to advise

colleagues nor the Spartan authorities at first attached any great importance to the capture of Pylos: it was a difficult place for the Athenians to hold, when it had to be supplied by sea. (Contrast our position at Gibraltar, connected with England by sailing-ships or steamships.) Similarly, Sicily, even if the expedition had succeeded, could scarcely have been held by Athens: not only because Athens had not enough soldiers nor administrators (especially the latter), but because the line of communications was too long; with a fleet of sailing vessels this would have been no difficulty, but the range of action of the trireme was too limited—not only was its voyage from Athens to Sicily much longer,[1] but it was dependent on the peoples of the coast. And we can understand why Greek fleets found it impossible to maintain an effective blockade, even when in command of the sea, why Peloponnesian squadrons were able to escape the vigilance of a superior Athenian fleet, why it was so difficult to keep the sea clear of pirates: triremes could not keep continuously at sea long enough for police work. The fact that the Mytileneans held most of the *land* increased the difficulties of the Athenian fleet that was blockading them: τὸ δὲ περὶ τὰ στρατόπεδα οὐ πολὺ κατεῖχον οἱ Ἀθηναῖοι, ναύσταθμον δὲ μᾶλλον ἦν αὐτοῖς πλοίων καὶ ἀγορὰ ἡ Μαλέα. They must have a friendly land-base near at hand, this time on the island itself.[2] Difficulties from exactly the same cause were envisaged or experienced at Pylos and Syracuse.[3] The remarkable thing is that Athens succeeded as well as she did, both in 'keeping her allies in hand' and in suppressing piracy.[4]

A word as to the Greek attitude to the sea and sea-adventure. Even Köster, a sympathetic writer, who does justice to

the King of Spain to secure Flushing before sending the Armada. But he does not note the special difficulty of the trireme. In the late war the allies had to have a base at Lemnos and Imbros for the attack on Gallipoli; but that does not mean that modern and ancient conditions of naval attack are the same, and it is the difference that needs emphasis. In fact, compare the strategical factors in the campaigns of Pylos and Navarino.

[1] There was not much difference in the average *speed* of trireme and merchantman —each from five to six knots. See Köster, *Seewesen*, pp. 125, 177 ff.

[2] Thuc. iii 6. 2.

[3] Thuc. iv 27. 1, vii 12. 3-5.

[4] Conversely, Alexander the Great defeated the Persian fleet on land, when finally by the capture of Tyre he had taken all but their island bases.

their actual achievements in navigation, agrees with the majority that the Greeks had no real love for the sea, were not true seamen, had no naval heroes; seamanship was not praised in their songs.[1] It may be so; I would not assert this view to be wrong. But it is worth while uttering a word of warning: fragmentary remains of a literature and an art can so easily mislead. Read the story of the storm at sea in *Amelia* (bk. iii, c. 4), in which 'the sailors were going to hoist out the boat and save themselves,' leaving the soldiers to their fate; as soon as it was brought alongside, 'the master himself, notwithstanding all his love for her, quitted his ship, and leapt into the boat,' and 'every man present attempted to follow his example'; of the two officers one 'appeared quite stupefied with fear,' the other was 'no less stupefied (if I may so express myself) with foolhardiness, and seemed almost insensible of his danger'; and 'as to the remaining part of the ship's crew and the soldiery, most of them were dead drunk, and the rest were endeavouring, as fast as they could, to prepare for death in the same manner.' So in *Comedy of Errors* i, 1: 'the sailors sought for safety in our boat, and left the ship, then sinking-ripe, to us.' Who would suspect John Bull of any connexion with the sea? Hesiod's Boeotian was not more a landsman than the English countryman; and not the peasant only, but the gentry—Sir Willoughby Patterne, Sir Thomas Bertram, above all Sir Walter Elliot—far stranger to the sea than Homer's heroes. If only a little English literature survives, but amongst it Jane Austen's novels, and it is known not only that she lived in the great days of Nelson, but actually had close family connexion with the navy, what will be thought from *Mansfield Park* and *Persuasion* of our English love of adventure at sea? How much would be suspected from Shakespeare? Nobles are generally landsmen: especially when the sailing-ship is a merchantman, and the warship is rowed. And literature, even history, can be very conventional. Characteristically Aristotle describes the training of the Athenian hoplite, but says nothing about the rowers, still less of their officers; yet they were more highly skilled than the soldiers. I suspect the Greeks had more of the sea in them than we

[1] *Seewesen*, pp. 80–3.

imagine. Aristophanes understood the sailors among his own countrymen (as he understood most things democratic):

δεῦρ' ἔλθ' ἐς χορόν, ὦ χρυσοτρίαιν', ὦ
δελφίνων μεδέων, Σουνιάρατε,
ὦ Γεραίστιε παῖ Κρόνου,
Φορμίωνί τε φίλτατ', ἐκ
τῶν ἄλλων τε θεῶν Ἀθη-
ναίοις πρὸς τὸ παρεστός.

And the Athenians were not the greatest of Greek sailors; Phokaians, Samians, Milesians would claim the prize.

XI

THE END OF THE CITY-STATE[1]

In the large majority of histories of Ancient Greece, both learned and popular, but especially in the latter, there is agreement on these three propositions: first, that Greek independence was ended by Philip's victory at Chaironeia, the battle 'fatal to liberty'; second, that the victory was, in the main, due to the degeneracy of the Greeks of the fourth century—Demosthenes' appeal to his countrymen was inevitably in vain, for he was calling upon them to act as though they were still the men of the age of Themistokles and Perikles; and thirdly, that it is remarkable that there was hardly a Greek of the time who saw what to us seems so obvious, that the day of the city-state was over, and though we may forgive and even sympathize with the patriotic ardour of Demosthenes, it is hard to understand the blindness of Aristotle. The year 338, it is said, marks the end of Greek history in the old sense, it is the close of an epoch; though the romantic career of Alexander, and the fact that both Demosthenes and Aristotle survived him, have induced most historians to carry their narratives down to 323. The latest important History in English, that edited by Dr. Cary, makes this year end the second of its three main divisions, though the Cambridge History made its sixth volume cover the period 403 to 301, the year at which Grote ended his great work. These three propositions can be summed up in the statement that the battle of Chaironeia is the end of an epoch; and I propose to examine that statement in its three aspects.

I. THE POLITICAL CONDITION OF THE GREEK CITY-STATES AFTER CHAIRONEIA

That so many historians who have held the opinion that the Greek states lost their independence in 338, have yet

[1] I agree with Wilamowitz that the term *City-state* is very misleading, but there is no convenient alternative. The German *Kleinstaat, Kleinstaaterei*, represent the idea much more correctly.

found themselves impelled to continue their narratives
further, that is to say, beyond what they felt to be the end of
classical Greek history, to the death of Alexander, should
itself make us pause. For there is one thing to which all
would agree, and that is that Alexander's career, if not
Philip's, opens a new epoch; the chapters which cover the
years from 338 to 323 in such histories are not the last act,
nor yet the epilogue, of the drama, which ended in 338, but
the first and glorious act of a new one; and they are tacked on
in an episodic manner which is both artistically and historically false. Why then have these historians not ended
their work with Chaironeia? Partly because of the fascination
of Alexander's career; but also, and this is for us more important, because they felt that, with both Demosthenes and
Aristotle surviving the battle by sixteen years, it was impossible to say that the city-state was dead. Had their accounts
of those sixteen years been written with Athens still in the
centre, Alexander only mentioned in so far as his actions
directly affected hers, Demosthenes and Aristotle the most
prominent figures, and so have closed with their deaths, that
would have been artistically sound, the epilogue to the drama,
but historically false; for Alexander's career outshines the
last years of the Athenian politician, if not those of the philosopher. Or rather, it would have been historically false, unless
they had expressly called their work not a History of Greece
(of which Alexander and his successors so obviously form a
part), but a History of the Greek city-states. For such a
history it would be correct to put the conquest of the East
into the background, important as that background was;
but it still remains to ask the question, whether, if we reject
338, the year 322 can properly be said to mark the end of
the city-state epoch. (Written histories, and separate
volumes of universal histories, must end somewhere; some
year must be chosen, however much we may feel that no
date is actually the *end*.) And, first of all, we realize at once
that epochs overlap: that the beginning of the Hellenistic
period as we call it, that is, politically, the period of the large
territorial *Greek* state (the large barbarian state had long
been known and played its part in Greek affairs), goes back
at least to the beginning of Alexander's reign, or to 334 B.C.,

if we would take a symbolic year, though more accurately
to that of Philip's; and that the end of the small state period
came some time later.[1] The beginning of the new epoch is
shown by the title of Theopompos' *History of His Times*—
Φιλιππικά. It is not only that a man's name takes the place
of the state's, but one state gives its name to the history of
the contemporary Greek world. Hitherto all histories of
Greece had been Ἑλληνικά; an Ἀτθίς, a Λακωνικά, were
local history, antiquary's work; but Theopompos' work was
not a *History of Macedon in the Reign of Philip*, any more than
it was a biography of the king, but a *History of Greece* at a
time when that was dominated by the activities of one people
and one man.[2] That two series of events overlap, and that
each series affects the other, makes the work of narration far
more difficult for the historian; but it does not do away with
the necessity of distinguishing the two series.[3] Here I am
concerned with one series only, the last years of the city-
state, and with the question—when may we conveniently, or,
if you will, conventionally, say that the city-state system ended?
The other series, which opens the story of the Hellenistic

[1] Just as within the city-state period, the struggle with Persia, 490 (or, if you will,
499)–449, overlaps the struggle between the Greek states themselves, which culmin-
ated in the Peloponnesian war and continued into the fourth century. The few
years that passed between the battle of Mantineia in 362 and the earliest activities of
Philip do mark a pause, as though a fast-flowing river which had just passed a
series of shoals and rapids were for a short space to widen out to a quiet stream
before resuming once more its still hurried but ever-widening passage to the sea.

Professor Toynbee, in *Essays in Honour of Gilbert Murray*, p. 299, says that the
Greeks who began a new era with Alexander's crossing of the Hellespont—who
made, that is, the archonship of Euainetos at Athens and the second year of the
111th Olympiad into Year 1—were saying thereby that 'it was the first event in
history worth recording.' This is a misunderstanding. They were very far from
turning their backs on the past: Alexander's first act was to·sacrifice to Achilles at
Troy (back to Homer), and there was always present the idea that his invasion was
the revenge (in the manner of Herodotus' preface) for the Persian invasion of Greece
—back to Marathon and Salamis; just as Napoleon made his son King of Rome,
though the Revolution had also started a new era. We must remember that the
Greeks before this time had had no era, and they were always making attempts to
solve the simple problem of dating. The author of the Parian Chronicle did not, in
dating events before 264 B.C., imagine that history would stop there.

[2] The *Cambridge Ancient History* entitles its fifth volume *Athens*, its sixth *Macedon*.
The Greeks would have accepted the latter, but not the former.

[3] There was every opportunity for making this distinction in the new Methuen
History of Greece. It is in three volumes, and each volume by a different
author. It would have been, at the least, an interesting experiment, if Professor
Laistner had carried the story of the city-states beyond 323 (to 262, in my opinion),
and Dr. Cary had then resumed from 336, to give the story of the Hellenistic
states. Similarly, though in this case it is not so important, Professor Ormerod
could have carried the story of the Persian Wars in vol. i down to 449.

states, will only be considered in so far as it affects this.

What, then, happened in 338? Did the battle of Chaironeia put an end to the independence of the Greek States? Did they become subject to Macedon? Was Greece now at last united, under the Macedonian crown—Beloch entitles his chapter on the second half of Philip's reign *Die Griechische Einheit*? A little thought only is sufficient to show that the question—for it is in reality one question only—must be answered in the negative. After the defeat, the Athenians hurriedly put their city in a state of defence; the walls were repaired where necessary, the reserve troops organized to man them, the country population began to move within their protection. The scene was a repetition of that of 431, though more hurried, more anxious and nervous; there was no need to desert the city and take to the ships, as in 480, for the long walls secured connexion with the sea. But unlike Xerxes, for he had quite different aims, Philip did not attack; instead he proposed terms of peace. We write 'he proposed very generous terms,' 'he spared Athens,' as though Athens lay at his mercy. In fact, he prudently refrained from what must have proved either a long and hopeless siege (hopeless, if Athens' morale held out, and while she controlled the sea), or from a difficult assault. He had tried new engines for the assault of walls; but he had only two years before experienced severe defeats at Perinthos and Byzantion in just such circumstances—against a steady defence of city-walls and a superior fleet. In 352 he had been easily rebuffed by energetic Athenian action at Thermopylai. He was a great soldier, none greater in his day; but he was not invincible. In truth he and Demosthenes were not badly matched: had he tried to conquer Athens, as he had conquered Olynthos, we need not doubt that Athens would have held out, and Philip have been baffled once more.

And to what end? For he had no desire to capture Athens. He had one aim now, and one only, the conquest of the East. (How much earlier he had formulated this aim to himself we do not know; certainly some years before 340 and his attack on Byzantion.) The capture of Greek cities and their incorporation within his kingdom was no part of it. He must be secure from Greek attack in Macedon, and he must have

control of the Hellespont and the Bosporos. He had failed
to achieve this in 340; he saw another opportunity in 339–8
and seized it by his campaign in Phokis. His victory at
Chaironeia decided not the question of independence for
the Greek states, but whether he was to be able to invade
Persia. It gave him the indispensable control of the Straits,
because he obtained by it the withdrawal thence of the
Athenians. He was a great strategist; and he was not the
man to let the glitter of immediate triumphs blind him to the
needs of his greater plan.

More than this. He had not only no desire to conquer
Athens, or Greece. He had a more positive aim—an active
alliance for the sake of his invasion. The conquest of Persia
was to be no merely Macedonian affair, nor a merely
military triumph. It was to be Greek; and the soldiers'
victory was to be followed by colonization. For this the active
support of the Greek states, and their moral backing were
all but indispensable—and especially the moral backing of
Athens, which was become by this time so clearly the most
distinguished state of Philip's world. His own Macedonians
might supply the best troops—certainly he could rely on
their loyalty in a way in which he could never have hoped to
rely on any from Greece. But they were only to be part, if
the best and most numerous part, of a Pan-hellenic army.
Hence his interest in Olympia and the Amphiktyonic
assembly of Delphi; Macedon must be part of the Greek
world. Hence the congress at Corinth and the Pan-hellenic
League. The league but renewed the old ideas of the Delian
confederacy at its inception (the treasurers of that confederacy were treasurers of the *Greeks*, *Hellenotamiai*, not of the
Athenians, or of the Allies), and was even more liberal than
that had been, more careful to preserve the independence of
the separate states; for there was no φόρος to pay in lieu of
military contingents. Philip was elected to supreme command of all the forces, just as Athens had occupied a different
position at Delos from that of any other state and had
supplied the military leaders; but it was an alliance of free,
autonomous states.[1] The Congress of Corinth was Philip's

[1]For the constitution of the League, see U. Wilcken in *Sitzb. Berliner Akad.*,
1927, 277 ff., and 1929, 308 ff.; and W. Schwahn, *Rhein. Mus.* lxxviii, 1929,
188–198, and *Klio*, Beiheft 21, 1930, together with a good critical review of the
latter's conclusions by F. Geyer in *Phil. Woch.*, 1932, 136–41.

triumph rather than the battle of Chaironeia, which only led up to it. Whether, if he had lived, or if Alexander had been a different kind of man, a cautious man, the league of 338 would have developed into a more or less closely organized empire, as did the league of 477, is another question.[1] Obviously Demosthenes might reasonably have feared that it would; it was (humanly speaking) inevitable that Athens should resist such a development, just as it was, to be more particular, inevitable that she should resist Philip's expansion towards Byzantion and the Chersonesos, defending thereby her own freedom of access to the Euxine through the Straits. As it was, nothing of the kind happened.

The Delian League had been converted into an empire, more or less closely organized; and it is worth considering for a moment, for the purposes of comparison, some of the measures adopted then by Athens. From the beginning the decision of so many of the allies to contribute funds rather than military forces resulted in an increase of the Athenian fleet relatively to those of the other states in the League; for though large numbers of citizens of these states served in the fleet, it was officered and trained by Athenians, the ships designed and built at Athens. She took every opportunity to increase the number of the tribute-paying allies and thereby to decrease that of the separate units in the whole force of the League; so that by 439 only Lesbos and Chios had their own fleets, manned and built by themselves, and these formed but a small proportion of the whole. Taken generally, the fleet—and that means the principal armed force of the League—was a unity, and was Athenian; and the allies who rowed in it joined as individuals, men attracted by the service (perhaps at times pressed into service), not as contingents from the several states. Secondly, where necessary and as occasion offered (not, in my opinion, everywhere), Athens used her power to modify the constitutions of the states, to set up democracies after her own model; and decided

[1]Equally interesting is it to speculate on what would have happened if Alexander *had* been Parmenion and stayed his advance at the Euphrates. The Greeks would not have been so dispersed; there might have developed a closely-built state from the Adriatic to the Euphrates under one ruler, and thereby a much happier and perhaps more creative time for its inhabitants; the Hellenization of the East was after all ultimately bounded there, when the Parthians recovered their independence. But there would have been no conception of the World-state; and that was to prove to be Alexander's greatest gift to Europe.

that all trials of crimes that could be interpreted as treason to the League[1] should be tried in her own law courts. Thirdly, she planted cleruchies of her own citizens in places of strategic or political importance—these cleruchies being not colonies in the older Greek sense, and not therefore independent communities, but extensions of Athens; for the settlers retained their Athenian citizenship. In addition, she encouraged trade within the league not only generally by the maintenance of peace and the suppression of piracy, but by commercial agreements between herself and the other members; and thereby encouraged the use of a common coinage (or a common standard of coins and weights and measures) until she finally imposed her own on all her subjects. The numerous foreigners, largely from the empire, who settled in Athens for purposes of trade, and were welcomed and honoured there, and who naturally retained numerous ties with their cities of origin, helped the growth of a common feeling. The Mysteries of Eleusis, if they could not be an international festival, the equal of Olympia, were at least made an imperial one; and, finally, Athens made the magnificent effort to persuade the cities that she was their cultural centre, a worthy capital, that they could share in her glory and that, as Perikles said, none could complain that they were subject to a city that was unworthy to rule.

All those steps, towards a common fleet, common political ideas, common trade and a common glory, were steps in the direction of unity. What Athens and her subject-allies would ultimately have made of the empire had circumstances been but a little different from what they were (had Alkibiades, for instance, been built more after the fashion of Perikles, or even of Kimon), we cannot tell; but we can say that even with these steps to unity, Athens was still far not only from creating, but even from thinking of the empire as organically one. If we contrast the position of the Roman governor of a province, from the earliest days of foreign conquest, with any Athenian official, we shall see the difference at once. Athens sent out no magistrate to rule her subjects, as Rome did; officers, yes, to assess and perhaps to

[1]Not, as generally interpreted, all cases involving the penalty of death or exile. See *C.R.*, 1936, p. 8.

collect tribute, to see that ordinances were obeyed, to command a garrison—to make, that is, Athenian domination
over the cities secure; but not magistrates to conduct the
administration. The division of the empire into districts was
made only for the convenience of tribute-collection and of
record; the districts had no other function as parts of an
organized whole—and of course there was no governor, or
even a tax-gatherer or assessor, of a district; the demos did
not delegate its powers. Nothing could make clearer the fact
that the league was in fact as well as in theory a union of
separate states than those treaties which also make clear
how real was Athenian domination: Erythrai and Chalkis
have their fates decided for them by Athens, but they are to
remain self-governing units. The trade agreements were
made as with states that were not only autonomous but equal.
When Perikles carried in the assembly his proposal to
summon a Pan-hellenic congress, to consider questions of
peace and of the freedom of the seas—'so that all should sail
the seas without fear and keep the peace'—it was taken for
granted that the states subject to Athens should be represented in the same way as Athens herself and as those of
the Peloponnese and Central and Northern Greece; Athens
could not speak for them—any more than she would have
thought for a moment that a Mytilenean or Seriphian
victor in the games at Olympia or Delphi, or at Athens,
should be anything but so described. Domination, not
absorption, was the Greek method, the opposite of Rome's.
That is why Athens did not offer her citizenship to her
subject communities: not because she was less 'liberal' than
Rome, but because she did not want to absorb them and
they would not have said thank you for the gift—except as
an honour without practical effect. On the one occasion on
which she did offer her citizenship to a whole community,
to Samos in 405, she guaranteed to recognize Samian
autonomy at the same time.

If we consider this, and reflect that Philip of Macedon did
not attempt even those steps towards unity which Athens
had taken—no encouragement of trade, no common coinage,
no magistrates, not even a common army; and imagine
Pella as an inspiring centre of culture for Greece!—we can

see how mistaken it is to speak of the Greek states having become subject to Macedon in 338, of the union of Greece having been accomplished by Macedon, of the blindness of Demosthenes in not seeing that this union was desirable. Philip had become the dominating figure in the Greek world, strong enough to interfere effectively with any state that might seek to cross his will; but he had in no sense altered the political structure of that world. In resisting him Athens was acting only as other states had acted in the fifth century against herself, and in the fourth against Sparta; and with this much more reason, that Macedon had but recently risen from a state of semi-barbarism marked not only by assassination and civil war, but by extreme instability (there had been fifteen claimants to the throne between the death of Archelaos in 399 and Philip's accession, and eight of them on it; twelve met with violent deaths, only one king dying in his bed). She had in any case little political experience of the kind that Greece would have welcomed; and no one could be glad of domination by a country which, for all he knew, might on the death of Philip revert to the anarchy of the forty years preceding his accession.

Alexander, indeed, soon showed that this was not going to happen; but after his destruction of Thebes, though he demanded the surrender of the active anti-Macedonian politicians as security for peace, he waived that demand rather than provoke Athens to a war he did not desire, and had no thought of altering the political status of any of the Greek cities who were members of the Pan-hellenic League. Athens, naturally, spent the years after 335, as a completely independent power, in a steady effort to strengthen her forces in view of the possibility of future conflict. A great effort was made; financial administration was reorganized, a more efficient training for the army was introduced, new kinds of warships tried. It is particularly interesting that the change was in the direction of a greater professionalism, from a desire for efficiency (they had had experience of the extremely efficient Philip), away from the old and persistent amateur methods which had been one of the likeable weaknesses of the Athenian demos and other Greek states. The ultimate effect of Alexander's conquest of the East on the Greek *Kleinstaaterei* no man as yet could foresee. The Greek cities were still in vigorous being; they must be made capable of effective self-defence.

But, if that is true of 338, is it also true of 322? Alexander before his death had, even from distant Babylon, shown his power in Greece by his demand for the restoration of exiles in all the states and his request to be recognized as a god (the political implication of this latter being however a very uncertain matter); but there had been no change in political status—the demand for the restoration of exiles meant, for example, far less interference with the autonomy of the Greek cities than the Athenian practice in the fifth century by which they themselves tried the cases among their allies which involved the penalty of exile. In 322, however, there was a change in Macedonian methods; and the question now becomes: If it is wrong to speak of Athens 'revolting' from Macedon in 323 as though she had already become a subject state, part of the kingdom of Macedon, would it be equally wrong after 322? Antipatros then at least took measures more like those of Athens and Sparta in their days of dominion: the constitution of Athens was violently altered, and a garrison installed in Munychia to control both constitution and policy. But neither was this an attempt at unity; the oligarchy was not secured in power because oligarchy as such was more agreeable to Macedonian ideas, as the democracies in the subject states of the Delian confederacy had been more agreeable to Athenian ideas, because with such a constitution it would be easier for Greeks and Macedonians to coalesce, but because it was easier to control and the democratic leaders had been in fact the leaders of active resistance. The garrison signified the occupation and control of foreign territory, not an alteration, even a contemplated alteration, of state frontiers. Both measures served, strictly speaking, not to modify Athenian autonomy, but to curb her power of doing harm to Macedon. No Macedonian citizen, for example, had any more rights within Athenian territory than he had had before, or than any other foreigner; contrast the position of Roman citizens and *socii* in the earliest provinces. Better still, contrast the position of the Greeks in the newly-founded or re-founded cities of Alexander's empire in Asia and Egypt. The events of 318 B.C., so vividly, and so incompletely, described by Plutarch—the quarrel between the Macedonian leaders, the rival Athenian delegations at the camp of Polyperchon, the trial and execution of Phokion—show as clearly as can be the political weakness of Athens and the dominance of Macedon, as clearly as they show the least attractive side of the Athenian character; but they show as well that in no sense was Athens incorporated within a Macedonian empire. Polyperchon, with the half-wit king Philip IV, for whom he was self-appointed guardian, was marching through Phokis towards Athens; Nikanor the new commander of the Munychia garrison had been sent there by Kassandros, to secure its loyalty to him against his rival Polyperchon.[1] Phokion, now over eighty years old, had for three years maintained peaceful and even friendly relations with the commander of the garrison, and had recently been guilty of an act which, honestly enough intended, even Plutarch admits to have been almost treacherous to his country. Polyperchon therefore, anxious himself to gain control of Athens, declared for the democrats, promising, of course, complete freedom; the latter, now led by a worthless demagogue, Hagnonides, welcomed the alliance, not seeing, says Plutarch, that it would be but a change of masters, that Polyperchon's promises were worthless.[2] They gained control of Athens, apparently without interference by the garrison—an obscure point in the story, which seems to show the limit of the garrison's power: for it made no attempt to hold the city against Polyperchon, whose troops were still a long way off. Two sets of delegates set out to meet Polyperchon, the one headed by Hagnonides, the other by Phokion (another obscurity: it is not clear what the latter's aim can have been). They fell in with him at a spot near the borders of Phokis and Boeotia:

[1]Nikanor did one thing that presaged the future: on the advice of Phokion, as ἀγωνοθέτης (perhaps officially so designated, perhaps it is only a descriptive term— Ferguson, *Hellenistic Athens*, p. 28, n. 4) he gave splendid games to appease and please the people (Plut. *Phoc.* 31).

[2]Up to this point in his *Life of Phokion* Plutarch has shown no sympathy with, nor understanding of the anti-Macedonian party in Athens. He at last allows himself to criticize Phokion's whole-hearted support of Nikanor; and his criticism of the democrats on this occasion too implies that after all the freedom of Athens was a thing worth striving for. See below, p. 228, n. 1.

There Polyperchon set up a golden canopy, and placing the king and his courtiers beneath it . . . gave audience to the Athenians. The latter started accusing each other, and there was a deal of confusion and noise in the council, till Hagnonides came forward and said, 'Throw us all into one cage and send us back to Athens to give account of our conduct.' At this the king laughed aloud; but the Macedonians and foreigners who were standing around, having nothing else to do, were eager to listen and nodded to the delegates to make their accusation then and there. There was nothing fair about it; for when Phokion was speaking he was frequently interrupted by Polyperchon, until at last, striking the ground with his staff, he withdrew and refused to speak further. And when Hegemon said that Polyperchon himself could bear witness to Phokion's loyalty to the Athenian people, the latter cried out angrily, 'Stop telling lies about me in the presence of the king'; whereupon the king leapt to his feet, and rushed upon Hegemon to strike him with his spear. Polyperchon, however, got hold of him and held him back, and the council was thereupon dissolved.[1]

Phokion and his friends were thereupon put under guard, and conducted back to Athens, as prisoners, and, according to Plutarch, in a particularly shameful manner, in carts. There, he was put on his trial for treason before a tumultuous assembly—a revival of the old system of impeachment before the sovereign ecclesia. The majority consisted of men who, because they were poor, had been deprived of their political powers—their full membership of the proud citizen body of Athens—in 322 at the behest of Kassandros and with the approval of Phokion.[2] Hagnonides, his most malignant prosecutor, had been, according to Plutarch, saved by him from death at the hands of the Macedonians in 321. Phokion and some of his closest associates were condemned (even torture, we are told, was proposed by some), and drank the hemlock. When they were drinking it the hemlock gave out, and the prison-warder refused to get any more unless he were given the money. 'Someone give it him,' cried Phokion; 'we cannot apparently even die in Athens without paying for it.'

[1] Plutarch, *Phokion*, 33. 5–7.
[2] Plutarch's description of this assembly τὴν ἐκκλησίαν ἐπλήρωσαν οἱ ἄρχοντες οὐ δοῦλον, οὐ ξένον, οὐκ ἄτιμον ἀποκρίναντες, ἀλλὰ πᾶσι καὶ πάσαις ἀναπεπταμένον τὸ βῆμα καὶ θέατρον παρασχόντες (*Phoc.* 34. 2) is no more than an oligarch's account of a meeting to which Athenians excluded from the citizenship since 322 were admitted, as a sign that the democracy had been restored; but we may believe that entry had not been very scrupulously regulated.

It is a tragic story: Athens at her worst and weakest—at the mercy of unscrupulous men, of warring Macedonian factions. But what is of interest to us, in our present enquiry, is that Phokion's trial was an Athenian one; he was not tried before a Macedonian magistrate. And after the final defeat of Polyperchon by Kassandros, which followed soon after, the democrats at Athens were once more driven from power and the garrison in Munychia strengthened; but she remained a separate unit, governed by an Athenian, Demetrios of Phaleron: in the interests of Macedon, that is, to see that she could not join forces with any of Kassandros' rivals for power, but no more incorporated within his dominion than before.[1]

The position was the same in the next crisis in Athenian history—the arrival of Demetrios, son of Antigonos, in 307; and even more clearly to be seen. War had broken out between Demetrios and Kassandros. Each king wanted Athens on his side, partly for her value as a naval station—her convenient geographical position and excellent harbour—and as military ally, perhaps more for the sake of her incomparable name. Athens decided for Demetrios, who promised to respect her independence. He arrived with a fleet; Kassandros' garrison had to withdraw from Munychia, the other Demetrios, who for ten years had acted as benevolent ruler of the city, retired to Alexandria, and the old democracy was restored. The war between the rival princes lasted for four years, from 307 to 304; Athens bore the brunt of it. Much of the fighting took place in Attica, and the city suffered a long siege, when Demetrios' fleet failed to keep the sea continuously open for food supplies. Demetrios won in the end, and Athens remained free. But he was now at the height of his power, and he was not a man who was averse to displaying and exploiting it. While in Athens he took up his quarters in the Parthenon—for he had been

---

[1]'Governed by Demetrios.' Yet we should be careful about our words; cf. Wilamowitz, *Aristoteles u. Athen,* i, p. 354: 'die späteren haben in der tat von einer zwölfjährigen herrschaft des Lykurgos (oder auch Demades) ähnlich wie von der herrschaft des Phalereers Demetrios geredet. Das ist eine übertreibung, vergleichbar der vierzigjährigen oder fünfzehnjährigen herrschaft des Perikles, aber etwas wahres liegt in all diesem zu grunde: die dauernde Vorstandschaft bestimmter personen, die dem staate schon wegen der stätigkeit regelmässig gut bekommt.' The later writers did indeed know nothing of the working of the Athenian constitution.

recognized as a god, he was brother to Athena—and the
virgin goddess' home was turned, men said, into a brothel.
The worst of place-hunters and flatterers ruled in the
ecclesia, men who combined brutality to their defeated
enemies with a gross servility to the powerful. A decree
formally excluding Demetrios from any interference with
the city's affairs was soon followed, if we can believe Plutarch, by another which recognized his will to be decisive.
The better democrats, among them Demochares, nephew of
Demosthenes, soon left Athens in disgust or were exiled. A
typical incident was the initiation of Demetrios into the
Eleusinian Mysteries. It was characteristic of the man that
he wanted to be initiated; it was a tribute to Athens' fame.
But there was a six months' delay between Anthesterion
and Boedromion that all candidates for initiation had to
endure, a qualifying period between the preliminary and the
final ceremony; and, further, Anthesterion was now over,
and Demetrios could not wait—he had to go on a campaign
against Kassandros. So a subservient ecclesia decreed first
that the present month be declared to be Anthesterion, and
· the first ceremony was performed; then that it be called
Boedromion, and the ceremony was completed. Demetrios
had his way.[1] But all was not black even in this dark hour of
Athens' fortune. The philosophical schools founded by
Plato and Aristotle had never been particularly friendly to
the democracy; and the Lyceum in particular had a long
tradition of friendship with Macedon, and Theophrastos,
Aristotle's successor at the head of it, had remained happily
in Athens between 317 and 307 and was an intimate friend
of Demetrios of Phaleron, who had himself been a pupil of
Aristotle.[2] One Sophokles now moved and carried in the ecclesia and before the *nomothetai*, a law that no philosophical
school be founded without the consent of the demos. It was

[1]See Ferguson, *Hellenistic Athens*, p. 122. I believe, however, that Grote was right
in thinking that this story of the juggling with the months, which is found only in
Plutarch (*Demetr.* 12), is based on jests in contemporary comedy. It is well known
how some of Aristophanes' jests were misunderstood by some historians, and are
misunderstood to this day. Diodoros (xx 110) only says that, by special decree of
the people, the officials were authorized to dispense with the usual interval between
the ceremonies in the case of Demetrios.

[2]The Academy, as always, was truer to the native Athenian tradition, and
Xenokrates had made a noble protest against Antipatros in 322, when he refused
the citizenship under the new constitution which he had done his best to prevent.

mainly a political move, as had been the attack on Sokrates in very similar circumstances nearly a hundred years before. But he was indicted by another, who brought a γραφὴ παρανόμων on the ground that the decree was contrary to one of the laws of Solon that declared the right of free association; Sophokles was supported by Demochares who made a bitter attack on all the great philosophers since Sokrates, as oligarchs and pro-Macedonians, but was beaten in spite of the natural unpopularity of a school that had for so long been friendly with the rulers of Macedon, and so badly that he had to pay a fine of five talents. No further attempt was made to control free thought; Athens was the natural home of philosophy, and the two new schools of the Athenian Epikouros and of Zeno the Cypriot were founded at this time. She was still also the home of comedy, not only of the social comedy of Menander, who, though himself, too, a friend of Demetrios of Phaleron, refused all the tempting offers of Ptolemy to settle in Alexandria, but of political satire as well. The right to think, and the right to laugh and to criticize, could still be exercised in Athens, and in Athens only. The difference between a Kleon and a Stratokles, and between Aristophanes and the pale shadow of political comedy at the end of the fourth century, is a measure of the decline of Athenian power, not of a difference in her spirit.

Demetrios soon left Athens to help his father Antigonos in his grandiose plans to restore the world-empire of Alexander, after an agreement with Kassandros that both should respect the autonomy of all Greek states and their freedom from garrisons. Antigonos was utterly defeated by the combination of rival princes at the battle of Ipsos in 301. Athens thereby lost a powerful and at the same time inconvenient and oppressive ally; and Kassandros still ruled in Macedon and had gained strength by the defeat of Demetrios. She attempted a policy of neutrality, even of partial disarmament. The demagogues who had flattered Demetrios disappeared from power; independent men, ready to be at peace with all their powerful neighbours, took their place. The two-centuries-old democracy, with its boulê, the strategoi, election by lot, rotation of office, dicasteries and all-

THE END OF THE CITY-STATE

powerful ecclesia, was still there;[1] but it endeavoured to
break with the democratic tradition in foreign policy and to
be friends with Macedon. The attempt succeeded for a short
time; but it could not be maintained in that violent and restless age. The death of Kassandros (in 298–7), was followed
by the quarrels among his sons. Three generations earlier
this common habit of Macedonian princes would have
meant a weakening of the kingdom. But now Demetrios
saw a chance of rebuilding his shattered fortunes, and aimed
at the throne of Macedon. For this he would like control of
Athens again. But Demetrios the ally against Macedon was

[1] I do not agree with Ferguson (*Hellenistic Athens*, pp. 129–30, and an earlier
article in *Klio*, v. 1905, 155–79, with a note by Ed. Meyer, 180–2) and others that
there was any serious modification of the democratic constitution in 301. Some
changes seem to have been made, but in the same spirit as those of 335. Nor, I think,
is there sufficient evidence to suppose further modification in 276 (*ibid.* pp. 161–2),
except in detail and perhaps in the same direction. At many periods of her democratic history Athens made (rather half-heartedly) changes with a view to greater
administrative efficiency, but in no oligarchic sense. In fact, a professional efficiency
in government was not in' Greece an oligarchic ideal, any more than it was a
democratic one. Oligarchs believed in yearly magistracies and rotation of offices
as much as democrats. For an extreme instance, we can examine the two proposed
constitutions of 411 as given in Aristotle's *Constitution of Athens*. A change for
instance from plural to single control of finance (οἱ ἐπὶ τῇ διοικήσει to ὁ ἐ. τ. δ.)
in the third century (Ferguson, *Klio*, pp. 169–73) is by no means an oligarchic
change. Lykourgos, to take an obvious instance, was an extreme democrat and
anti-Macedonian. Ferguson also argues that 'no explanation of Demochares'
failure to return in 301 is possible, if we retain the ordinary view that at that time
the party, of which he was the recognized leader, got possession of the government.'
But there was to be a new policy, one of neutrality and neighbourly relations with
Macedon: Demochares may well have disapproved of it, and the new government
not have welcomed his return to Athens. Ferguson throughout assumes that any
change of policy towards Macedon implies not only a change in personnel of the
'government' at Athens, but in the constitution. In fact neither is inevitable. There
were always a few prominent people in Athens (not many) who had some diplomatic wisdom and tact, and were prepared neither to provoke Macedon nor to be
subservient.
    The decree in Demochares' honour refers to his never having held office under an
oligarchy; but this does not necessarily mean that there was a period of oligarchic
government in Athens after his return in 289. It may refer to his refusal to do
anything to help Demetrios of Phaleron. Lehmann-Haupt (*Klio*, v 375–91, and in
'Ἐπιτύμβιον Swoboda, 142–65) has an ingenious solution of the difficulty of the
'oligarchic' government's alliance with Egypt, 275–2 B.C.; but a good deal of his
ingenuity is wasted, if we but remember that Athens was autonomous. (His connexion of events in the East with those in Greece, however, is valuable.)
    Ferguson now (*Class. Phil.* xxiv. 1929, 1–31) would place the rise of Lachares to
prominence in the spring of 301, and his seizure of power in 300 (but with no change
in constitutional forms!) on account of *Ox. Pap.* xvii 2082 and of Menander,
Περιοχαί, 105–10—the dating of his Ἴμβριοι in 302–1, though it was not
then produced 'owing to Lachares'. I am not yet however convinced of the value of
2082, even if fragment 3 is rightly placed and understood, and even if Eratosthenes
is its author (de Sanctis, *Riv. di Filol.* vi, 1928); and I find it hard to believe that
the writer of the summaries of Menander's plays wished to say that one of them was
written in 302–1, but only ready for the Dionysia of 301–0.

one thing—his conduct might have to be tolerated to keep his support; Demetrios as king in Pella was quite another. Athens was not allowed to be neutral; she must choose, and now as ever anxious to prevent the domination of Macedon, was compelled to be an enemy. She was compelled also to seek for allies, especially for one who would dispute with Demetrios the control of the Aegean, so that her food supply would not be at his mercy. She could only find one amongst the rival princes; and Ptolemy, a distant and therefore a less dangerous power, promised support and entered into an alliance with her. But he proved as broken a reed as great powers often do who are pledged to support weak but distant countries; his fleet appeared off Aigina, when Athens was closely besieged by Demetrios, but his admiral refused to engage the latter's fleet in battle, and retired. His support was conditional on his not being involved in war. After a long siege Athens was starved into surrender. Demetrios was now all-powerful; he announced his decision to the people in the theatre of Dionysos: the democratic constitution was to be restored once more—it was easy to denounce Lachares and the other leaders who had fought the Macedonians as oligarchs and tyrants—and a garrison was to hold the Peiraeus; but this time Demetrios' troops seized the city-end of the long walls as well, and fortified the Mouseion hill just within the city. And Demetrios became king of Macedonia.

This was in the spring of 295; and both garrisons remained for five or six years, when the Mouseion fort was captured by Athenian troops, though the Peiraeus was still held for Demetrios. Are we to say that now at last Athens was Macedonian? Demetrios issued a new coinage with the statue of Athena Promachos in the design, as though to show that he regarded the city as his Greek capital. When in 288 and 287 he was preparing for his campaign in Asia, he had warships building in Peiraeus as well as in Demetrias and Macedonia. Wilamowitz thought that 295 should be regarded as the end of Athenian independence, as closing an epoch: in one of his masterly footnotes he wrote, 'Dass dieses Unglücksjahr in der Geschichte Athens Epoche macht, ganz anders als 321 oder der Unterwerfung durch Gonatas (geschweige 338, das nur die Phrase für epochemachend halten kann), ist erst durch CIA II b deutlich geworden. In welchem Sinne die Athena γυμνὴν ἐποίησε Λαχάρης, lehren die Schatzverzeichnisse; die ταμίαι haben nichts mehr zu verzeichnen. Die Trierarchie hört auf: Athen hat keine Flotte mehr. Die Arsenale sind leer; sie sind nicht wieder gefüllt worden. Die Institution der Metoeken verschwindet, wie wir noch näher sehen werden. Ob dem Lachares eine moralische Schuld tritt, ist zu bezweifeln: aber sein Name ist mit der Katastrophe verknüpft, welche dem Staate Athen den Todesstoss gab. Das Menschenalter bis zur Eroberung durch Gonatas ist die Agonie.'[1] Ferguson speaks of Athens as Demetrios' and his son's 'Greek capital' in 290 and 277, and as a 'rebellious city' in 288–7; of Antigonos, when Demetrios left for Asia in 287, assuming the title of king and taking over 'the management of Greek affairs'; and, after the overthrow of Demetrios in Macedonia by Pyrrhos and Lysimachos the year before, 'even though Macedon was lost Greece might still be held.'[2] All this suggests complete subjection; and we must not forget as well that for the last generation the Macedonians had controlled with garrisons Demetrias, Chalkis and Corinth, the three fetters of Greece. Moreover, just as we cannot help feeling that, on account of the deaths of both Demosthenes and Aristotle, 322 does mark the end of an epoch, for there is only Theophrastos to follow at the Lyceum and no more political oratory *is preserved* and we feel in consequence that there was none, that therefore the days of αὐτονομία and παρρησία were over: even so, with 294–3 the long list of Athenian archons is broken; henceforth, though we know the names of most, their years are uncertain or only recently after infinite labour and research to some degree re-established; we seem to be back in the dark ages, with no contemporary narrative and the very skeleton of history in fragments—it must appear that Athens, and all that Athens had stood for, is past.

Yet immediately after her capture, when Demetrios was dominant, during the period 294–288, Athens was negotia-

[1] *Demotika der Metoeken, Hermes,* xxii (1887), p. 218, 1.
[2] *Hellenistic Athens,* c. iv.

ting first with Ptolemy in Egypt, then with Lysimachos in Thrace and with Seleukos; large supplies of corn and money were sent by these princes,[1] past the Macedonian garrison; the fort on the Mouseion was captured and Eleusis recovered (289 or 288); and when in 288 or 287, after he had lost Macedonia, Demetrios attempted to recover Athens by force, in spite of his still holding Peiraeus, he failed. Once more a Macedonian king refused a direct assault on the Athenian walls,[2] and he was too impatient for a siege. Among those who helped Athens then by fighting Demetrios was Pyrrhos of Epeiros; who visited the city and sacrificed on the Acropolis, and gave to the Athenians the hollow advice not again to admit a king within their walls. A year later Demetrios left for Asia to meet his final defeat at the hands of Seleukos, and he disappears from history. His son, Antigonos Gonatas, was left in Greece with but little power, and controlling only a few garrisons. No Macedonian force was able to prevent the Gauls from invading Greece in 279–8, and it was Athens and Aetolia, with some help from other Greek cities, who were responsible for their defeat and expulsion, on their own initiative as well as with their own forces. But the Gauls had overthrown Demetrios' successor in Macedonia; and Antigonos was strong enough to take advantage of this and of the retreat of the Gauls to recover the throne there. For some years he remained at peace with Athens. He often visited the city, being on friendly terms with Zeno, and his son by Demo (an Athenian) was brought up there. It is an extreme instance of the uncertainty of the history of this period that we do not know when nor in what circumstances the Macedonian garrison was withdrawn— we know of one unsuccessful attempt to expel it, begun and frustrated by treachery, ending in heavy Athenian losses— and there have been many who have doubted whether it ever was withdrawn before the Chremonidean war. But we

---

[1] Also by some others, including Audoleon, king of the Paeonians, who were once more trying to free themselves from Macedonia. The latter never succeeded in consolidating her rule on her northern boundaries, and this was one cause of her weakness in Greece.

[2] Like Philip in 338 and Alexander in 335, he is said to have 'spared' Athens, owing to the entreaty of ambassadors. Is it probable that he would thus have allowed himself to be jockeyed out of his own 'Greek capital'?

know that even when it was there it was unable to prevent
supplies reaching Athens (either in 290–89, or later, if it
was still there, after war broke out with Antigonos in 267),
and was quite powerless to control her policy; and it was
during this time, probably in 280–79, that on the motion of
Demochares, who had been the determined enemy of
Demetrios and had left Athens in 303 and returned some
ten years later, a statue was at last erected in honour of his
uncle the great Demosthenes, to celebrate the long struggle
with Macedon; and on Demochares' own death in 271,
one was set up to him too to honour his unswerving loyalty
to the Athenian democracy. We say that Antigonos
'allowed' this, for he was a moderate and wise man; did he
also allow his 'capital' to be in alliance with Ptolemy II
against him in 267?

It is the year 262 (or in whatever year it was that the
Chremonidean war ended with her capitulation) that marks
the end of Athenian independence. It is not simply that
Macedonian troops now occupied the city itself and Peiraeus,
and many places in Attica—Sounion, Phyle, Panakton,
Salamis—and controlled the assembly and the magistrates;
but it appears that the assembly met but rarely, and above
all Athens ceased to issue her own coins—her autonomy
was gone, as well as her trade, and she never recovered it.
Even so there was no absorption into the Macedonian
kingdom, only domination now complete; the form of the
πόλις remained,[1] so that it was easy for an apparent
autonomy to be restored in 229, on the strict condition of a
quiet neutrality. But it was now a gift of the King of
Macedon. The year 322 marks the end of Athens as an
important power—her last big fleet was destroyed. During
the next two generations she is a small power, struggling to
maintain her independence against much stronger ones, and
she does not succumb till sixty years after the crushing defeat

___

[1] A particularly interesting example of the way in which the forms of the old
Greek administration were preserved by the Macedonians is the decree published
by Kougéas in Ἑλληνικά, vii, 1934, 177–208. It comes from Chalkis (always held
by Macedonian garrison) and is an edict issued by a high official—the governor of
Euboea—in the name of the king (probably Philip V); it relates to the military
stores of the garrison. In spite of the king's autocratic powers, the form of the
decree and its general tone, with its fines for disregarding the regulations and its
order for publication, are in many ways the same as those of an independent *polis*.

of Amorgos. Within a year of Antigonos' victory, there died Philemon, the last of her great line of writers of comedy, Philochoros, the last of her scholars, and Zeno, the last creative philosopher. The Muses left Athens when her independence was gone, just as the last great politician and the last political philosopher died when she lost her position as an important power.

But even this year did not see the end of the city-state, for there were others besides Athens, even if their glory is pale in comparison. Argos, Sparta, Messene, Boeotia, were still active; Byzantion, Kyzikos and Rhodes not only active, but playing a more important and independent part than they had done heretofore. Side by side with these were the Achaean and Aetolian leagues, which were not 'city-states'; not because they were federations, for the federal idea had long been known in Greece (in Boeotia and Thessaly), but because as they increased in power they absorbed their neighbours, by persuasion or by force, into their own polities, as Sparta and Athens had not done; theirs was a true territorial expansion. All these states were in active life when the Romans first crossed the Adriatic, and their activity continued till the Roman conquest. The significance of Greek History from the time of Philip III to that of Philip V does not lie in the union of the Greek states (even in Greece proper), which the Macedonians neither achieved nor attempted. They sought only to dominate, not to unite, and, essentially, they failed even in this. For they did not secure peace. Their rise to power meant only another factor, and the most disturbing factor, in the political confusion of the Greek world. They made the Roman victory easier; the newcomers from beyond the Adriatic did not find one united power to oppose them, but as always before in Greece, many separate ones, quarrelling among themselves in spite of eloquent appeals for unity; and it was fitting that Philip V, one of the most energetic and the least statesman-like of Macedonian kings, should have been the one who saw the Roman victory achieved, and was chiefly responsible for it.

The importance and the interest of this period (especially after the death of Alexander) are that during it we can watch

—fitfully, so broken is the record of it—the struggle of small powers to maintain their independence against great powers who were perpetually warring among themselves. Ferguson, entitles the fourth chapter of his *Hellenistic Athens*, which covers the years from 294 to 262, *The Crushing of Athens between Macedon and Egypt*. That is correct, and little consistent with the view that Athens was the capital of one of the two powers. She was a small independent state, not part of Macedonia, nor under her suzerainty. This is not a matter of words only; and here the analogy from modern Europe (for once) will help. When in 1914, the great powers went to war, one of the small ones, Serbia, was a direct object of conquest; two others, Belgium and Greece, not immediately concerned in the quarrel, were quite unable to prevent their territories being invaded and made the battleground of other interests. At the present day it is obvious that there are many countries whose territories, if they were left to themselves, could with equal ease be overrun by stronger neighbours; many whose policy is from time to time determined by their neighbours. But that does not mean that the independence of the smaller powers is unreal, only nominal. The political problems of to-day would be very different if Europe consisted in fact of half-a-dozen great powers who had divided the continent between them, instead of twenty-eight, of which some are very strong and some very weak. It is exactly the existence and the independence of the small powers which create one of the problems. So it was in the Greek world of the third century B.C., however different in other respects the conditions were. There were large territorial states, generally antagonistic to each other; the old *poleis*, now weak states, were unable to save themselves from being involved in the wars and being easily overrun and ultimately defeated if they could not rely upon help from others. None of the big powers was strong enough, or statesmanlike enough, either to unite the small states by conquering them, as Rome did, or to leave them alone.

In a well-known passage, often quoted, Polybios censures Demosthenes for assuming that the interests of Greece were identical with those of Athens; for not seeing that Philip's

Q

ascendency meant the protection of many small states against stronger neighbours, and for denouncing as traitors all politicians who sided with Macedon.[1] That Polybios should have written this after the Roman conquest is remarkable. It is true that Philip, except where he directly dominated affairs, as in Thessaly, supported the autonomy of the small state, especially Messene and Megalopolis against Sparta, who refused to give up the struggle for her old supremacy in the Peloponnese. It was a policy that succeeded for him; for there was no Sparta at the head of the Peloponnesian League to oppose him, and perhaps decide the issue, at Chaironeia; and Athens had been weakened and distracted by the struggles in Euboea fomented by him. But it means that far from uniting Greece, he was assisting its division into the smallest fractions; and his successors on the Macedonian throne continued his policy. When Demosthenes claimed for Athens her proper place as the champion of Greece, he was thinking of her past as the head of the Delian confederacy and advocating a policy that had far more chance of uniting Greece than ever the Macedonians did. It is his opponent Aischines who could see nothing beyond the old city-state with its narrowest limitations, who saw in Thebes only the natural enemy of Athens, condemned all co-operation, and aided her destruction at whatever cost to the whole of Greece. As Wilamowitz saw long ago,[2] Macedon did not in most cases restrict autonomy as much as Athens and Sparta had done; and her supremacy did not therefore seem so disastrous to one who believed in the small city as the proper form of state. And Isokrates? 'In little more than twenty years,' we read in the Preface to volume vi of the *Cambridge Ancient History*, 'Macedon became strong enough to impose unity upon the Greeks and to lead the West to the conquest of the East. The city-state with its insistence on particularism surrendered the lead to the military monarchy. The orators of Athens had used their powers either, as Isokrates, in advocating union, or, as Demosthenes, in striving to inspire with new life the ideal of the city-state. A Macedonian now carried out the aspirations of the one

[1] xviii 14.
[2] *Aristoteles u. Athen* i, p. 355.

and defeated the efforts of the other.' But Isokrates' ideal too was a Greek world full of little states, each autonomous. There is sincerity in his constant plea for the cessation of war between them, as in his pathetic belief in the virtue of war against the barbarian; but little else of value in all his writings. His appeals for war against the 'national enemy' had about as much actuality and chance of success as would a modern crusade for peace in Europe based on a Christian war against the infidel; and his choice of leaders—as he says, he appealed to everyone, even Jason and Dionysios— shows the worth of his political judgement. No wonder that little notice was taken of him. It is indeed one of the curiosities of the history of Greece that the shallowest and wordiest of her men of letters should apparently have anticipated the achievement of the most brilliant and decisive of her men of action. But it is only a curiosity and a coincidence. Alexander did not in fact realize the ideas of Isokrates; and the latter, had he lived yet longer, would have been still lamenting the state of his world in 323, as, with more reason, he would have lamented it in 300 or 260. His dream had been of little city-states living in peace with each other, and joining forces only for a glorious war against inferior races (how far he was from the humanity of Herodotus!); and that dream was far more effectively shattered by Alexander and his successors than it had been by Athens and Sparta.[1]

II. THE 'BLINDNESS' OF ARISTOTLE AND DEMOSTHENES TO THE SIGNIFICANCE OF CHAIRONEIA

It is true enough that by the battle of Chaironeia 'the city-state surrendered the lead to the military monarchy,' and that this surrender was confirmed and made complete at Amorgos and Krannon in 322. The large territorial state, ruled by a military autocrat, was now the dominant factor in politics. In that sense, the day of the city-state was over—it had now to play a subordinate part. Many reforms had been

[1] See P. Treves, *Demostene* (1933), c. i., for a sound appreciation of Isokrates' position. Others too, as Mathieu, *Les idées politiques d'Isocrate* (Paris, 1925), Wilcken (*Sitzb. Berl. Akad.*, 1929, and *Alexander der Grosse*) and Momigliano have properly distinguished between Isokrates' ideas and those of Philip; but the older view still prevails, as shown by the quotation given from *C.A.H.*

introduced into the Athenian administration after 335, to
secure a greater efficiency and to profit if possible from the
lessons of the war with Philip; Athens was alive and energetic. We, who know the results of the war of 323–2, feel
how useless this was: it all came too late. And most modern
historians say, not only too late, but obviously too late; that
is, that it should have been clear after 338, if not before, that
the day of the small state was past—an intelligent man would
already have seen it. So of what use all these reforms, what
use the renewal of the struggle in 323? Those who praise
Demosthenes speak of him, generally, as fighting gallantly
for a lost cause; those who blame him, say he was a politician
of narrow vision, and praise Isokrates and the pro-Macedonians: for the future lay clearly with the large state. Yet
the Greeks were intelligent if anything, and Isokrates not
more but less intelligent than most; and three men, all
intelligent, but of very different stamp, agreed in their
blindness, and they may be taken as typical of their time—
Demosthenes, Phokion and Aristotle. Demosthenes' attitude
is clear, and needs no description; but we should keep in
mind the fact that it was not based on any foolish optimism,
on an under-estimate of the enemy and over-confidence in
the strength of the Greek forces. He knew well enough the
weaknesses on his own side and the advantages on Philip's.
Phokion was a very different man. He was old already in
338—over sixty; he was a pacifist in the circumstances of
the time, a realist; later at least ready to work with Macedon.
Yet he said to his countrymen after Chaironeia: 'You agreed
to attend the Congress of Corinth, and you must abide by
that. But do not be resentful nor despondent; remember
that our ancestors too were sometimes rulers and sometimes
ruled, καλῶς δὲ ἀμφότερα ταῦτα ποιοῦντες καὶ τὴν πόλιν ἔσωσαν
καὶ τοὺς Ἕλληνας.' He was clearly not anticipating the end
of Athens' usefulness as a state. Was that, if brave, yet
stupid? Aischines said, 'All was over.' Was that vain and
pompous man more intelligent than Phokion?[1]

---

[1]Plutarch, *Phoc.* 16. 5. The limitations of Plutarch are more noticeable in his
Phocion than in most of the *Lives*: admirable in anecdote, it is only a puzzle to the
historian. As elsewhere, he shows little understanding of the political conditions
which determined his subject's actions; but in this as well there is profound inconsistency. For the description *defeatist* can be properly applied to his Phokion,

Lastly Aristotle: the friend of the Macedonian kings, one who had no sympathy with Athenian politics and politicians, who was himself ἄπολις and content to remain so, with all the advantages of the outside observer and a profound philosopher of τὰ πολιτικά—why was he so blind as to think the *polis* still important? Not only in the *Constitution of Athens*, but in the *Politics* too he regards the small state as that best suited to his countrymen and superior to other forms; he is quite unconscious that, in our modern phrase, it did not *work*, just as he is that it was already moribund, if not dead. Yet there was Alexander's career, only too plain for all men's eyes. Why did he—the wisest man of his day, divorced from the passions of national politics—why did he not either welcome the advent of Macedon to end the *Kleinstaaterei* that was ruining Greece; or, if he did not think it was ruining Greece, why did he not fear Macedon, and especially Alexander? Not surely just because Macedon respected autonomy, where it suited her, more than dominant Greek states had done; the example of her behaviour in Thessaly, Euboea and Thebes (where it did not suit her) would have saved him from such a blunder. It was partly that no doubt, but the reason is more complex.

First a word on the question whether the small state system was, for Aristotle, a mistake, a ruinous mistake; or rather, why he did not think so, for he obviously did not. For him, the question whether a political system 'worked,' was not, primarily, a question whether it secured an efficient administration or even whether it would survive external attack; but did it fulfil its purpose? A man can be killed by a lion, or a good man by a bad one; but that does not show he was not, till the moment of death, fulfilling his proper purpose; and if a man, in order to survive, must spend all his time hunting lions or on his guard against a

as to but few; he is the most unhelpful of statesmen, an honest man with a knack for the apt retort, but with no consistent policy. (Some even of his retorts are at the most apt only for the moment, as in 16. 2: 'Sir, he replied to Demosthenes, we must not ask where we are to fight, but how we can win the war. If we win, war will be anyhow far from our doors; when men are defeated, every terror is close at hand'— a truth that Demosthenes had more than once recognized.) Yet this noble appeal to Athens in 338 is the appeal of an optimist, as well as a brave man; Plutarch does not see the contradiction, and the saying is isolated—nothing that Phokion later proposes should be done is consistent with it.

bad man (and so behaving like the latter), he cannot fulfil his proper purpose. The business of the state is to provide conditions in which the best possible life is open to the citizens; and in his view, as in that of most Greeks, though himself ἄπολις, public life, politics, was part of this best life for most citizens, not a few only. It was not a matter of a few able men (whether democratically elected, or in office by birth) securing a tolerable government for the masses of their fellow-citizens; still less could an efficient autocracy organized to defend the State against neighbours be considered a desirable form (but at the most the necessity of a moment); but every citizen should take his share, not only as a duty to the state, but as part of the good life for himself. This was not obtainable under any constitutional system that he knew except the Greek—certainly no more in Macedon than in Persia or Egypt; and a political system that did in fact foster the activities not only of the politicians, but of a Sophocles, an Aristophanes, and a Plato, cannot be said not to work.

Why, then, did he not fear Macedon, see that she was ruining the Greek system? Because it would not have appeared so to a contemporary. Philip had indeed been a danger, or had seemed so; but Alexander was now carrying out his father's plans, conquering Persia and creating a new state, and at the same time getting further and further from Greece. Alexander was the successor and heir of Dareios, he was another Great King; and Greeks were quite familiar with the huge territorial, monarchical state on their eastern borders. In an earlier day it had attacked them and been defeated; thereafter they had lived fairly well at peace with it, on reasonable terms: with some fighting, some victories and defeats, but on the whole with less anxiety, with fewer interruptions of neighbourliness than amongst themselves. There had been for many a generation now little or no danger to the autonomy of most of their states; and they might reasonably expect that Persia ruled by the Greek-speaking Alexander would be yet more friendly than the old empire. The huge state indeed must have come to seem almost a necessary complement to their own small *poleis*.

But in fact something else happened, something that

neither Aristotle nor Demosthenes nor Phokion foresaw: something which did ultimately ruin the Greek states; which had they foreseen, they would certainly have feared and opposed, each in his different way. First, owing to the genius of Alexander, came the idea of the world-state, the most fruitful political idea of the new age. But secondly, the realization of the idea was immediately made impossible by the events that followed Alexander's death. The birth and, so to speak, the exposure to almost certain death, of the new idea were together disastrous to the old Greek *polis*. Men capable of thought, already disgusted with the endless twists and turns of small state politics which had not even realized its own trivial aims, turned to the world-state in the hope that there men might live in peace; to them ἀπραγμοσύνη seemed now the supreme virtue. Thoughtless men, who prided themselves on their contempt for politicians and their empty phrases—freedom, equality, the rule of law—rushed off to serve and admire the new leaders, the impatient men of action, neither knowing nor caring whether these men of action were, as Alexander had been, inspired by the civilization which had been, with such constant effort, built up with these phrases, or, like Lysimachos and many another, were ignorant of their very meaning. Both classes alike deserted the city-state; and immense numbers of men actually left Greece as soldiers of fortune or, even more commonly, as settlers in the newly-conquered East. This migration would not of itself have harmed, on the contrary would probably have benefited the cities of old Greece, as the earlier colonization of the Mediterranean had done; but, just when it was at its height, it was accompanied by that series of dynastic wars which were so destructive both of the prosperity and of the self-respect of the Greek states. It was these wars that Aristotle had not foreseen, the history of the Greek world after Alexander's and his own death; the position of the city-state in a world of big states, whose quarrels in the end made not only all real independence, but almost all genuine and honourable public life impossible. Not one of the men of the fourth century would have been happy: not Isokrates, because there was no peace; not Demosthenes, because the last hope of Athens leading Greece in defence against an alien system and in peaceful progress was gone; not Phokion, because honour in public life was gone; not Aristotle, because philosophy had become the *only* occupation of a reasonable man. All would have been unhappy, because freedom and the rule of law had both disappeared, violence had taken their place, and it must have seemed that all that Greece had stood for, at least in the political sphere, had gone for ever. For neither union nor peace was the lot of the Greek city-states in the third century.

It is, perhaps, legitimate to complain that Aristotle always assumes the superiority of the small state and never argues it. He does not, that is to say, ever stop to consider the relative advantages of the small and the big state, even if he were ultimately to come down decidedly on the side of the former. For some of the advantages of the big state, and not only the obvious material ones, must have been clear to him. The pan-hellenic activities of the artists and thinkers, and the careers of men like Iphikrates and Chabrias, who, though loyal citizens of Athens, yet because they were not politicians, found their own city too small for their energies, would have suggested them to him. It is the same with his discussion of slavery. It was because he had so high a conception of the functions of the free man, of *all* free men, because he made such demands on him and in consequence conceded him such privileges, that he thought of those who were not equal to these functions and privileges to be by nature not-free, slaves. He is in effect asserting no more than the natural inequality of man, and assuming that all free men should be equal, should have equal rights and duties, should 'rule and be ruled in turn.' It is legitimate to say that, even if we grant both the major and the minor premisses implied, that men are unequal and so unequal that some must always be among the rulers and others be the ruled, it does not necessarily follow that the relation between rulers and ruled should be that of master and slave. This step in the argument Aristotle has omitted to prove. In a similar way he has omitted to prove that the advantages of the small state, great as they are, are yet greater than those of the large one; he does not consider the latter at all: he assumes that the best, if not the only state for free men must be the *polis*, that because man is a political animal, the state must be part of his life, and its political life must be such that every citizen (that is, ideally, every free man in it) may take a personal part in it. Macedonia was an ἔθνος, not a πόλις, though she might be a very powerful one and a very uncomfortable neighbour, just as Persia had often been to the Greeks of Asia. She was not for that reason a state of the kind best suited to free men. But so long as Alexander was conquering Persia, so long as he could be regarded simply as the successor to Dareios, and was not destroying the autonomy of the Greek states, there was no danger to fear; but rather a cause for optimism, that states that had become subject to Persia might now be freed.[1]

III. THE 'DEGENERACY' OF THE GREEKS IN THE FOURTH CENTURY

The Greek states, and more especially Athens, were decisively defeated in 338 and in 323–2. It need not be said that decisive military defeat is no proof of decline or degeneracy, or all peoples will have been declining when at their prime. But the Greek states did not recover after 322; was the cause of this, or the principal cause, internal or external? I have already explained that in my opinion it was external: in place of the old Persian Empire, which had been

[1] If Aristotle ever gave to Alexander what has been called 'the truly Greek' advice to treat the barbarians whom he was to conquer as slaves but the Greeks as free men, he meant it politically: that is to say, regard the Persians as your subjects, as Dareios did before you, but restore and preserve the autonomy and freedom of the Greek states.

It is true of course that Aristotle did not appreciate what was greatest in Alexander, his dream of the union of mankind, which is no part of my subject in this essay. 'If the things Alexander did were great,' says Tarn (*C.A.H.* vi, 437), 'one thing he dreamt was greater. We may put it that he found the Ideal State of Aristotle, and substituted the Ideal State of Zeno. It was not merely that he overthrew the narrow restraints of the former, and, in place of limiting men by their opportunity, created opportunities adequate for men in a world where none need be a pauper and restrictions on population were meaningless. Aristotle's State had still cared nothing for humanity outside its own borders; the stranger must still be a serf or an enemy. Alexander changed all that. When he prayed for a union of hearts and a joint commonwealth of Macedonians and Persians, he proclaimed for the first time, through a brotherhood of peoples, the brotherhood of man.' On which, however, I would make two comments: when Alexander's dream in part came true in the Roman Empire, it can hardly be said that men profited by their enlarged opportunities as well as they had within the old narrow limits of the city-state; secondly, it is not true that 'the stranger must still be a serf or an enemy.' He could be, and often was, a guest. Zeno himself was one.

on the whole a good neighbour to the Greeks, they had, not the world-state, Greek in culture, of Alexander's planning, but three or four great powers whose constant quarrels involved the whole Greek world, and fatally weakened or destroyed the old city-states. In view, however, of the prevalent opinion that these states were already so degenerate by 338 that their defeat, and final defeat, without hope of recovery, was inevitable (and easily to be foreseen), it is worth while discussing the question, more particularly as it involves a nice problem of evidence.

First, what meaning are we to give to the term degeneracy or decadence, when applied to a people? Only one, I think: loss of creative energy, of vitality. We can, for example, reasonably speak of Greece being decadent by the first century B.C. There was then no manifestation of original genius, no great activity of mind: only a philosopher or two of the second class, like Philodemos, only a few minor poets such as Meleager; and no great achievements in other branches of human activity. What a different picture is presented by the fourth century and the first half of the third. There are some ages in which a magnificent energy is displayed throughout almost the whole range of human activities. The fifth century in Greece is clearly one of these. But it is almost, if not quite, as true of the fourth. There was a remarkable recovery from the disasters of the Peloponnesian War; philosophy and science reached even greater heights than before; sculpture and painting were as fresh, as skilful and as fertile as in the previous century; Demosthenes, Hypereides and Menander showed what yet could be done with the flexible Greek language; manufacture and commerce flourished, and knew how to make use of the fresh opportunities provided by Alexander's conquest; Greek engineers and scientists revived the prosperity of agriculture in Egypt, and doubtless in Asia as well, only we have not the evidence. Greek soldiers, both as officers and in the ranks, were showing themselves as good as any in the world, both in Greece and abroad.[1] Further, there was the immense

[1]When Persia reconquered Egypt in 343–2, the best soldiers on both sides were Greek. And, when we speak of citizens refusing to serve in person and committing their wars to mercenaries, we must remember that these latter were Greek, and that we are considering a general decadence of the people.

vitality shown in the settlement and hellenization of the
newly-conquered lands—a work comparable on its scale
with the colonization of North and South America in
modern times. This alone should have been sufficient to
prove how idle is talk of Greek decadence; when the first
generation of the third century had passed away, it must
still have seemed that their energies were inexhaustible,
their powers undimmed.

But what of public affairs? Had not their conduct so
declined that we may properly talk of decadence, and see
in it not only the cause of the defeat, but a proof that it was
inevitable, and desirable? Does not Demosthenes himself
provide the evidence? There was indeed much vacillation
and weakness in the conduct of the war with Philip; but not
more than appears in Herodotus' narrative of the war
against Persia. The differences in the results of the two
wars are not to be explained by any decline in the morale of
the individual Greek, nor by failure in leadership. But now,
on the one side, there was a general and statesman of the
highest class, with a well-trained army, and operating not
far from his base; then there had been Xerxes with his
heterogeneous forces, operating far from home and in a
country strange to them and unable to supply them ade-
quately. On the other side, there was this important difference: the absence of Sparta at Chaironeia. Thebes took her
place, and her troops, as they had always done, proved
themselves as good soldiers as the Spartans; but she had not
her influence in Greece, and what influence she might have
had was weakened by her long friendship with Philip. She
had herself destroyed the ability of Sparta to help the
national cause by her campaigns in the Peloponnese after
Leuktra; not only was the Peloponnesian League ended,
but its former members were nearly all of them paralysed
by mutual suspicion; they could have no influence nor active
policy outside the peninsula. That is the story of the
military defeat at Chaironeia, and with but few changes, of
the Lamian War as well.

It will be said, there is all the evidence of Demosthenes
for the corruption and incompetence of Athenian administration—not only in his public speeches, when he is advoca-

ting a policy, but in some of his law-court speeches in which damning facts come to light incidentally, where even if a particular statement is not true, the fact that it could be asserted may be equally enlightening. The absurdities of the trierarchic system, the 'usual desertion' of crews when a warship returned to the Peiraeus,[1] the difficulties of recruitment; the unwillingness of the masses to serve in the army and navy, of the rich to pay their taxes; a frivolous assembly that wasted precious time in debate, would vote for war when the time for decision had gone by, and send an expedition but fail to provide its finance; weak and corrupt politicians bending to every breeze of popular favour, generals either too incompetent or too much harassed by incompetence at home to carry out their duties. That is the picture drawn for us by Demosthenes, and we sigh and say, 'the spirit of the age of Perikles was not there, and Demosthenes was appealing in vain.' Especially do we think of citizens refusing to serve, and of those mercenary armies— the brilliant narrative of Demosthenes of these mercenaries unpaid, leaving the objects of the expedition unattempted to go off on some marauding foray in which they might win both pay and loot, καὶ ὁ στρατηγὸς ἀκολουθεῖ. All that Demosthenes says may well be true; his general picture (a very different thing) may be true; but the conclusions that we draw from it false. They may be false in two particulars: we may be wrong in supposing the corruption and incompetence to be peculiar to that age; and we may be wrong therefore in supposing that they are signs of decadence.

I will only briefly refer to the last century of the Roman Republic, when there was continual violence, disregard for law and order, and a standard of corruption such as Athens never knew; yet whatever was wrong with the Romans of that time, they were not decadent; they had not lost their vitality. I will give instead some comparable instances from the history of our own country.

No-one can open the pages of Pepys' Diary without immediate astonishment at the state of the English navy in his day. 'Pepys would drive to the Exchange, there to surprise a truant captain whose ship was already due at sea.

[1]Dem, l. 11.

. . . They would . . . board a warship there—where
"found all things out of order and after fighting the officers
there, we left them to make more haste." '[1] 'The store-
keepers and clerks of the Cheque and Survey at Woolwich
and Deptford . . . the deals which they undervalued and
then sold, the multitude of servants and decrepit old men
whom they kept on musters and whose pay they retained,
the old cables which they stole and subsequently retailed to
the King as new.' 'The Government contractors—the flag-
makers' genial cheat of charging threepence a yard more
than was allowed for in their forgotten contracts.'. . . 'And
the great Sir Richard Ford, who provided the navy with
worn-out yarn, skilfully covered over with new hemp,
found himself confronted with the cheat before his very
friends, the Principal Officers.'[2] Two of the Principal
Officers themselves—Admirals both of them—joined in the
cheating, and defended it, doing little other work; one of
them, Sir Wm. Batten, kept to himself large sums from the
Chatham Chest for disabled seamen, to which each serving
seaman paid 6d. a month from his wages.[3] The contractors
could not be altogether blamed, for payment for goods
delivered was often long in coming and sometimes in doubt
to the end; and the Government could not be altogether
blamed, for they often had no money in the Exchequer
because Parliament had not voted it. Pepys—who, after two
years in office as Clerk of the Privy Seal, at the age of
twenty-nine, went to school again to learn the multiplication
tables by rote from a discharged mate whom he had known
on the *Naseby*[4]—spent much of his time exposing and
fighting these frauds; well might he exclaim in his Diary,
'But, good God, what an age this is, and what a world is
this, that a man cannot live without playing the knave and
dissimulation.'[5] And this same Pepys who did so much to
stem the corruption, was himself taking all the usual per-
quisites, including presents of money from the honest
merchants for whom he had at last succeeded in getting

[1]Bryant, *Samuel Pepys*, p. 174.
[2]*Ibid.*, pp. 171–2.
[3]*Ibid.*, p. 178.
[4]*Ibid.*, pp. 175–6.
[5]Diary, 1681 (*Ibid.*, p. 161).

Government contracts against the competition of the dishonest ones and their friends. At first, at any rate, 'he was more interested in the honour and profit of his place than in the work it brought him. When Mr. Mann offered him £1,000 for his post, it made his mouth water, and he only refused it in deference to the objections of Lord Sandwich (then *Head of the Navy*), who told him it was not the salary that made a man rich but the opportunities of getting money while he was in place.'[1] Sandwich himself got into as many financial difficulties as had the Athenian admiral Timotheos, and had no better or more dignified ways of getting out of them. So when in 1665 the Dutch were prepared to fight at sea again, the English fleet 'was forced to return to harbour for the ignominious, but unchallengeable reason that its victuals had given out weeks in advance of the time allowed for in the victualling contract.' There was no money to pay discharged seamen nor dockyard-workers nor contractors; there were riots and strikes while the war was still on; and no fleet could put to sea later in the year. At last Parliament voted the money; but there were no means of raising it.[2] When they were at sea, if they captured an enemy ship, the admirals and the crew, and Pepys, all rushed for the plunder before they reached port.[3] When the Dutch were in the Medway in 1667, many of our seamen deserted to them: 'English seamen . . . stood on Dutch decks and shouted to their countrymen on shore that they had fought hitherto for tickets, and now they would fight for dollars.'[4]

Another story of Pepys throws light on a different aspect of Stuart politics: 'In 1677 Titus Oates and a notorious ruffian, Colonel Scott, charged Pepys and Sir Anthony Deane with betraying secrets of the Admiralty in France. Their covert intention was to strike at the Duke of York. Atkins, Pepys' clerk, had been employed by the Duke to collect evidence against Scott. Pepys and Deane were admitted to bail in February, 1680; but the charge seems to

[1]Bryant, *Samuel Pepys*, p. 123.
[2]*Ibid.*, pp. 265–82.
[3]*Ibid.*, pp. 267–8.
[4]*Ibid.*, p. 333. And for the general manners and life of the times, see the incident of Pepys surprising Lady Sandwich making an emergency use of the chamber-pot in his dining-room (p. 223); and his hurrying down to his family in the country to bury his stores of gold safely in the cottage garden (p. 334).

have hung over them for years, for Pepys was committed to the Gatehouse in June, 1689, and released in July on the ground of ill-health. Pepys, accused of high treason, was put to great expense in collecting evidence of Scott's character, and he employed Joyne as one of his agents in this detective work. He seems to have paid Joyne generously, and was rewarded later by blackmailing threats.' Scott, it seems, was himself a deserter from the army, and had gone to Paris taking with him 'Draughts and Platts of severall Towns in Flanders, by which he gained very good reception among the French' (Joyne's report).[1] How wisely we should moralize over such a tale told of ancient Greece.

In 1695 Captain William Kidd a well-to-do merchant of New York, 'was recommended to Lord Bellomont as a trustworthy person to take command of a ship to be dispatched against the pirates of the Indian Ocean. No man-of-war could be spared for the service, and it promised to be a profitable venture for a privateer. So Kidd sailed in command of the Adventure galley, owned by a syndicate of which he himself, Bellomont, Admiral Russell, and other noblemen were members, with a commission from King William III to exterminate pirates, and letters of marque against France. Three years later, rumours having reached England that so far from fighting against pirates he had turned pirate himself, Kidd was arrested in Boston and sent to London for trial. The evidence against him was weak. According to his own account of his proceedings his captures were all lawful prize under his letter of marque; but his documents had been impounded and suppressed and he was allowed no advocate for his defence. For political reasons a scapegoat was needed to placate the Government of the Great Mogul, whose just resentment at the pirates' depredations might otherwise be vented upon the East India Company. It may well have been that Kidd's noble associates in the ownership of the Adventure galley were only too glad to sacrifice him to that need.' He was convicted and hanged at Execution Dock, Wapping, in 1701.[2]

[1] See the account by Mr. George Sherwood in *The Times*, May 3rd, 1935.
[2] Review of *Captain Kidd and His Skeleton Island*, by H. T. Wilkins, in *The Times*, May 24, 1935.

Marlborough was a great and successful commander; and Parliament was prompter in voting money for his campaigns than it had been for the navy of Charles II. But the raising of troops was not begun till after a campaign had been decided on, and recruitment was left to the individual efforts of the colonels of regiments; the commissariat was still in private hands, and Marlborough distinguished himself among other captains of his age in the care he took to see that his men were properly clothed and fed and received their pay. Later, the American War exposed the weaknesses in our conduct of public affairs; above all we employed mercenaries. These, the 'damned Hessians and Prussians,' 'were expensive and mutinous; when they arrived in America, they failed to distinguish between loyalists and rebels, and by looting both alike they lost us what allegiance remained in every province through which they passed. But these were minor drawbacks: in the realm of policy the consequences were calamitous. In the first place, the employment of these boorish huns, coming on top of the incitement of the Red Indians to scalp and disembowel their masters, removed the last ounce of compunction that such men as Washington, who had won fame in fighting the French at Fort Duquesne, could feel at the thought of enlisting the French against the mother-country. In the second place, it exposed our weakness to the gaze of all Europe. Catherine of Russia bluntly informed George III that she would not send a single soldier to help him make a fool of himself; Frederick the Great sarcastically levied a cattle-toll on those of the mercenaries who passed through Prussia: France exulted.'[1] This was by no means the only evil. There is the well-known story of Lord George Germain's week-end, who was Minister for War. 'Burgoyne's surrender at Saratoga made him that occasionally necessary part of our British system, a scapegoat.' The explanation of his defeat given in the play is founded on a passage quoted by De Fonblanque from Fitzmaurice's *Life of Lord Shelburne* as follows: ' "Lord George Germain, having among other peculiarities a particular dislike to be put out of his way on any occasion, had arranged to call at his office on his way to the country to sign

[1]Chr. Hobhouse, *Fox*, p. 95.

the dispatches; but as those addressed to Howe had not been fair-copied, and he was not prepared to be balked of his projected visit to Kent, they were not signed then and were forgotten on his return home." These were the dispatches instructing Sir William Howe, who was in New York, to effect a junction at Albany with Burgoyne, who had marched from Quebec for that purpose . . . The policy of the English Government and Court for the next two years was simply concealment of Germain's neglect. Burgoyne's demand for an enquiry was defeated in the House of Commons by the Court party; and when he at last obtained a committee, the king got rid of it by a prorogation. When Burgoyne realized what had happened about the instructions to Howe . . . the king actually took advantage of his being a prisoner of war in England on parole, and ordered him back to America into captivity.'[1]

Further as to the friction between the fighting services and the executive ministries: 'With an attainted coward [Germain] at the War Office, and an army asked to fight against Englishmen with whom they had fought shoulder to shoulder twelve years back, perfect harmony could hardly be expected. Amherst refused to serve; Carleton in Canada was not on speaking terms with Germaine; . . . Burgoyne and Howe both served under protest; and when Burgoyne was brought back to England to face an enquiry obviously designed to save Germaine's face,[2] Howe threw up his command as well, loudly declaring that his honour was not safe in the hands of the Secretary for War.

'General Howe had a brother, Admiral Lord Howe, who was commanding in American waters. At the outbreak of war with France 1778, the Toulon fleet set out for America, while the Brest fleet continued its preparations for invading England. Lord Howe was not informed by the Admiralty of the departure of the Toulon fleet, of which he was totally unaware until they hove into sight off Sandy Hook. Not without reason, Lord Howe decided that his honour

---

[1] From Bernard Shaw's *Notes to the Devil's Disciple* in *Three Plays for Puritans*, pp. 77-78 (Standard Edition, 1934).
[2] There seems to be a small discrepancy between this account and Mr. Shaw's. I have no idea which is right.

R

was not safe in the hands of the First Lord of the Admiralty, and joined his brother in England.'[1]

After the battle off Ushant in 1778 Admiral Keppel was court-martialled by the Tories as a retort to the shooting of Byng twenty-one years before by the Whigs. His accuser was a junior admiral, Sir Hugh Palliser, who had disobeyed an order and torn out a page of his log-book; whom Keppel had praised in his despatches but abused in private. Charges of treason were made by both sides. Keppel was acquitted, but Palliser remained in command at Greenwich Hospital.[2]

Prize-money was for long a source of trouble in the army and navy. 'Cromwell sent a filibustering expedition to San Domingo in 1655 to replenish his empty treasury. Three parties divided the command: the commissioners of the Treasury, the Admiral and the General. When they reached their objective the admiral was for running in at once and taking the town by surprise. The Commissioners objected because in that case the soldiers would get all the plunder. Thereupon there was nearly a mutiny among the troops, who made their attack on another plan and were disgracefully routed. The admiral then offered to take the town alone; but the commissioners and general would not hear of it; and thus all three parties were by the ears, and nothing was done.' Other expeditions in 1693 and later were similarly wrecked by quarrels between the different services; on one of them 'the commodore and the commissary [representing the Treasury] took sides against the general. First they inveigled him ashore at Madeira and tried to leave him behind; and, this plan having failed, the commissary, who was in control of all supplies and stores, wrecked the general's plans by declining to land any of them.' The disastrous expedition to Cartagena in 1741 was mainly undertaken for the sake of the prize-money; and the successful one against St. Eustatius by Rodney in 1781 led only to a dangerous weakening of the English forces in the West Indies because the admiral had to detach a part of his fleet to carry home the plunder. Later 'in the Mediterranean naval commanders were always calling upon generals to aid them

[1]Hobhouse's *Fox*, p. 110.
[2]*Ibid.*, pp. 111–3, and *Encyclopædia Britannica*, s. v. Keppel.

in some unsound operation which promised lucre, and were very angry indeed when the generals declined to participate in them. St. Vincent and Nelson were as bad as any.'[1] We remember as well the general desire for renewal of the war on the part of the younger naval officers in Jane Austen's *Persuasion*, owing to the prospects of a fortune from prize-money. And for the conditions under which the crews lived, we have the story of the mutinies at Spithead and the Nore in 1797: there had been no increase in pay since the time of Charles II in spite of the great increase in the cost of living, and that scanty pay was almost always months in arrear; pay was stopped during sickness, even when it was the result of wounds in action; there was no shore-leave, and the men were often five to ten years at sea; the food and the quarters were alike poor, and there was much sickness; even at this the pursers were often dishonest; the system of punishments was a brutal one, and even so they were generally illegal—for example, flogging without a court-martial.[2] No wonder the press-gang was still thought by almost everybody to be a necessity (it was not abolished till 1836), in spite of its tyranny and its inefficiency; no wonder that villages were deserted by men of military age when it was rumoured that the Press officers were near ('citizens reluctant to serve in person.)' 'Till impressment be declared illegal,' wrote *The Times* on March 6, 1834, after the matter had been debated in Parliament, 'we shall never be secure from its terrors on sailors, or its damage to the mercantile service of the country. . . . But in every pro-position to maintain the numbers and to improve the discipline of our Navy by the abolition of impressment, we must include likewise an abandonment of the practice of manning it with profligate, disreputable, or criminal characters sent to it as a place of punishment. While our fleet is partly recruited from gaols and houses of correction —while the King's naval service is made a substitute for transportation, or the deck of a man-of-war an auxiliary to the treadmill—while our naval officers are ordered to receive among their crews the sweepings of our courts of justice, and

[1] Sir J. Fortescue, article in *The Times*, September 25 and 26, 1928.
[2] *The Floating Republic*, by Manwaring and Dobrée.

to act as assistants to the beadle or the executioner—while poachers, smugglers, and rioters, whom no law can bind on land, are sent to the fleet as to a great penitentiary on the ocean—while our vessels are obliged to have on board bodies of marines as much to overawe these turbulent characters as to fight the external enemy, it would be vain to expect that cruel or brutalizing punishments can cease, and, consequently, that our Navy can be manned by voluntary enrolments.'[1]

Since public speaking in the ecclesia and the law-courts was such an important element in Athenian life, let me add these few passages (all from *The Times* extracts of a hundred years ago). 'Great as the improvement of the Criminal Court is, it will yet be incomplete without some reformation of manners. The Old Bailey has long been a scandal to the country, and a by-word expressive of everything coarse and indecent in the business of advocacy. The personalities, the wranglings, the explosions of brutal intemperance, have been a disgrace to the bar. Considering the station of the individuals, it would be hard to say in what society the parallel of such outrages against the proprieties could be found. The nearest example is the ready and copious abuse of the omnibus cads, but the cads are not conscious that anything better should be expected of them. It is but just, however, to add, that though the main blame lies with certain irritable and foul-mouthed members of the bar, the whole blame does not attach to them, for the bench has had some share in it, though certainly not in the person of any of the superior judges.'

'Sir F. Pollock (in an action in the Court of King's Bench). —There were some kid-gloves; most people used this article, though perhaps persons in the profession of the law wore the worst.

'The Attorney-General (Sir John Campbell).—I don't wear them.

'Sir F. Pollock—His friend did not wear gloves. His friend came from a country where they not only did not wear gloves, but did not wear either shoes or stockings—they went bare-handed and bare-legged; but in the south a

[1] Quoted in *The Times* of March 6, 1834.

gentleman of education was compelled by the usages of society to cover hands and feet.'

From an article on Daniel O'Connell: 'Our boisterous bully. . . . What a blubbering slave is this—what a mean, crawling, drivelling reptile . . . a Jew extortioner, a cheating pedlar.'[1]

'It is now some weeks since the Tory journals followed up the announcement that Mr. Norton had commenced an action for criminal conversation with his wife against Lord Melbourne by triumphantly declaring that the result of the trial must inevitably be the retirement of that statesman from office. Their object was to poison the mind of the public before the question could be tried. Disgusted as we are with this conspiracy, and shocked as we must utterly be by this immolation of domestic happiness at the shrine of political opposition, we boldly say that it but fairly represents that mode of party warfare which the Tories have recently adopted. Failing all other means, they now persevere in efforts to wound the Government by assaults on private character.'[2]

Take that kind of evidence by itself (and it is far more scandalous than any we actually have of Athens, as well as more copious and more varied), add something of the manner of life of the large majority of our fellow-countrymen only a hundred years ago, the story of the Tolpuddle Martyrs, the conditions of life in mines and factories, and the conclusion is inevitable: this nation was in decay, its defeat was certain, and not only certain but desirable. Yet this greed, inefficiency and misery, though it led to some immediate disasters, and to one great defeat, in the American war, did not even lead to ultimate disaster, but to victory; because there were greed, inefficiency and misery among our rivals. Still less can it be taken as evidence for degeneracy; some of the worst scandals of our naval history belong to the great days of Nelson. It is true enough as well that Athenian foreign policy was uncertain and feeble in the extreme after 355 (though not more so, probably, than much of ours in the eighteenth century when we were

[1]November 4, 1834; June 27, 1836; and July 19, 1836.
[2]From the *Observer*, June 26, 1836.

building up and losing an empire); neither the peace policy of Euboulos nor the war policy of Demosthenes was at any time consistently adopted, but bits of each so that nothing effective was done. Men were weary of a number of small wars, from which they seemed never to be quite freed, which whether ending in victory or defeat, seemed to decide nothing. There was no lack of energy, courage, intelligence, patriotism. There was a general and sensible fear and dislike of war, accentuated by the recent inconclusive fighting that left nothing but irritation on both sides. Into such a Greek world, industrially prosperous, or at least active, in science, art and letters as active as ever, but politically weak—Thebes bullying but not commanding, Sparta destroyed for good but not for harm, Athens disillusioned, wayward, provoked and provoking—entered the strong figure of Philip. Athens longed for peace, but there was no denying the force of the great orator's warnings, the very real danger from Macedon. Therefore: 'we must do something; but let us not get ourselves involved in a big war. Let us send a small force, just to defend our legitimate interests. Isn't there a professional force somewhere immediately available? No need to waste time calling up the citizens.' Actually Athenian citizens must have served in person in the fourth century, especially after 355, rather more than in the fifth; for there were no subject allies to be persuaded into the fleet; and there is plenty of evidence that this was so. But in any case, feebleness of policy, resulting from a strong desire for peace at a time when peace can perhaps be attained only at too great a sacrifice, is no proof of decadence (a thought that may be of some comfort in Europe to-day); any more than are extreme incompetence and corruption in public affairs. We are bemused by the fact that most of the Greek city-states, and in particular Athens, did not recover power after the defeat of 322; but this, as I have tried to show, was due to external causes, of a novel and special character, and not to be foreseen. Actually the Greek soldiers were the equal of the Macedonians, as brave fighters and as well disciplined, both mercenary and citizens, as they proved at Issos and Krannon and many a later battle. And when we recall all that the Greeks were achieving in the

many fields of human activity outside war and politics we
should realize that it is idle to talk of decadence, even to the
smallest degree, in the fourth century. There was decline,
and apparently rapid decline, after about the middle of the
third century; but into the phases and the causes of that it is
not the purpose of this essay to enquire.

A NOTE ON THE EVIDENCE

If one well versed in English history of the seventeenth
and eighteenth centuries, and possessed of historical sense,
should see the foregoing pages in which I have quoted
passages illustrative of that time and country, he might well
object: But this is a hotch-potch of evidence. Some of it
original documents, some of it from later writers; some
quoted direct, some at second or even third hand; the
historians used of unequal merit, or not historians at all, but
journalists; newspaper evidence—that should be treated
with care. Above all, even though every incident may be
true, the resulting picture may be false, because the incidents
are not seen in their true perspective. The whole of Pepys'
diary must be read, not a few short extracts; and Pepys does
not provide the only evidence for his time.[1]

This, and much else of a similar kind, might be said.
But I have quoted those pieces of evidence from our own
history of set purpose, because it is just that kind of evidence
we have for the picture we draw of Athens in the fourth and
early third centuries. Political and law-court speeches and
fragments of speeches, isolated lines quoted from comedies
of whose context we know nothing, the tittle-tattle enjoyed
by some scribblers of the third century, inscriptions which,
even when well preserved, are of uncertain interpretation in
the complete absence of all contemporary narrative, the late
compilation of a man of such little judgement as Diodoros,
the biographies of Plutarch, who did not even profess to be

[1] It would of course be easy even for a casual reader of English history like myself
to quote passages of apparently equal historical value to those quoted above, from
which very different conclusions would be drawn. For instance, Admiral Rich-
mond sent a letter to *The Times* in which he called much of Fortescue's article 'a
travesty of the facts' (Oct. 2, 1928): and foreign observers of both the sixteenth and
the seventeenth centuries admired the organization of our fleet as well as the devoted
courage of the sailors.

a historian, whose knowledge and understanding of the political conditions in which his heroes lived was, inevitably considering the political conditions in which *he* lived, of the smallest.   (His manner of comparison of the lives of Demosthenes and Cicero and of Phokion and Cato show this as clearly as anything; and he knew nothing of the methods of government by discussion.) That is what we have to deal with; and with it an immense amount of most valuable work, work which arouses our constant admiration, has been done by modern historians, especially in the reconstruction of the history of the city-states after the death of Alexander. But we must be aware of its limitations; and, perhaps not unexpectedly, our judgement is more often at fault where there is a little more evidence, about the age of Demosthenes and Aristotle, than about the two generations after their death.

XII

MENANDER[1]

When the considerable fragments from Menander's plays, recovered from Egypt, were published, we could only wonder at this new manifestation of the Greek genius. When by the labours of many scholars, Lefèbvre (the principal discoverer), Körte, Capps, van Leeuwen, Sudhaus, Wilamowitz and Jensen, the fragments had been placed in their right order, many doubtful readings had been restored, and the whole interpreted, our admiration grew. There was that kind of freshness in them which we feel at once when another piece of Greek sculpture comes to light— οὕτως ἐπανθεῖ καινότης ἀεί τις ἄθικτον ὑπὸ τοῦ χρόνου διατηροῦσα τὴν ὄψιν, ὥσπερ ἀειθαλὲς πνεῦμα καὶ ψυχὴν ἀγήρω καταμεμιγμένην τῶν ἔργων ἐχόντων; and, for skill, we found that he was, in his field, the equal of the other great writers of Greece. We found in fact, though we still only possess so small a part of his work and no complete play, that the ancient judgement of him was correct.

He has not, however, been much appreciated in this country, in contrast to Germany, France, Italy and America.[2] And the depreciation has generally taken the form of implying, if not of saying in so many words, that the discovery of Menander has added little to what we already knew of the New Comedy from Plautus and Terence; that we have just three more conventional comedies of intrigue, of the type so familiar to us, pleasantly written but not in essentials different from the Latin plays. Mr. Angus, for example, in the *Cambridge Ancient History*, quotes Ovid's

> So long as fathers bully, servants lie,
> And women smile, MENANDER cannot die,

as though it were not only the first, but also the last word to be said about Menander; and continues: 'Feeling therefore

---

[1] I have to thank my colleague, Mr. Kitto, for reading this paper through in ma nuscript, and making many fruitful suggestions.
[2] For the latest example, see the deprecating page in Rose's *History of Greek Literature*.

free to include in our evidence the Latin plays which have survived as well as the Greek fragments, new and old, we may attempt to summarize very briefly the main features of the new comedy.'[1] One would have thought that, quite apart from Menander, Plautus and Terence were sufficiently different from each other to prevent their plays being lumped together to give a general picture of Greek comedy; while, when we include Menander, we must reflect that there can hardly have existed two writers of comedy so divergent in their aims, their methods, and their effects as he and Plautus. Wilamowitz in a fine study has stressed the individuality of Menander;[2] but his words have not been appreciated here. It is to various aspects of this individuality that I wish to draw attention in this paper.[3]

First, two words of warning. I am concerned with Menander's special characteristics; I am therefore compelled frequently to contrast him with Plautus and Terence. This implies no criticism of Plautus, for his aims were other

---

[1] Vol. vii, pp. 227–8. Yet he has just quoted from Gellius (ii 23. 5 ff.): 'We were reading Caecilius' *Plocium*, with pleasure to all present, and we thought we would read the original by Menander also. Heavens! how flat and dull Caecilius immediately appeared, and what a change after Menander.' Gellius' extracts make it clear how freely Caecilius adapted his original.

[2] *Die Kunst Menanders* in his edition of *Das Schiedsgericht*, and in *Berliner Sitzungsberichte*, 1916.

[3] Not only do men still write as though nothing of Menander had been discovered; but they will not learn from experience. Mistakes were often made by confident and unnecessary conjecture about Menander before the discovery of the papyri—to take a conspicuous example: Leo, *Plaut. Forschungen*,[1] p. 126, 4—'Zeichen einer ähnlichen Reaktion oder bewussten Abweichung von den ausgebildeten Typen zeigt ausser den Captivi die Hecyra Apollodors: der in seine Frau verliebte Jüngling, der neugierige Sklave, der statt als Vertrauter eingreifen zu dürfen, immer fortgeschickt wird und nichts erfahrt, die Hetäre die ihrem treulosen Liebhaber zur Frau verhilft, das ist alles neu und, soweit unsre Kenntniss reicht, antimenandrisch. Bacchis hebt beständig ihre Abweichung vom Hetärentypus hervor; Menanders 'Επιτρέποντες, eine *fabula similis argumenti* (Apoll. Sid. ep. iv 12. 1), hatte gewiss andere Charaktere.' (It had; but not quite as Leo guessed. It is further remarkable that Leo did not think this note needed any modification in the second edition of his work, which appeared in 1912—p. 141, 2.) But this does not prevent similar conjectures being still made about other unknown writers; and it is characteristic of our fallible human nature that Jachmann is properly cautious about Menander and will write 'so weit er uns erkennbar ist,' yet has no doubts about Diphilos (*Plautinisches u. Attisches*, 100–4, 117–8); and does not see that even if he had succeeded in isolating the original elements of Diphilos from the additions and alterations made by Plautus (and the difficulties of this task are obvious), he would have thrown a flood of light on the methods of the latter (while leaving his *plays* as they are), but would have done next to nothing to restore the former to life; who must for ever remain a bloodless shadow, till some considerable amount of his own writing be discovered. (Cf. above, pp. 164–5.)

than Menander's; and though, in so far as Terence was attempting to reproduce Greek comedy on the Roman stage, there will be some criticism of him, I am well aware that there are many virtues in him which I shall not touch at all. I am not attempting a judgement of Terence.[1] Secondly, I am not directly concerned with the problem of the relationship between the Latin plays and their originals, with what is or is not *plautinischer* or *terenzianischer Zutat*; though I may mention it on occasions. In general I follow the lead of Fraenkel and Jachmann in this;[2] but whether the differences between the Latin writers and Menander are due to their own alterations of their originals or to the fact that they were adapting Greek plays that were themselves different in character from Menander's, does not matter for my purpose; not even, strictly speaking, when they are adapting plays of Menander himself, for he may have written comedies different from those which have been preserved; some of them doubtless inferior to them—he wrote a hundred. For I am dealing with the art of Menander only, and with

[1]'Reproduce' is perhaps the wrong word, even with the qualifying 'in so far as.' Terence was not saying 'See what a good dramatist Menander was'; but 'Here is a new Latin comedy; the best way we can obtain that is by adapting from the Greek.'

[2]But with a strong feeling for the wisdom of Fraenkel in concerning himself more with the general methods used by Plautus in his adaptations, with *types*, than with the detailed analysis of particular plays attempted by Jachmann and after him by Drexler (*Philologus*, Supplbd. xxvi, 1934). Fraenkel gives one a vivid picture of Plautus; Jachmann adds but little to that, and his picture of the lost Greek dramatist is anyhow of a shadow; and the most ingenious argument may be upset by the discovery of an original play. Besides, a microscopic gaze often leads to blindness: consider the two following examples. Fraenkel (pp. 307–8) regards *Casina* 767–72 as 'von Plautus eingeschachtelt' in the original Greek monologue—as they stand, ll. 759–21 are 'ganz chaotisch'; 'so lässt kein Dichter erzählen, der über einen ausgebildeten Erzählungsstil verfügt.' Jachmann (pp. 113–5) objects (rightly, in my opinion); but one of his reasons is that the excision of ll. 767–72 would leave *illarum* in l. 775 in the air! Was then Plautus a nitwit?
   Secondly: Drexler (p. 25), in his analysis of the *Adelphoe*, objects to ll. 266–7
                         quid fit, Ctesipho?
         in tutost omni' res: omitte vero tristitiem tuam,
on the grounds (1) that the question is 'sinnlos'; and (2) that Ctesipho knows what has happened, 'muss also die tristitia schon abgelegt haben. Dass dies Postulat richtig ist, zeigt erstens 252: Syrus sieht Ctesipho die Freude an—Aeschinus dagegen nicht? . . . Also auch hier Widersprüche über Widersprüche.' But the two brothers are contrasted: Ctesipho is a sentimentalist, and is already looking lovesick again; Aeschinus is a realist in his loves (and *quid fit?* means no more than 'What is the matter?'). It is an excellent point.
   In fact in all three writers, even in Fraenkel, everything that is found to be *chaotisch, sinnlos, ungeheuerlich, gedankenlos*, every contradiction or improbability, is attributed to Plautus and Terence. Each becomes *ein Narr*. Wherein then does their merit lie? Fortunately much of their criticism is mutual.

that as exhibited in the fragments of the surviving plays. Unless I am directly discussing some adaptation of him by Plautus or Terence (or unless it is otherwise obvious), when I say Menander in this paper I mean only Menander in the original Greek, not as we can guess him to have been from the Latin comedy.[1]

I begin by noticing his treatment of certain theatrical conventions. These can, I think, be conveniently grouped into two kinds, dramatic conventions and stage conventions. By the former I mean those demanded by the μῦθος, the story of a play—as for example that next-door neighbours know everything or know nothing of each other, according to the author's will;[2] by the latter I mean those demanded by the exigencies of the stage used—to take the obvious example, that in the Greek theatre the scene did not change and was always in the street, not indoors; so that actions that would 'naturally,' that is in real life, have taken place in different places, or indoors, are supposed all to take place just outside one or two particular houses—so that, so to speak, as the stage cannot go to the drawing-room, the drawing-room must come to the stage.[3] To take this latter kind first. Stage conventions, however, 'unnatural,' will not disturb an audience provided that two conditions are fulfilled (1) that, through familiarity or, exceptionally, by a dramatist's peculiar skill, they do not strike the audience as either funny or picturesque, and (2) that they are not underlined, that attention is not drawn to them, either directly or because a particular action, in that setting, seems at once to be absurd.[4] In the matter of the scene of a

[1] I shall use Greek lettering for the titles of Greek plays, to avoid confusion; thus Ἀνδρία will mean Menander's play, Andria Terence's. The numbering of lines in Menander's plays is according to Jensen's edition.

[2] An extreme case of ignorance is in Mostellaria, in which Theopropides had never seen his neighbour's house, and did not know it was a particularly fine one till told by an architect. In Andria Simo finds a difficulty in finding out what is going on in Chrysis' house, and his son has to be introduced there by friends; but later Mysis and Glycerium, though busy with other things, soon learn of the preparations for the wedding in Simo's house.

[3] It is a pity that in English the phrase 'theatrical convention' is also used for something quite different—the constant use by all or most dramatists of an epoch of *typical* stories or *typical* characters, or for mere conventionality of treatment of story or character. I shall deal with this very important question later.

[4] *Spontaneous* illusion is the life of the theatre: see H. Granville Barker in *Essays in Honour of Gilbert Murray*, pp. 237–8. This is an excellent essay on the conventions of the theatre.

play in the New Comedy, the first condition was amply
fulfilled—it was, as far as we know, always the same or
nearly the same: a street scene, in the country or the town,
including the homes of the principal characters; occasionally a temple or shrine would be added.[1] So long as the scene
was so familiar that the audience would scarcely notice it, it
was as easy for them to accept the convention that all action
would take place there, as for us to accept the curtain
'scenery' of the Elizabethan stage. When we *read* Shakespeare, we have stage directions—'a street in Venice,' 'a room
in the palace,' 'the battlefield,' 'another part of the battlefield'; on the stage everything was performed before the
same curtain, and, normally (except when he takes the
opportunity for some fine poetry in describing natural
scenery), Shakespeare takes no trouble to tell us where we
are supposed to be.[2] Nor is it necessary that he should. On
the Greek stage the street scene is almost as conventional as
the Elizabethan curtain; it is scarcely more 'unnatural' for
everything to take place in front of some houses as for
characters to be conveniently meeting in 'another part of
the town.' And this one street scene must be quite conventionally represented; the houses must not be individualized,
not be made 'characteristic' of particular persons, Demeas
or Chairestratos or Euclio; that would be to draw attention
to them, with disturbing results. I saw Sacha Guitry's play
Le Nouveau Testament, produced by him in London in 1935:
the scene was the same throughout, a room in a doctor's
house; as it was the same throughout, it had to serve as

[1] It gives I believe a wrong impression to say that the scene simply represents two
(occasionally three) *houses*, belonging to the principal families of the play. It is
rather a street, of indefinite length, in which these houses, which may or may not be
next to each other, are situated. This helps several of the conventions mentioned
below—characters on the stage not seeing each other, a man asking where so-and-so
lives when he is in front of the house, even the plot discussed outside the house of
the man from whom it must be kept secret.

I suppose too that in some plays, as *Mostellaria* (cf. 774 ff.) and *Truculentus* (cf.
386–7), the houses were represented with a walled garden or courtyard round and
in front of them; whereas in others the houses share a party wall when the fact that
the families are next door neighbours is essential to the plot.

It is interesting to note that in *Ecclesiazusae* we have a scene with two houses; but,
in the manner of the Old Comedy, they belong to different persons in different
scenes—another kind of convention. See Ed. Fraenkel, in *Greek Poetry and Life*
(Essays in Honour of Gilbert Murray), p. 257 ff.

[2] Nor does Molière. *Le Misanthrope* can be taken as a good example; in which
everybody comes and goes at will in Célimène's house.

drawing-room, for the family and friends, as waiting room for patients, as consulting room for the doctor, his patients, and his secretary. That was a convention we should have been very ready to accept—very gladly, for it would have been restful—but for one fact: the room was individualized; it was the room of this particular intelligent, cultured doctor. This meant not only that we were too often reminded of his intelligence and culture (as though certain lines intended to make this clear were repeated in every scene), but it made us aware of the convention, it drew our attention to it; it disturbed us that the drawing-room and the consulting room were one and the same. The Greeks, as far as we know, did not make that mistake.[1]

But there is another way of drawing attention to this convention; and in this we can observe a very interesting difference between Menander, Terence and Plautus. It is not always easy to give an adequate motive for the appearance of a character on the stage—for his coming out of his house, for instance; but it is necessary for the play's sake that he should. How does Menander do it? In the best possible way, in the same way that Shakespeare and Molière do, by saying nothing about it—the character just enters; and we accept the fact without difficulty: Onesimos' entrance, for example, in the second act of 'Επιτρέποντες (l. 166), and those of Habrotonon and Syriskos in the third (ll. 213, 225); and many another.[2] All very convenient for the story, and just happening that way. Very private matters are thus discussed in the open, and we are not disturbed by it. Plots can be hatched under the very windows of the intended victim, and by already suspected persons. Or take the convention by which one character is detected by another a long way off, before he reaches the stage, or, alternatively, is not seen when he is already arrived and is not half-a-dozen yards away;[3] and with this the con-

---

[1] Cf. Plaut. *Men.* 73 ff., quoted below, p. 258.

[2] We must of course distinguish between this kind of appearance, and that where it is important that the audience should know the reason of it—for example, Sosias' first and second appearance in Περικειρομένη (ll. 52, 164): there he explains his arrival.

[3] A good example is *Ad.* 537, 542, 553: Syrus and Clitopho see Demea before he arrives on the stage; Demea does not see them till some time after. See also *Curc..* 301 ff., *Miles* 609, *Pseud.* 960; where the elastic length of the street scene (above: p. 253, n. 1) is clear.

vention by which a dialogue or even a monologue is over-heard by a third party who is unseen. All these are accept-able enough, *provided that attention is not drawn to them*, and that probability is not strained. Menander is entirely at his ease in this respect; especially with regard to the un-seen third party. There are only some ten lines in Act iii of Ἐπιτρέποντες during which Onesimos and Habrotonon each speak without seeing the other, and Habrotonon overhears the dialogue between him and Syriskos because she is naturally inquisitive, and because Onesimos is excited and talking in a loud voice. The scene in which Pamphile finally refuses to accede to Smikrines' command to leave Charisios, which 'unnaturally' takes place out of doors, must do so; for it is both the central scene of the play and it is necessary that Charisios should overhear it (it being natural enough that he should listen when he sees Pamphile with her father). So what is unnatural is not alluded to.[1] So with his admirable monologues: which are of two kinds (excluding the formal or semi-formal prologues). The one represents a man thinking to himself, talking quietly; such are not over-heard. The other is the action of a man so excited by his emotion that he talks aloud, tells the world of his happiness or misery; that may be overheard. Nor does Menander overdo the monologue as a device simply for telling us what has happened off the stage; apart from the semi-formal prologue, such as that of Demeas in the Σαμία (l. 1 ff.),[2] he uses it sparingly, and can make it dramatic, as that mono-logue of Onesimos which tell us of Charisios' surprising behaviour (Ἐπιτρ. 494 ff.).

Compare with this the frequent practice of Terence. How often do we find lines such as these spoken by a character on entering:

Enim vero Chremes nimi' graviter cruciat adulescentulum
nimi'que inhumane: exeo ergo ut pacem conciliem. optime
ipsos video;[3]

or

proviso quid agat Pamphilus. atque eccum.[4]

[1] It is probable indeed that we have lost a few lines, perhaps as many as six, at the beginning of this scene; but we can be confident of their nature.
[2] For this, which I think—contrary to most scholars—is the opening of the second (not the third, or fourth, act), see *C.Q.* 1936, pp. 64–72.   [3] *Heaut.* 1045–7.
[4] *Andr.* 957. This line is spoken by Charinus, a character invented by T———

Terence cannot manage these entrances naturally; he has to explain; he is uneasy with the convention which he found in his Greek models. In the same way there is a clumsiness about the movements of Chremes at the end of the first scene of *Heautontimorumenus* (168–74), to explain his staying for the next one;[1] still more in the way in which the unlikelihood of Clinia's appearance and actions in 230 ff. is underlined by the warning:

> etiam caves ne videat forte hic te a patre aliquis exiens?

just the convention to which all Greek plays must avoid drawing attention. Or take the opening lines of *Eunuchus* iii 5 (549 ff.): there is not really any motive for Chaerea to appear at all; he should be with Pamphila (cf. 575 f.); but let that pass—he must tell everyone of his pleasure, that is, he indulges in a monologue that can legitimately be overheard, and it is overheard; but it is spoilt by the opening lines (549–50):

> Numquis hic est? nemost. numquis hinc me sequitur? nemo
> homost.
> iamne erumpere hoc licet mi gaudium?

when in fact Aeschinus is on the stage at the time. It strains probability to call our attention in this way. If the scene is a translation of Menander, I feel confident that he began with l. 550, and that 549 is Terence's own, unable to let things alone.[2]

Plautus too. *Cas.* 879–80:

> operam date, dum mea facta itero: est operae pretium auribus
> accipere,
> ita ridicula auditu, iteratu ea sunt quae ego intus turbavi.

---

[1] On the other hand, the departure of Menedemus in l. 167, which seems badly designed—he should, to be in character, remain digging as the curtain falls—is due to a real weakness of the Greek stage: there was no curtain. No one can just be left on the stage at the end of a scene.

For a modern example of an ill-managed exit, see *School for Scandal*, v. 2, 'I see Lady Teazle going to the next room' (she is off stage); an interesting case, for normally Sheridan wisely leaves such things alone.

[2] Another instance of a somewhat clumsy explanation is *Andr.* 412–5, which it is interesting to compare with Περικ. 52 ff., which is dramatic. But how well the short following scene is managed (416–25), in which the hesitations of Pamphilus and the natural surprise of Simo at his son's acquiescence give the right opportunities for the asides of Byrria and Davus.

What an elaborate introduction to a narrative monologue! *Aul.* 133:

> eo nunc secreto te huc foras seduxi.

That underlines the convention that private matters may be discussed in the street. So do several passages in the *Miles*:

> cohibete intra limen etiam vos parumper, Pleusicles,
> sinite me priu' perspectare, ne uspiam insidiae sient
> concilium quod habere volumus. nam opus est nunc tuto loco
> unde inimicus ne quis nostri spolia capiat consili (596-9).

> circumspicedum ne quis nostro hic auceps sermoni siet.
> nam hoc negoti clandestino ut agerem mandatumst mihi (955-6).

> sequimini, simul conspicite ne quis adsit arbiter (1137).

Similarly ll. 1196-8: et vos abite hinc intro, when they have only come on to the stage to talk of secret plans; and immediately after: commodum aperitur foris. Timely indeed. And in *Epidicus* (an excellent play) it is in itself absurd that Stratippocles, not wanting his father to see him, should talk with Chaeribulus and Epidicus in the street, just outside his father's house (104 ff.). That, however, we could tolerate, or barely notice; but it is fatal that at the end of the scene the latter should point out the danger:

> ibo intro atque adulescenti dicam nostro erili filio,
> ne hinc foras exambulet neve obviam veniat seni.[1]

Take a different convention: how unnatural it is that in *Truculentus* (711-9) Astaphium should talk to herself just when Diniarchus is waiting to hear her; still more unnatural that Euclio should allow himself to be overheard and thus let out the whole secret (*Aul.* 605-16)! What is a secret worth, if it can be discovered from a man's private thoughts?[2]

---

[1] Ll. 567-9 also strain the open-street convention:
> eho! istinc, Canthare,
> iube Telestidem huc prodire filiam ante aedis meam,
> ut suam videat matrem.

Or again: Plautus was seldom loath to explain the obvious—his characters and his plots; he left little to his audience's intelligence. In *Miles* 874 ff. we get the whole intrigue over again (and in 932 and 1162 ff. as well); and in 878 ff. and 914 ff. he actually draws attention to the repetition.

[2] Ll. 667 ff. are not, in a way, more sensible; but they are in character, they suit Euclio; and that makes all the difference.

It is very interesting to observe similar difficulties with the conventions in Euripides—especially the presence of the chorus. *Medea* is a well-known case;

Plautus did not manage the Greek convention any better than Terence (or Terence in his earlier plays). But he had a gayer spirit; and the vigour of his comedies enables them to digest these crudities better. More than that: he liked laughing at, guying, the conventions which he did not understand, or the value of which he did not appreciate. An obvious instance is from the end of the prologue to *Menaechmi*:

> haec urbs Epidamnus est dum haec agitur fabula:
> quando alia agetur aliud fiet oppidum;
> sicut familiae quoque solent mutarier:
> modo hic habitat leno, modo adulescens, modo senex,
> pauper, mendicus, rex, parasitus, hariolus.

The *Poenulus* prologue is an elaborate jest, which gives the facts required at the same time.[1] Other conventions are laughed at, as the convenient meeting with someone you have been looking for: *Bacch.* 1104:

> certo hic prope me mihi nescioquis loqui visust; sed quem video?
> hicquidemst pater Mnesilochi.

Mercator 857–864:

> Ev. Cogito quonam ego illum curram quaeritatum. Ch. certa rest
> me usque quaerere illam . . .
> Ev. nescioquoia vox ad auris sui advolavit. Ch. inuoco
> vos, Lares uiales, ut me bene tutetis. Ev. Iuppiter!
> estne ilic Charinus?

equally interesting is *Electra*, 292–9, to which Mr. Kitto drew my attention. Orestes asks Electra for information about happenings in Mycenae; and the chorus chime in—

> κἀγὼ τὸν αὐτὸν τῷδ' ἔρον ψυχῆς ἔχω.
> πρόσω γὰρ ἄστεως οὖσα τἀν πόλει κακά
> οὐκ οἶδα, νῦν δὲ βούλομαι κἀγὼ μαθεῖν.

The explanation makes it worse. How much better to have left the chorus out of it or let them say only, 'Yes, do; it is right to tell strangers what they ask,' as Aeschylus and Sophocles would have done. This uneasiness was due to the fact that Euripides was trying to make a realistic use of a non-realistic form. He was an innovator, as Menander was not.

[1]How can one doubt that the majority, at least, of the Plautine prologues are not late, but the poet's own, freely invented or freely adapted from the Greek original? Cf. ll. 22–3 from this same prologue:

> ut quidem ille dixit mihi qui pueros viderat:
> ego illos non vidi, ne quis vostrum censeat.

That is not only in Plautus' own vein; it is obviously *an author's* jest. So, I think, is *Plautus noluit*, l. 65, of the *Casina* prologue; the lines written for the later performance of the play may be only the first twenty. I cannot at all agree with Ernoux (ed. Budé, i, 1932).

Miles 1132–6:

> Nunc ad me ut veniat usust Acroteleutium aut
> ancillula eius aut Pleusicles. pro Iuppiter,
> satine ut Commoditas usquequaque me adiuvat!
> nam quos videre exoptabam me maxume,
> una exeuntis video hinc e proxumo.

Very convenient, for it had all just been arranged.

Then the secret-in-the-open-street convention—*Merc.*
1005–8.

> Ev. eamus intro, non utibilest hic locus, factis tuis,
> dum memoramus, arbitri ut sint qui praetereant per vias.
> De. hercle qui tu recte dicis: eadem breuior fabula
> erit.

This last was a jest Plautus was fond of, as in *Pseudolus*
387–8:

> temperi ego faxo scies.
> nolo bis iterari, sat sic longae fiunt fabulae.

And 720–1:

> Cali. quo modo? Ps. horum caussa haec agitur spectatorum fabula:
> hic sciunt qui hic adfuerunt; uobis post narrauero.[1]

Not that Plautus is not generally only too ready to explain
the obvious, whether in the intrigue or in a character, and
not always in jest. In the *Poenulus* (almost the weakest of his
plays) he has a long passage, with the same joke, which,
however, does not save us from a repetition of the plot
(550 ff.).

> Adv. omnia istaec scimus iam nos, si hi spectatores sciant;
> horunc hic nunc caussa haec agitur spectatorum fabula:
> nos te satius est docere, ut, quando agas, quid agas sciant.
> nos tu ne curassis: scimus rem omnem, quippe omnes simul
> dedicimus tecum una, ut respondere possimus tibi.
> Ag. ita profecto est. sed agite igitur, ut sciam vos scire, rem
> expedite et mihi quae uobis dudum dixi dicite.
> Adv. itane? temptas an sciamus? non meminisse nos ratu's
> quo modo, *etc.*

He was extremely careful of this intrigue; see ll. 579–81,
590, 597–9, and finally 920–2, which laugh at all this business:

---

[1]Ben Jonson was fond of jests of this kind, in the Plautine tradition: e.g., *Every-man Out of His Humour*, 247 ff.

ibo intro haec ut meo ero memorem. nam huc si ante aedis evocem,
quae audivistis modo, nunc si eadem hic iterum iterem, inscitiast.
ero uni potius intus ero odio quam hic sim vobis omnibus.

Inscitia indeed!

Funnier is his laughter at the convention that the stage
may represent almost any length of street you like; so that
a man can enter and walk and talk for an age before he
finds the house or the friend he has been looking for; as in
Act ii sc. 1 of *Stichus* (note especially l. 307—

sed spatium hoc occidit: breuest curriculo; quam me paenitet!);

Act iv sc. 3 of *Trinummus*:

Stasime, fac te propere celerem, recipe te ad dominum domum;

the admirable monologue of Curculio (280 ff.); and the
very funny scene at the beginning of *Mercator*, in which
Acanthio pretends to run hard (racing with his legs, I
imagine, without advancing), to push people on one side,
to stop for breath, to run again, knocks violently at the door
and calls loudly for his master Charinus ('I have never seen
a house so badly run!') and then turns to him as though
he had known all the time that he was on the stage; the
very picture of the *servus currens*.[1]

---

[1]Laughter at other conventions is to be observed too in *Poen.* 1075 ff., I think (at
the ordinary recognition scene), in *Cistell.* 149–53, and *Miles* 79–82, at the formal
and semi-formal prologue, and in *Miles* 1435 ff., at the epilogue—here it is of a
kind that Plautus often wrote seriously, but in the mouth of Pyrgopolynices it is
jest. Compare the epilogue of *The School for Scandal*, which is in Plautus' manner
(as is also the character of Charles Surface).

In *Phormio* 179–96 is Terence following Plautus in making fun of the convention? or does Geta pretend not to see the others and talk aloud so that they may
hear? or is Terence just using and straining the convention of convenient meetings
and of players not seeing each other and monologues overheard? Probably the
second answer is right; Terence was more skilled when he wrote the *Phormio*. So
Ad. 364–73: Syrus' natural impudence makes him pretend not to see Demea?

Hec. 866 ff. is a jest at a different kind of convention—the ordinary finish to a
comedy:

placet non fieri hoc itidem ut in comoediis
omnia omnes ubi resciscunt. hic quos par fuerat resciscere
sciunt; quos non autem acquomst scire neque resciscunt neque scient.

And perhaps *Heaut.* 536–8, at the conventional story of slave deceiving his master.

Both Fränkel (*Plautinisches im Plautus*, p. 144) and Norwood (*Art of Terence*,
29–30) give *Andr.* 490 ff. as an instance of the poet's laughing at the stage convention that private matters are talked about in the open street (though for Fränkel the
poet is Menander, for Norwood, of course, Terence); and they both add that at the
same time, like the good artist he is, he makes use of the convention to help the
plot: Simo, overhearing the midwife giving instructions how to look after the
baby just born, thinks he was intended to overhear, so that he may be deceived; he
fancies that he sees through the trick. But we cannot have it both ways: laughing at

A good instance, on the other hand, of the *understood* conventions of Greek comedy, where there is neither underlining nor laughter, and therefore no difficulty, is the second scene of *Eunuchus*: where Thais *sends* for Phaedria as though from a distance, yet he lives next door; and he having come, they talk over intimate personal matters, outside Thais' house, that is really, outside both houses. But we accept all that.

That is Menander's way, making use of the stage conventions naturally and easily. It is the same with the dramatic conventions, those demanded by the *story*; but here the question is more complex and more interesting. The superficial excuse for treating Menander, Plautus and Terence as belonging to one school of comedy, with only Plautus displaying a vigorous, *Latin* individuality, is that their plots are all alike. But what does that mean? Are all the plots of Greek tragedy alike? In a sense, yes. But do we therefore deny individuality to Aeschylus, Sophocles and Euripides? And if tragic plots are all alike, what did Aristotle mean by saying that the μῦθος is the most important element in a tragedy, even more important than character? We know what he meant: it is the treatment of the story *in the play*, the solution of the difficulty, the untying of the knot—it is in this, he says, that the dramatist's skill and individuality are best shown. It is only the preliminaries of the plot, what is ἔξω τοῦ δράματος, what the dramatist

a convention is extra-dramatic, a direct appeal to the audience (permissible enough on occasions, especially in Plautus), something quite outside the story; to make use of it is to remain dramatic—an admirable device, but possible only because the poet is confident that the audience will *not* be conscious, at the moment, of the absurdity of the convention, because it is well understood and accepted. If Menander, or Terence, was attempting two incompatible things at the same moment, he was making a mistake, for he was putting the audience into the wrong mood. Actually, I am convinced, he was making use of a well-understood convention, not laughing at it. The convention is indeed somewhat strained; but Simo's discovery is well-managed, and then turned to excellent account when he thinks the discovery was intended.

There are many instances in Aristophanes too of an apparently clumsy use of conventions, as *Equit.* 36 ff.

βούλει τὸ πρᾶγμα τοῖς θεαταῖσιν φράσω; κ.τ.λ.
and 146–7,
ἀλλ᾽ ὁδὶ προσέρχεται
ὥσπερ κατὰ θεὸν εἰς ἀγοράν.
But Aristophanes was laughing, or at least did not trouble himself about such things.

takes from tradition, that may be very similar or actually the same for different poets. Menander also, we are told, in an anecdote that may well be true, thought the μῦθος most important: a friend met him only a short time before the Dionysia and asked him how his play was going. 'Excellently,' said Menander, 'I have thought out the plot; and I now only have to write the verses.' What did this mean if all his plots were taken from stock, and a stock containing but small variety of goods and no exclusive models? Simply that in comedy as in tragedy, the Greeks were generally concerned only with the last part of a story, with the solution, not the tying of the knot; the first part was all put into a prologue or one or two exposition scenes. Only occasionally, as in the *Andria*, does the comedy consist in the complication; and in that half the complication is Terence's own.

Take for example the plot, a simple one, of 'Ἐπιτρέποντες: the quarrel of a devoted husband and wife owing to a discovery of something that was true, but only half the truth. Had Menander been writing this play on the lines of the normal modern comedy, he would have shown, certainly, Charisios and Pamphile immediately after the marriage, the former very happy, the latter trying to be happy, but conscious of her secret and knowing that it must soon come to light, becoming more unhappy as she learns to love Charisios; her nurse comforting her to no purpose with trite commonplaces and foolish promises that all will go well; Smikrines, vain of the large dowry he has given his daughter and very glad to have found a son-in-law like Charisios, so steady and good, so different from his friend Chairestratos. (It might have begun even earlier, with Pamphile at home with her father, happy and innocent, while plans for her marriage were being made.) Then the tragedy, the birth of the child in Charisios' absence abroad, the dreadful decision to expose it in spite of Pamphile's own better instincts and judgement, the busy Onesimos finding it out and his discovery of it to Charisios on his return; and Charisios' despair. And only in the last part of the play the estrangement, followed by enlightenment and reconciliation. That is, most modern comedies are essentially narrative, the Greek dramatic (just as *Macbeth* is narrative but not *Hamlet*). The Greek dramatist made his play only of this last part; the rest is the situation presupposed and explained at the beginning. Therefore it is not dramatically important; and can be taken from a common stock of conventional stories, as the tragedian took his preliminary plot from a common stock of traditions. It is the treatment and conduct of this last part of the whole story that forms the μῦθος, and it is here that the dramatist shows his skill; note the variation in the structure of three of Menander's plays, ῞Ηρως, Πλόκιον and ᾽Επιτρέποντες (or four, if the original of the *Cistellaria* was his), all of which spring from the same story, a night *affaire* followed by the marriage of the parties; that is, all are *similis argumenti* (for that is what *argumentum* amounts to): in the first the parties are of the older generation, and the story is about their daughter, now grown up; in the second, they are young and the birth of the child and the consequent quarrel takes place before marriage; in the third (as in the *Hecyra*) they are also young, but the quarrel is subsequent to the marriage;[1] while in the *Cistellaria* the parties recognize each other and therefore marry (after their child is grown up). It was by the management of the plot that one writer of comedies may differ from another almost as much as from a tragedian. It was often pointed out by ancient critics that Euripides' plots are many of them forerunners of the later comedy; this is quite true of the preliminary story—that of the *Ion* for example could quite well be the prologue of a comedy by Menander; substitute conventional names, Demeas, Myrrine, Moschion, for the traditional ones, and a comedy might follow. But that does not make the *Ion* at all like a play by Menander.[2]

Menander, then, like other Greek writers of comedies, was content to take his preliminary plots from a convenient and conventional stock. More than that: he was content

---

[1]Sidonius Apollinaris (*Epist.* iv, 12) calls ᾽Επιτρέποντες a play *similis argumenti* to the *Hecyra*; and in a sense it is (cf. below, p. 276, ff.). But how different is the conduct of the story.

[2]Leo compares the *Helena* with Greek comedy; and of course there are points of similarity. But a comparison of the *Ion* is much more instructive: it is that kind of plot which the ancients were thinking of when they said Euripides foreshadowed comedy; and the entire difference of treatment show what they meant when they spoke of the importance of the μῦθος. The *Iphigenia* too can be compared with comedy (especially with the *Rudens*, the original of which was by Diphilos, and which of all Plautus' plays comes nearest to the Greek type).

with a conventional social relationship for his characters. Most characters in Greek comedy are members of a family; by which I mean that their place in the family group is essential to the story, which is the story of a family rather than of individuals, or rather of those individuals in relation to their families. We speak of the 'old men,' the *matronae*, the young men and the young women as eternally recurring in ancient comedy; rather should we group them as parents or uncles (or old family friends) and as children. The essential is not their ages (many of the 'old' men are clearly not thought of as more than fifty at most—Demeas in the Σαμία is hardly fifty, whereas Smikrines in 'Επιτρέποντες may be seventy), but simply that the two groups belong to different generations, and that the relationship between them depends on this fact. Hence the young are very young, barely twenty in most cases, not yet, even in Greece, independent of their parents;[1] the assumption is that the unity of the family is all important, that even after his marriage, the young man forms part of his father's household (note how in the *Hecyra*, Sostrata and Laches agree to leave the town house to Pamphilus and Philumena; there is no suggestion that the latter might set up house on their own). The slaves equally are servants of the family. The only classes of persons who are independent of these family ties (and who can therefore be of different ages, between say twenty-five and forty) are the *hetairai* and the soldiers of fortune, as well as those hangers-on of society, cooks, parasites, flatterers, and panders. Furthermore, these families all belong to the same social class, the leisured class. They are not particularly wealthy, nor aristocratic; they are not specially persons of rank and fashion; but they have plenty of time and plenty of servants. It must be remembered, however, that this is largely a dramatic convention; comedy studied individuals; it did not give a picture of a social class as such, nor of the family as an institution.[2] In all this

[1] Especially I think in Terence must the *adulescentes* be regarded as mere boys; which helps to make understandable some otherwise surprising conduct. Moschion in Σαμία is also very young, though, as we should expect, he is more independent of his father than the Latin *adulescentes* are of theirs. Moschion is σώφρων; Pamphilus in *Andria* only obedient.

[2] So much a dramatic convention that even those who, for the purpose of the plot, are said to be poor have several servants, as Demea in *Rudens*, who starts with one

Menander too, like his fellow-dramatists was content with the conventions. They gave him adequate material, and there was no need for innovation.[1]

But he was far from content with conventional plots or conventional characters. Here he shows his individuality and his greatness. The problem of the plot is, as Aristotle says, to make the incidents appear probable in themselves and follow each other in an apparently natural and inevitable sequence; or rather that is the negative side of the problem, the positive side being to hold the interest of the audience through to the end. Both parts of the problem depend for their success on careful structure and drawing of character; incidents and characters must be both probable and interesting. The same rule does not apply to the preliminaries of the story—there improbabilities may abound (again as in tragedy, as Aristotle points out with reference to the *Oedipus Tyrannus*). It is highly improbable that Glykera in Περικειρο-μένη should on becoming Polemon's mistress find herself living next door to her brother from whom she has been separated since they were both exposed as infants, and that her lover should be the friend of a man who turns out to be her father. It is equally improbable that the two parties to an *affaire* at a midnight festival should afterwards marry and that without recognizing each other, however dark the night may have been, as in "Ηρως, Πλόκιον, and 'Επιτρέποντες;[2] still more improbable that in the latter Charisios could happily marry Pamphile without discovering that she was already four months with child. But we accept these things, as we accept the improbabilities of the *Oedipus*, without difficulty because they are not brought before our eyes, we are only told that they have happened before the play opens.[3]

---

old and faithful retainer, but later is discovered to have many; a detail that may well be from the Greek original. We may remember that old Philokleon of *The Wasps*, who should be poor as the typical dicast, has servants and a gentlemanly son.

[1] That is why as well the Greek comedy-writers did not bother to make use of more than a few stock names for their characters: *Moschion* or *Pheidias* will do for any young man of this class. But it has a psychological effect on us, by creating a feeling that all Moschions must be alike; which is a very different matter.

[2] Sometimes they do recognize each other, as in *Cistellaria*.

[3] Hence that imaginary 'Επιτρέποντες in the form of a modern play sketched above would not in fact work, for the improbability of Charisios not knowing that Pamphile was with child would at once be obvious; it would be part of the story, instead of being preliminary to it.

So in such a matter as the exposure of children Menander runs a risk in bringing before us the circumstances of the exposure in Περικ. 359 ff.; but he does it very skilfully, and makes it credible and human, not simply conventional fiction; contrast this passage with the formal statement of the facts in the prologue. Within the play itself, the incidents and characters are probable and self-consistent, and properly related to each. It is consistent with his character and his feelings that Charisios should act as he does—leave Pamphile for the gay company of Chairestrates, but not be gay; so that though Onesimos discovers the ring early in the play, he delays showing it to his master; which gives Habrotonon the chance to develop her scheme, and to find Pamphile first, and gives Charisios the chance to overhear the scene between Pamphile and her father: the whole admirably designed to delay the solution of a simple problem and to hold our interest.[1] And how excellent too is the manner in which the true characters of Charisios and Pamphile (on which the main structure of the play depends) are shown or suggested in

[1] I would not suggest that the structure of the 'Επιτρέποντες is perfect. Although the most mature of the three plays preserved to us, it is not the best constructed. The coincidence of Habrotonon having been at the festival of the year before, though not in itself remarkable, and of course not to be compared with the coincidence of the marriage of Pamphile and Charisios, yet strains our credence because it is so convenient to the plot; and the scene between Habrotonon and Pamphile, when the latter learns both that her child has been saved and that Charisios is the father, the key scene to the plot of the comedy, is hurried—they both go indoors before Pamphile realizes what has happened. There is a technical reason for this, that the audience already knows what Habrotonon has further to tell Pamphile; but it is none the less somewhat mechanical; though doubtless the loss of the greater part of the preceding scene between Pamphile and her father and of her monologue, makes us feel this scene to be more hurried than we should if we had the whole play.

I feel also that the action is too long delayed by the otherwise excellent arbitration scene; for the play scarcely gets under way before Onesimos' appearance and sight of the ring at the end of the second act; and that the last act in its turn is too long drawn out—the play is over by the end of the fourth act: the freedom of Habrotonon was certain, and the satisfaction of Smikrines, delayed by the moralizing of Onesimos, is of very minor interest. But Menander had a weakness (and a gift) for moralizing, of which the best and best-known example is the passage beginning
τοῦτον εὐτυχέστατον λέγω (fragm. 481)
so admirably translated by Gilbert Murray. (Ad. 806–35 is a good example of Terentian translation. O, Gripe, Gripe, etc. (Rud., 1235–48) lookes like Diphilos writing in Menander's manner, and Gripus' retort spectavi ego pridem comicos ad istunc modum looks like a jest by Plautus at Menander's expense, as O scirpe, scirpe (523–4) looks like parody; but parody earlier than the lines parodied! Cf. too Aristophanes, Av. 1238, Iris addressing Peithetairos: ὦ μῶρε, μῶρε, μὴ θεῶν κίνει φρένας δεινάς.)

the first three acts without our once seeing them, by hints or statements, in themselves quite natural, made by the others. In fact the structure of the ᾿Επιτρέποντες is in one respect of very great interest: the whole play turns on the characters and fate of Charisios and Pamphile; all the other incidents and persons, numerous and various as they are, and well as the characters are. drawn or sketched—Onesimos, Smikrines, Daos and Syriskos, Habrotonon above all, Simmias and Chairestratos, Sophrone the nurse and Karion the cook—are, it is made quite clear, subordinate to these two, their activities of interest only in so far as they concern *them*, retard or help *their* happiness. Yet they themselves each make but one appearance, both in the fourth act: Pamphile first, in the long scene with her father in which she shows herself at once so gentle and so firm, in her monologue of which we have but the one line, so full of pathos,

$$ἐξετύφην μὲν οὖν$$
κλαίουσα,

and in the short following scene in which she learns the truth from Habrotonon; then Charisios appears, after Onesimos has forewarned us, to show his remorse and self-abasement and then in his turn to hear the wonderful news from Habrotonon, and to rush in and beg forgiveness from Pamphile.[1] It is a most interesting variation in the conduct of a plot, even though it does result in too much weight being given to one act, with the last act left somewhat in the air.[2]

In the Περικειρομένη the very first scene shows us the lovers' quarrel, the furious and despairing soldier and Glykera defending herself but unable to tell the whole truth; then by a curious device, the formal prologue informing us of the play's preliminaries;[3] then the plans for Glykera to take refuge with Myrrine; and the knot is thus

[1] I feel confident that Wilamowitz was right in reading *KAP* (for Karion the cook) as the speaker of l. 405, in Act iii, in place of *XAP* (Charisios).

[2] Only a stage performance however could make clear how this would work out. (The fourth act is not longer than the second and third, the number of verses in each act being—i, perhaps not more than 150; ii, c. 240; iii, c. 290; iv. c. 260; and v, 160–70.)

[3] The postponing of the formal prologue may be intended by Menander to mark the passage of the night between the opening scenes and those that follow the prologue.

tied. The conduct of the play after this is well enough, but (so far as it is preserved to us) calls for little comment; and it contains one of those recognition scenes by means of tokens of which the Athenians were so strangely fond (a scene avoided by the way in 'Επιτρέποντες; partly because there had already been discussion of the tokens between Syriskos and Onesimos, but partly perhaps because Menander had grown out of such scenes). But the characters are excellent—Glykera, young but with such poise and such intelligence; her excessively vain brother—an admirable contrast, these twins—and the sympathetic, kind-hearted, mistaken Polemon; what a relief he is after the *milites gloriosi* of Latin comedy! How excellent that it should be his fond and foolish sentimentalizing over his love for Glykera that leads her father to her discovery. The Σαμία is a more youthful play, and in a lighter vein; our emotions, our sympathies are not stirred as in the two others;[1] the fun is often farcical. But it is an exceptionally well-constructed play. Four persons—the two fathers, the boy, the girl—all intensely desire the marriage, which is being hurried on; each in turn, imagining something that is not, delays it by refusing his part; the innocent and unfortunate Chrysis driven from her house to her neighbour's, then back to her own, stands between them all and was probably the means in the end of bringing everyone together reconciled.[2] All is excellently devised, though no character is deeply thought out.

Contrast with Menander Terence's *Andria* and *Heautontimorumenus*. If this paper were intended to include a judgement on Terence, that would not be fair; for these are not his best plays, and he was young when he wrote them. But they will serve all the better as a comparison, to bring out the strength of Menander's work, more particularly as they are adaptations from him. The *Andria* is a *contaminatio* of his 'Ανδρία and Περινθία. These two plays had similar plots;[3]

[1] And, I am sure, in the Ἥρως: there it is the character and fate of a slave that moves us. I cannot understand how, even with the one scene left us, so many can have thought of Daos as a crafty character.

[2] For my analysis of the plot of this play, which in some respects differs from that of other scholars, see *C.Q.* 1936, p. 70.

[3] But when Terence says

qui utramvis recte norit ambas noverit:
non ita dissimili sunt argumento, et tamen
dissimili oratione sunt factae ac stilo,

but, whereas Ἀνδρία opened with a monologue spoken by Simon (if this was the name of the character corresponding to Terence's Simo)—one of those semi-formal prologues which introduce us both to the story and to the man's character, which he managed so well (as in Σαμία)—Περινθία had a more dramatic opening, a dialogue between the old man and his wife, which equally served to explain the story. Terence, afraid of a long monologue, borrowed this opening scene from Περινθία; but, presumably because Simon's wife did not appear in Ἀνδρία, and Terence did not want to introduce her into his play, he invented the freedman Sosia to take her place.[1] A device legitimate enough; and Donatus says (on l. 28): *in hac scaena haec virtus est ut in argumenti narratione actio scaenica videatur, ut sine fastidio longus sermo sit ac senilis oratio.* But, in fact there is no virtue in the scene, and not a little tedium. It is not that the arrangement itself is artificial—the introduction of a freedman expressly to talk with Simo so that we may learn the situation with which the play opens; nor is there really any harm in the fact that he is a πρόσωπον προτατικόν who does not appear again in the play. What is wrong is that he is quite colourless, has no character, and serves only, as Prof. Norwood says, to 'interject "Hum!" and "Ha!" and the like at intervals'; that the scene is not in fact dramatic, that it is really a semi-formal prologue spoilt by pretending to be dramatic—particularly at the end when Sosia is asked to watch the conduct of Pamphilus, as though he were really to take a part in the play. Terence was at sea with a Greek convention and not bold enough or not yet clever enough to put something else in its place. As Croiset said: 'En donnant directement au public les explications nécessaires . . . le poète s'affranchissait de certaines exigences gênantes qui l'auraient obligé à charger son drame d'entretiens peu animés. Il se débarrassait des difficultés qui auraient entravé son génie, et il lui assurait ainsi un jeu plus franc et plus vif.'[2]

this is rather a measure of his youthful understanding than of Menander's powers of invention. For *fabulae similis argumenti*, cf. above, p. 263.

[1] What a pity it was not the other way about; then we could have said that the Greek poet naturally had no interest in women characters.

[2] *Rev. des Deux Mondes*, 1909, p. 818, quoted by Norwood, *Greek Comedy*, p. 353, n. 6. (Norwood, however, does not appreciate Croiset's argument.)

Secondly, we are constantly being confronted with the highly improbable story that Simo and Chremes arrange that their son and daughter shall marry that very day: everything—decision, preparations, ceremony—is to fall within a few hours. The length of a day in a Greek play could be as elastic as that of the street which is the scene of it; and Demeas and Nikostratos in Σαμία had similarly made all arrangements for a wedding within the day. But there the decision is, probably, part of the preliminary story and we are therefore the more ready to accept it, and besides that all the principals are longing for it and the hurry is an essential part of the comedy.[1] But in the *Andria*, the decision is part of the play, opposition to the marriage by one of the principals is the whole story, and, as well, attention is drawn to the improbability: Pamphilus is given to the wedding day itself to hold out against it (155 ff.);[2] his servant Davus explains to him, in the second act (387–8),

> nempe hoc sic esse opinor: dicturum patrem
> 'ducas volo hodie uxorem'; tu 'ducam' inquies;

and tells Simo how he has made some trifling objections (453)—

> 'quem,' inquit 'vocabo ad cenam meorum aequalium
> potissimum nunc?'

whom, indeed, at such short notice? It is true that Simo's hurry is part of his offence:

> pro deum fidem quid est, sic haec non contumeliast?
> uxorem decrerat dare sese mi hodie: nonne oportuit
> praescisse me ante? (237–9);
> nam quid ego dicam de patre? ah
> tantamne rem tam neglegenter agere! praeteriens modo
> mi apud forum 'uxor tibi ducendast, Pamphile, hodie' inquit; 'para,
> abi domum' (251–5).

But these naïve complaints of Pamphilus none the less seem to underline the improbability, and so far to weaken

It is interesting to observe that Euripides has the same device as Terence in an early play, *Medea*, where the nurse of the prologue is only a πρόσωπον προτατικόν and without individual significance: she is only there to listen to Medea. Later he adopted the simpler method of the formal prologue. Cf. above, p. 257, n. 2.

[1] At the end of *The School for Scandal*, Sheridan has: 'We'll have the wedding tomorrow morning'; in itself unnatural, but again, outside the story, *after* the play.

[2] As in *Aulularia*; but that is farce, and Plautus is as careless of plot as, in his different way, is Aristophanes.

the story.[1] In *Adelphoe*, too, the marriage can be fixed to take place within an hour or so of the child's birth; and again the difficulty is noticed (920–2); but at least this is when the main problem of the play is solved.

Lastly, the solution, the appearance of Crito with the news that Glycerium is a citizen. Norwood points out that he has a good reason to come to Athens, as he is the nearest relative and heir to Chrysis. Of course he has; indeed anyone might with a good reason come to Athens from Andros. But it doesn't help. If Crito had been in the play from the beginning, but in some way (made sufficiently probable) had not met or not recognized Chremes, nor Glycerium, all might have been well. As it is, we have a very cleverly woven plot, with everybody in difficulties (and, as in 'Ἐπιτρέποντες, it is the clever servant who gets them into these), and the only solution is the opportune arrival of someone to tell them there are no difficulties. It is the worst kind of woodenness; and not even in details is probability observed:

> eadem haec, Chreme,
> multi alii in Andro tum audiré (930-1).

Just so; so might Chremes have known from Crito, an old friend.[2] Crito is given scarcely more character of his own than Sosia at the beginning of the play; both are but artificial limbs.[3]

---

[1]Pamphilus is a good case to show that we must think of these *adulescentes* as very young. Nothing else would make tolerable his willingness to obey his father at the very end:

> tibi, pater, me dedo: quidvis oneris impone, impera.
> vis me uxorem ducere? hanc vis mittere? ut potero feram (897–8).

We are not asked to regard this filial obedience, this readiness after all to desert Glycerium and her child, as anything but amiable. In 687–90 even his youth will not excuse his conduct. *Phormio* 693 is another case: Antipho is the legal husband, yet has apparently no say in the matter—because he must not break with his father.

[2]There are of course many other improbabilities which are half suppressed, as that Chrysis in spite of her declared intentions had made no attempt to find Glycerium's father on moving to Athens, though she had only to ask after a brother of Phanias Rhamnusius.

[3]Donatus noticed this opportune arrival of Crito: ad v. 844.

I am not forgetting that some of these weaknesses were perhaps to be found in Menander's 'Ἀνδρία or Περινθία. But, as I said at the beginning, I am comparing only Terence as we have him with Menander in his original work. What saves Terence's play is the extreme liveliness of the first four acts—the greater part of it; and this must be largely due to him, as it was he who introduced the two characters, Charinus and Byrria, who add much to the humour of the story. We may, I think, surmise that the sudden shutting down of the story by the arrival of Crito is also due to Terence, unable to extricate himself from his own excellent weaving of the plot.

It may be said that the conventions of Greek life or of Greek drama anyhow made these recognitions or similar devices inevitable; that they are all artificial, and this example from the *Andria* only a little worse than the rest. Greek girls did not meet Greek men in ordinary society, so an innocent love affair to end in a happy marriage is impossible to represent on the stage; or would have been but for the convention of the girl lost in childhood (kidnapped, shipwrecked, or exposed) and apprenticed to a *hetaira*— for in the *demi-monde* of course young men and women meet.[1] 'Menander and his fellows,' says Norwood,[2] 'were compelled to evolve' this 'stock female *dramatis persona*' to meet this difficulty; who 'had been brought up amid poverty and the resultant *sans-gêne*, so that she could with ease be encountered by her future husband,' and in the end will be rescued by revelation of her birth and the recovery of her parents. 'None of the ancient dramatists (for whatever reasons) seems to have conceived and worked out a mere love-story between mere man and mere woman. Marriage, and even sexual affection, are for them necessarily entwined with, and governed by, social status; if the woman's parents are undiscoverable or not Greek citizens, no course is open but demoralizing irregularity. The discovery at the end, that she is not the daughter of some deceased Milesian or Perinthian, but the offspring of the ridiculous old man who lives next door to us in Athens, is indispensable. All this is now obsolete enough, but we must beware how we smile. It is entirely analogous to the nineteenth-century mechanical conception of the marriage ceremony.'

I quote this at length because it seems to me typical and incorrect. Of the four plays of Menander of which we are certain of the plots, *Ἥρως* ends in recognition of citizen

---

[1] The convention in a case like that of the *Andria* is that Pamphilus and his friends have ready access to the house of Chrysis, because she is of the *demi-monde*; and there (almost by chance) he meets Glycerium, who is being brought up in as orthodox and proper a manner as if she had belonged to the most respectable family in Athens; Glycerium does not herself 'go out.' When Pamphilus meets her out of doors it is at a religious ceremony (the funeral of Chrysis), of a kind at which he could have as easily met a girl of good family. In fact τὸ οἰκουρεῖν is as characteristic of the self-respecting hetaira as of the virtuous. (We may note in passing that in *Heaut.* 1061–5, the young Clitopho seems to know his respectable neighbours' daughters well, just as in *Andria* Charinus knew Philumena.)

[2] *The Art of Terence*, p. 24.

birth and marriage with a citizen, in accordance with this convention; 'Επιτρέποντες is a love-story between a man and a woman (whether or no a 'mere' story) without any recognition (of this kind); in Περικειρομένη there is a recognition but marriage with a foreigner, again a love-story of a man and a woman; in Σαμία, Demeas the Athenian and Chrysis the Samian are living together at the beginning and continue living together, a fond couple, at the end, without any recognition: a state of affairs that is neither demoralizing nor irregular.[1] Even if we adopt the entirely unnecessary suggestion that Chrysis was recognized at the end as Athenian, so that she may marry Demeas, this has nothing to do with the *play*, but is a mere convention when the play as such is over, the story complete, like the marriage of Moschion in Περικειρομένη; the convention, that is, was not adopted to make the play possible. To say that for the Greeks 'marriage and even sexual affection were entwined with, and governed by, social status' is scarcely to distinguish them from other civilized people; and is as irrelevant to Menander as to Homer or Sophocles. Of course, if he wished, he could make use of Athenian citizenship laws and social customs to make a play out of the conflict arising from a man's reluctance to marry a foreigner, a *hetaira*, or a servant (as in "Ηρως), or, more frequently, from his wanting to and his parents' opposition (as, presumably, in 'Ανδρία and Περινθία); just as a modern story can be, and has been, written about a prince wishing to marry a commoner and a young man of wealth not wishing to marry a servant girl. But Menander and his fellows did not evolve a 'stock character' to get over an insuperable difficulty; they found the story as it were to hand, and were content, as I have said, to accept a conventional preliminary story for their plays as the tragedians had been to accept a traditional one—partly because of its similarity in outline to certain tragic plots, because the audience liked that kind of story (it had in it an element of the spectacular and was immediately provocative of interest), and partly because of its rela-

---

[1]When Norwood speaks of 'the *ridiculous* old man who lives next door,' he is of course thinking of Plautus though writing of Menander. There is nothing, or scarcely anything, of the kind in the latter.

T

tion to real life: at a time when the selling of prisoners of
war as slaves was frequent, piracy not uncommon, and the
exposure of unwanted children not unknown, it is probable
enough that many hetairai had taken to their profession
because of such an accident and not impossible that some of
them were recognized and rescued.

For if it were true that such conventions were *necessary*
for the play, were of its essence, and that they are 'obsolete
enough now,' then neither Menander nor Terence would be
readable, or only in patches. To account for the convention
as Norwood has done would be to give its historic origin,
but it would not turn a poor play into a good one, a
conventional play depending upon a dead convention into a
living one. No amount of explanation of this or that curious
custom can do that; it can lessen a reader's surprise at an
unessential detail, but if what needs explaining (in this way)
is of the essence of a work of art, the work is dead. When, in
the *Odyssey*, Telemachos sneezes and it is regarded as a
good omen, that may need a learned note; but if the whole
significance of the poem lay in the importance of sneezing,
it would long ago have lost its meaning and would be read
only for its antiquarian interest. So would *Antigone*, if the
understanding of it depended (as some have supposed) on
our knowing the importance of burial to the Greeks; and
Prometheus, if we had to be as interested in the geography
of the East as Aeschylus at that moment was. *Evan Harring-
ton* is a romantic comedy, about persons, not a social study;
but it has as its basis a class prejudice, a social snobbery,
with which we can all, whether we like it or not, sympathize;
without it the story is incomprehensible. If ever it becomes
necessary to explain that, and not only certain accidental
characteristics of it, to a generation to which it is foreign,
then for that generation the story is dead, it can only be a
historical curiosity. Similarly, we have to explain one or two
particulars incidental to the society which Menander
depicts—for example, the Athenian law of citizenship,
the general disorder and unrest of the age; we do not have
to explain the conduct of his men and women: that is common to humanity.[1]

[1] It does not necessarily follow that his plays would succeed now on the stage, for

The *Heautontimorumenus* is for us of even greater interest. It has some of the usual improbabilities: everyone overhears everybody else (note especially 512–5, 517, 679 ff., and 614 ff., where as well Sostrata's appearance on the stage to talk about the ring with her nurse is clumsily managed); no story is told Chremes to explain the presence of Antiphila (if she is just one of Bacchis' *ancillae*, why is she especially placed with Sostrata?);[1] the solution of the problem begins all too soon (626 ff.), before there is any real difficulty—in fact there is no real problem except the automatic one, automatically solved by the ring. But more interesting is the inconsistency of tone between different parts of the play. Terence promises us high comedy in the prologue:

> adeste aequo animo, date potestatem mihi
> statariam agere ut liceat per silentium,
> ne semper servo' currens, iratus senex,
> edax parasitu', sycophanta autem impudens,
> avaru' leno adsidue agendi sunt seni
> clamore summo, cum labore maxumo.

The first act and the opening scenes of the second are in this vein, good comedy of manners, in which our feelings are engaged. But with the appearance of Bacchis and her train, the play becomes farce, for which we are not prepared; sometimes amusing, as the descriptive passage 448 ff., and her passing from one house to the other, but generally trite: one *senex* telling the other of his son's plot to do him out of money (through the slave, of course), the

---

the Greek methods of production, which Menander had in mind when he wrote, may be too foreign to our taste; though I should like to see the experiment tried. Just as a production of one of Pindar's odes in the original manner might fail, if Greek music and dancing made no appeal to us; but this does not mean that the odes are dead as poetry.

I do not wish to imply that Professor Norwood thinks the convention excuses the poor construction of the *Andria*, though he puts all the blame for it on to Menander and his fellows (of whom he is curiously jealous), which is inconsistent in one who so much insists on the originality of Terence. Indeed, I think he overdoes his criticism of the play in this respect, for he finds the introduction of the new characters, Charinus and Byrria, purposeless. True, they might have been used to better purpose; but they serve to add to the general muddle in which everyone gets involved through the well-meaning activities of Davus; and that is the main thing in the plot.

[1] Superficially the situation is similar to that in Περικειρομένη, a girl in a difficult situation taking refuge with a *matrona*. But how much more probable are the circumstances of the Greek play!

senex abusing his wife (623 ff., 879, 1006), and so forth. Comedy has fled. The whole idea of bringing Bacchis to a respectable house, is farcical, and still more her transference from Chremes' house to Menedemus', without Menedemus being asked; it is impossible, except in farce, that Clinia should agree, and that he should not at that point (722) go in to see Antiphila. It is incongruous with the comedy with which the play opened, which led us to expect probable (as well as interesting) characters and incidents; Menedemus' fears and self-tormenting have come to nothing. It is a fatal defect when an author cannot decide what sort of play he is writing. And it is this play which recent scholars have regarded as an almost word for word translation of Menander—the only comedy of Menander completely preserved![1]

Consider a much superior play of Terence's, the *Hecyra*. There are weaknesses both in structure and in characterization in this too, but of a different kind from those of the *Andria* and *Heautontimorumenos*. It is most interesting to compare this play with 'Επιτρέποντες, and that not principally on account of the similarity of the plot in outline (noted by Sidonius)—that in both the hero and heroine have met before marriage at night without seeing each other's faces, then married without recognition, and the child she bears is the cause of the quarrel between them. There is much more than this: the *Hecyra* opens with 'I never thought Pamphilus would *marry* while Bacchis was alive,' 'Επιτρέποντες with 'I never thought Charisios would *take a mistress* so soon after marrying,' for both were steady, dependable men and in love; then we learn that Pamphilus will have nothing to do with his wife, nor Charisios with Habrotonon. And this is no mechanical copy the one of the other, for in the *Hecyra* the mistress is later forsaken for the wife, who, in character very like Pamphile in 'Επιτρέποντες, wins Pamphilus' affections. If this variation of Menander's theme is, as seems probable, due to Apollo-

---

[1]See for instance, R. Walzer, *Hermes*, lxx, 1935, 197–202. His main thesis is that the play illustrates Menander's pupillage to Aristotle and his followers in ethics: his characters illustrate the doctrine of τὸ μέσον. As though he were incapable of understanding and portraying a δύσκολος, a δεισιδαίμων, a φιλάργυρος, a φιλάνθρωπος, without previous study at the Lyceum.

doros, he was a most ingenious dramatist.[1]   But we can
already note a weakness: whereas in Menander we hear,
in a very natural manner, of Charisios' coldness to
Habrotonon from her own lips, and indeed everyone of
the party must have noticed it, Terence has to suppose that
Pamphilus told his servant Parmeno the secrets of the bridal
chamber; and we must not only suppose it, but it is emphasized (136 ff., then 410–1; and compare 393—a general
rumour of the truth). Secondly, the birth of the child during
the course of the play strains our powers of belief unduly;
not only has Philumena been with her husband's family
for some months without her pregnancy being discovered,
but when she returns to her father's house for the last
month or two before the child's birth, it can still be kept
secret from her father though her mother and the servants
(excitable creatures—367 ff.) know of it, and he can talk
with her an hour or so before the event (243–5)! And attention is drawn to this (530, 641).[2] After that Phidippus'
scolding of his daughter an hour after the birth (623–6)
seems almost commonplace; though we cannot in this case,
or ought not to, make allowance for the elasticity of stage-

---

[1] It will be remembered that the *didascalia* attributes the original of the *Hecyra*
to Menander, and it may be that Terence borrowed from both dramatists; a variation of this kind would be in Menander's manner; but Donatus does not suggest
any author but Apollodoros.
   There are other interesting points of similarity or contrast between the two plays:
the characters of the two heroes (*Hec.* 152: *pium ac pudicum ingenium narras Pam-
phili*), and the gentle conduct of the two heroines (*Hec.* 165 f., 302 f.); the journey
of the hero abroad (*Hec.* 173); ll. 138–42 of the *Hecyra*, which might well come,
mutatis mutandis, from Ἐπιτρέποντες; and the talk between Bacchis and Parmeno
(808 ff.), which it is interesting to compare with the plot devised by Habrotonon and
Onesimos, and the contrast in the attitude of the two fathers towards their daughters:
Phidippus' words to Philumena—

   Etsi scio ego, Philumena, meum ius esse ut te cogam
   quae ego imperem facere, ego tamen patrio animo victu' faciam
   ut tibi concedam neque tuae lubidini advorsabor

                                                                (243–5),

and Pamphile's to her father in Ἐπιτρ.. fr. Z 1–2 (p. 35, Jensen)—

   ἀλλ' εἰ με σῴζων τοῦτο μὴ πείσαις ἐμέ,
   οὐκέτι πατὴρ κρίνοι' ἂν ἀλλὰ δεσπότης.

[2] It is possible enough that this emphasizing of an improbability (410–1 and 641)
may be due not to the original but to Terence, uneasy with it as he was with the
stage conventions and making matters worse by drawing our attention to them.
   Note that in Ἐπιτρέποντες there is no such improbability; not only is the child
born before the play opens, but Smikrines' ignorance of the event is natural, for he
was not living in the same house.
   The other improbability, Pamphilus' own ignorance of his wife's pregnancy,
scarcely matters, for like that of Charisios, it is ἔξω τοῦ δράματος.

time, for it is necessary to the story that this visit to the unfortunate young mother should be immediate—otherwise the child would have been taken away.[1]

Again, the *narrative* monologues are awkwardly managed, well-written though they are. Terence (or Apollodoros) was trying a new method—keeping *the audience* in the dark about the past as well as the players, and letting the facts only come to light gradually in the course of the action; but he can only manage that by plain narrative, not dramatically; he does away with the narrative prologue, only to substitute for it three pieces of prologue inserted into Act iii (377 ff.), Act iv (572 ff.), and Act v (816 ff.)—excellent narrative, especially the last, but very ill-fused in the whole amalgam of the play. The first of these, that of Pamphilus, begins well enough: he is crying out his indignation and misery, the very stuff of a monologue; but that he should go on to quote sixteen lines of what Myrrina had said to him, including such careful explanation as:

> parturire eam nec gravidam esse ex te solus consciu's:
> nam aiunt tecum post duobu' concubuisse mensibus.
> tum, postquam ad te venit, mensis agitur hic iam septimus:
> quod te scire ipsa indicat res:

that is hard to stomach. Terence had advanced far when he was no longer afraid of the monologue; but his use of it, or of part of it, to take the place of a formal prologue is no better than the jejune dialogue with which he preferred to open the *Andria*. Contrast Menander: the monologue of Moschion in Περικειρομένη (276 ff.) is narrative—it tells what has happened indoors; it is thus far a substitute for drama, an interlude, most like that of Pamphilus in the *Hecyra*; but it is not so long, and it only tells us what has just happened and

---

[1] Glycerium in the *Andria* has to receive two visits immediately after the birth of her child, one of them from a stranger (818, 951).

The stage-conventions too are somewhat strained in the *Hecyra*: (1) that Phidippus and Laches should be near neighbours; for Philumena leaves the latter's house for the former's in order to get quite away and to keep her secret, which must of course be discussed on the stage (cf. esp. 314–8; emphasized 336, 341); nor was there any need to make Bacchis a neighbour too (720); (2) the out-door scene: by one use of this convention the scene between Myrrina and Pamphilus (Act iii 3) must be related, not acted, because it takes place indoors, by another she leaves the house, and the talk with her husband is clearly not one which would naturally take place in the street (Act iv 1—again awkwardly drawn attention to, 522). The great secret of course is mentioned out loud (388); but here the monologue is not overheard.

prepares for the next scene.[1]   In Σαμία we have the first
monologue of Demeas, which is narrative, but is semi-formal
prologue; then his second (110 ff.), which is outburst, that is,
dramatic, most cleverly giving us information with it; then
Moschion's, which is reflective (271 ff.).   In 'Επιτρέποντες,
a short narrative by Onesimos (202 ff.), quite naturally
managed; Onesimos' reflective monologue (340 ff.); the
long speech of Pamphile; and finally the excited narrative of
Onesimos, which he cannot keep to himself, followed by the
great monologue of Charisios: all of them as dramatic as
any dialogue could be.

There is a more serious fault, however, in the structure of
the *Hecyra* than these, and it is in part due to this use of the
monologues. The opening dialogue (between two *meretrices*
who, like Sosia in the *Andria*, are introduced only for the
sake of this expository scene)[2] tells us of the loves of Pamphilus and Bacchis, and his unexpected marriage. In the
next Parmeno, the confidential servant of Pamphilus,
confirms the affection for Bacchis by the coldness towards
Philumena; for though Pamphilus learnt later to love his
wife (chiefly, though, because of Bacchis's coldness since
his marriage) and has indeed transferred his affections
thither, still there are hopes of a permanent separation once
more as she has left his house for her father's during his
absence abroad. Throughout Act ii, when the parents,
Laches, Sostrata and Phidippus are on the stage, disputing
the cause of Philumena's departure, we are left wondering.
Not till Act iii, when Pamphilus returns, do we learn (very
perfunctorily in a line and a half, 297-8) that his affection
for her is genuine, and then later of the birth of the child
and its effect on his feelings. The second half of the play is
dominated by his refusal to have his wife back and his
chivalrous resolve not to state the real cause; it is a complex
situation admirably managed, especially when her father
learns of the child's birth and thinks now everything will

---

[1] I do not agree with the usual account of this monologue (for example, Jensen's).
See *C.Q.* 1936, pp. 67-8.
[2] But how much better done is this scene and the following one with Parmeno
than the corresponding scene in the *Andria*. Besides, by suggesting the conventional
picture of the *meretrix*, it adds point to the very different conduct of Bacchis in the
event.

be well, unlike Smikrines in 'Επιτρέποντες who holds out to the end because he does *not* know of the child. But it is spoilt because Pamphilus' conduct is not made clear: not only is the reconciliation after the original coldness only briefly referred to (169–70, 297–8); but we are not once shown his jealousy. It is natural enough to assume that a man will be jealous when he learns that his wife whom he loves has had a child by another man, especially one conceived before their marriage. But it is not enough for a play to assume a feeling; it must show it. As it is, the change in Pamphilus, from the first conflict of affections to love for his wife and then to jealousy, are but briefly related or assumed, when they are the very source of his actions; he is at the crucial moment, from scene 3 to scene 5 of Act iii, almost an automaton—'naturally I cannot have my wife back after this'—without real emotion.[1] How different from Charisios, whose feelings and conduct are so well displayed, even though he does not himself appear but in the one scene in Act iv.

There are also faults in characterization which are particularly interesting to note. Laches might have been drawn as the kindly but crochety man that is suggested by his words to his wife

> abi rus ergo hinc: ibi ego te et tu me feres (610);

but in general he is the conventional *senex*, surly to his wife only because the convention demanded it. Nor is Phidippus more sharply drawn: he shows no natural indignation at Pamphilus' ἀγνωμοσύνη (*inhumanus* 499), and is absurdly indifferent to his daughter's fate— quite ready to give up the child to its father and leave her a widow and childless (508–9, 665 ff.); his weakness, that is (cf. 243–5), is not effectively visualized.[2] Pamphilus himself

---

[1] It is this, as well as the management of the monologues and the variations on the theme of the 'Επιτρέποντες noted above, which makes me think those scholars may be right who, in spite of Donatus, have thought the *Hecyra* a *contaminatio* of Apollodoros' play and another by Menander (though not, of course, the 'Επιτρέποντες). If it is, Terence has made a most interesting play of it, notwithstanding these weaknesses in construction.

[2] There is one admirable touch: he is trying to persuade his wife to tolerate Pamphilus' liaison with Bacchis—

> audisti ex aliquo fortasse qui vidisse eum diceret
> exeuntem aut intro euntem ad amicam. quid tum postea?
> si modeste ac raro haec fecit, etc.,

is better done, a self-absorbed, self-pitying young man, who expects everyone to bestir himself to make him happy; priggish to a degree at times—

> quod potero faciam, tamen ut pietatem colam;
> nam me parenti potiu' quam amori obsequi
> oportet (447-8; cf. 470 ff.);[1]

and lyrically happy at getting back his wife, for whom he has shown no sign of anxiety during the birth of the child. He does not at all deserve Philumena. This might well have added point to the play; but—a fatal defect— Terence does not seem to be at all aware of it: for him the good young man will make a perfect husband.

Bacchis might have been delightful—she is kindly, gracious, well-mannered, especially to Laches, whose rudeness to her, if he were a living figure, would be intolerable (note the conventional jest in 737–8); and, like Philumena, much too good for Pamphilus. But she is spoilt for us, at first by Parmeno's description of her (taken from stock)—

> sed ut fit, postquam hunc alienum ab sese videt,
> maligna multo et mage procax facta ilico est (158-9),

then by her own self-consciousness of the fact that no other *meretrix* would behave as she has done: three times she says this, twice to Laches and once more to herself, to us, to make certain of our applause (756, 775–6, 834). Is it Terence apologizing, thinking an apology necessary, for putting on the stage a *meretrix* who is not mercenary? It is difficult to believe it can be a countryman of the man who created Habrotonon.[2] And Sostrata? That calm, kindly, sensible woman who has to manage a surly husband and a priggish son? Her character too is marred, not so much by anything she says, as by the trite jests about husband and wife, of

when the affair was notorious, as he himself says it was a moment later
  quicum tot consuesset annos (550-5).

[1] His general sense of the duty of obedience to his parents is part of the dramatic tradition—he is a member of a family, even after marriage (see above, p. 264); a tradition which also accounts for the fact that the simple solution of the difficulty between his wife and mother, namely, that he should have a house of his own, is not suggested.

[2] Isidore, *Origines*, said of Terence: *quinetiam solus ausus est, etiam contra praescripta comica, meretrices interdum non malas introducere.* It is clear that he did not appreciate the 'rules' of Greek comedy; not so clear, that he misunderstood those of the Latin adaptations.

which one might have supposed an intelligent man would
have had enough in Plautus:

> So. non, ita me di bene ament, mi Lache,
> itaque una inter nos agere aestatem liceat. LA. di mala prohibeant
>
> (206-7);
>
> LA. Gaudeo, ita me di ament, gnati causa; nam de te quidem
> sati' scio peccando detrimenti nil fieri potest (233-4).

So her own foolish moralizing—

> edepol ne nos sumus inique aeque omnes invisae viris
> propter paucas, quae omnes faciunt dignae ut videamur malo, etc.
>
> (274 ff.)

Yet Laches can say, with equal sententiousness, that he
approves of Pamphilus' respect for his mother (482–3).
All this is quite out-of-place and undramatic, for Sostrata is
altogether a sympathetic character: as undramatic as the
similar jests in *Adelphoe* (30–1, 43–4, 867), and as the trite
humour of Demea in the *Rudens* at his wife's expense (recognized by most as Plautus' own addition), as the conventional
traits of the *meretrix* in Adelphasium and Anterastilis in the
Poenulus, though they are of gentle birth, and of the slave in
Tyndarus in *Captivi*, though he is no slave.[1] Anything for a
laugh, though you spoil the tone and colour of a scene. The
fact is, Roman comedy seldom rose above the music-hall
level for this particular kind of joke: the level that is marked
by a lack of wit in the writer, and in the audience by equal
pleasure at endless repetition. Donatus makes an illuminating
comment on one such jest of Terence's, at the end of the
Adelphoe, where Micio is being persuaded to marry:

> Ego novo' maritus anno demum quinto et sexagensumo
> fiam atque anum decrepitam ducam? (938-9).

Apud Menandrum, he notes, *senex de nuptiis non gravatur:
ergo Terentius* εὑρετικῶς; and on *anum decrepitam*: *facete
hoc addidit, tanquam faciendum hoc esset, si puella duceretur
seni.* Alas, for Roman inventiveness and Roman wit![2]

---

[1]It must not be forgotten that a good many of such passages in Plautus are in
song, not in dramatic dialogue; this makes a lot of difference in our reaction to
them.

[2]There is much in English comedy to parallel with the Latin in contrast to
Menander—the jests of Teazle about Lady Teazle in *School for Scandal*, i, 2, *init.*,
and indeed all the laughing at Mrs. Malaprop, which would be cruel if not so
obvious. The intrigue in *The Rivals* is also in Terence's manner; Trip, in the

But if there are many faults to be found in the *Hecyra*, there is this which distinguishes it altogether from the *Andria*: we are judging it by a high standard. There is a quality in the *Hecyra*, and also in the *Phormio* and the *Adelphoe*, which is lacking in the three other plays, and marks a very great advance in Terence's art.[1] How is it to be described? Consider an earlier criticism, one of twenty similar ones: 'If from style,' wrote Papillon in 1870, 'we turn to matter there is less to be said. His plots are marked by tiresome uniformity; in each play the same stock characters play out the same stock rôles of immoral intrigue and unfilial deceit which in the end are triumphant: so that however elegant the language, however artistic the by-play of character, the story has but little interest or profit. The cause of these defects lies in the sources from which Terence drew, the literature of the New Attic Comedy; which reflected the degeneracy of a society whose political, social, religious and domestic life had alike become demoralized and decayed.'[2] Now quite apart from the obviously false judgement of Greek comedy (an error however from which we are not yet free, as can be seen from the quotations from the *Cambridge Ancient History* with which I opened this paper), quite apart from this, such a criticism has an old-fashioned air; it seems ῑ us, so much younger, and therefore so much wiser than Papillon, to leave Terence very much where he was. Yet, if we were

School, is like the Latin slave. And it is interesting to note how Sheridan's language often recalls Plautus, although the whole tone of his plays is so different: 'I hate such an avarice of crime; 'tis an unfair monopoly, and never prospers'; 'deviated from the direct road of wrong'; and many other instances.

Ben Jonson is, of course, closer to the Latin comedy. It may be worth while noting a few points in two of his plays. In *The Case is Altered*, we have narrative monologue, telling us the essentials of Rachel's birth (ii 1), very well managed, and another, cruder one later (iv 4); and there is a good monologue, spoken by Angelo, in Menander's manner (iii 1). There is the very conventional betrayal of Paolo by his friend Angelo (v 8)—the characters do not live; and the recognition scene (v 12) is not better managed than in Greek or Latin plays. Finally the marriages are all rapidly arranged at the close, in eight lines. *Every Man in His Humour* is in many ways very like Plautus: Bobadill is the *Miles*, with Mathew as his parasite, ever at his heels ready to praise all he has done; in iv 7 they are both arrant cowards. Brayneworm is the clever slave, and fools the old master for the sake of the young one (see esp. iv 6); Act iv 10 is pure Plautus (l. 42, 'this hoary-headed lecher, this old goat'). But note this difference: for a play of this kind Ben Jonson did not put his characters into respectable society; Plautus did—that is, he transforms his Greek original, takes its society and the surroundings, which are respectable, and makes their conduct disreputable.

[1] This development in Terence has been properly emphasized by Norwood.
[2] Edition of *Andria and Eunuchus*, pp. xv–xvi.

candid and honest with ourselves, we should admit, I think, that it has some truth, some point; or rather that it has some point, when applied to his three earlier plays. What is at bottom wrong with the *Andria*, the *Heautontimorumenus*, and the *Eunuchus* (leaving out of account faults of construction and characterization), what Papillon and others felt but did not sufficiently express, is that, unlike the three later plays and still more unlike those of Menander, they are not *about* anything. There is much good writing, some good scenes, clever development of plot up to a certain point, some amusing characters (the slaves); but we are not interested in any one, and in consequence the oft-repeated situations and characters—the helpless young man, the too helpful servant, the autocratic and silly father, the mercenary harlot and the colourless young woman, the whole general air of self-conscious virtue combined with childish intrigue and deceit—become tedious. We feel it plainly in those comedies of Plautus which are failures. That genial playwright had the Shakespearean gift of making a good play—or rather a readable and actable play—out of a very poor story; but he could not always carry it off, as in the *Poenulus* and, in a different way, the *Captivi*. Then we have forced on our notice the well-worn elements from which his plays derive, the rags and tatters of the material upon which he drew. I have no doubt that if there were discovered now any considerable number of the hundreds of Greek comedies written, say, in the century between 350 and 250 B.C.—not a selection, but a chance collection of them—we should find much of it tiresome in the extreme (interesting as the discovery would be to the historian), as tiresome as nine-tenths of Restoration comedy. That Terence himself felt this is clear from his prologues to the *Heautontimorumenus* and the *Eunuchus*:

> quod si personis isdem huic uti non licet:
> qui magi licet currentem servom scribere,
> bonas matronas facere, meretrices malas,
> parasitum edacem, gloriosum militem,
> puerum supponi, falli per servom senem,
> amare odisse suspicari? denique
> nullumst iam dictum quod non dictum sit prius.

qua re aequom est vos cognoscere atque ignoscere
quae veteres factitarunt si faciunt novi.

Terence is referring to Latin comedy; but it seems also
clear that he did not see, or had not yet seen, when he wrote
the *Eunuchus*, that this would be a very superficial and therefore an essentially false judgement on Menander and,
perhaps, some of Menander's fellow playwrights. It would
also be a superficial judgement (as is Papillon's) on his own
later plays; in which, with the same materials as he had
already had at his disposal, he not only succeeded in making
his people real, but made their purposes and therefore their
actions interesting.[1] His development is evident: from the
beginning he was a master of style, but either he adapted
weak plays or failed in his adaptation; then, perhaps
suddenly, he saw what the best Greek writers were aiming
at, and half succeeded (*dimidiatus Menander*) in adapting
their work for the Roman stage. It was a tragedy that he
died so young; his last play is his best constructed.

But it is still only half Menander.[2] It is not simply that
the latter's plots do not consist in 'immoral intrigue and
unfilial deceit'; for intrigue and deceit may be good matter
for comedy. Actually, of the five plays of which we can
reasonably reconstruct the whole story ("Ηρως and Πλόκιον
in addition to the other three), there is only one in which a
father is deceived by his son, in the Σαμία; and that in
the preliminary to the play, and for a worthy end—a dramatically worthy end, that is: we are interested in the result,
not asked simply to admire the cleverness of the deceit.[3]
It is *that* which becomes tedious with repetition; for it is

---

[1]Note for example, *Phormio* 477, *confutavit verbis admodum iratum senem*: the
usual story, with the parasite taking the rôle usually played by the slave. But how
much more subtly managed; and how much more *significant!*
[2]'Caesar's well-known characterization of Terence as "Menander halved" is not
so much an exact arithmetical valuation [indeed?] as a reminder of his adroitness in
weaving two dramas into one'—Wight Duff in *C.A.H.* viii 414. He should look at
Caesar's lines again. And why not 'Menander doubled'? If it referred to *contaminatio*
at all, it would mean Terence left out half of Menander in every play (as he must
have done, for example, in the *Andria*).
[3]The only surviving scene of *Fabula incerta*, from the end of the play, is one of
deceit of an old man by two other men to get his consent to his son's marriage, and
of confession when the consent is gained. In its liveliness and the rapidity of the
action (which would be unconvincing if we were asked to take it seriously) it recalls
Plautus; but it recalls him largely because it is all that we have of the play—we
know nothing of its general tone.

fundamentally uninteresting, it touches neither our feelings nor our intelligence. On the contrary, in Menander we are in a world of reasonable men and women, with human feelings and emotions; and these men and women are most subtly observed. The Romans saw things in black and white; not so the Greeks. In Plautus there is little real observation of character (any more than there is in Restoration comedy and in Sheridan). It is what interested Menander most. Least of all men did he deal in *bonas matronas, meretrices malas, parasitos edaces, gloriosos milites*.[1] His Habrotonon is one of the most lively and charming characters in comedy; his Polemon sympathetic, simple, impulsive—very different from the *Miles* of Plautus and the youthful Terence. Another of his soldiers was Thrasonides in Μισούμενος, perhaps yet more subtly drawn; for he appears to have failed in the beginning, through his roughness, to win the affections of Krateia, and only succeeds in the end: that is, she (and we) perhaps had to overcome a repugnance to something that was really repellent in him, not only to forgive a too impulsive action, as in Περικειρομένη. There are fine shades of difference between the two Moschions: in the Σαμία, a vain but likeable boy whose happiness with Plangon is assured and who will make her happy (contrast Pamphilus in *Andria*, so unworthy of Glycerium); in the Περικειρομένη a vain egoist, whose marriage, noted at the end of the play, is of no interest. Smikrines, though not Demeas, suggests that perhaps his older men were more conventional; but there is none of the trite quarrelling of husbands and wives.[2] Above all, no *servus currens*. This truly comic character, the deviser of ingenious schemes, the controller of events, the

---

[1]But this did not prevent commonplace minds from labelling his characters in this fashion. See the *Periochai*, in Jensen's edition, p. 4: τὸ δὲ δ[ρᾶμα τῶν] ἀ[ρίστων. ἔχ]ει δὲ πρ[εσβύτην] εὐ[όργητο]ν, νέαν κ[αὶ νέους] φι[λεράστο]υς, οἰκέτη[ν φι]λο[δέσποτο]ν καὶ παν[οῦργον] (ll. 96–100), according to the ingenious restorations of Körte.

[2]Demeas could not possibly have spoken the words
κατάξω τὴν κεφαλήν, ἄνθρωπέ, σου
ἄν μοι διαλέγῃ (Σαμία 173–4)
to Chrysis, as many have supposed. This could be taken as a test of one difference between Menander and the Latin playwrights. The only jest of this kind in our papyri is Κιθαρ. 61–2; where we may note as well a certain awkwardness in the way the meeting between father and son is managed. An early play?

commanding officer of his young master and his friends—

PSEUD. Nunc, Calidore, te mihi operam dare volo. CALID. ecquid
imperas?
PSEUD. hoc ego oppidum admoenire ut hodie capiatur volo;
ad eam rem usust hominem astutum, doctum, cautum et callidum,
qui imperata ecferta reddat, non qui vigilans dormiat.
CALID. Cedo mihi, quid es facturus? PSEUD. temperi ego faxo scies.

(*Pseud.* 383 ff.)—

the man who must be ready at times even to make love
on the helpless young man's behalf (*Poen.* 353 ff.), this
greater than Ulysses and Agamemnon: he is a creation
of Latin comedy, especially of Plautus.[1] He was based of
course on his Greek original: the Italian observed the
free speech and easy ways of the Greek servant, the easy
relations between him and his master; and he saw
the possibility of comic exaggeration.[2] But Menander
did not like exaggeration. His servants play an important
part—Parmenon helping his mistress and his young master
to conceal the truth from Demeas, Daos helpfully doing
nothing to assist Moschion, Onesimos busily telling his
master Pamphile's secret and so getting everyone into
trouble, the kind and sentimental Daos of the *Ἥρως* in
love: they are all interesting; but their relationship with
their masters is throughout a natural one.[3] In no one of his
plays is there a sign of the slave who holds the will and the
conscience of his master, to whom the latter not only defers,
but is helpless without him.[4] The old line 'Menander and

---

[1]Not that Terence's slaves are not good too; and the excellent device in *Hecyra*
of making Parmeno achieve nothing—always *currens*, but to no purpose, always
being sent on profitless errands—has often been noticed. Parmeno's flourish at the
end is admirable:
immo vero scio, neque inprudens feci. PAM. ego istuc sati' scio. PAR. an
temere quicquam Parmeno praetereat quod facto usu' sit?

[2]How far the character of the comic slave had already been developed in Old
Comedy, we cannot say, though the many hints of it in Aristophanes, especially in
the opening scenes of the *Knights*, suggest that it was familiar: for example, the
managing, helpful slave, *Equit.* 229—
κἀγὼ μετ' αὐτῶν χὠ θεὸς ξυλλήψεται.
And the story of the play often recalls the familiar plot of the clever servant out-
witting a foolish old master.

[3]One instance, slight in itself, perhaps illustrates this: cf. *Ad.* 364–73 with *Σαμία*,
81—in both the slave blandly pretends not to have seen his master; the former is
exaggerated and very funny, the latter is more naturally done, and raises a smile.

[4]*Γεωργός* gives a chance of such development, for the young man is at a loss
(20–1).

Life, which of you imitated the other?' is the right way to approach his work. It is possible that he did not attempt that type of comedy which gets its effect by simplification and concentration on one character or situation, by ignoring the secondary and magnifying the essential feature—Ben Jonson's *Humour*—the type of which the *Aulularia* is (in spite of everything, we may say) a triumphant example, of which *Tartuffe* is the classic:

> 'As when some one peculiar quality
> Doth so possess a man, that it doth draw
> All his affects, his spirits, and his powers,
> In their confluctions, all to runne one way,
> This may be truly said to be a Humour.'[1]

Euclio may be borrowed from one of Menander's *avares*, or the whole play be adapted from him; but, if we may judge from Menander's extant work, the intensifying of the one element in his character, the heightening of the comedy in this way, is the work of Plautus.

Yet, even within the compass of the little that is left, we can see the great variety of Menander's plays. Σαμία, an early work, is light comedy—a marriage, much desired by all four principals to it, and being hurried on, is delayed through a misunderstanding by each of them in turn; in the third act a farcical scene where the faithful Chrysis, turned out of her home by Demeas just before and kindly received by Nikostratos, is now driven out by the latter in a fury and rescued by Demeas, who goes on to assure Nikostratos that the father of his daughter's child is probably Zeus. Περικειρομένη is almost pure romance, the story of a lovers' quarrel: Ἥρως and Γεωργός may have been similar in tone, and these developed too the contrast both in conduct and circumstances between rich and poor. Ἐπιτρέποντες is the most mature, and contains the finest observation, a comedy of character, not of situation. It is not, as I have already remarked, the best constructed: it takes a long time for the story to get under way, and the arbitration scene is developed at length rather for its own sake than for its contribution to the plot; the central scene, in which Pamphile learns of the truth, is too hurried; and

---

[1] *Every Man Out of His Humour*, 105 ff.

the last act, after we know that all is well, is too long drawn
out.[1] But the unfolding of the situation, as it depends on the
characters, is admirable. Greek drama 'did not interest itself
in the development of character, but it did gradually reveal
an already developed character.'[2] In the *Epitrepontes* we
have an excellent example of this—the manner in which we
learn what sort of person Charisios is, differentiated from
his two friends Simmias and Chairestratos, who are themselves also different, the latter the ordinary young man about
town, cheerful and ready for any spree, the former more
serious, with some regard for consequences, with some
conscientiousness as a man, and not only with the manner of
a gentleman; the optimistic, good-hearted, nicely-behaved
Habrotonon ('sie ihr sehr dezent,' said Wilamowitz); the
almost tragic figure of Pamphile, stirring our sympathy
to the very limit of comedy; and Charisios—his general
steadiness and good conduct is real if a little self-conscious,
his love for Pamphile strong, his reaction to her apparent
deceit natural—his harshness to her, and his ill-mannered
roughness to Habrotonon, his self-torture; when he discovers
the truth, when he is forced to remember his own lapse from
virtue (perhaps the only lapse in his life, but how easy for a
man to forget and forgive himself), how sincere his remorse!
how passionate his desire for Pamphile's forgiveness, for
reconciliation! And he ends his great speech—

ὁ δὲ πατήρ

προπετέστατ' αὐτῇ χρήσεται.   τί δέ μοι πατρός;

ἐρῶ διαρρήδην· ' ἐμοὶ σύ, Σμικρίνη,

μὴ πάρεχε πράγματ', οὐκ ἀπολείπει μ' ἡ γύνη.

τί οὖν ταράττεις καὶ βιαζῇ Παμφιλήν; '

He puts all the blame for the quarrel on to Smikrines. There
is no finer comedy in all Jane Austen.

---

[1] On the other hand the manner in which Onesimos sees the ring on which the
whole dénouement turns is very well devised. Syriskos goes over the ornaments one
by one with his wife, and this is the technical means by which Onesimos finds the
ring; but it is made to appear natural, because it is in accordance with Syriskos'
nature—the poor peasant, the slave, who prides himself on being a connoisseur in
art as well as an orator and a lover of classic drama.

The stage conventions too, especially that involving only the single, outdoor
scene, with its consequences that indoor scenes must be narrated and all that is
acted must be in the street, are excellently managed. And see above, p. 267, for the
bold and unique feature of this play's construction.

[2] Quoted from a forthcoming book by Mr. Kitto.

There have been many, even among his admirers, who
have thought that it in some way diminishes Menander's
greatness, that his world is a small one, the narrow world,
it is said, of the Athenian bourgeoisie; that he was blind to
the great movements which even then, in his own day, were
shattering that world to pieces. *Kleinbürgerlichkeit, Philis-
tines*, are often on the lips of these critics—though they
may at the same time note his cosmopolitan outlook; and
if he had that, he was sensitive to the most important of the
changes taking place in his time. This criticism is not only
inaccurate, in applying to ancient Athens words that
properly belong to modern society. It is irrelevant to
Menander; as irrelevant as are similar complaints made
about Jane Austen. She is indeed a writer with whom
Menander can be profitably compared. She has neither the
wide range, the well-filled canvas of Fielding, nor the
intensity of Charlotte Brontë; she is content with her own
world—the gentry, the narrow little society of a small part
of England, that was blind to the great movements of *its*
generation.   But when we have said that, we have said very
little. 'Accident—the accident of birth—dictated the scene
and scope of her novels, but did not restrict their power.
She was a very rare example . . . of intelligence articulating
with the social personality; she was one of those happy
natures whose very stuff is intelligence, with which nothing
goes to waste, that everything aliments. Provinciality is a
malady of being too much engaged with one's surroundings.
. . . To be unprovincial is to know what is important, to
see the exact importance of everything that you see. To
underrate a deliberately quiet life is, absurdly, to confuse
experience with knowledge.'[1] That might almost have been
written of Menander. He was not the author of social
studies; he was concerned with humanity as such, ordinary
men and women, their characters and emotions, their loves
and hopes and fears, their reactions to the average chances
and accidents of human life. For that any class of society
would do, and he (like all good authors) took that with
which he was familiar. The dramatic convention that his
principal characters are persons of leisure, with plenty of

[1] Elizabeth Bowen, in *The English Novelists*, ed. D. Verschoyle (1936).

servants (or rather that his groups consist of the leisured and their servants and dependents), that their actions and emotions are not interrupted and complicated by the necessities of a full day's work, is one which, when you come to think of it, has been adopted by all but a small group of imaginative writers. The story of a man whose passion and despair is complicated by his having to catch the 8.30 train every morning and work all day in an office, may well be matter for comedy; that of one whose love is accompanied by grinding poverty, for tragedy. But they would be stories proper only to a particular time and a particular class. Menander was dealing with the universal, with every man and woman; so was Jane Austen, even though in externals her stories so obviously belong to a particular age, and a particular class and country. He may, for all we know, have had strong opinions on politics and social questions; indeed, quite apart from his obvious sympathy with poor or oppressed persons (as the slaves), we can perhaps still catch glimpses of a discerning social criticism in some isolated fragments, as

$$εὐκαταφρόνητόν ἐστι, Γοργία, πένης,$$
$$κἂν πάνυ λέγῃ δίκαια· τούτου γὰρ λέγειν$$
$$ἕνεκα μόνου νομίζεθ' οὗτος, τοῦ λαβεῖν·$$
$$καὶ συκοφάντης εὐθὺς ὁ τὸ τριβώνιον$$
$$ἔχων καλεῖται, κἂν ἀδικούμενος τύχῃ$$

$$(Γεωργός, fr. 1),$$

and in some stray lines from the Latin comedy:

dum licitumst ei dumque aetas tulit,
amavit; tum id clam: cavit ne unquam infamiae
ea res sibi esset, ut virum fortem decet.
nunc uxore opus est: animum ad uxorem adpulit

(where I am not sure that Terence was aware of the irony[1]); and in traces of a sympathetic treatment (sympathetic at least in contrast to Aeschinus' conduct) of the slave-dealer Sannio in the *Adelphoe*;[2] all of which suggest that he could

---

[1] *Andr.* 443–6. It is interesting to compare this with the very different tone of Oscar Wilde's 'It is your duty to get married; you can't be always living for pleasure'; and with the conventional view of marriage that we get in *Andr.* 191, 395–6.

[2] Compare also *Phormio* 533 and 561–2, which is from Apollodoros, and shows some understanding of the slave-dealer and the parasite; and contrast the superficial

understand not only the poor as well as the rich, not only
the prostitute as well as the young gentleman, but the pander
no less than the girl he owns; that he was not content with
the conventional morality which both allowed a gentleman
to make use of a pander and excused any dishonesty
and ill-manners towards him. But he was not primarily
concerned with such things, nor with class struggles
and political upheavals, nor with moral revolutions. He
belongs to his own time and society as closely as Jane
Austen does; neither can be imagined away from it. But
they are both at the same time classics, timeless.

Schnitzler is another modern writer whose work he
recalls, especially the Schnitzler of *Spiel im Morgengrau* and
similar tales, though in them there is more romance and less
comedy than in Menander.[1] The young subaltern in an
expensive regiment, seen against a background of his
fellow-subalterns and his senior officers (and their servants,
but the rank and file do not appear), and of the light-hearted,
fashionable world of Vienna; from which comes to him
tragedy, the immediate consequence of gambling or some
unhappy love-affair (from which he was just successfully
emerging, to a purer love and happy marriage, when, alas,
discovery was made and his castle crumbles to ruins), at
bottom caused by a careless irresponsibility, a weakness
which prevents him first from seeing, then from facing the
consequence of his own actions; the story mainly of an
individual, told with such delicacy and justness of observation because Schnitzler was able not only to understand the
individual, but to see behind the façade of conventional
moralty which contented his characters; yet would not let
the implied social criticism intrude upon the romance.
Willi in *Spiel im Morgengrau*—the self-centred young officer,
so vain and so likeable, with such charm of manner, and
interpreting everybody's every movement as it affects his
particular trouble: the dialogue between him and Consul
Schnabel, an older man, on the way home after the gambling; the scenes with Leopoldine, especially the last—with

passage ('would that there were the same law for men as for women!'), *Mercator*
817 ff.: which may well be Philemon's own, not Plautus—Philemon was the
popular dramatist, not Menander.
[1] Norwood well compares Schnitzler's style with Menander's: *Comedy*, p. 351.

what mastery it is handled: it moves almost to tears, there is a critical irony for the intellect; but the romance remains. Note too the touch of social criticism, when an officer makes an insulting remark about consuls of obscure countries and Schnabel answers: 'Warum frozzeln Sie mich, Herr Leutnant? Haben Sie sich schon erkundigt, ob ich satisfaktionsfähig bin?' So with Menander—a comedy of men and women, of all types and classes, but not a play about classes (the slave-*world* is absent, as the rank and file of the army from Schnitzler); indeed he gives but a sketch of the *milieu* of his characters, of Athenian society of his day, whereas Schnitzler drew a more vivid picture of pre-war Vienna;[1] he almost strips his characters of the inessential in their surroundings, or, if you will, fails to give them a satisfactorily living background.[2] That is a possible criticism; though, even so, he is less formal and less abstract than Molière. But he was a wonderful observer of mankind, with a gift for clear portraiture in a language exactly suited to his purpose: a language of just the right range, full of charm, never sublime, never 'pure' poetry, seldom rhetorical;[3] an instrument of which he was the complete master. An easy

[1] Whether the fact that Menander and his peers all wrote comedies with happy endings and Schnitzler romances that ended in death—and generally the emptiest form of death, by suicide or in a duel—has anything to do with the comparative energy and vitality of ancient Athens and modern Vienna, I leave for others to discuss.

[2] Let me give two instances in which modern writers have misunderstood this characteristic. Körte (*Hellenistic Poetry*, Eng. trans., p. 60) says of the arbitration scene in 'Επιτρέποντες: 'First of all, the idea that slaves can come to a legal settlement of a dispute strikes him (Smikrines) as curious.' That is exactly wrong: it is making the scene particular to Athens and to the classical period; in reality the legal status of slaves is not thought of; Smikrines only shows the uppish amusement of rich men of all ages and places when poor men have a dispute and want it settled in the regular fashion to which *they* are accustomed.

Of the end of the *Heautontimorumenus* Norwood (*Art of Terence*, p. 47) says: 'Another objectionable element is the solution of Clitopho's scrape. He hurriedly agrees to marry; the lady selected is unknown to us, and almost anyone will answer the purpose. Bacchis simply disappears. Very like real Athenian life this may be; dramatically it is huddled and threadbare.' How can a man be so perverse? An arranged marriage, such as we are never tired of saying all Athenian marriages were, needs time for the arranging. This rapid marriage has nothing to do with life; it is a dramatic convention (as much so as the *deus ex machina* of Euripides). It is generally harmless enough, as that of Moschion in Περικειρομένη, though it is always pointless; if it *appears* threadbare in the *Heautontimorumenus*, that is because Terence (perhaps Menander in his original) mismanaged it.

[3] Smikrines' speech in 'Επιτρέποντες (Z, 5 ff.) has some rhetoric in it; so has *Papyrus Didotiana* (esp. l. 19 ff.), though rhetoric beautifully in control. And of course, in Syriskos' speech, where it is gently laughed at.

mastery, both of his material and his language, is his most notable characteristic: how apt, in fact, is the story that 'he had only to add the verses.' He never stumbles, never appears to be at a loss. You may say if you like that his range was not a wide one; if it is necessary to point out that he was not an Aeschylus nor a Shakespeare, by all means let it be done. There is much comedy in Plautus, too, that he eschews—the exuberance of language, the variety of metre and song, the slave on the heroic scale, that excellent back-chat, *velitatio*, between the servants and other humble folk or, occasionally, between master and servant, which recalls much in Shakespeare (though there is always sentiment in Shakespeare, and as little of it in Plautus as in Vanbrugh or Wycherley, dramatists in other ways so different from him); Plautus' general air of carrying off improbabilities and absurdities instead of avoiding them, as though to avoid them was to be timid and cautious. Truly Menander's *vis comica* was very different.[1] Nor was he witty in the manner of Restoration comedy and of Oscar Wilde. He was himself, and that is sufficient; and his province was the same as Molière's. Within his chosen range, even in the little that is left of him, he shows wonderful variety of character and situation. He seldom or never strikes a false note; and it is remarkable how high a standard he maintains, not only in the three plays best preserved, but wherever enough is left, a scene or part of a scene, to enable us to form a judgement. He can move us near to tears, he can make us smile or laugh, he can keep us in anxious doubt though we know the end of the story; the master of the ἰδιωτικῶν πραγμάτων ἀκίνδυνος περιοχή: 'comedy shows us life, not at such a distance that we cannot but regard it coldly, but only so far as we may bring to it a ready sympathy free from terror or too overwhelming a measure of pity.'[2] He always appeals to the intelligence, and to a cultivated and sensitive intelli-

---

[1] Where he does approach (without getting very near) the manner of Plautus, he is not, I feel, very successful, as in the fooling of Laches in the scene (from the last act?) in *Fabula Incerta*, which is lively, but hurried and unconvincing. Compare too Κόλαξ, 86–8, and the leno's speech, 96 ff.; and the threats to torture Daos for his deceiving of the foolish old man (13 ff., and fr. 1) in Περινθία, which are in the Latin manner.

[2] Dobree, *Restoration Comedy*, p. 130; quoted by Post in *Trans. Amer. Phil. Assoc.* lxv, 1934, p. 16.

gence; ἀγνωμοσύνη, in its full range of meanings, was his
enemy. He was one of the princes of comedy.[1]

[1]There is one important matter on which I am completely at a loss: how did
Menander treat those birth-scenes in which not only does a birth take place during
the play, but we hear the cries of the mother in pain from behind the scene? Whether
in Plautine farce (*Aulularia*, perhaps from Menander, though at a long distance) or
Terentian comedy (*Andria* and *Adelphoe*, as well as the *Hecyra*), they are, to me at
least, intolerable. What they were like in the original I cannot guess; anything of
the kind is so unlike the Menander that we have. It seems certain that there was
such a scene in Πλόκιον; at least probable that there was one in Ἀδελφοί and
Ἀνδρία or Περινθία or both, on account of Donatus' note on *Andr.* 473 *Juno
Lucina: obstetriciam hanc potestatem Junoni attribuit, quamquam illam Menander
Dianam appellet.* (I say *probable* only, because the birth may have been managed,
as I believe it was in Γεωργός: where, I think, it occurred between Acts i and ii,
and so was only *reported*: see ll. 87 and 122. We have τὴν Ἄρτεμιν in l. 118, clearly
after the birth, and some such line in Ἀνδρία could have occasioned Donatus' note.
If the birth were only reported in Menander's play, Terence's alteration, to make
the action more 'vivid,' would be similar to that he made in Ἀδελφοί, by the
introduction of the abduction scene from Diphilos.) All we can say is that such
scenes were probably not so frequent as Körte, for example (ap. Pauly-Wissowa,
art. *Menandros*, p. 758), has stated—that there was none in Σαμία, Ἥρως or Fab.
Incert., and perhaps not in Γεωργός; and that they involve as well, at least in the
Latin plays (see above, pp. 277–8), a wild improbability that is as foreign to the
Menander that we have as is the harrowing of our feelings.

XIII

TWO LETTERS TO *THE TIMES*

I HAVE only written two letters to *The Times* and neither was published. As both were concerned with matters of interest to classical scholars, I print them here, the first as it was written, the second somewhat expanded.

THE SMUGGLING OF ANTIQUITIES

SIR,—The account sent by your correspondent of the recent smuggling of antiquities out of Greece raises an important question. If there were not several museums, in different countries, and a few individuals, ready to buy such smuggled goods, there would be no profit in them, no motive to break the law. By their action they are aiding and abetting law-breakers, well knowing the law that all antiquities discovered are declared the property of the state—a poor return to make to a country so hospitable to archaeologists of all nations as Greece. This, however, is sentimental, and the protest will be scorned. There is fortunately another side to the question—the scientific. All scholars are familiar with accounts of objects, appearing from time to time in learned journals, of which the circumstances of discovery cannot be given, sometimes because they are not known, sometimes because publication would give away the smuggler. But the circumstances of discovery, giving the historical context, are always important and often more important than the object discovered, considered in itself. We often congratulate ourselves on the superiority of modern methods of excavation over the old, and just in this, that we no longer dig only for objects, but excavate a site. All museums and individuals who buy smuggled antiquities are directly encouraging an unscientific method, and contributing to ignorance instead of to knowledge.

Jan. 12, 1933.

THE RETURN OF THE ELGIN MARBLES

It depends on how you look at the matter. If you think of the Acropolis buildings as a collection of specimens of architecture and sculpture, of none of them as a whole but as so many specimens, of columns, capitals, architraves, roof-tiles, low-relief, high-relief figures, as museum pieces in a word (if, that is to say, as Mr. Edward Bell once said in *The Times*, you would, if possible, put the whole of the Parthenon in a museum—as if it were not only too easy! a gigantic concrete building could cover the whole of the Acropolis summit, to preserve it for ever, or the buildings be pulled down, lovingly, stone by stone, and re-erected elsewhere): then, naturally, you would see no sense in the restoration of the Elgin marbles to where they belong. But if the Acropolis is to you an organic whole, a sacred spot, its history woven in with the history of Greece (so that even the marks of damage done in the War of Independence, the last occasion on which the hill played a living part, have their own significance), if that is, you are sensitive to the past and its continuity with the present, then a removal of any part of the whole, from whatever motive, is an act of vandalism. Elgin was an enlightened vandal, who had no feeling for the Acropolis, only for specimens of sculpture and architecture to be preserved in a museum; that is why he cared nothing for what he had to leave behind. To complain of the neglect with which the buildings were being treated, and himself to do his best to destroy them in order to preserve little bits and pieces! Supposing someone about 1900, foreseeing the European War, had, in his anxiety to preserve them from obvious danger, wrenched away the sculptures of Reims and carried them off to America? Or supposing, during the war, France had been so weak that enlightened allies had removed those sculptures, and refused to return them when the war was over? Yet Reims stands still in greater danger of bombardment than ever Athens did (and so, for that matter, does the British Museum, though I have not yet heard an Englishman advocate the removal of its treasures to America). It would not be tolerable, not because the sculptures are not worth preserving for their own sake, but because they belong to the cathedral, and the cathedral to Reims, and nowhere else. Will anyone suggest that Westminster Abbey should be removed from the destroying soot of London, or parts of it be taken down and preserved out of harm's way? Even when some historic building is carried off and re-erected in America, for want of anyone to look after it here, we cry out upon the vandalism. The Theseion, in fact, was in equal danger when Elgin was in Athens with the temples on the Acropolis: do we now wish that he had carried off a column or two?

But as we cannot now go back upon the past, how do these considerations affect the question of the return of the Elgin marbles to Greece? The sculptures of the Parthenon could not, at least for the present, be restored to their places on the temple (Elgin is in part to blame for that); they would therefore, if restored to Greece, only be transferred from one museum to another: with considerable advantage, in the Greek climate, and because all parts of the building would then be together; with some disadvantage, for fewer would see them—London is more central for Europe and America; in essentials (leaving out the morality of the matter) there would be little change. But it is different with the architectural fragments: the capital from the Parthenon, the column and the Karyatid from the Erechtheion. *They* could be restored to their places. No one can look at the Erechtheion without feeling it truncated and despoiled, wanting a column on the east front, with that cheap and accusing substitute in the Karyatid porch on the south. The useless damage done by Elgin can be undone. It would be a generous, a gracious, and a sensible act.

DATE DUE

9 781013 992223